Eva Webb Dodd

Mary Comfort Leonard   *Anna Boyd Ellington*

This portrait of the Founders, done by Barbara Hutchinson Grein-
er, Epsilon-Ohio State, hangs in the Delta Gamma Archives Room
at Executive Offices. Other pictures of the Founders are individual
portraits painted by Helen Humphreys Lawrence, Lambda-Min-
nesota, which hang in the Memorial Room of Alpha Psi chapter,
University of Mississippi, and a daguerreotype of the Founders,
done in 1874, and also displayed in the Archives Room.

A History
of
Delta Gamma

presented by
The Anchora
Winter, 1973

Contents

On History

From time to time during her 100 years, Delta Gamma has recorded for her membership an account of her past. Sometimes these have appeared originally—like this one—as an issue of the Fraternity journal, *The Anchora*, later to be permanently bound as a single volume.

The first issue of *The Anchora*, April, 1884, was, in fact, a series of histories of individual chapters. This sort of accounting, tied together by editorial comment, appeared from time to time until 1901 when a small, hard-bound volume appeared, including as much history as was available and a directory of Delta Gamma membership.

It would seem that less than thirty years of history could be recorded with ease and accuracy, but this was not the case in 1901. Delta Gamma, as a national organization, was virtually out of contact with its origin. Through the sad incident of 1889 when the Mother Chapter in Oxford, Mississippi, was removed had come a complete severance of ties with these first members. Thus, important early records and correspondence (which have come to light since) were missing, and it was impossible to put together a complete history based on memory alone.

Shortly after the appearance of this first attempt at a Delta Gamma history, Blanche Garten, K-Nebraska, became Delta Gamma's president. From the moment she took office her efforts were concentrated on re-establishing the lost tie with the South and the early Delta Gammas still living there. After ten years of searching, corresponding, and cataloging—and even a visit to Oxford—Blanche Garten and Anchora Editor Ethel Tukey put out in 1915 a monumental volume which carried the complete and authoritative record of Delta Gamma's early years as well as clear insight into more current happenings. To this history, published in 1915, subsequent historians are much indebted.

To celebrate Delta Gamma's sixtieth birthday during 1933-34, another history appeared, An Historical Sketch of the Delta Gamma Fraternity. The committee in charge, former President Nancy Brown Woollett, Φ-Colorado; Editor Leulah Judson Hawley, Λ-Minnesota, and long-time Fraternity officer, Alice Perry Gradle, Ξ-Michigan, did an admirable task. Mrs. Woollett states in the Foreword: "This brief history of Delta Gamma Fraternity is offered at this time in lieu of the expected detailed and comprehensive one, to fill a requirement for data and information covering the period between 1915 and 1934."

With the January, 1945, *Anchora* came another history, edited by Alta Gwinn Saunders, I-Illinois, with a large committee of officers assisting. This volume necessarily competed with World War II and its accompanying paper shortage, but it is nevertheless remarkably complete.

In 1950, with the Publications Department of Central Office only a year old, the Convention decided that the surplus in the Alta Gwinn Saunders Memorial Fund might well be applied to a new historical volume. Thus began our efforts toward The Record which appeared, as an issue of *Anchora*, in 1955. The hopes at that time was that at intervals of ten years the Delta Gamma story might be brought up to date with a new historical edition.

It was actually eleven years later, 1966, that a sixth edition of the Delta Gamma story, *A History of Delta Gamma,* appeared. It was remarked that discerning readers would note that this was an embellishment of the 1955 volume, and with the publication of this seventh history the same remark might be made. In both 1966 and 1973 the historians were able to go forward from the basic work completed in 1955. At that time we depended heavily on the aid of an Editorial Board of Review (all former Presidents, Editors, and Historians)

whose experience and knowledge stretched back over many years, and so the two volumes since have become opportunities to enlarge and adorn as well as to bring history up to date.

If we were logically inserting a history into the *Anchora* schedule each decade, then why this one only seven years after the 1966 edition? This is 1973, the end of our first century, and it seemed a logical time to package in one volume Delta Gamma's first hundred years.

Once more we give thanks to the Editorial Board of Review (1955) for the basic plan and the second group of reviewers who served in 1966. Our current Editorial Board of Review consists of the Presidents, Editors, and the Executive Secretaries who have held office during the 1966-73 period, and we especially want to thank for their aid and support former Presidents Elizabeth Kloppenburg and Marcia Strickland, President Kathryn Gary, and Executive Secretaries Roberta Abernethy and Carmalieta Brown. As to the Editors— this is a different story. All three who represent the decade are here to make some claim on a part of this history: Fran Stevenson and Barb Carvill who have taken it from start to finish and Mary Ann Shepard who has just returned to the Executive Offices staff in time to get us to the printer on time and then to refile an enormous quantity of pictures and miscellaneous information and records in the Delta Gamma Archives.

Frances Lewis Stevenson, Z-Albion
Barbara Carvill, θ-Indiana
Mary Ann Dalton Shepard, N-Idaho

THE EAGLE on the cover is the editor's version of an old Delta Gamma sign. This is pure poetic license, for the first Delta Gamma eagle was a "hieroglyphic symbol of an eagle enclosed in a Delta." We hope you agree that our version is an appropriate historic symbol.

Fig. 1.   Fig. 2.   Fig. 3.   Fig. 4.   Fig. 5.   Fig. 6.   Fig. 7.

Ladies' Own Magazine---Fashions for December, 1873.

(From Demorest, for December.)

*It was Christmas time, 1873. The Lewis School,
Oxford, Mississippi. Three weatherbound girls isolated
in a girls' boarding school for the holidays . . .*

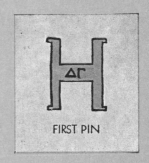

FIRST PIN

In 1873, when a girl ventured away to school, she became virtually an exile from her family. A look at the map shows us that, while Oxford was on the railroad, Kosciusko—the home of Anna Boyd, Eva Webb and Mary Comfort—was sixteen miles over uncertain roads from the nearest junction. Travel to this point must be by stage or private carriage, and in seasons of bad weather—like December—it was best not to attempt such a trip.

This was a period in the United States of severe depression and the trials of early reconstruction in the South only added to the universal financial difficulties. On the other hand, it was an exciting decade, for inventions were coming rapidly—the radiator, the self-binding reaper, the typewriter, the Westinghouse air-brake, the Duplex telegraph, the phonograph, the gasoline carriage. Most of these—as well as the electric light—would not be in general use for years.

These early Delta Gammas studied primarily the classics and arts, and a little, if any, math or science. Though they were educated to be gentlewomen, the curiosity which nurtured a thirst for further knowledge is evident in the tasks they assigned themselves in their fraternity meetings—for they considered their fraternity a means of adding something to their education which could not be gained solely through the academic curriculum. These girls, and others like them in other places and wearing other emblems, sought through their fraternities to maintain high ideals and standards of conduct and to encourage intellectual interests in order to exemplify the college woman at her best.

Eva Webb Dodd

Eva Webb, the daughter of Mr. and Mrs. R. B. Webb, pioneer residents of Attala County, Mississippi, was born July 5, 1855 in Kosciusko where she made her home throughout her life.

At eighteen she was part of the trio from Kosciusko—she and her cousin, Anna Boyd, and their friend, Mary Comfort—at the Lewis School in Oxford. These three, with their highest ideals shining with the spirit of Christmas, became the schoolgirl founders of Delta Gamma.

Eva's two years at the Lewis School completed her education, and on October 12, 1875, she was married to the Honorable S. L. Dodd, until his death in 1928 a prominent attorney of Kosciusko. They were the parents of eight children.

At the time of her death, her friend Mary Leonard wrote, "She was a charter member of the Twentieth Century Club and for a long time led the civic work of the club. She also took an active part in the organization of the Mississippi Federation of Women's Clubs in 1896.

"She was a devout and consecrated member of the Presbyterian Church and she lived the religion she professed."

With Mrs. Leonard, Mrs. Dodd was a Fraternity guest at most of the Delta Gamma Conventions between 1909 and her death January 28, 1934.

Among the mementoes of Eva Webb Dodd's busy life are her gold thimble and scissors. An expert needlewoman, this crocheted cuff is undoubtedly one of many produced by her during the period of their popularity. The daguerreotype is of Eva at about eight. These are among the gifts to the Archives from her granddaughter, Mrs. J. Y. Waugh of Eskridge, Kansas.

Anna Boyd Ellington

Anna Boyd was born near Kosciusko, Mississippi, on January 22, 1856. Her early schooling took place in Kosciusko and later, after a year at school in Alabama, she went with her cousin, Eva Webb, and her friend, Mary Comfort, to the Lewis School in Oxford.

Her education completed, she taught in the public schools until her marriage to Mr. D. A. Ellington in 1882. Four daughters were born to them (Caroline, Lillian, and Lena later became members of Delta Gamma), and Mr. Ellington died in 1890, leaving her with the four small girls to rear—a task she accomplished nobly.

After a few years in California to regain her own health, she returned to Kosciusko. Years of struggle followed to make possible her goal of properly educating her four daughters. And with this task nearly completed—the first two graduated, the third a sophomore and the fourth ready to begin college—she died, August 12, 1907.

Anna Boyd Ellington was a useful woman and a useful citizen wherever she lived. She was a handsome brunette, but her greatest charm was that of mind and heart. She possessed a fine and strong personality and a bright mind and quick wit.

*Anna Boyd Ellington's many talents are evident
in the tangible memories of her life found in the
Delta Gamma Archives. Her sketch book, used at Lewis School,
displays artistic ability. It appears here with the chocolate
pot used by the Ellington family; these and other mementoes
were donated by her daughter, Miss Lena Boyd Ellington, ΑΨ-Mississippi*

Mary Comfort Leonard

Mary Comfort was born the same day as her friend, Anna, January 22, 1856, in Kosciusko, Mississippi, one of thirteen children. After completing her early education at home, she was sent to Lewis School in Oxford where she was a student for three years.

While in Oxford, she met Charles H. Leonard, a University student, who became a teacher. After their marriage in 1880, they taught together, later moving to Florida where nine years later, Mr. Leonard died. Mrs. Leonard, left with three small boys to educate, returned to Kosciusko where she taught for 16 years.

Mrs. Leonard is well remembered by generations of Kosciusko children, members of her Bible class at the Presbyterian Church. She was a stern but inspiring teacher and enriched the spirit and understanding of all who knew her.

For years she worked in the Twentieth Century Club and other civic activities. *The Anchoras* over a period of twenty years contain personal messages from Mrs. Leonard and Mrs. Dodd, confirming their devotion to the principles on which Delta Gamma was founded. Mrs. Leonard passed away August 4, 1940, after living to see her granddaughter initiated as a charter member of the reinstated Alpha Psi chapter.

Like Anna Boyd Ellington, Mary Comfort Leonard showed considerable artistic talent—the hand-painted bowl and fan products of her brush which are displayed in the Archives. An enthusiast for all Delta Gamma projects, she was a notable cook and a number of her recipes appear in the Delta Gamma Cookbook, 1912 edition. Mementoes of Mrs. Leonard's life were the gifts of her grandchildren.

LEONARD---COMFORT---At the residence of the bride's father, Mr. D. B. Comfort, on the 28th of Jan., 1880, by Rev. J. H. Alexander, Mr. C. H. Leonard, of Memphis, Tenn., to Miss Mary E. Comfort, of Kosciusko.

We heartily congratulate our worthy young friend and old school-fellow, upon his distinguished success in securing a partner for life so eminently fitted to fill and adorn all departments of the position she has thus assumed. One of the brightest stars has been plucked from the galaxy of Kosciusko's social system, to form a jewel in a new sphere. The happy couple left on Wednesday evenings train for Memphis, carrying with them the best wishes of many friends.

As the train that bore them moved away,
Their radiant faces seemed to say:
"Here are two hearts whose movements thrill,
In unison so sweet,
That pulse to pulse responsive still,
They both must heave, or cease to beat."

The original
minute book of
Psi Chapter,
Oxford, Mississippi
is in the
Archives.

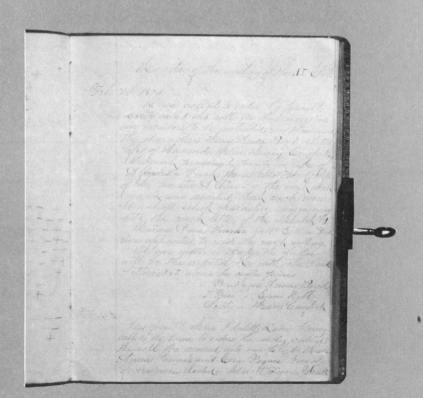

Barnes Co

Garnets $ 2⁰⁰
Pearls 2.50
Turquois 8⁰⁰
Rose Diamonds 12⁵⁰
Attach pins with setts
Extra $ 1.50
with rose diamonds
$ 1.50 per stone

*Corrinne Miller's first negotiations
of an "anchor pin" were simple. The drawing
shown here was issued to other jewelers authorized
by Conventions to produce the badge. Thus, we
find considerable variance in styles of the old large size badge.*

C. P. BARNES & BRO.,
Gold Pen Makers, Jewelers,

AND DEALERS IN

FINE "KEY" AND "STEM-WINDING" WATCHES.

SPECTACLES A SPECIALTY.   224 MAIN STREET,

Louisville, Ky., Feb 7 1877

Miss Corinne Miller

We can make the Anchor
Pins for $40 per Dozen
The A Pin with chain attached
we suppose you only want
one of, that would cost $250
made of solid Gold
If you wanted a dozen
of the A Pins with attaching chain & Pin they would
be made for something
less

Respy
C P Barnes & Bro

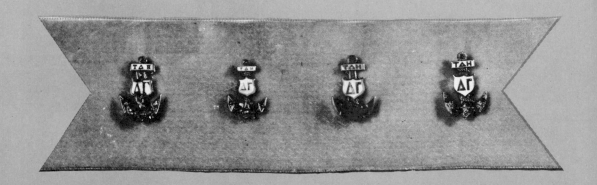

Corinne Miller was not only
the designer of the Delta Gamma anchor,
but she was also the Fraternity's
first active expansionist, having
been instrumental in establishing
several of the earliest chapters.
A memorial fellowship bears Corinne
Miller's name.

Called the "corner stone of the Archives,"
this metal box—battered but still bearing
the lettering "ΔΓ"—stored under lock
and key the papers and letters of value
of the first chapter. When this chapter
was withdrawn in 1889, Minnie Wohlleben Carter
locked it and put it in her attic where it stayed
until 1937 when she presented it with its contents
to President Marguerite Winant.

WOOLLEN & BANTA,
ATTORNEYS AT LAW.

Franklin, Ind. Mch 12 1879

Miss Miller.

You will doubtless be surprised at my presuming to address you but matters of importance to both of our respective fraternities are involved and under existing circumstances I think it best to inform you. Emma has been dangerously ill for some weeks with pneumonia and cannot attend to affairs as she expected to. She has been suffering for two weeks with hemorrhages of the lungs, and towards the latter part of last week they became so frequent and severe that on Sunday we did not think that she could live more than two or three days. She has however been growing better since Sunday and, will I trust, be well soon.

The matter which I deem so urgent as to necessitate my informing you is This. Mr H. A. Kelley of our Ohio Eta chapter writes me this morning, informing me that they ~~are~~ (the ΦΔΘ chapter) are trying to persuade some of the young ladies of Buchtel College to organize a ΔΓ chapter. He requests the ΔΓ ladies to write immediately to Miss Mary Laughead Akron, Ohio, Care Buchtel College. He says that you will have the persuasive eloquence of 15 ΦΔΘ to support you and thinks that a fine chapter could be started at once and be well supported. The KKΓ is already located there. Please write to the young lady mentioned above at your earliest convenience.

Very Respectfully

Geo. Banta

George Banta (above) was responsible for Delta Gamma's expansion to the North. Lillian Vawter (below) his fiance, was the first Northern initiate.

An early charter was an ornate affair designed and printed by Psi-Mother Chapter.

This symbolic anchor was for some time used as an emblem on stationery. Note error in date of founding.

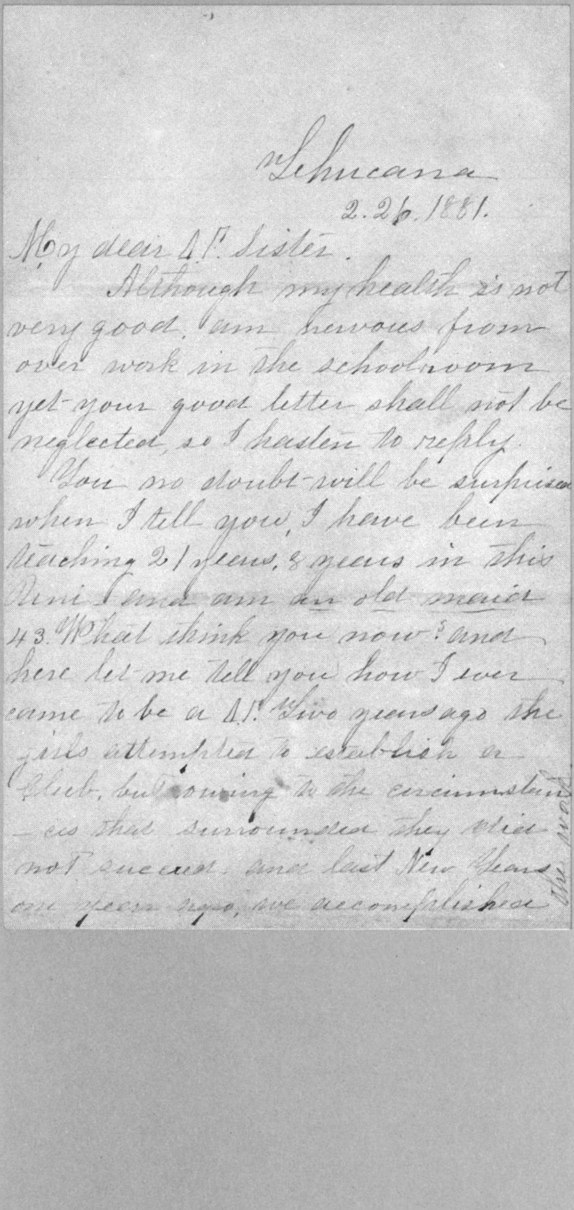

Correspondence between
these early chapters
contained newsy bits
as well as business.

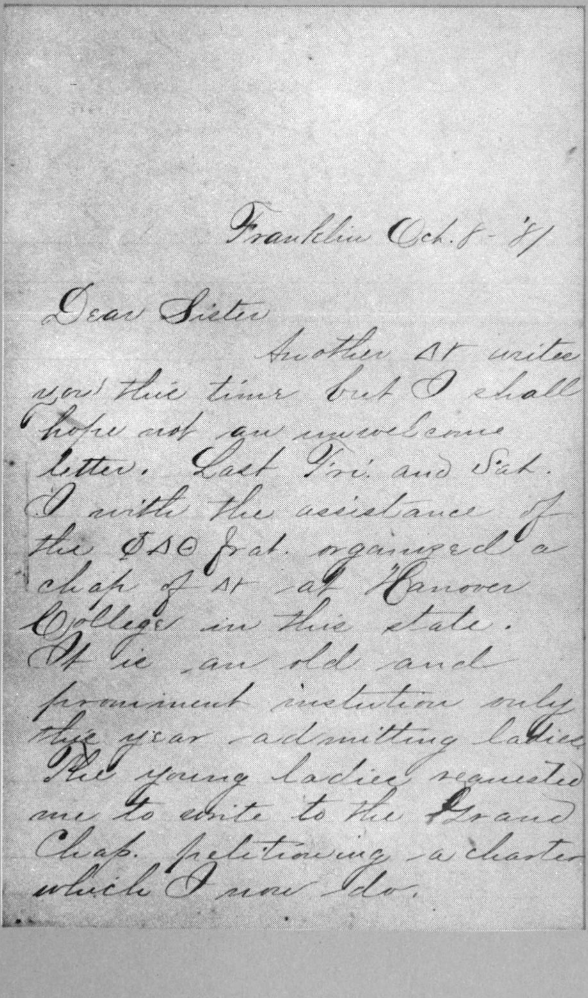

Tehuacana
2.26.1881.

My dear Λ Γ Sister.

Although my health is not
very good. I am nervous from
over work in the schoolroom
yet your good letter shall not be
neglected, so I hasten to reply.

You no doubt will be surprised
when I tell you, I have been
teaching 21 years, 8 years in this
Uni. I and am an old maid
43. What think you now? and
here let me tell you how I ever
came to be a Λ Γ. Two years ago the
girls attempted to establish a
Club, but owing to the circumstanc-
-es that surrounded they did
not succeed. And last New Years
one year ago, we accomplished

Franklin Oct. 8 - '81

Dear Sister
Another Λ Γ writes
you this time but I shall
hope not an unwelcome
letter. Last Fri. and Sat.
I with the assistance of
the ΦΔΘ frat. organized a
chap. of Λ Γ at Hanover
College in this state.
It is an old and
prominent institution only
this year admitting ladies.
The young ladies requested
me to write to the Grand
Chap. petitioning a charter
which I now I do.

The first Convention was
a glorious affair, for
the hostesses—and apparently
all their friends in Oxford—did
their utmost to entertain royally
the guests from the North. Shown together
are Mary Thompson Stevens, the first
Anchora editor, and Fannie Mulliken
Thompson, whose father made the first
Convention possible by transporting his
daughter and other Eta members to
Mississippi in his private railroad car.
Fannie was, until her early death, an
energetic Delta Gamma, serving as president
of the last Convention she attended.
Below is the Second Convention assembled. Lillie
Wohlleben, who served as second president, is
seated second from left. Though others were
present, this is the official body.

The cover of the first issue—a single issue varied in cover color, depending on what paper the printer had on hand.

Delta Gamma Anchora.

M. E. THOMPSON, ... Editor-in-Chief
MARY DOW SIBLEY, . . . Vice Editor-in-Chief
MAY C. BOCK, ... Managing Editor

*.*TERMS.—$1.00 per year, in advance. Single copies, 35 cents.
. Address all communications to M. E. Thompson, 39 South State St., Ann Arbor, Mich.
. Matters pertaining to subscription and advertisements should be sent to May C. Bock, 800 East Market Street, Akron, Ohio.

AKRON, OHIO, NOVEMBER, 1884.

ADVERTISING RATES.

We offer our advertising space at the following rates:
One page, 1 year (four insertions)............$25
Half " " " 18
Quar. " " " 8
Business Cards, 1 year 5

DELTA chapter has our heart felt sympathy for having so unwisely (?) chosen their fraternity. Will the members of Delta Tau Delta of Albion please accept our thanks for their brotherly commiseration of the Albion chapter? Girls, how could you have taken such an important step without first receiving counsel and permission from the "dear boys"? How sad to think their sensitive organisms should have received such a shock! Will they ever recover? "Dear Girls," never be so cruel and unkind again. However, we will gladly forgive you this time; but the next time you contemplate joining a fraternity, be sure to get the little boys to select the proper, world-renowned one, fit for you to link your fortunes with.

UNFORTUNATELY we were unable to fulfil our intentions in regard to publishing another number of the ANCHORA before the close of the school year; but, partly from the illness of the editor, which necessitated a cessation from all school duties, and partly from the great press of work incident to commencement time, which left the other members of the corps little time for editorial work, the accomplishment of our design was flustrated. We hope to make up the loss, however, by the increase of interesting matter relating to commencement with its attendant festivities.

We trust that "the fates" will be less unkind in future, so that the ANCHORA may make its appearance with due promptness and regularity.

THE ANCHORA desires, on this its second appearance, to thank all who have given it such hearty support and encouragement, and especially the other fraternities and exchanges which have so cordially welcomed the young stranger into the journalistic field.

In some respects the ANCHORA was all we had dared hope for our

Masthead—and editorial comment.

An early back cover

But let me tell you that for a long time my editress was sick and when she became well again she did not return to Buchtel College but went to Ann Arbor, and although she did not forget me, I missed her very much, and my assistant editresses were so busy that they did not lavish the care on me which I deserved. Nor was it wholly their fault that I was so late, for some of my friends who live away from Akron, were neglectful in not sending messages to me, hence I was delayed a few days, for when I came to see you I wanted to bring you tidings from all the homes of my little world. But after all my trials I am here to see you and hope my visit may prove a pleasant one.

Among the Hellenes.

A song book has recently been published under the auspices of Kappa Alpha Theta.

The Delta Tau Delta Cresent is responsible for the following:—"Two Chinese students at Kenyon college have been initiated into Alpha Delta Phi. Can this be a move of this very "conservative" Fraternity eastward?"

We are sorry to learn that the charter of Sigma Chapter, Mt. Union, of Delta Tau Delta, has been withdrawn.

It is rumored that another journal will soon make its appearance in the Greek World under the management of the Tufts Charge of Theta Delta Chi. It has our best wishes.

A tax of $3.00 is imposed on each active member of Phi Delta Theta to defray convention expenses.

The Beta Theta Pi has a subscription list of two-thousand. The Betas seem fully to appreciate the fact they have a journal of real merit.

It is rumored that Phi Delta Theta expects to enter Ann Arbor, where she already has several men attending. It seems to be the general opinion that now is no auspicious time for such a move on the part of any fraternity, as the present complement of eighteen fraternities must make the field comfortably crowded.

"In the Michigan Chapter o Delta Upsilon at Ann Arbor a committee of five is appointed, whose unanimous recommendation is sufficient to admit a candidate to membership in that Chapter."—Sigma Nu Delta. This may be one of the distinctive features on which this fraternity bases its stand as being among the "antis."

The following Fraternity Journals receive outside subscriptions;—the Beta Theta Pi published at 11 Apollo Building, Cincinnati, O; the Sigma Alpha Epsilon Record, Sewanee, Tenn; the Crescent of Delta Tau Delta, box 144, Meadville, Pa.; the Golden Key of Kappa Kappa Gamma, Greencastle, Ind.; the Delta Kappa Epsilon Quarterly, 52 William St., New York, N. Y.; the

Alpha Tau Omega Palm, Richmond, Va., and the Delta Gamma ANCHORA, Akron, O. The above publications are sent to any address at the uniform price of one dollar.

As the political mania runs high, it may be interesting to our readers to know that Arthur is the first United States president who was a "legitimate member" of a fraternity, entering the mystic brotherhood of Psi Upsilon at Union College in '48, the cradle of that fraternity. Garfield became a member of the mother chapter of Delta Upsilon at Williams College in '56. Washington and Jefferson College is the Alma Mater of James G. Blaine, at which institution he graduated with the class of '47. The Delta Kappa Epsilons are said to have the "Plumed Knight" enrolled among their honorary members. Jefferson is regarded as the founder of the now reverend Phi Beta Kappa, the honorary society of college presidents and class prize men.

December 5, 1776, the first American college fraternity, Phi Betta Kappa came into existence at William and Mary College, Va., with Thomas Jefferson as its founder. Beyond these few facts its early history is almost entirely shrouded in mystery. Chapters were afterward organized at many other institutions, among the earlier of which were Harvard, Yale and Dartmouth. A convention was held at Cambridge in 1881, the centennial of the Harvard chapter. It no longer retains the distinctive features of college fraternities, but limits its membership to college presidents and professors and honor men of senior classes. President Eliot of Harvard University has been elected president of its National Senate. Kappa Alpha founded in 1825 at Union College forty-nine years after. Phi Beta Kappa was the second college fraternity established in this country and the first of the "latter-day" fraternities.

The National Convention of Kappa Kappa Gamma was held at Canton, N. Y., commencing Aug. 27 and continuing five days. Fifteen chapters were represented.

The next convention of Kappa Kappa Gamma will be held, August, 1886, with the Lambda Chapter of Buchtel College, Akron, O.

Wishing soon to publish a catalogue of our members, we request each chapter to send the name, residence and general statistics of every person who has ever entered the chapter.

Exchanges.

The Golden Key extends to us a warm and cordial greeting, and kindly offers congratulations upon our advent. We acknowledge the kindness and hope when the ANCHORA becomes older and more experienced that she will be more worthy of praise from her only fem-

I — an oft told tale nearly a century old

The Founding

The story of the founding of Delta Gamma has indeed been a much told tale. The Founders themselves repeated it many times; not long before her death Mary Comfort Leonard wrote of it like this:

"I have told it so often, I am afraid it has become stale, however, I am always happy to do anything in my power for our Delta Gamma sisters. As I have now reached the evening of life, I naturally live a great deal in the past and derive great pleasure from most of it. You would know that I dwell much on that period when Anna Boyd, Eva Webb and Mary Comfort (Anna and Eva were cousins) at The Oxford Female Institute and so especially on the Christmas of 1873 when we were guests of our lady principal for the holidays, the days before coeds. We had no railroad to Kosciusko, and we went to boarding school in September and there we stayed until the next June. But we were a happy trio. We had many friends among the students and our friends of our classmates were very kind. . . . Our greatest pleasure was our work in forming our club as we first called our sorority for mutual helpfulness. How patiently we worked to embody into it all our highest ideals our Master had given us! We wrote our constitution and by-laws, adopted a name and motto, and Delta Gamma was born. We received no help from anyone—only borrowing a Greek grammar to find the Greek initial letters for our name. If the smile of the Infinite has been on Delta Gamma—and it seems to me it has, judging from its miraculous growth—we may be sure it is because of its high ideal, rendering service to others—trying literally to live the motto—Do Good.

"After the holidays were over we held our first meeting in January, 1874,* taking in our first members, several fine girls. We went to a local jeweler and had our pin made—the dear little letter H which stood for Hope, for we hoped

---

* These first four initiated January 2 were Idelette and Lucy Lyons, Mary Skipwith and Anna Towns.

great results and have not been disappointed. . . ."

Part of a picture

It is doubtful that Mary, Anna and Eva saw themselves and their venture away from home for higher education or their newly formed society as part of a spreading movement toward freedom of thought and activity for women. Prior to the Civil War higher education for women was by no means general, and co-education the exception rather than the rule in colleges and universities. The great conflict brought about some fundamental changes in the general attitude toward higher education of women, for time and again they had proved beyond question their ability to think and act independently and efficiently. Also the dearth of men teachers, due to the high mortality of the war years, made a wide demand for women teachers and it became expedient to educate women.

Delta Gamma had come into existence in the South at that period after the Civil War when the Southern states were again raising their heads and seeking their rightful place in the nation after the terrible disorganization of the immediate post-war period. While the education of women on an equal footing with men was no longer debatable, still few universities or colleges were opened to women in 1873. However, select schools to provide for the higher education of women were numerous, and it was one of these, The Oxford Female Institute, known as The Lewis School, which Eva, Anna and Mary attended.

This school was founded before the War between the States and eventually was absorbed by the University of Mississippi, a few blocks away, when the latter became co-educational. The Lewis School management changed a number of times and also changed its name. At the time of Delta Gamma's appearance it was known as The Oxford Female Institute. A little later we also find it referred to as "Warren Institute."

Unaware of others

On a number of occasions of pleasant reminiscing Eva Webb Dodd, Anna Boyd Ellington and Mary Comfort Leonard recall that they were unaware of the existence of other fraternities for women. They didn't know that the first of all fraternities, Phi Beta Kappa, had been organized in Williamsburg only five months after the first Fourth of July, 1776. They did know of men's fraternities, for the three girls' "lady principal" and holiday hostess was a Mrs. Hayes whose son was a student at Ole Miss and a member of one of the fraternities there. It is evident that young Mr. Hayes and the girls' other gentlemen friends at the University provided a good deal of the incentive for forming their own Greek letter society. The trio asserted, however, that they received no help—just pondered their project sitting in the middle of "Old Father Noah" as they dubbed the huge four-poster bed in their room.

Fraternities for women

During the period of the Civil War in the United States college fraternities then in existence suffered greatly, their development was retarded and in some cases their very life threatened. By the time their recovery was well advanced the secret society idea had spread and taken form within groups of young women like the trio in Oxford. By that Christmas, 1873, two local groups, Phi Mu and Alpha Delta Pi, had been in existence for more than 20 years at Wesleyan College in Georgia (neither expanded to other campuses until the turn of the century), and others were appearing in other parts of the country: Sorosis in 1867 at Monmouth (becoming Pi Beta Phi in 1888), Kappa Kappa Gamma in 1870 also at Monmouth, Kappa Alpha Theta the same year at DePauw, Alpha Phi in 1872 at Syracuse, and in 1874 Gamma Phi Beta also at Syracuse and Sigma Kappa at Colby. It was this scene, then, in which Delta Gamma was born.

At the end of the academic year 1873-74 Delta Gamma's three founders ended their schooling in Oxford, leaving behind a thriving society which owed to them its origin. The minutes* of these first meetings record gatherings of a literary nature and high-minded discussions of the intellectual and moral aims and ideals as well as the congeniality of potential members. Some business was transacted:

February 14, 1877. . . . Our Box was then produced and duly examined, proving not to be the thing desired. Necessary arrangements were made to obtain one suitable to our wants. . . .
March 7, 1877. . . . All business having been attended to satisfactorily and as a certain number of our sisters were very anxious to go through the city before—well, we don't know what reason to give, but I suppose the secret of it all is they wanted to see their sweethearts, we adjourned to meet on the following

* The original leather-bound minute book, with ornate Victorian lock and key, is on display in the Delta Gamma Archives.

Wednesday at the usual hour. . . .
February 27, 1878. . . . Under the head of miscellaneous business we were discussing the propriety of establishing a chapter at Water Valley. It was suggested that the most certain and satisfactory way of accomplishing this would be to send a delegate. The vote was taken and Miss Mary Skipwith was elected and the amount furnished. . . .

Evidently Mary failed to make the trip, for later is recorded:

May 1, 1878. . . . It was decided to send Miss Corrinne Miller, a hardworking sister, to Water Valley, hoping through her energy and determination to establish a chapter there. She promised to leave May 2nd and several sisters were to meet her there. . . .
January 22, 1879. . . . We were made happy by the presence of one of our sisters from Water Valley Club. As she will henceforth make Oxford her home we hope to have her with us every meeting. . . .
February 26, 1879. . . . This week several young ladies are going to order badges soon so we discussed that subject. . . .
September 17, 1879. . . . Miss Miller desired to borrow all the money in the treasury. This was put before the house which decided to loan it on interest. A resolution was then put before the house which was readily adopted: that no member shall repeat any unpleasant slander concerning an absent member. . . .
September 24, 1879. . . . Miscellaneous business was next in progress, resulting in the introduction of three amendments into the Constitution. 1st, that the house fee be reduced to 35 cents, 2nd the initiation fee to 50 cents, third that no one should be admitted into the club under 13 years of age. . . .

Each meeting from the beginning records criticisms at the close of the session. In later years two of the founders reminisced that this began during those first Christmas holidays in 1873 in their earnest efforts, through the bonds of Delta Gamma, toward self-improvement. Each paid five cents when she used slang; this kept Eva in pocketfuls of change. The criticisms are enlarged upon—

November 5, 1879. . . . Our criticism box was quite full of good and sensible criticisms this week. Several young ladies were criticized on the way they conduct themselves in the hall during club meeting. Hope they have not forgotten as requested. . . .

Youthful members

During these early years in Oxford observers from elsewhere note a peculiarity in the Mother Chapter—that the "actives" are in reality the inactive members of the group and the alumnæ or inactive members are really most active in the chapter. This is attributed to the youth (those over 13 years of age) of the members, for we must remember that the Institute was really a prep school. In the early 'eighties when the University began to admit women, many of Psi's members were entered in classes which is the reason letters to the *Anchora* are datelined during this period "University of Mississippi." Actually, the chapter itself was still established at the Institute and was never moved to the University—until it was installed many years later as Alpha Psi. Hence the disgust written into the following—

March, 1880. . . . Found a note on the table from the school girls asking or rather commanding the young ladies of the town to become honorary members. Our vice-president was disgusted with the command so would not allow it to be voted on. She threw it aside and proposed an adjournment. . . .

December 27, 1880*. . . . Had quite a nice pleasant chat and letter was read from our much beloved Franklin sisters, Miss Lillie Vawter wanting to have a national Convention and also telling us of a good field in Vermont where a chapter would do well. . . .

2 — Unity through correspondence

First mortar

For a time it seemed that the adhesive on the back of a postage stamp was the mortar which held together the foundation of Delta Gamma.

Long-faded letters written in the careful hand of the 'seventies and early 'eighties herald expansion, transact business of badges and charters and answer the technicalities (Do we have a fraternity grip?—from Akron to Oxford in 1879) as well as form an intercollegiate camaraderie among these pioneering coeds.

Naturally, much of that early correspondence does not live to tell its fascinating tale. For much of what remains we are grateful to Minnie Wohlleben Carter in whose guardianship the Delta Gamma strong box remained from the time the Mother Chapter was withdrawn from Oxford in 1889 until many years later when contacts were renewed and firmly established with Delta Gammas elsewhere. It had been Minnie's older sister, Lillie, who had handled the chapter correspondence during the period when Psi was most active in expansion, and it was her busy pen which inspired the organization and activities and soothed the troubles of half a dozen or so small but eager groups of Delta Gammas. Lillie Wohlleben had been initiated into Psi in October, 1875, and from that time until her marriage in 1883 she held some office in the chapter.

Expansion is simple

In those days the organization process was a simple one. One of the earliest remaining letters is dated May 29, 1878 and is written by Kate Thompson who had been initiated at Oxford during a vacation from Fairmount College at Monteagle, Tennessee.

Dear Clubmates,

Last Monday evening we organized a chapter of the Delta Gamma Club at Fairmount. I received into it five girls, Jennie Ramorth of Vicksburg, Miss., Dellie McCoy of Mobile, Ala., Warrene Anderson of Greenville, Miss., Georgia Sterling of Lake Washington, Miss., Laura Skipwith of Little Rock, Ark. They are among the nicest girls in school and are all charmed with our Club. Mrs. Yerger and Kells were much pleased that we should establish a literary club in school and gave their hearty approval. We wish to get our chapter fully started before we receive any new members. Will you please tell us the lowest price which we can get the badge, chain and chapter pin? We have not named our chapter yet but intend to do so at the next meeting. We also could not possibly meet on Wednesday as it would interfere with the practice hours, so chose Monday evening in one of the recrea-

* Can't help wondering if the chapter was once more weatherbound for the holidays—Ed.

tion hours. Miss Laura Skipwith, our Cor. Sec., will write once a week to our clubmates in Oxford so you will hear all the news. We also will send the rules back as soon as possible.

Psi chapter was choosing carefully the institutions which were to make Delta Gamma national, and Fairmount was one which maintained the highest standing. When the extensive Delta Gamma history was compiled in 1915, Fairmount, then Fairmount School for Girls and still enjoying its high standing, was under the management of a former member of this chapter, Susie Du Bose. In 1877, Psi had sent a delegate to Water Valley, Mississippi, 18 miles from Oxford, to establish a chapter at the Water Valley Seminary, the first Chi chapter. The Fairmount group became Theta and later in 1878 a group at Bolivar College, Bolivar, Tennessee, became Upsilon chapter of Delta Gamma. All three of these chapters were extinct by 1880-81 because of prejudice against fraternities in girls' schools in the South.

With a thoughtful backward look, the historian wrote in 1915: "In judging the character of Delta Gammas in her early days we must remember that this period of our history occurred during the Reconstructive Period of the South after the Civil War. Southern schools had a hard struggle to exist and it was only a natural result that Delta Gamma could not grow stronger although she had expanded to the extent of four chapters.

"In order for a national fraternity to develop and become a permanent institution, it must be established in institutions of collegiate rank. As college education for women met with bitter opposition in the South until recent years, Delta Gamma had no opening for a permanent growth. It probably would have become extinct as a national fraternity if a group of girls had not written to Corinne Miller a petition for a chapter of Delta Gamma at Franklin College, Franklin, Indiana."

The role of George Banta

It took the strong, guiding hand of a man to bring about this important move to the North. That man, George Banta*, a prominent Phi Delta Theta worker all of his life, wrote of his Delta Gamma experience in 1907: "Let me say at the outset that I am compelled to rely much upon my own memory of the events of 1878-82 with which I had to do, and which I trust it may not impute me to egotism if I say were of great importance to the sisterhood. (Recently), I have spent much time reviving memories and while

---

* It was this George Banta who later founded the George Banta Publishing Company of Menasha, Wisconsin, which has since 1908 printed *The Anchora*.

there is yet much that eludes me, I am now sure of the main outlines of all the really important facts.

"As it is true of many of the important events of all our lives, the transplantation of Delta Gamma was the result of a trivial cause. In the latter 'seventies the great event in collegiate politics in Indiana was the election held annually in May at the time of the Indiana State Oratorical Contest. The fraternity of which I am a member, in those days seemed to always find the delegates belonging to either of the two sororities then in the state, combined against them at these elections. Of course, this was merely consecutive accident for two or three years, but it led me to consider methods of securing organized affiliation on the part of the young ladies. The local Greek-letter society was unknown in Indiana in those days except through the most vague hearsay, and I most naturally turned to the national idea as the only way out. The accidental combination of the two then in the state was the very thing I was planning to defeat, so that I had to turn to the outside field.

The initial contact

"In May, 1878, I was returning from the national convention of my fraternity which had just adjourned in Ohio. In the homeward bound party was Monroe McClurg of Mississippi University at Oxford. To him I related the political difficulties I have recounted and asked him if there was a sorority in his institution or state that might be transplanted into the North and which might be made our special ally in our college warfare. . . .

"Mr. McClurg was able to give me the name of a sorority having a chapter at Oxford Institute, and of a young lady. I cannot be sure as to the lady's name he gave me, but I think it was Miss Corinne Miller. At any rate, I was in correspondence with Miss Miller, as attested by one letter I still have from her. The sorority, of course, was Delta Gamma.

Correspondence opened

"I at once opened correspondence with Psi chapter at Oxford, Miss., which was then the Grand Chapter, and very quickly received reply that Delta Gamma was glad to contemplate extending her chapter roll and boundaries. . . . I at once took up the matter with a group of young ladies in Franklin College, and my preliminary overtures were received with immediate success. I gave these young ladies the name of my correspondent at Oxford and withdrew from active participation in the movement. A correspondence between the Franklin girls and Delta Gamma ensued which dragged over several months without issue satisfactory to me or Delta Gamma. I can recall that the Franklin girls told me that Oxford was too far away. I had the idea at the time that the correspondence was haltingly and lamely conducted on both sides. I have sometimes thought that the yellow fever epidemic which raged in Mississippi in 1878 may have been partly to blame for this. But I could see that the wide distance separating the correspondents and the imperfect and crude understanding each had of Greek methods was the main stumbling block. These negotiations terminated abruptly when the Franklin girls accepted the overtures of another national.

"As soon as this occurred I wrote Psi chapter that I had failed. By this time I had lost sight of the political end I at first had in view, and felt much chagrined over the lame and impotent conclusion because of the disappointment I feared it was to the girls at Oxford. I explained to them the causes I had observed working for failure and said to them I would be glad to begin all over again. The absence of direct personal communication having been potent for unsuccessful issue, I suggested that I be clothed with sufficient authority to act personally and directly. In doing this, I did not have in mind more that being made a sort of minister extraordinary to deliver to a new group I had in mind, the sealed packets containing the necessities for membership without myself knowing the contents or participating in the active work of Delta Gamma.

Honorary members

"I may explain here that in that elder day of thirty years ago, here in the West at least, fraternities on special occasion affiliated students in colleges in which they had no chapters, by registered mail. This, of course, will seem most strange to fraternities members in this day. But it was then the day of rapid extension and fierce rivalry. Fraternities were not centralized as they are today, and methods were then more lax and crude. Every fraternity and sorority in the West initiated honorary members and many men and women, valuable to them in their fight for not only growth, but existence as well, were oft quoted and oft boasted members. Nearly every member of the faculty of Indiana University in 1875 was a member of a fraternity and not more than one of them had been a member of his fraternity in college days, and I am really doubtful if that one had been.

"Then it will afford light on what follows, and show precedent if I say there was in Oxford, Mississippi, at that time a young lady, Miss Bessie Carrothers, who was a member in full standing of one of the promiennt national men's fraternities and whose name appears in catalogue of that fraternity, issued in 1878. Such a precedent was right at home in Oxford in daily view of Psi chapter of Delta Gamma.

"With this lengthy premise I come to what has always remained to me the pleasantest compliment I have ever received in my life. In due time there came from Psi chapter a formal answer to the letter I have last mentioned, dated May 27, 1879, notifying me that I had been elected to full membership in Delta Gamma and welcoming me as the first masculine member of the order. The letter was signed by Corinne Miller. I will not need to say to you that the letter is one of my most prized treasures today. I have never valued the honors paid me by my fraternity of the sterner sex more than I do the graceful compliment of the girls of Oxford chapter paid me then.

"Of course, correspondence followed and I was speedily given authority to organize and initiate a chapter at Franklin College. The three girls I first interested were Miss Mary Vawter, her cousin Miss Lillian Vawter, and Miss Kitty Ellis, my own cousin. Their initiation was extremely simple, consisting as I recall it of my communicating the few secrets to one, who in turn communicated them to the others. . . . As Miss Lillian Vawter was my fiancée, it is probably not difficult to conjecture who the first Delta Gamma north of the Ohio River was, after myself. . . . I clearly remember that we were told we should select our own chapter letter and we promptly chose Phi, in honor of the familiar name applied to my fraternity.

"We at once started to found other chapters.° I cannot now recall when nor in what order the organizations were effected at Hanover and Buchtel (Akron). In both cases it was through the direct and active effort and cooperation of members of my fraternity. At Hanover the sister of one of the boys interested and Miss Lillian Thompson went to Hanover, I think, and organized the chapter. I am sure the Buchtel Chapter was organized by correspondence. . . . (Here follows a detailed account of circumstances surrounding the organization of Delta Gamma at the University of Wisconsin, which we have recorded elsewhere.—Ed.)

"Naturally I have always had a profound interest in Delta Gamma, her progress and success. While the very peculiarities of the case would not permit me to approach the Delta Gamma of today with unreserved freedom, no one of you who in these later years have taken her pledges, has a deeper or more affectionate interest in her welfare than I. I cannot number the times I have seen the badge of Delta Gamma passing me and wished that proper convention did not forbid my greeting its wearer. On such an occasion I feel precisely as you feel when you suddenly see the emblem away from college. Doubtless you cannot understand it more than in part, but the feeling I have is in almost all respects the same as when I suddenly meet a stranger wearing the pin of my fraternity.

"So I rejoice with you today in Delta Gamma's strength and glory, and I hope neither can ever be weakened or dimmed."

George Banta

° All approved by the Grand chapter in Oxford.

3 — Foundations are built

The move to the north

And so Delta Gamma's move north had begun. During 1879-80, Phi Delta Theta connections aided with the founding of one more Southern chapter—the first Delta chapter at Trinity College, Tehuacana, Texas—but this was to be the last installation in the South for many, many years. Like the Mother Chapter's other southern expansion, the Trinity group was to return its charter within a year or so.

Buchtel College (Akron University)

With the installation of Phi at Franklin the foundation was laid for a permanent, national fraternity. As Mr. Banta has mentioned, it was through Phi's efforts (Lillian Vawter's, in fact) that Delta Gamma entered Buchtel College, now Akron University, in 1879.

On March 12, 1879, George Banta wrote to Corinne Miller as follows:
. . . "The matter which I deem so urgent as to necessitate my informing you is this. Mr. H. A. Kelley of our Ohio Eta chapter writes me this morning informing me that they (the Phi Delta Theta chapter) are trying to persuade some of the young ladies of Buchtel College to organize a ΔΓ chapter. He requests the ΔΓ ladies to write immediately to Miss Mary Laughead, Akron, Ohio, Care Buchtel College. He says you will have the persuasive eloquence of 15 ΦΔΘ's to support you and thinks that a fine chapter could be started at once and be well supported." And so it was.

George Banta and his fiancée were also instrumental in the establishment of a chapter at the University of Wisconsin in 1880, through again a Phi Delta Theta whom they met at the ball which closed the 1880 Phi Delta convention in Indianapolis, Dan S. McArthur. This chapter did not really establish itself until a year later, however.

Days at Franklin

During the early Delta Gamma days at Franklin, Mr. Banta was evidently furnishing Phi Delta Theta stationery for the Delta Gammas' reports back to the Mother Chapter in Oxford. Competition was evidently stiff and after it was all over Correspondent Emma Taggart gives forth a slightly wordier "whew" than might be

heard after a rugged rush season today:
"However, the enemies' forces are completely routed and they have given up in despair. There are only three left, and one of them we actually wouldn't have as a Delta Gamma anyway!" This letter accompanies Oaths of Secrecy and Obedience, which had been entrusted to Mr. Banta, signed by the newest members.

Emma Taggart was the faithful correspondent at Franklin for several years until that duty was taken over by Lillian Vawter, who writes their friends in Oxford, "Miss Taggart is still sick (consumption) with no hopes of recovery. I believe a letter from you would make her feel better." Later another letter from Miss Vawter tells of Miss Taggart's death and eulogizes a strong and faithful member.

Emma Taggart's energies in behalf of Delta Gamma were quieted only a little during her long illness. Earlier in the year she wrote her sisters in Mississippi, "Others have managed to get organized here, but as they can't keep their own secret I know what they intend doing. Yesterday I understood they were after two girls we wanted and though I was sick, I jumped up out of bed and went to see them and gained a promise if they joined any they would come with us. . . . I haven't heard from Greencastle yet, hope I will this week. . . . The Phi Delta Thetas edit a monthly called 'The Scroll' and as Mr. Banta was very busy he asked me to write for him in 'Opposition to College Fraternities.' I did so, signing the nom de plume 'Delta Gamma.' The piece came out in the December number and I thought no more of it until the other day I received a letter from the President of ΦΔΘ fraternity, Clarence J. Redding of Pennsylvania, thanking me for the piece and offering his assistance in establishing a chapter at Wilson College, Chambersburg, Pa."

University of Wisconsin

Early in 1880, letters from Wisconsin begin to appear in the aging collection, but it was not until the following year that the chapter we know as Omega was firmly established in Madison. Most of the members of the corresponding group, chartered in 1880, were either graduated or left school after the close of the 1880-81 school year, and the three who remained felt it best to return their charter. In November 1881 another group of girls petitioned (some of whom had been rushed by the earlier Omega chapter the year before), and once more Omega chapter was established at the University of Wisconsin. It wasn't as simple as it would seem, however, for anti-fraternity feelings compelled them to resort to secret meetings outside campus precincts until conditions were more favorable for fraternities in Madison.

A great portion of each letter was usually devoted to family and other personal items of news and particularly matters of religion. From Akron to Oxford in 1880: "You asked in your last if I am a Universalist. I am. Are you?" This was typical.

Agitation for a convention

By 1880 agitation was beginning for a Convention, and through the year enthusiasm gained momentum. But even the important fact that the Convention which this enthusiasm was to inspire in May 1881, was the second held by a women's fraternity, the more important business of daily chapter problems persisted. From Akron in March, 1880, come these perplexing thoughts, "Have you any fraternity colors? Will you send us your coat of arms or a drawing—we are anxious to know positively. Send us your coat of arms by express at our expense. The seniors are about to issue a paper. They want all the information they can get concerning the number of chapters, where located, etc. . . . The Phi Delta Theta boys are anxious for us to show our badges. . . ."

And from that small, isolated group at Trinity College in Tehuacana, Texas, a few months later, "Now can you not suggest something that will add interest to our meetings. Please excuse me for being inquisitive, but is it obligatory upon the president that at each meeting she read an essay or can this be required of someone else? What is meant by the clause, 'Ask the question?' Is some question to be proposed. . . . The Phi (Delta Theta) delegate returned from their convention much elated, and the consequence of his visit will much edify and improve his brethren. . . . There is mention of us in *The American College Fraternity* that we are now an organization, and here comes another question, how will we stand upon the roll, who receives our name, what Greek letter is ours?"

Several weeks later another hurried letter from the Texas correspondent, Sallie R. Young, indicates the beginning of difficulties which later brought an early end to the chapter's minute book . . . "false reports have gone to our president with such a story as this—that our sole object was to meet and discuss the pupils of the school, etc. I shall not go into detail, but suffice to say, we are in trouble and for fear he, not knowing our motive, may forbid our meeting, I appeal to the Oxford chapter to let us show him

our Constitution. I think this will appease him."

Surprise from Texas

In short order, the permission was evidently given by the Oxford girls via Lillie Wohlleben, and for a time did succeed in appeasing the school's president who promised to be the Delta Gammas' "true friend." Once again the Phi Delta Thetas were the loyal supporters of the Delta Gammas, and among other activities Sallie reported to her mail-time friend in Mississippi, "We, the ΔΓ's and Phis, had a soiree, an interesting affair, December 23. The other frats here had been in the habit of having suppers, but we determined to have something new. There is an account published of it I wish you all could read, would show you our status, I think."

Throughout the 1880-81 school year this was a lively correspondence between the two representatives of their respective chapters, but when the secretarial office passed on to someone else in Tehuacana, it comes to an abrupt halt—in Tehuacana, at least. It is with some glee, however, that Sallie surprises her friend Lillie in her last letter—"You no doubt will be surprised when I tell you I have been teaching 21 years, 8 years in this university, and *am an old maid* 43. What think you now?" Miss Young goes on to relate the history of the Texas chapter and indicates that one careless step on their part—even in rumor—may mean its exodus from the school. For that reason, she feels that the prudent thing to do is not to send a delegate to the approaching Delta Gamma Convention in Oxford.

Scholarship program suggested

What representation from Tehuacana could have meant to Delta Gamma's first Convention can only be guessed, for it was a group which early in its existence had shown a maturity of thought and goal which brought forth ideas that did not materialize in the fraternity world until some years later. A scholarship program was one of their earliest suggestions: "*We are thinking of taxing ourselves a small sum, putting that out at interest, and seeking some noble, worthy Delta Gamma and to educate her to prepare her for a field of responsibility, we will claim her as our property. We hope you will approve of our motive to say the least of it. I think it is duty we feel will give us prestige at home and abroad.*"

Not always were the letters from these outlying chapters answered with such speed and attention as was received by the Trinity Delta Gammas. Lillie Vawter during the same year scolds the Mississippians soundly for their neglect, not only of the chapter at Franklin, but of the group whose organization she herself instigated at Wisconsin. The chief cause for complaint was the lack of the long-promised charter itself. A letter to Oxford a few days later affirms Miss Vawter's accusation and states that it is the cause for the failure of Delta Gamma in Madison to get a real start in spite of the enthusiastic groundwork done by Miss Vawter. Without delay apologies were made and accepted and the charters were in the mail.

Competition at Wisconsin

In the midst of all this, the first Omega chapter became the indignant victim of mail-snatching by competing Greeks also living at the Ladies' Hall in Madison. Says the Wisconsin correspondent, "Isn't it provoking? I don't think I care to have any more Delta Gamma mail come to Ladies' Hall and shall appropriate Mr. McArthur's box again. So when you write me again please address me as 'Dan S. McArthur' with the ΔΓ Mark, and I don't believe it will fail of reaching me."

The arrival of charters from Mississippi was not the end of this affair. In mid-January, 1881, Lillian Vawter, her fraternity spirit kept at high pitch by her active Phi Delta fiance, George Banta, writes to the other "Lillie" in Oxford, "My dear girl, you did nobly getting up the charters. They are very pretty indeed. There are one or two things might be added which would improve them. One is, there should be a seal on them, but we will let the Convention fix that as it will fix a great many other things." The Franklin Delta Gammas had been duly impressed by attendance at the Phi Delta Theta Convention in Indianapolis a few months before this.

First Convention Special

During the spring of 1881 pre-Convention excitement grew, particularly in Akron when it was learned that Fanny Mulliken's father, Mr. J. B. Mulliken, was making it possible for an Eta delegation to make the trip to Oxford. At this point, however, something caused the members of the Mother Chapter to cancel Convention plans, the reason unapparent in the collection of yellowed correspondence in our possession today. The tearful pleas of the girls planning to board Mr. Mulliken's "Special" train (actually a private railroad car) as well as agonized cries from chapters who, though unable to send delegates, felt a convention necessary at this moment for the survival of the Fraternity, must have caused Psi to reconsider, for the Convention invitation from Oxford was reaffirmed.

Among the most insistent that this Convention must be held as soon as possible—though she was unable to send a delegate—was Omega. Upon the action that could be taken by the delegates and upon the comaraderie and spirit which could develop from such an assembly, she felt the future strength of Delta Gamma depended. These sentiments are voiced again and again by Omega's enthusiastic correspondent, Eloise Johnson, who, in making suggestions for the Convention's agenda, said that Omega would be agreeable to any action taken—most important is that there be some action. Nor was Omega alone in these thoughts; others, viewing rising Greek competition on their own campuses, were echoing the same ideas but without the same vigor displayed by Miss Johnson. As we muse over the Texas Delta Gammas' absence from this first Convention, we may also wonder what Omega might have contributed had she been able to make the long and costly journey to Mississippi.

Lillie Wohlleben's own thoughts are recorded under the lock and key of the Psi minute book, for she was serving as secretary at this time:

January 12, 1881. . . . There was much talk of Convention. We must all work if we hold this Convention by the first of May. I know the girls will take new interest and help the Club grow. . . .

Minnie Wohlleben Carter, Ψ-Mother Chapter, was a special guest at the 1911 Convention. It was she who had guarded safely the early records and treasures of the Mother Chapter, introducing them to Blanche Garten in 1905 and many years later, just before her death, presenting these things to Marguerite Winant, then President of the Fraternity.

4 — The first sorority convention — May 25, 1881, Oxford, Mississippi . . .

A gavel falls

The first General Convention of the Delta Gamma Fraternity convened in the parlors of Mr. H. Wohlleben at 4 p.m. on Wednesday, May 25th, delegates from Ohio and Mississippi being present." Thus Delta Gamma met as a national organization.

The first minutes continue, "As the Convention was not organized the body proceeded at once to organization and elected the following officers by secret ballot: Sister Mollie Laughead, H-Akron, President; Sister Anna Bowen, Υ-Oxford Institute, Vice-President; Sister Carrie Hawk, H-Akron, Secretary."

Mulliken honorary member?

Since it was the father of one of the Akron delegates, Mr. J. B. Mulliken of Detroit—father of Fannie Mulliken—who had made the Convention possible by providing his private railroad car for the transportation of the Akron girls to Oxford, the first item of business concerned him. Mr. Mulliken was unanimously elected an honorary member of the Fraternity. Unfortunately, no certain record can be found of his acceptance of this honor though later Mrs. Mulliken's name was also proposed for honorary membership.

The Convention disposed of much business in a most energetic manner—largely organizational matters, such as securing books for the Convention Treasurer and Secretary, selecting a committee to work on a Coat of Arms, etc. Probably the most important action was the decision to hold a second Convention in 1883. The results of the conscientious work carried forth in Mr. Wohlleben's drawing room in Oxford were to show in the progress of Delta Gamma during the next two years. Psi was elected Grand Chapter, Eta Deputy Chapter and Delta of Trinity College (though not represented) was to be Historian. The terms of office were for two years.

Convention report

When the Akron girls returned home, Carrie Hawk, recounted in *The Akron Beacon* the happy affair. For many years this clipping was the only account on record of the Convention, for a fire in Akron destroyed all of Eta's possessions, including these early records. At the time of the fire, Psi had been withdrawn, and feeling among Delta Gammas in Oxford ran high. Many years later, when old friendships were renewed, the original Delta Gamma strongbox was found in the possession of Minnie Wohlleben Carter (Lillie's sister), and in it the original minutes of the first Convention.

It is, however, to Carrie Hawk's account that we must turn for the social part of Convention—which, inevitably set some precedents. Here are a few extracts:

"On the evening of May twenty-second, we, Misses Fannie T. Mulliken, Mollie M. Laughead, and Carrie B. Hawk, accompanied by Mr. J. B. Mulliken of Detroit, started on a trip to the 'Sunny South.' The immediate cause of our adventure was a convention of the Delta Gamma Fraternity to be held in Oxford, Miss., where the Grand Chapter is located and to which the three young ladies were delegates. Our little company was very happy as we moved away from the Akron Depot, where 32 of our friends stood to bid us farewell. We arrived at Oxford, Miss., at 9:10 p.m., Tuesday. A delegation met us at the depot, and we were most warmly received. . . . The excellent manner in which we were entertained attests that Oxford people appreciate the true spirit of hospitality. There is a tone of refinement and culture that seems to pervade the very air that we breathe. . . .

The convention, which as all important to us, opened Wednesday, May 25, at 4 p.m., though there had been an informal meeting from nine to twelve in the morning. The convention was in session from four to seven on Wednesday and Thursday evening and from nine to twelve Thursday and Friday morning. There was also a short business session on Friday afternoon. The convention from a business point of view, was a complete success. The ladies confined themselves closely to the business at hand and a great deal was accomplished. . . . We received reports, histories and essays of every chapter in the Fraternity. . . . The convention has done much to put the Fraternity on a firmer basis and has given us much pleasure. A reception was given us at Mr. H. Wohlleben's on Thursday evening. It was quite a brilliant affair. The evening was spent in social chat, interspersed with music, for the young people of Oxford are fine talkers: indeed it is a characteristic of Southern people. . . . On Friday we dined with General Skipwith, whose wife is the daughter of General Volk. The spread was elegant and in unique style. . . . In the afternoon, we visited the university. The campus is very large and the drives under the grand old trees are particularly cool and pleasant. . . . The university has just closed its twenty-ninth session, having an attendance of 347 students. . . . . In the evening, we were again tendered a reception at Mr. Blakely's and we spent the time until

the 'wee sma hours' in blissful social entertainment. We met many of the prominent citizens of Oxford and everyone seemed to lay aside everything that could interfere in the least with our entertainment. But all good things have an end and at 6 o'clock next morning we were on our way to Chattanooga. Though we left so early, a large delegation was at the train to see us off. . . ."

Those attending the first Convention were: Eta, Mollie Laughead, Carrie Hawk and Fannie Mulliken; Psi, Anna Bowen, Lillie Wohlleben, Aslee McLeod, Mollie Blakely, Madie Blakely, Mary Dulaney, Millie Richmond, Minnie Wohlleben, Lillie Andrews, Julia Johnson, Cora Pegues, Mary Skipwith, Minnie Chapman, Ida Milbourn, and Ida Howell.

5 — Convention inspired real and rapid progress

New vigor

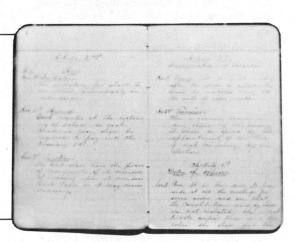

It was with new vigor that Delta Gammas returned to fraternity business following that first Convention. Just how much more rapid and real the progress of the Fraternity had become as a result of this meeting is probably best evidenced by the expansion during 1881 and 1882.

Hanover College

Hanover College at Hanover, Indiana—a "neighbor" of Franklin—had seemed a suitable field and, as has already been recorded by George Banta, Delta chapter was installed there in the fall of 1881. Delta Gamma was the first women's group to enter Hanover but it was quickly followed by Kappa Alpha Theta. The active membership of either chapter never exceeded six and both Delta Gamma and Kappa Alpha Theta turned in their charters six years later. As the 1915 historian relates, "This was the second time that Delta was chosen for a name of a chapter in Delta Gamma, but fate seemed to decree it an unlucky choice, for later a third chapter dared to choose this Greek letter, and each in turn passed out of existence."

Northwestern University

Northwestern University in Evanston, Illinois, already the home of a year-old Alpha Phi chapter, welcomed Delta Gamma in the spring of 1882. Again this was an instance of hearsay from another campus—Catherine Stoneman having heard from a Chi Psi friend at the University of Wisconsin of the great attractions of young Omega chapter, "and besides, their pin is about the prettiest I ever saw," he remarked. Catherine's enthusiasm was quickly caught by a group of her closest friends, and after some correspondence with Omega, they appointed Catherine along with Leila Crandon to go to Madison to be initiated and bring back the "authority and enlightment" necessary to introduce to the other six of the group into the mysteries of the organization. Omega was evidently delighted with this novel experience—she herself having heretofore been an outpost of Delta Gamma—and entertained the pair royally with a banquet, dance, what must be recorded as a "rough" initiation complete with much goat-riding (a sawhorse).

Fulton Synodical College

Fulton Synodical College in Fulton, Missouri, received Pi chapter in 1882, but neither records nor correspondence remain to enlarge upon its three-year existence. . . .

Mt. Union College

Mount Union College at Alliance, Ohio became, in June, 1882, the home of Alpha chapter. Alpha remained sub rosa for six months, "but our weekly rendezvous was not unmarked by the members of the gentlemen fraternities, in whose footsteps we were but following, and who finally succeeded in wresting from us the veil of concealment under which we were quietly hiding until we should acquire strength sufficient to stand side by side with the gentlemen fraternities, two of which exist in our college." Thus reported the *Anchora* correspondent in that Journal's first issue in 1884.

University of Minnesota

University of Minnesota in Minneapolis, Minnesota was simultaneously receiving a Delta Gamma chapter which chose the letter Lambda. Since the term was nearly over, its first two members let matters rest until fall when they quickly increased the membership to ten. This again was the result of a Phi Delta Theta contact—Max Vanderhoock, a Minnesota Phi Delta, receiving a letter from Omega alumna Eloise Johnson MacArthur (Mrs. Daniel S.—she married the owner of the mailbox to which early Delta Gamma mail went!) asking him for the address of some girl who might be interested in establishing a chapter of Delta Gamma at the University. He turned the letter over to Louise Cady, a sophomore, who wrote Mrs. MacArthur for information and instructions.

Eta chapter evidently distributed these charters as part of her task as Deputy Chapter—though they were, of course, signed by officers of the Grand Chapter. Shortly after the 1881 Convention Carrie Hawk, H-Akron, wrote to Anna Bowen in Oxford, delighted that "We can get 15 charters for $1.50 not including parchment!"

Delta Gamma bids First Lady

George Banta has written of the fierce competition of the day in initiating as many as possible persons of note for added prestige for the various Greek-letter groups. In the summer, 1881 Delta Gamma made the grand attempt at this by bidding the wife of President Garfield. Before any sort of reply could come from the First Lady, the President was assassinated. In Psi's minutes we find the following:

"November, 1881—Miss Mary S. read a splendid letter from our sister Delta Gamma Miss Carrie Hawk of Akron, Ohio. In it was enclosed a letter of consolation to our deceased President's wife, Mrs. Garfield, who has been heretofore solicited to join our club. Miss Carrie asked our advice and permission to send said letter

which we willingly granted though our hearts are as loyal as ever to the Southern Democracy."

Second Convention
1883—Akron, Ohio

And so it is a confident and spirited national organization which met in its tenth year for its second Convention—May 24-26, 1883 in Akron, Ohio. Phi Delta Theta played its part once more, and sessions were held in the Phi Hall. The president of the Grand Chapter (Psi), Lillie Wohlleben, presided, and Mollie Scofield, H-Akron, recorded the proceedings. At the time, and through the years, Delta Gamma looks upon this Convention as one of great success with 6 of 9 chapters represented, and 37 attending the Convention banquet. Of utmost importance was the national spirit it ignited. Of equal note were the more tangible milestones marked in the Convention proceedings:

- **Initiation** fee was raised from one to two dollars.
- **Grand Chapter** location was to be changed every four years.
- **A Fraternity Journal** would be published to be known as the *Delta Gamma Anchor*, the first number to appear in the fall of 1883 with Eta chapter as editor.
- **Official jeweler** would be Bunde & Upmeyer Co. of Milwaukee.
- **Fraternity colors** would be bronze, pink, and blue, bronze having been added as some felt we might be confused with the pink and blue of Beta Theta Pi.
- **Expansion** included a vote to establish a chapter at the University of Michigan.

Elections

Omega was elected Grand Chapter for the coming term, thus furnishing the next Convention president. Sigma would become recording secretary and Alpha treasurer. Eta, along with its editorial duties, would again be deputy chapter, and Psi would serve as historian.

Adelbert College

The quick pace of expansion continued after this second Convention. Eta had reported at the meeting the initiation of a young lady from Adelbert College, Cleveland, Ohio, a Miss Cornelia Wadhams, but it was not until December 17 that she assembled a group to be initiated, with Eta's assistance, as charter members, the second Theta chapter.

St. Lawrence University

Earlier in the fall, through correspondence Delta Gamma had installed Upsilon chapter at St. Lawrence University, Canton, New York. Though its charter was returned in 1887, correspondence living to tell the tale gives evidence of an energetic and fervently interested group whose enthusiasm in 1885-86 aided in the campaign to add Delta Gamma to the women's fraternities at Cornell.

Albion College

Simultaneously a charter was granted to a group of young ladies at Albion College, Albion, Michigan. For a year or so the chapter was Xi but through an error in recording it became Zeta and so it remained. This was a case of direct colonization by a member of Sigma chapter—Ella M. Tarr whose sister, Cora Belle Tarr, was among the petitioners. The Tarr name reappears later in connection with the installation of another Delta Gamma chapter, the third Delta at the University of Southern California.

On Zeta's fiftieth anniversary charter member Elizabeth Masters Swarthout wrote, "A drive around town, a meeting where the secrets were whispered in our ears and important words of caution, counsel and direction were spoken, and then she departed leaving behind Zeta (then called Xi) of Delta Gamma. I have heard the 'eighties spoken of as the 'genteel eighties.' But when I think of our first initiation in the basement of 'Mud Palace' on Erie Street, which we stealthily entered by a basement window, and the subsequent goings-on there, I must conclude that 'genteel' was a misnomer or we were misfits." Reminiscences of early initiations similar to those recorded by Mrs. Swarthout can be found in the annals of all these early chapters.

Co-education struggles

Of this group of new chapters the one at Adelbert is particularly interesting in its reflection of a terrific struggle for co-education to gain a foothold. Delta Gamma appeared on campus during the first year women were able to maneuver entrance to classes. The correspondent reports twelve women enrolled in the college, a division of Western Reserve, and then lists seven in the membership of Delta Gamma—a good percentage! Delta Gamma remained until the feeling against co-education stifled it completely and a ban was placed on women attending classes.

The Anchora

Assembling funds and literary material proved a longer task than anticipated, and the first issue of *Delta Gamma Anchora* (no record of why the change in name since Convention) appeared in April, 1884, with Mary E. Thompson as editor, assisted by Mary Sibley and Mary Bock. In January, 1885, Abby C. Soule became editor with the same assistants. Delta Gamma was the second women's fraternity to publish a journal, Kappa Kappa Gamma having initiated *The Key* two years earlier.

Cornell University

In 1885, too, a new chapter appeared on the chapter roll—Chi at Cornell University, Ithaca, N.Y., which remained sub rosa for two months in order to increase its membership (from five to

eight) and to announce themselves by wearing their anchors publicly. Their desire was to make this first appearance at the Sage reception. Afraid that the pins might not arrive in time, they asked Eta to loan hers for the occasion. Both packages arrived the day of the reception, and the announcement was duly made.

Third Convention
1885—Madison, Wisconsin

Once more it was Convention time; this time Delta Gammas were traveling to Madison, Wisconsin, where Omega was to be hostess. Meetings of this Third Convention were held in the Chapel of Ladies' Hall, and Emma Goddard, Ω-Wisconsin, presided.

Once more, too, Fannie Mulliken's father provided a Convention "special car"—he and Fannie's brother bringing fifteen Delta Gammas from Detroit. Among these were Fannie and Mary Thompson, the first *Anchora* editor, both of whom had transferred to the University of Michigan the preceding year fired with the possibility of establishing a chapter there. Also among the fifteen was Clara Glover, a student at Michigan, who had decided to join the prospective chapter and was to be initiated at Convention.

More important milestones were marked on these days of June 24-26, 1885, at Delta Gamma's third Convention:

- *The Anchora* would be edited by Eta for another two years.
- "Fraternity" would be used in reference to Delta Gamma rather than the newer term, sorority.
- The history of Delta Gamma, written by Anna Bowen, Ψ-Oxford Institute, was read, and each chapter was urged to start its own book of history.
- The flower was to be the cream colored rose.
- Petitioners for Delta Gamma chapters would, in the future, be investigated by official delegates assigned to this duty. In the past desirous groups had simply been installed by correspondence.
- No men were to be initiated as honorary members in the future.
- The symbol of an "Eagle within a Δ" used by the fraternity prior to this time was to be discontinued.
- Recognition sign among members would be as follows: First, put the handkerchief to the right cheek. Second, in reply, first finger of right hand to lips.
- Annual dues were raised from fifty cents to one dollar and charters from five to ten dollars.

Elections

Theta (Adelbert College) would become deputy chapter and would provide the president for the next Convention. Alpha was elected secretary, Chi treasurer, and Lambda historian. Others would remain the same.

University of Michigan

So for the third time Convention was adjourned and Delta Gammas went forth with greater energy for fraternity activity. The Michigan girls returned to Ann Arbor in the fall and acquired as their first pledge Helen Lovell—whose daughter, Helen Million Preston, many years later was to become President of Delta Gamma. They also acquired three other pledges, and so initiating the four, Xi chapter had seven charter members.

University of Colorado

Two more chapters were to appear before the next Convention. The fraternity began a long move westward, and Phi chapter was installed at the University of Colorado in June, 1886.

In the recollections of a charter member, note is made for the first time of initiates clad in white: "white flannel, elegant but warm in June heat." When Phi celebrated its Golden Jubilee, its historian remarked on what Delta Gamma had found in Boulder in 1886: "Dr. Sewell, as president of the university, heading a faculty of 13; a student body of forty-seven; five buildings. . . . 'Four of these were supplied with bathrooms and three with hot water,' says the catalog of University of Colorado, 1886; and a group of eight eager girls who became our charter members."

State University of Iowa

Later in the same year Tau chapter was installed at the State University of Iowa—the charter granted November 9, 1886, though the charter members were not initiated until January, 1887. The group receiving the Delta Gamma charter had been contacted and "rushed" by correspondence by several national groups simultaneously, but these first members relate that they chose Delta Gamma because of its fine reputation. Again an initiation (Tau's first) was informal in an extreme sense of the word, concluding with the formal ceremony.

*A game of cards
for five Kappa chapter founders
and two initiates . . .*

A slumber party at Cornell in the 'nineties.

6 — Sadness in the South as Psi is withdrawn

Survival of the fittest

It was the mid-'eighties, and Delta Gamma had not only survived and endured but even thrived and grown during these rugged days in the field of education for women. Coeducation was by no means a certain thing though in most places the young ladies had earned a secure footing in the eyes of administration and faculty. On some campuses they had not fared so well. The governing chapters of Delta Gamma agreed that it was a vital matter to be considered before the next Convention.

Fourth Convention
1887—Cleveland, Ohio

And so action was taken at Delta Gamma's Fourth Convention in Cleveland, Ohio, May 29-31, 1887, which caused the return of two charters, that of Delta chapter at Hanover College and Upsilon at St. Lawrence. Other business transacted in Adelbert's Beckwith Chapel (Sarah McKinney, Θ-Adelbert, presiding) did not make the fourth Delta Gamma conclave a particularly important one. Socially, on the contrary, Theta chapter hostesses made it a great success. However, among the records of business we find:

• **Editing** the Anchora was transferred from Eta to Lambda chapter.

• **A catalogue** of members was to be published during 1888 by Omega.

• **The Constitution** was revised, particularly with emphasis on improving the journal. A committee for revisions was appointed of representatives of Eta, Xi, and Sigma chapters.

• **The Charter emblem** currently used would be replaced by an Anchor. A comment on this: "The old cut had been the representation of a fair damsel poised in a hazardous attitude who guided, with the assistance of an angel, a gondola across the water. The objective point apparently was a spectral figure in the sky surrounded by the Greek letters of the Delta Gamma pin."

Elections

Sigma became Grand Chapter; Xi, deputy; Sigma, general treasurer, and Eta, historian.

It is certain that an effort to make the most of their time was uppermost in the delegates' minds, for they packed their lunches so that they could work straight through the Convention day! We must note, too, that instructions to delegates were explicit: "Reduced rates have been secured on all railroads. Each person going to Convention must obtain a certificate from the ticket agent at her station of the Central Traffic Association form to the effect that she had bought a first class ticket. Then at Convention, a secretary must sign the same, certifying that she has attended Convention. If she does this, she can obtain a return ticket for one-third the regular fare." Conventioners recall that the practice of reduced rates of this sort continued for many years.

University of Southern California

Less than a year passed before the Fifth Convention was to be held, and only one chapter was installed. The letter Delta, so recently withdrawn from Hanover, was given to a chapter in the promising institution in California, the University of Southern California. Again one of the Tarr sisters—the same who figured in the organization of Zeta and Sigma chapters—was active. Ella Tarr, Σ-Northwestern, had gone to this new University of Southern California to be its dean of women and had straightway organized there a chapter of her own fraternity on the growing campus—a somewhat more direct approach than might be approved in today's rules for a successful dean of women!

Fifth Convention
1888—Evanston, Illinois

Sigma was hostess when the Fifth Convention met at the Odd Fellows Hall, in Evanston, Illinois, April 10-13, 1888, with Caroline Hunt, Σ-Northwestern, presiding. Only six years before Miss Hunt had been the then new Sigma chapter's first pledge—and initiate. Sixty Delta Gammas were present.

Request alumnæ charter

Since this Convention seems to reflect so sharply the trends of the day and growing organization strength of the Fraternity, we turn to our 1915 historian for a detailed account:

One of our strongest and most promising chapters, Theta at Adelbert, applied to Convention for a charter of an alumnæ chapter as the active chapter was doomed to go out of existence.

"A strong feeling in Adelbert against coeducation started a movement in 1885 to exclude women from the classes, and though the movement was defeated, the feeling was still an undercurrent. In 1888 coeducation was completely abolished in Adelbert college. There was no alternate for Theta chapter but to slowly go out of existence as its members left college or were graduated. The young women who composed Theta were among the most charming and cultured members of Delta Gamma and no greater loss could come to the Fraternity than the non-existence of Theta of Adelbert college. So intense was their interest and enthusiasm that they conceived the idea of forming an Alumnæ chapter in order to be part of the actual organization of the Fraternity.

"The constitution of Delta Gamma did not provide for alumnæ chapters, so an article providing for them was incorporated in the constitution and the Alumnæ of Theta at Cleveland granted a charter. It was a happy arrangement for both. Fraternity and chapter were left in touch with each other and Delta Gamma did not lose the support of such valuable members."

The chairman of chapters and charters, Susie Wegg, Ω-Wisconsin, reported favorably on the application from the University of Nebraska and "recommended that the case of Psi be investigated by Grand Chapter, the charter of Psi to be withdrawn at the discretion of said Grand Chapter. On motion, the report was accepted."*

Conditions in the Oxford Institute where Psi was situated had changed when the school in 1880 became Warren Institute. This caused the Fraternity to investigate conditions.

Founders Day established

One of Eta's most enthusiastic workers and a former editor of *Anchora*, Abby Soule, had made a plea in *Anchora*, March, 1887, for a reunion day for Delta Gamma. Eta probably introduced the subject at Convention and spoke of the custom in that chapter of observing March 15, the date on their charter as their reunion day.

Convention decreed that one day be set aside for an annual reunion, a day all chapters should observe. As a tribute to our oldest living chapter which had accomplished so much for Delta Gamma, March 15 was chosen. The celebration of that day has been an unbroken custom, and one of the most loved traditions of our Fraternity.

* Minutes of 1888 Convention.

Other Convention business included:

- **A Council** was added by Constitutional revision. The original plan of government in Delta Gamma had provided for a Grand Chapter to be assisted by a Deputy Chapter to transact the business of the Fraternity between Conventions. The 1888 Convention added a Council, a body consisting of "one active member and one alumna member from the Grand Chapter, one from the Deputy Chapter, one from the Editing Chapter, and one from one of the Alumnæ Chapters. The term of office was to be two years. The Council shall have power of final decision referred to it by the Grand and Deputy Chapters and by the Convention." This power was never really enforced until 1895.

- **Official jeweler** authorized by the Convention was J. F. Newman. This list of official jewelers grows with each Convention; manufacture of the Delta Gamma badge was not an exclusive right as it is today.

- **Songbook** arrangements were made, after considerable discussion at every Convention. Soon after a "pathetic little pamphlet" was issued, containing a few songs. It was the only one until 1895 when another weak attempt was made. This was not much of an improvement on the first publication according to later historians.

- **The Constitution** had been completely revised by a committee, was accepted and printed during the following year. This is the first printed Constitution for Delta Gamma; previously they had been hand-written.

Psi chapter to be investigated

Though at the time it was only a case of a committee chairman reporting to the Convention assembled, Susie Wegg's recommendation concerning Psi chapter which was accepted by this 1888 Convention probably caused more reverberations over the Mason-Dixon line than had been heard since cannon fire had ceased twenty-three years earlier. Many words have been written and voices have rung, pro and con, sweet and bitter. Years have slipped by and the wound has been healed; we will never know—though original handwritten reports are still on file—who was right and wrong. At first it was Psi who paid a heavy penalty for its lack of attentiveness to national fraternity matters, and later we are well aware it was the fraternity which paid even heavier penalty for its loss of contact with the South. The years of rebuilding have been high toll for harsh words in 1889.

To keep this record full and complete, we turn again to the 1915 historian's open and understanding account of the affair —

Report of investigation

"The Committee on Chapters and Charters recommended at the 1888 Convention that the case of Psi, the Mother Chapter, be investigated by Grand Chapter and the charter be withdrawn at the discretion of Grand Chapter. This motion was accepted. In recording it in the minutes and copying the same, a mistake was made. Some of the copies sent to the chapters omitted the last clause of the motion. These copies were hand written and a mistake could easily have been made. Grand Council sent a committee to investigate Psi and gave them authority to act. This authority the committee used. It naturally aroused resentment from those chapters which had received an incomplete report of Convention minutes as they considered that Grand Chapter, then Sigma, had over-stepped her authority in withdrawing Psi's charter between Conventions. When the subject was discussed in Convention at Madison, 1889, Sigma realized that, as Grand Chapter, she was strongly criticized by the major portion of the chapters. As a result, Sigma presented her resignation as Grand Chapter, "feeling that it is for the best interests of the Fraternity at large." Sigma was asked to reconsider her resignation. This, Sigma refused to do until the affair was threshed out in the sessions and Grand Chapter cleared of all blame and by general consent, the trouble-making clause inserted in the official minutes of the 1888 Convention.

"The feeling in Convention must have been intense as it related to two vital subjects. One, the severing of all relations between the Fraternity and the Mother Chapter, Psi—a subject which must have aroused the most decided personal feeling among delegates and visitors, as many had formed close friendships with many of Psi's loyal workers. Another, the question of the justice of the action of Grand Chapter, besides the precedent which would have been established if it had acted without authority."

Though, the official report states, the committee composed of Susie Wegg and Fannie Mulliken was appointed in the fall of 1888, they were unable to arrange their ill-fated expedition to Mississippi until February, 1889. They wrote friends in Oxford of their anticipated visit but apparently the full import was not made clear—possibly the investigators assuming that Psi had seen the Convention minutes which later proved never to have reached her.

Weaknesses of Psi

Fannie Mulliken, of course, felt extremely close to the older members of Psi and requested full particulars as "I would probably have a large share in the final decision and I wished to use my influence in behalf of Psi." Susie was unbiased in attitude, even grim in approach, but even Fannie's definite prejudice in favor of Psi could not blind her to certain weaknesses in the chapter as it existed in 1889.

The chapter originally organized at the Institute had only two actives enrolled there in 1889 while five others were pupils in the Oxford public school. These seven ranged in age from thirteen to seventeen. All offices were held by non-active members, and during the investigation they did all the negotiating. Financially Psi had been negligent for some time, but Fannie and Susie were told of elaborate annual banquets given their gentlemen friends and could not help noticing members wearing "handsomely set" badges. Psi had not seen the magazine since its removal to Minneapolis, but her minutes recorded receiving reminders for literary and financial contributions. There seemed to be disagreement on every point within the chapter itself.

In Psi's favor—

On the other hand, Psi stood extremely well socially in Oxford, and the citizens of the town took pride in "the club" of which daughters of the "best families" were members. But as Fannie states in her official report, "the trouble was it was looked upon as a local institution, and not as a unit of a national sisterhood of wide-spread and varied interests. The chapter was isolated by her own neglect of sister chapters; she was not at all in touch with the spirit of advancement which characterizes the Fraternity; she was local and stationary." On the last day of the investigators' visit the final and fatal meeting was held, and "having been assured that all was said that could be said on either side," the two retired to deliberate—their sympathies and judgment in sore conflict. It was Miss Wegg who expressed sincere and deep regrets that such action was necessary and who read the resolutions the committee had drawn up declaring Psi no longer an active chapter.

Returning to the 1915 record, "The members of the Mother Chapter after hearing the decision of the committee felt that their side of the question had not been properly brought before the fraternity as a whole. They therefore prepared a letter stating their understanding of the case and giving several resolutions which they had drawn up. This letter was sent to all chapters of the Fraternity. It said that Psi chapter was essentially the same that she always had been; that she had created the Fraternity and was part of the whole not by inheritance or grant; that she had made a constitution and by-laws and designed the badge; that as a southern chapter she could not be ruled or be judged by the same laws by which a northern chapter would be ruled or judged; that she had not made the laws which she was accused of not obeying; that she never could have made these and expected to live up to them; that in the South people reached maturity much earlier than in the North and that a girl was very old to graduate at twenty so she could not be criticized justly for taking such young girls; that she had not been given a chance to defend herself; that her promises to try to live up to the rules of the Fraternity were apparently of little weight; that her excuses were not considered; that if Psi could not be a part of

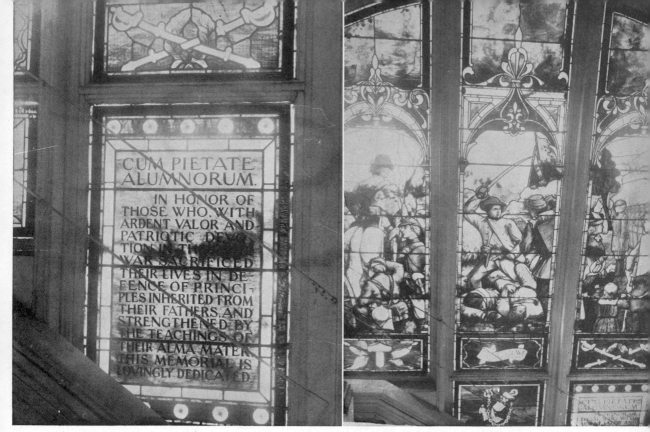

During the year 1889, which brought so much unhappiness both to the Fraternity and to the Mother Chapter, the members of Psi, with the help of University of Mississippi alumni, erected a beautiful memorial window to the University Greys. The "Greys" were a group of students in the University who, when the Civil War began, formed a company and went out known as the "University Greys." It is a tribute of which every Delta Gamma may be proud and was placed in the end of the hall of the Law building, then in the course of construction. At the bottom of one of the three panels of the window is the Anchor of Delta Gamma with the chapter letter "Psi" attached to the Anchor.

the whole she would exist as a separate organization as she had before granting northern chapters; that she had been judged by those standards by which a new chapter seeking admission should be judged and not by those things which she as Mother Chapter and a southern chapter should be judged.

The end of an era

"Minnie Wohlleben Carter in speaking to me of the last days of Psi said that the scene would always be impressed upon her and 'Although it was a beautiful day in the early spring of the South, how sad were our hearts—at least Miss Anna's and mine. Fannie Mulliken sat with the tears streaming down her cheeks, while Susie Wegg read the decision of the convention. I am afraid that I felt for a long time a very bitter feeling for my Delta Gamma sisters in the North. But you know time heals all wounds and here I

am loving everyone of you and trying to do everything I can for you and hoping to be able to attend another Convention some day."

Minutes continued in Psi's locked book into the 'nineties, and in our files today in Executive Offices we have some correspondence from Mrs. Carter to Mary Skipwith Buie in Chicago. Mary is apparently in a position to appeal Psi's case and has written her old friend Minnie for all evidence of Psi's early existence. She even mentions the purchase of a new outfit in which to make her presentation of an appeal. Minnie highly approves this and tells her of a group of girls enrolled at the University of Mississippi—none members of the Mother Chapter—who would like to petition to Delta Gamma for a new chapter in Oxford, this time officially at the University. What came of all this activity we shall never know, for it was thirty years before Delta Gamma again returned a charter to Oxford.

7 — New things appear on all sides

"Spirit of advancement"

DELTA GAMMA LODGE
ALBION COLLEGE
ALBION, MICH.

"The spirit of advancement which characterizes the Fraternity . . ." Fannie Mulliken had written in her report on her trip to Oxford. This was indeed true, and though the Sixth Convention held in Madison, Wisconsin, May 28-31, 1889—Belle Flesh, Ω-Wisconsin, presiding—does not on the surface seem to have taken many important steps (the exception being the unhappy withdrawal of Psi chapter), it does reflect this spirit of advancement.

University of Nebraska

Eleven chapters were present (Delta of Southern California absent)—including the one alumnæ chapter in Cleveland and one new collegiate chapter at the University of Nebraska, Kappa. This group, aided by Phi Delta Theta on that campus, had petitioned the 1888 Convention, was duly investigated according to rigid standards, and was installed by Susie Wegg on October 19, 1888.

Caution in expansion

Here was a tangible advancement, this caution which had become the byword of Delta Gamma expansion within two or three short years, and from this time onward increasing care is taken in studying the institution and group being considered. As early as June, 1885, an editorial in the *Anchora* carried the following comments: Good solid extension cannot be made too rapidly; every strong chapter is an added element of power to the Fraternity. Great emphasis is put upon good institutions, but the editorialist also notes that the expression "good institution" should be qualified. "In the East, by good institutions we mean those which have lived through the struggle for existence, established their reputation, and are everywhere recognized as the leading institutions of our land. By good institution in the West we mean those which in all human probability will in the next decade or two rank favorably with any eastern institutions. Then, to the established colleges of the East and the growing ones of the West, let us turn our eyes and lose no golden opportunity in either of these sections."

First chapter housing

Housing, too, was part of this spirit of advancement at the 1889 Convention, for one chapter was able to report the successful operation of its own house (rented) for the past three years. In March, 1887, Zeta chapter at Albion had reported to the *Anchora* the hiring of a chapter house—though the idea had seemed pretentious at first. Financial figuring proved it anything but pretentious.

The correspondent wrote that besides their three resident (of Albion) members, eight of the girls boarded in the college building, and the expenses of seven of them for room, board, heat, light and laundry amounted to five dollars a week, or $525 for all of them for a term. The eighth person tutored, etc, and she nearly canceled her own expenses. They discovered that with that sum they could hire a house with ten rooms and a good cook, and by practicing economy pay for their own fuel, light and food and have from five to ten dollars left each month for extras. They were in despair as to how to furnish the house until one of the girls announced that she'd been corresponding with her mother on the subject, and her mother had promised to furnish the sitting rooms and bedrooms and donate the kitchen stove and dining room table, and she also suggested that the girls bring what kitchen utensils and dishes they could from home and purchase the rest after they returned in the fall.

Promises fill the larder

So finally they found a house the size they wanted for $30 a month, and before they left that June (1886), each girl solemnly swore that she would make during the summer, jellies, preserves and pickles for the following year, and that she would gather together all the unneeded kitchen utensils and dishes she could find and that she would bring at least one article for the fraternity hall, for which they had set aside the large front room. The girl who furnished the house also brought her own piano from home for the place. It wasn't too long after this, a matter of five years, that Zeta had built its own lodge in addition to the residence which it rented. Delta

Gammas at Michigan followed Zeta's plan in the fall of 1889 and rented a house, too.

Convention business

This Sixth Convention also revised the Constitution and referred to a committee some additions and changes suggested in the initiation ritual by the chapter at Southern California. Though these additions were not accepted at that time, they were eventually incorporated into the ritual. Great care was taken to order the collection and destruction of old Constitutions when the new ones were printed and distributed.

The fall following Convention, September, 1889, the alumnæ of Eta petitioned the Grand and Deputy Chapters for an alumnæ chapter at Akron, but they were refused on the grounds that it was not advisable to have two chapters in one place, giving two votes in this way to a single chapter at Convention. It was many years before the Fraternity realized the great strength Alumnæ chapters gave the collegiate groups.

First Founders Days

Concerning the first year Founders Day was officially celebrated, this appears as Sigma's chapter letter in the April, 1890, *Anchora*:

"The idea of a reunion day was an inspiration. There certainly was not a girl of the twenty-seven who came together at the beautiful new home of Elizabeth Whiteley who did not go away prouder than ever of her chapter and more than ever in love with the girls. We were so fortunate as to have eleven of the 'old' girls with us. . . . All the active chapter and nearly all our pledged girls were present.

"The roll was called from the beginning of the chapter and letters were read from many absent members. Those present answered with quotations. But there is no way of describing the groups of girls, half of them sitting on cushions, or according to our girlish custom, on the floor; no way of telling of the jokes and laughter that mean so little and yet so much; but all Delta Gammas have the power of creating the picture, and know how full of it life should be."

To honor an initiate

A social fete to honor initiates reflected the social pace of Los Angeles' young university. From the June 16, 1889, Los Angeles Times.

"One of the most recherche social events of the college year of the University of Southern California was the annual reception given by the young lady members of Delta Gamma fraternity on the 15th inst, at 537 Jefferson street. The lawn and piazzas were illuminated with man-colored Chinese lanters. Indoors the large house was decorated with palms, roses, and magnolias. About one-hundred guests, including the faculty, were present in full evening dress in honor of the occasion, as the Delta Gammas comprise many of the most popular young lady students of the university."

Delta chapter letter adds to this, "The old members of Delta Gamma wore evening costumes of light blue, while the three new members were attired in pale pink which served as a delicate background for the three new gold anchors which glistened upon it."

Rushing is a problem

Through this period much attention was given in the *Anchora* to growing rushing problems. In 1887, the exchange column commented on the headache concentrated and frenzied rushing at the opening of the year had become and heartily approved the suggestion of the Kappa *Key* of sending new students in each institution a card stating that the fraternity issues no invitations to membership until a certain date—as for instance, November 1. Or it was suggested that the fraternities of an institution unite in some way whereby a longer time is secured in which to become acquainted with the new students and in which the latter in their turn might become better acquainted with the fraternity members and also gain some ideas of the nature of the fraternity and the size of membership and such data of each society.

First panhellenic meeting

All of this, of course, was ground work for the Panhellenic which eventually emerged. The first crystallization of such an idea occurred early in 1891 when Kappa Kappa Gamma called a meeting which took place in Boston, April 16-17. Delegates present represented Gamma Phi Beta, Alpha Phi, Delta Delta Delta, Kappa Alpha Theta, Kappa Kappa Gamma, Pi Beta Phi and Delta Gamma. This group recommended: the annual publication of an Interfraternity Directory in which were to appear the names of general officers, chapter secretaries and governing boards; that each fraternity and each chapter make a formal expression against "lifting"; that each fraternity make formal expression against double membership without honorable dismissal; the abolition of the practice of pledging and initiating preparatory students. Suggestions were also made to protect fraternities against persons without authority purchasing fraternity badges. There was also some discussion of plans concerning a Panhellenic Congress in 1893 at the World's Fair.

Another important measure introduced was the exchange of fraternity magazines among the different fraternities. Chapters of the various individual groups were quite ignorant of the strength and work of the fraternities and the exchange of magazines would tend to educate them concerning the Greek world.

The delegate of Delta Gamma was Bertha Reed, X-Cornell, a senior at the time of the meeting. Tirzah Sherwood, Ω-Wisconsin, was also present, and she and Bertha both served on committees.

Seventh Convention
1891—Ann Arbor, Michigan

A month later, May 13-15, 1891, Delta Gamma's Seventh Convention met in Ann Arbor, sessions convening in the Presbyterian Church parlors. Fannie Mulliken, H-Akron, presided, though Sara Foster, Σ-Northwestern, was Grand President at the time. The hostess chapter for the last time was furnishing the presiding officer of Convention. At this Convention the following change was made in this form of government: A Council was created to consist of the Secretary and Treasurer of the general Fraternity, elected from the Grand Chapter, the editor of *Anchora*, a member from the Deputy chapter and one from the alumnæ of the retiring Grand Chapter. Slowly, the influence of the alumnæ was overshadowing that of the collegiates in the governing of Delta Gamma. From this time forward the President of the Fraternity was to preside at Conventions, and the officers of the Convention were to be the President, Secretary and Treasurer of the Fraternity.

Women's College of Baltimore (Goucher)

The pace of expansion had slackened considerably, and at this Convention a charter was granted for the first time since 1888. Under the guardianship of Helen Lovell, Ξ-Michigan, a member of the faculty at Women's College of Baltimore (later Goucher College), a group on that campus petitioned Convention. Their charter was granted and the chapter was installed during the week after Convention. The new chapter being the only one now existing south of the Mason-Dixon line, took the name of Psi from sentiment for the Mother Chapter which had been withdrawn two years before.

This Convention recorded sixty Delta Gammas attending the banquet—attendance was slowly increasing.

Other Convention action included the following:

* **Incorporation** was reported to be of such slight value that no action had been taken by the committee appointed by the 1888 Convention to look into the matter.
* **The editor** would be paid a salary, the account to be raised by doubling the annual dues.
* **The alumnæ chapter,** Theta of Cleveland, registered its desire to give up its charter as there never seemed to be more than two members in Cleveland at the same time. Delta Gamma was most reluctant to lose Theta and urged its members to delay the matter of returning the charter.

Eighth Convention
1893—Akron, Ohio

Since the Convention of 1891 had decreed that henceforth the President of the Fraternity should preside at Conventions—and since the Constitution was interpreted to mean that the Grand President should be an alumna, Sara Foster Briggs resigned just before the 1893 Convention, and on very short notice, Aurora "Rho" Fiske Zeublin, Σ-Northwestern, was elected. She would then preside at Delta Gamma's Eighth Convention which was to meet at Akron, May 11-12, 1893, in the Universalist Church parlors.

Conservative expansion continues

Delta Gamma's conservative policy concerning expansion continued, and though this Convention approved Bryn Mawr and the University of Chicago, both of these fields were later realized not feasible. Delta Gamma continued, too, to refuse far more petitions than she considered, and often complicated situations arose. One of the most confusing had been in connection with DePauw University. In 1884 a group at DePauw had petitioned, and withdrew the petition in 1885 because they resented an investigation. A second group petitioned in 1886 but the affair became very complicated as two sets of girls were corresponding with two different chapters of Delta Gamma. Naturally, the Fraternity refused both groups. Again in 1892, a third group applied, which was followed by a long correspondence between Delta Gamma and the group with no result. Delta Gamma did not enter DePauw until 1949.

Convention action

It almost seemed that Convention could not be a success unless many changes were made in the Constitution, and the 1915 historian comments that this steadily increased until "no one dared suggest another change!" The 1893 Convention recorded the following:

* **The badge** would be worn by no one but a Delta Gamma. (On some campuses it was the custom to exchange pins with one's fiance.)
* **Men,** it was emphasized once more, could not become either active or honorary members of Delta Gamma.
* **Initiation practices** were discussed, and Convention agreed to "disapprove of any cruelty in any form during initiation."
* **Annual dues,** from chapters, were raised to five dollars.
* **The Constitution** would once more be completely revised before the next Convention. Again, a committee was appointed for this purpose.
* **Expansion** was discussed, and Convention favored considering Leland Stanford, Jr., University of California and Tufts College.

Resolution regarding the Mullikens

A resolution concerning the death of Fannie Mulliken Thompson and that of her father, Mr. J. B. Mulliken, both of whom had died since the

1891 Convention at which Fannie had presided, were incorporated into the minutes.

New format for Anchora

In the fall following Convention the *Anchora* took on a new format—no longer two columns, but a single page. During this period the appearance of the *Anchora* is frequently a matter for heated discussion during sessions of Convention. In November, 1893, the magazine carries a report of one of the early meetings of the Congress of College Fraternities. The program the first day opened with seven addresses: The Legal Status of the Fraternities, History of Fraternities, Fraternity Catalogue Making, Fraternity Finance, Advantages of Non-Secrecy, A Permanent League, and the Women's Fraternities. Two more days followed with a similar number of learned lectures each day. The second day was devoted to the seven phases of fraternity journalism.

Development of panhellenism

The next issue of the *Anchora*, January, 1894, carries an extensive article on the Women's College of Baltimore and her fraternities—of which the first was Delta Gamma. Almost every *Anchora* during the nineties carries some promotional material or some word of the development of Panhellenism among the women's groups. All this, of course, is leading up to the organization in 1902 of Panhellenic as a concentrated Fraternity force. Consequently, a great percentage of each issue is devoted to exchange of what other groups are doing—both men's and women's.

Anti-fraternity feeling

Through these years, the growth of anti-fraternity feeling was reflected, too, in our magazines and chapter letters. "Exclusiveness in Fraternities" opened one issue, and began, "Fraternities we all know are the subject of adverse criticism from many quarters." We had seen, of course, during the decade just prior to this the falling off of several chapters—and, usually simultaneously, the withdrawal of other Greek groups—for this reason.

Alumnæ organization

Alumnæ groups were making slow starts in some of the larger cities, often by running notices in the *Anchora:* (April, 1894) "The alumnæ of Delta Gamma residing in or about Chicago are requested to send their names and addresses to Miss Caroline Hunt, 5700 Kimbark Ave., Chicago, Ill. The alumnæ of Chicago are endeavoring to form a chapter and desire the assistance which all chapters can afford in furnishing names and addresses." The same issue of *Anchora* contained the first alumnæ chapter letter—from Lincoln, Nebraska, though a charter was not actually granted to this group until the 1895 Convention and then with strong opposition.

Convention attendance promoted

Promotion of Convention attendance appeared for the first time in the spring of 1895, though it was of a much more serious nature that what we carry today. Articles indicated what was to be expected of the delegates sent on a serious mission by their chapters. "A Suggested Preparation for the Convention" outlined the aims of the Convention—what shall we aim for—unity, uniformity, and a close organization. Thus Fannie Mulliken's "spirit of advancement" was presented in literary form to all of the members who are on the *Anchora*'s circulation lists.

Mary Power, Ξ-Michigan, President 1895-97, gave a lifetime of loyalty and service to her Fraternity.

Constitution and council

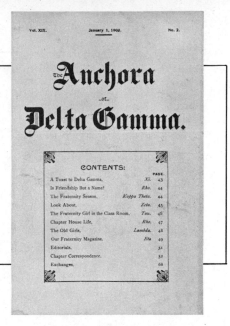

Vol. XIX.   January 1, 1903.   No. 2.

The Anchora ...of... Delta Gamma.

CONTENTS:

Eighteen-ninety-five was a year which proved good to Delta Gamma—though possibly at the time the resignation of President Rho Fiske Zeublin, a strong Fraternity force, just prior to Convention was not a particularly good omen. Mary Power, Ξ-Michigan, most ably replaced Mrs. Zeublin, and Ethel Baker Andrews presided at Convention.

Ninth Convention
1895—Minneapolis, Minnesota

The Ninth Convention was held at Lambda's invitation in Minneapolis, held May 8-11, 1895, at the Hampshire Arms. Practically a new constitution was adopted, the most important change being the abolition of the Grand Chapter and the investiture of authority in the Council. This was to go into effect October 1, 1895. At this time it was still to be the chapter rather than the individual who was elected to office, and then the chapter elected in this way would select the person to fill the office: the first Grand Council thus was composed of President and Vice-President, Xi; Secretary, Chi; Treasurer, Kappa, and Fifth Member, Lambda. *Anchora* was still with Lambda with Ina Firkins as editor. In 1899 this plan was changed so that no chapter could hold two offices at once.

This Council was to meet two days before each Convention and also in the intervening year between Conventions. It was composed of the officers listed above whose terms were to be four years—the President and Treasurer being elected for the first time for two years so that a rotation would follow which did not cause all offices to change at once.

Other Convention action appeared as follows:

- **Incorporation** was brought up again for discussion, but the decision of Convention was unchanged in the matter.
- **Expansion** was, as always, an important subject. The committee on chapters and charters reported unfavorably on Stanford University on account of its unstable financial condition at the time—this was during the period when the Stanford estate was in litigation.
- **The fee** for active chapters was raised to $25.
- **Alumnæ chapters** were to pay $15. Actually, at this time the only provision for alumnæ chapters was in the clause in the Constitution, "Delta Gamma shall be composed of collegiate and alumnæ chapters." There was no provision for representation at Convention though this was to come at the next Convention. We have already noted that the 1895 conclave did grant a charter to alumnæ in Lincoln who were to call themselves Kappa Theta. For many years alumnæ chapters chose two identifying Greek letters when they were chartered, in the same manner as collegiate chapters.
- **A directory** was to be published by the editing chapter.
- **A revised Constitution** was accepted at this Convention, a Constitution which for the first time contains a complete description of the badge.
- **Official jeweler** accepted at this Convention was Wright & Kay of Detroit.

1915 historian relates of the 1895 Convention, "The guests of convention were beautifully entertained throughout the week at the Hampshire Arms and enthusiasm for future conventions ran high. The attendance again topped all previous conventions."

The status of women

The *Anchora* of these days reflects a constant emphasis and interest in the position of women not only on campus but in the community as well. In the letter from the University of Michigan chapter in April, 1896, issue of the journal—an extremely lengthy discussion of the subject—is a report that three women had recently been ap-

Ethel Baker Andrews, Σ-Northwestern, presided at the 1895 Convention and later served as Fraternity President, 1897-98.

pointed to self-government positions in the university. The correspondent remarks that this is regarded as an innovation, not so much in the actual state of affairs for a few women have held similar positions in the past, but as a policy which in the future will direct the management of the university.

Let us not be led to believe that the Delta Gammas of this generation focused their attention only on such high-minded matters, for we find as complete reports of the horrors of initiation, always complete with "billy goat" (usually a borrowed saw-horse). The term "active" had by then become a generally accepted noun in speaking of collegiate affairs.

First Council meeting—
"Los Angeles boom over!"

The newly formed Grand Council held its first meeting in Chicago during July, 1896, more for an opportunity to organize itself than to transact much fraternity business. It did have called to its attention, however, the condition of Delta chapter at the University of Southern California. The school had been founded during the Los Angeles boom, the boom had subsided and the young university was left without material means of existence. We had one Greek rival whose chapter had been reduced to one member. The school's future was quite dubious at this point—though some of our strongest members had been initiated by Delta. Council and the chapters voted in December, 1896, to withdraw the chapter from the University of Southern California. Delta Gamma's exodus from the campus was quickly followed by the withdrawal of the other sorority.

Growing Panhellenic

Throughout this decade the *Anchora* maintained a close watch on the growing panhellenic organization—though the actual NPC as such did not materialize until 1902. However, the *Anchora* noted with interest each time one of the chapters entered into a local compact with other groups on that campus—always with particular regard to the rush season, rushing rules, mainly the time to which rushing should be limited.

Tenth Convention
1897—Ithaca, New York

Delta Gamma was again approaching Convention time, this one to be held with Chi chapter at Ithaca, New York, May 19-21, 1897, with sessions at Barnes Hall, and Council President Mary Power, Ξ-Michigan, presiding. This was Delta Gamma's Tenth Convention.

Stanford University

For the first time Grand Council met for a day before Convention opened. It was reported that on March 6 a charter had been granted to the nine petitioners at Stanford University. It has taken the group nearly four years to achieve this status as a chapter of Delta Gamma, years of cloud-high enthusiasm to darkest gloom as the settlement of the Stanford estate dragged on. The vote on their petition dragged, too, but persistence won, and from this strong charter group came a national President (Rose Smith) and the matriarch of the Los Angeles Nursery School for Visually Handicapped Children, Dr. Lillian Ray Titcomb. The three other Greek groups greeted Delta Gamma enthusiastically into their Panhellenic association—and a year later when, of the three, Pi Beta Phi gave up her charter she presented her punch bowl and glasses to Delta Gamma!

Convention business

But to return to this Convention to which the new Upsilon chapter had sent her first delegate. . . . Among other petitions was one from the previously mentioned group at the University of Mississippi. Convention deemed it unwise to encourage the group and later the petition was refused. Convention also had on its agenda:

- **Editing chapter** would be Psi. Lambda's resignation as editing chapter was accepted—this position she had held most ably for ten years, the last seven being under the editorship of Ina Firkins.

- **Alumnæ chapters** were provided for within the organization, and their place in Delta Gamma government was enacted at this Convention.

- **Honorary members** were restricted to women who were college graduates or connected with a college where there was a collegiate chapter. Later the first clause was dropped.

And Convention adjourned with the historian reporting that Delta Gamma was composed of thirteen active chapters and one alumnæ chapter; four chapters occupied houses—Alpha, Zeta, Xi, and Chi, and Zeta alone owned property, a lodge where meetings and social events were held.

Indiana University

The next year, 1898, was marked on the Delta Gamma calendar by the addition of Theta chapter at Indiana University—Theta being chosen by the petitioning group because they had been so aided in their plea for a charter by the University's President Swain and his wife, she being a Kappa Alpha Theta. They had earlier been discouraged by a Pi Phi friend (or Theta chapter might have been Pi chapter!) in Ann Arbor who reported on the fine members Delta Gamma had there, but she doubted very much if the group could get a charter from Delta Gamma as they were very conservative. But nothing else was worth the trouble, she added. The group was duly inspected and the charter granted December 10, 1898. During the same year petitions from the University of California and Sophie Newcomb were, among others, refused.

Eleventh Convention
1899—Albion, Michigan

For some reason, Council omitted its 1898 meeting and instead convened just prior to Convention at Albion. This was the Eleventh Delta Gamma Convention and it met in Zeta's lodge, May 9-11, 1899. Nina Howard, Σ-Northwestern, Council President, wielded the gavel.

Though it had been only four years since the major renovation of the Constitution had taken place, again the obsession for change took possession of the delegates. Along with this came the time-worn demand to change the Fraternity colors—a matter which recurs at every Convention until 1907. As the 1915 historian recollects, "The pleas from the younger members, who had not been associated with the traditions of Delta Gamma long enough to love them for their history invariably complained that the bronze was a difficult color to secure for use in decorating and other trivial purposes. This subject always aroused the old timers who were triumphant when their plea for the colors influenced Convention. This biennial bone of contention always started the sessions with more spirit. So it had its mission."

Convention business

Also on the records of this Convention:

- **Convention expenses** of official delegates were to be hereafter paid by the Fraternity with no more than two-thirds of the money in the treasury going for this purpose.
- *Sub Rosa,* a publication which would be published each month, would carry Fraternity business which could not appear in *Anchora.*

Nina Howard, Σ-Northwestern, President 1899-1901, served as Delta Gamma's delegate when NPC officially organized in 1902.

- **A Certificate of Membership** had been drafted and presented by Kappa chapter and was accepted by Convention.
- **The Editor of Anchora** would hereafter hold the position which had been known as "the Fifth Member" of Council.
- **Official jeweler** accepted at this Convention was Fetting of Baltimore.

One hundred and fifty Delta Gammas attended parts of this Convention, possibly because Michigan, having two of the oldest living chapters, was well populated with Delta Gammas.

Sigma entertains Council

Council's "Convention interim" meeting in 1900 was held in Evanston where the officers were guests of Sigma chapter. Business at these Council meetings was serious; the change in government was indeed taking effect.

Imposters

It seems impossible to us today that imposters could become a problem of concern to all fraternities, but this is a matter worthy of considerable mention during the 'nineties and through the early part of the new century. A girl (or more frequently, a man) might arrive on campus, go to a particular house, and announce that he was an initiate of another chapter. He was, of course, accepted without question, until it became apparent that he didn't know quite enough about the fraternity in question. Kappa chapter at one point of this period initiated what they called the "Graft Cup" which was presented to Blanche Garten in honor of her astute methods of discovering two such imposters. A 1900 *Anchora* reports a case of attempted dual membership, a member of one group who transferred to a campus where no chapter of her group existed, so she desired membership (and was offered membership) in another group on this campus.

Kappa Kappa Gamma Litigation

Apparently of supreme interfraternity interest during 1899 was a lawsuit against Kappa Kappa Gamma following an attempt by Kappa officers to withdraw its chapter at St. Lawrence. A complete report of the litigation is contained in the *Anchora* (and apparently most other fraternity journals), including in full the judgment of Mr. Justice Russell of New York in favor of the chapter which did indeed remain at St. Lawrence.

Twelfth Convention
1901—Lincoln, Nebraska

In 1901, for the first time, a collegiate and an alumnæ chapter were together Convention hostesses. Delta Gamma's Convention was meeting in Lincoln, Nebraska, May 15-17, as the guests of Kappa chapter and Kappa Theta alumnæ. Meetings were called to order at the Hotel Lincoln where Convention guests were entertained. Nina Howard once more presided.

Members of Kappa recall that Delta Gammas in Lincoln had spent the two years since the Albion Convention—when their invitation to Lincoln had been accepted—planning and working for this Twelfth Convention. Competition socially was at a high pitch in Lincoln—who should have the honor of entertaining for the delegates? The success of the affair is best recorded in the fact that Council decided that hereafter the social part of Convention would have to be limited or the Fraternity would be able to accomplish nothing at its biennial meetings!

Convention action

That nothing was accomplished during those full days in Lincoln cannot be said. Policy discussions were heated, "but always ladylike," it was reported.

- **Membership in organizations,** secret and intercollegiate in nature, with the exception of honoraries, was prohibited for members of Delta Gamma. This action was the result of difficulties with Omega Psi (an intersorority group which promoted panhellenism and its own enjoyment).
- **Initiation ceremony revisions** were accepted by Convention. These were presented by Upsilon chapter, the same additions which had been brought to Convention several years before by another California chapter, the ill-fated Delta of USC. Florence Whittier, Δ-

Edna Polk Wilson, K-Nebraska, Delta Gamma President 1901-02, resigned in mid-term and was replaced by Kappa's appointment of Blanche Garten.

Southern California, who had originated them, had transferred to Stanford, bringing these ideas with her. The Stanford Delta Gammas had embellished the ceremony and made it more adaptable for national use.

- **Pledge pins,** of various shapes and sizes, had been in use by a number of chapters for several years, and so a national pledge pin was at this Convention recommended. It was, however, several years before one was submitted which was accepted.
- **Chapter Roll Book** had been in use in Kappa chapter for some time, and she presented the form to Convention which accepted it and put it into universal use in the Fraternity. It was further decided that these roll books should be inspected by a national officer at each Convention.
- **Fraternity examination,** given annually, was also a Kappa chapter practice. This was introduced at this Convention and adopted for all chapters at this time.

Syracuse University

A new charter was granted to petitioners at Syracuse University. This group had organized in 1899 for the specific purpose of petitioning Delta Gamma. In 1900 they were inspected by the *Anchora* editor, Joe Anna Ross, Ψ-Goucher, who carried their cause to Council meeting and to Convention where the charter was granted.

In Miss Ross's honor, the initial Rho was chosen as the chapter's identification. That she was indeed their guardian angel and lost no time in transporting their charter to Syracuse is evident in these dates: Convention closed in Lincoln on May 17, and on May 23 she installed the group in Syracuse.

No Council meeting

During 1902 Council resignations and reappointments caused enough confusion to postpone Council meeting which would normally have been held that year. The volumes of correspondence which remain, however, reflect anything but an idle year. Another die had been cast, and a revitalized organization has sprung from this new form of government.

New York Alumnæ meeting in 1901

"We all met at the Montclair station of the D.L. & W.R.R., where a comfortable wagonette, with a fine pair of horses awaited us to carry us on a most delightful drive over the mountains back of Montclair. It was one of the most perfect of the real fall days, and the keen air gave us a fine appetite for the picnic supper which we ate at Eagle Rock.

9 — A look to the future — and to the past

A real Panhellenic

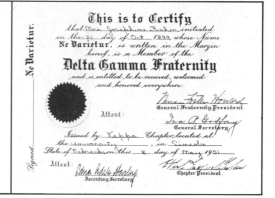

Another meeting in 1902 quite overshadowed Delta Gamma's lack of Grand Council meeting. This, of course, was the meeting called by Alpha Phi in Chicago of all women's fraternities to form a permanent Panhellenic conference—or Intersorority Conference, as it called itself then.

Nina Howard, Σ-Northwestern, recently retired President of Delta Gamma, represented the Fraternity; by-laws were formulated, and a working plan was submitted to member groups. Alpha Phi's primary purpose in assembling this group of fraternity representatives—the delegates were from the same seven nationals which had attended the 1891 meeting—had been to discuss pledging and rushing problems, so emphasis was pointed in this direction. The meeting in itself did accomplish the formation of a permanent Panhellenic, a turning point for the fraternity world, for as yet the men's groups—though dating back many more years than the women's—had no such organization. It was arranged that similar meetings would follow, to be called by the various member groups in rotation.

Thirteenth Convention
1903—Madison, Wisconsin

For the third time Omega was hostess and Madison the site of a Delta Gamma Convention, the Thirteenth which convened at the Grace Church Guild Halls, May 13-15, 1903, Blanche Garten, K-Nebraska, presiding. Now two alumnæ chapters were represented, Kappa Theta of Lincoln and the newly chartered Chi Upsilon of New York City. Once more expansion provided the most important debate of the day, the addition of a chapter at the University of Washington in Seattle and the possible withdrawal of Alpha at Mount Union. Charges were made against the latter, but those filing complaints were not sufficiently prepared to defend their charges, and Alpha made a splendid defense for herself. So Alpha's position was, for the time being at least, safe.

University of Washington

The advisability of going into the far Northwest with a chapter at Washington absorbed a session of heated debate. It was Susie Wegg Smith, Ω-Wisconsin, a name familiar in connection with the expansion question in earlier days, who had officially inspected the group and presented the case which won for the petitioners their charter. Delta Alpha, the local petitioning, had been organized in 1900 by Eleanor Hancock, a transfer from Michigan, with the express purpose of petitioning Delta Gamma. Finding the very active Delta Gamma, Mrs. Smith, in Seattle was a happy discovery and probably the reason that Delta Gamma was, by a few hours, the first national to enter the campus in 1901.

Blanche Garten, K-Nebraska, Delta Gamma President 1902-05, gave much to Delta Gamma during her lifetime. It was she who renewed contact with the members of the Mother Chapter and through this contact, brought to Delta Gamma much of her early history. Miss Garten also served from 1922-26 as Installation Officer. A Memorial Fellowship was named for her.

This action, too, was to pave the way for our entering other fields in the Far West. After Convention, Susie Wegg Smith returned to Seattle to install Beta chapter—so named to honor Mrs. Smith's and Mrs. Priest's (the chapter patroness) Beta Theta Pi husbands.

The petition from the University of California had been referred to nearby Upsilon at the 1901 Convention, and once again this action was taken. Several years of controversy on this question had occupied Council business, and many became so discouraged as to feel we would never enter the Berkeley campus.

New interest in Anchora

A great deal of attention was given to the *Anchora* during the Madison meetings—even to a discussion of format and cover design and color. The editor's great vigor had been felt not only on Council, but in the interest she had aroused in the magazine. It was she who had introduced illustrations during the second year of her editorship (1898), and now new provisions were made for its expansion and interest directed towards its welfare. A Board of District Editors was set up to assist not only in editorial matter but in collecting subscriptions and aiding in other ways.

History comes alive

During this period a great interest in our history had become apparent—possibly because we were now acquiring enough age to feel that we had some history, and efforts were made to renew contacts with the early members in Mississippi. In 1901 a board-bound history and directory had been published—much of the history containing unavoidable inaccuracies in our early history largely because it was not until later that solid contacts with the Mother Chapter were established and the correspondence brought to light. At this 1903 Convention George Banta, our only male member, attended several sessions and told of that transition to the north of which he had been such a vital part. His Delta Gamma wife had died not long after their marriage, and in the ensuing years he had had no personal contact with Delta Gamma. His attendance at this convention was primarily to speak on behalf of a group petitioning from Franklin College, some of whom had been members of the old Phi chapter there. Evidently though the Convention was much enlightened concerning this first northern chapter, they were not impressed enough with the status of Franklin in 1903 to desire reinstatement of the chapter.

Two hundred Delta Gammas attended the Convention banquet—a number which was not greatly exceeded for many years.

Secretary compiles records

At the 1903 Convention Lambda had been elected Secretary and had made, for the Fraternity, a most happy choice in its selection of Gratia Countryman to fill the office. Miss Countryman, fifty years later the recipient of Delta Gamma's Order of the Rose, was Librarian of the City Library of Minneapolis, and obviously had the talent and interest for reviewing all of Delta Gamma's sometimes scattered and incomplete records. Her understudy at the Library was another Delta Gamma, Ruth Rosholt, who aided her in this project and succeeded her in the office from whence her library work forced her to resign in 1905. This same spirit reached out to the other officers, and by 1905 a great improvement was noticeable in correspondence both between Council members and the chapters and Council. But still, writes the 1915 historian who was at this period President of the Fraternity, conditions were far from what the Council desired as it took time for this spirit of promptness and responsibility to be felt throughout the Fraternity. By 1905 the Secretary's files were in complete and perfect order and in a case suitable for office or shipping purposes.

Second Intersorority meeting

During the fall of 1903 the *Anchora* carried the complete minutes of the Second National Intersorority Conference to which Delta Gamma's delegate was President Blanche Garten. It is interesting to note that it was Delta Gamma who was credited with urging that the alumnæ become an integral part of this great Panhellenic movement and be enlisted in the attempt to bring about a better understanding among sororities.

A World's Fair

In April, 1904, Council traveled to Baltimore to be entertained by Psi and Psi Omicron (Baltimore Alumnæ) during its sessions there. An item of business was the setting aside for the St. Louis World's Fair in 1904 the dates August 24 and October 5 as "Delta Gamma Days" when at 11:30 Delta Gammas could meet at the southwest corner of the Inside Inn porch for luncheon.

One "No" hampers expansion

Probably most important business at this meeting was the subject of petitions for charters. Berkeley had become a perplexing problem. The ultra-conservative spirit had infiltrated all sections where Delta Gammas were organized, and for a farsighted Council this was a frustrating problem. Their realization of an institution's potential and complete endorsement of a petitioning group was not enough to combat one or two votes "No" which were then enough to refuse a petition. When this Council reported the next year at Convention, the following petitioning groups had been definitely refused just in this 1903-05 Convention interim: Illinois Wesleyan College, University of South Dakota, Colby College, University of California, University of Texas, Mary Baldwin College, Colorado College, Columbia College (later George Washington University), Colorado State Normal College, Swarthmore College, Randolph Macon College, University of Kentucky, Lake Forest College and Allegheny College.

Two more alumnæ chapters were, however, recognized—Chi Sigma in Chicago and Lambda Nu in Minneapolis.

Complete Anchora collection

During Joe Anna Ross' editorship of the *Anchora* a great effort had been made to gather complete sets of the *Anchora* to date. Four complete sets had been collected, and Council decided to place one with Upsilon, the chapter on the West coast; one with Xi, a centrally located chapter; one with the Historian, and the fourth, to be kept in the files of the *Anchora* office—at that time representing an East coast chapter.

More chapter visits

The 1915 History records this innovation at this time: Prior to this, chapters had never been officially visited except to install or in case trouble arose. The 1903 Convention desired the Council to visit chapters but at that time did not provide for the additional expense. The chapter visits that were made had to be combined with travel to and from Council meetings or Convention.

Delta Gamma calls conference

It was Delta Gamma's turn in 1904 to call the Third National Intersorority Conference. Alpha Chi Omega and Chi Omega had been added to the membership the preceding year, and Alpha Xi Delta would attend for the first time this year. This group of ten assembled in Chicago September 16-17 with Grace Telling, Σ-Northwestern, presiding. Again the conference attacked with vigor the ever-present rushing and pledging problems. The plan for rotation of office according to membership in the Conference was established; co-operation with college authorities, particularly deans of women, was stressed, and a spirit of democracy with regard to college activities was urged.

Fourteenth Convention
1905—Evanston, Illinois

These were busy years for everyone, particularly this hard-working Council, and soon it was time for another Convention. Once more delegates were to be the guests of Sigma at Evanston, Illinois. Blanche Garten, K-Nebraska, presided at sessions held at the Orrington Lunt Library, May 16-19, 1905. Miss Garten herself writes of the strenuousness of this Fourteenth Convention because of the issues at stake. This was accomplished:

- **Expansion** was much discussed during this period, and Delta Gamma was rapidly earning its traditional reputation of extreme conservatism. The petitioners from Berkeley, who had been refused, made a plea through a member of their organization, but Convention did not reconsider the refusal which stood on the records. The University of Illinois was to be investigated, a petition having come from a group there.

- **A uniform badge** had become a necessity because of the many sizes and differences of design which came from the many authorized official jewelers—and probably some who were not official. The form used by Bunde and Upmeyer, our oldest authorized jeweler, was accepted.

- **A pledge pin,** to be used by all chapters, was finally selected, a white shield with the now familiar Pi Alpha in gold. Ione Dille, Upsilon-Stanford, was the author of the motto.

- **The pin of a deceased member** was to be returned to the member's chapter unless the chapter made other provisions.

- **Annual dues** of active members were raised one dollar to provide a fund to meet the expense of a biennial visit to each chapter by a member of Council.

- **A Convention tax** would hereafter help finance Conventions. This biennial meeting had grown so much in four years that the expense had become too heavy for one chapter to be sole hostess. In the future a small tax of $3.00

would be levied on all members attending Convention.

- **Official jeweler** authorized at this Convention was the firm of Burr-Patterson, bringing the total to six.
- **Four alumnæ chapters** reported, as well as five alumnæ associations.
- *The Anchora* would be transferred to Kappa chapter for editing, with the understanding that Grace Abbott, recognized as being particularly well qualified, be editor. Psi had resigned as editor after having served, in the vigorous and interested person of Joe Anna Ross (recently becoming Mrs. Pancoast), for eight years.
- **A songbook** had been published in 1904 by Chi chapter, but Convention requested some additions and improvements—a request no doubt discouraging to Chi who had put years of effort into this publication. The second edition did not appear until 1911.

A *Delta Gamma Gavel*

At this time Blanche Garten had only served for three years, and many plans which she had started for the development of the fraternity had not been completed. Convention, aware of the strength she had given the growing organization, offered her the Presidency for another term, but she declined with the feeling that there was need for the enthusiasm of a new member on Council. She felt, too, that this re-election might establish an unwise precedent. Here we must turn to Miss Garten herself for the account of a milestone which occurred at this Evanston Convention, the presentation to the Fraternity of the gavel which with each Convention since has become a greater part of Delta Gamma tradition:

"While I was in office, I realized that the Fraternity possessed no memento of the founding of Delta Gamma. Our information of our early days was meagre and so many times varied, yet all intercourse with members of the Mother Chapter seemed forbidden by tradition which had arisen after Psi's withdrawal. For sometime I hesitated to make an advance to any one whose name appeared on Psi's chapter roll, yet I knew that only through the help of some of the early members of Psi, could I be aided in my quest for something of historical value to Delta Gamma. I decided to try to find a piece of wood large enough to make a gavel but farther than that I groped in the dark. To Mary Comfort Leonard, one of the two founders who lived, I wrote, stating my mission and hoped the sentiment of the idea might arouse her interest. As she lived in Kosciusko, some distance from Oxford and had been in school such a short time after the club started, she could do no more than write to a friend in Oxford stating my request. Mrs. Leonard succeeded in obtaining a spindle from the stairway which led to the upper floor where the room was located in which Delta Gamma was organized.

"When Mrs. Leonard wrote in such a kindly spirit and told me the piece of historic wood was actually on the way to me, I was delighted but alas, when it arrived, I discovered that the wood was soft and impossible to use for my purpose. I had made Mrs. Leonard some trouble and hesitated to tell her the failure and ask her to try again.

"Several months went by and as Convention time was near, I made another attempt and asked Mrs. Leonard if she could give me the name of a member of Psi who lived in Oxford and might be interested in my quest. She replied that Mrs. David Carter (Minnie Wohlleben) had been one of the most loyal and enthusiastic workers for Delta Gamma and could help me if anyone could. The short time in which to act gave me the courage to approach Mrs. Carter on the subject, but I realized that she would be one who had felt bitter towards her northern sisters and I did not expect a response much less an offer to assist me. You can imagine my happy state of mind when I read Mrs. Carter's immediate reply offering to do all she could to secure the wood.

"She first tried to trace the school desks and wrote to the last owner of the school, Mrs. Lancaster, then a very old lady. But the desks had been scattered to the four winds as had all the other school furnishings. The building used for the school had long since become a residence and one could scarcely demand a part of the house. Just as Mrs. Carter was about to write that she had failed, she walked over to look at the property and saw that the owner was remodeling the building. Mrs. Carter stated her case and the owner willingly gave her a piece of the wood from the woodwork in the room used as the Study Hall.

"Mrs. Carter was as happy as I was over her success. This opened a correspondence in which she told me that the years had softened her feelings on the subject of Psi's withdrawal, but through all these years when she had known nothing of Delta Gamma, she had kept every record of the Mother Chapter in a safe place as she cherished them among the dearest of treasures. The original constitution and ritual, the minutes of Psi from 1874-1889 which were recorded in a big book which is locked by a big lock and key, and innumerable relics of Psi's days she had kept. Mrs. Carter loaned me the constitution and ritual which I exhibited at the Evanston Convention.

"The wood, I had made into a gavel which is banded with a silver band on the head with the inscription "Presented to Delta Gamma by Blanche Garten, May 17, 1905 in memory of your Mother chapter, 1874." On the handle is a band with the inscription "Wood from the building occupied by Oxford Institute, Oxford, Miss. Given by Minnie Wohlleben Carter." The gavel I presented to convention to be used by Grand Presidents at convention."

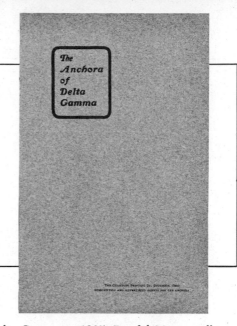

10—New records, new chapters . . .

Strengthening from within

It was an able Grand Council which continued the work of strengthening Delta Gamma from all points, the task so well carried on by the preceding Council. Rose Smith, Υ-Stanford, was the new President and Blanche Garten continued to work with the official group, representing Grace Abbott in the office of Editor when the latter was unable to attend the next Convention.

Two chapters were added to the roll before the time came for that Convention—Iota at the University of Illinois and Gamma at the University of California.

University of Illinois

The group at Illinois had been colonized by correspondence by a local sorority which had existed in an Eastern school for some time and desired to become national by the simultaneous establishment of many chapters. The meagre information given the colony and the feeling that a charter was being thrust upon them led to so much dissatisfaction that the colony "bolted" just prior to their scheduled installation. At about this time, one of the members attended a Delta Gamma formal at Northwestern—and suddenly others remembered that they knew a lot about Delta Gamma. So they voted to refuse the proffered charter and to petition Delta Gamma. With the dean of women's aid, contacts were made with local Delta Gammas; a lengthy investigation followed and finally in April, 1906, came the telegram affirming the granting of a charter. On May 12, Iota was installed.

University of California

At California while an anxious group of petitioners placed their plea for a charter again and again in the hands of a discouraging Delta Gamma, the Pie del Monte Club—the first organized women's house club on the growing campus—lived happily unaware of it all. Then after anxiety and discouragement became impossibility for the petitioners—with the final "No" from

Delta Gamma in 1905, Pie del Monte, still unknowing, began talking fraternity, too. At a special meeting in January, 1906, the club voted to petition Delta Gamma. The encouragement of the nearby Stanford chapter and of Delta Gammas in the San Francisco Bay area together with Delta Gamma President Rose Smith being at their side to cheer and advise made this a comparatively short petitioning period—only fifteen months until Gamma's charter was granted in April, 1907. This was the first time a charter group was a property owner in its petitioning status, so an important part of the first meeting after installation was the deeding over to Delta Gamma all Pie del Monte property.

Council meets, 1906

When Grand Council met in June, 1906, in Minneapolis as guests of Lambda and Lambda Nu alumnæ, there were four more petitions to consider—Adelphi, Swarthmore, University of Idaho and Ohio State. Though all four were eventually chartered, Swarthmore and Idaho were definitely refused at this time and Ohio State discouraged.

Fifth Intersorority Conference

Margarethe Shepard, Delta Gamma's Treasurer, was the Fraternity's delegate to the Fifth Intersorority Conference in Chicago in September, 1906. The interest of Delta Gamma in Panhellenic affairs was reflected in the great amount of space these matters received in the Anchora. Probably more interesting reading for West Coast Delta Gammas in the April, 1907, Anchora was an article concerning the reconstruction of Stanford University which had been partially destroyed in the 1906 earthquake.

Fifteenth Convention
1907—Boulder, Colorado

The custom of a May Convention was broken when the Fifteenth Delta Gamma Convention

Rose Smith, Υ-Stanford, President 1905-09, had been a charter member of Upsilon. Through her years of office she worked tirelessly for the advancement of Delta Gamma.

Consider Alpha's future

Once more the matter of Alpha chapter was brought up, and Council met with the chapter representative, discussing the charge that Mt. Union lacked sufficient material to support adequately a Delta Gamma chapter. Once more the matter was deferred, this time for further consideration by Council.

Convention program grows

By this time sessions devoted to discussions of the Intersorority Conference had a permanent spot on the business program, and other discussions also focused on alumnæ work and organizations. As Blanche Garten relates later, "Convention has become such an important as well as expansive factor of our fraternity because of the large attendance that the business program is well planned and different sessions are placed under the supervision of prominent alumnæ."

The following was accomplished at this 1907 Convention:

- **Constitutional revisions** had once more been made, this time under the direction of Lambda and Lambda Nu (Minneapolis alumnæ). Actually, they put into better form the changes made at previous Conventions. Their report was accepted and the changes incorporated in the Constitution and By-Laws.
- **Initiation ritual** in complete form was presented before Convention by Upsilon, using the form which the chapter used. A permanent ritual committee to serve four years was appointed. This committee was to work toward a perfect ritual, the work to be presented before Convention at the end of four years.
- **A directory** was planned, in Rho's charge, and the directory committee was to install a card catalogue system recording each member's data.

Because of its location, Phi was able to offer this Convention a great deal in the way of "tourist attractions" for delegates, including trips into the Rockies and a trip to Denver for the banquet and for more social affairs after Convention was officially over.

More alumnæ chapters

Conventions seemed to echo alumnæ enthusiasm, and in the year following the Boulder Convention Seattle alumnæ were chartered as Beta Sigma, Denver as Phi Omega, and Akron as Eta Upsilon. Kappa Theta had tendered its resignation to Convention as it drew material entirely from Kappa and many of Kappa's members were out of town girls. Kappa Theta became an association, however, and did remain active until many years later when she regained chapter status.

Alpha loses charter

The days of Alpha chapter finally came to a
(Continued on page 97)

was called for April 24-26, 1907. Phi chapter was to be hostess in Boulder. Meetings were held in Gilbert Hall, and Rose Smith, as Grand President, presided.

Of the 1907 Convention a Phi historian wrote many years later, "The Convention of 1907 was held in April, and we were all allowed to take a week off from school work in order to make it a success. I do not know how many were in attendance. Our visitors were housed in the Beta Theta Pi and Sigma Alpha Epsilon houses. Teas were given for us by practically every group on campus. To these we traipsed about in the mud, ruining our best shoes. There were few sidewalks on University Hill at that time, and it rained all during the Convention excepting when it snowed. It snowed the day we took our guests on a chartered train up to Mt. Alto, the present Glacier Lake. All the wraps from our homes went on that trip—our guests had come prepared for spring!

"We had a reception and dance in Citizens' Hall, downtown. Unfortunately for us the Elks had a dance that same night and brought up the four available cabs every time they passed the Twelfth Street corner. Our National Officers finally arrived at the function about 11:30 P.M.—and one beautiful auburn haired lassie from Wisconsin refused to go to the dance because her escort, who was trying to be very stylish, arrived for her at so late an hour. Most of us went on street cars and hence arrived in time."

Conventions

A Pictorial Section
*showing brief glimpses of
people, pleasure, programs, and projects
of some of Delta Gamma's Conventions*

DELTA GAMMA CONVENTION.

Banquet.

✳ TOASTS ✳

✢

MRS. H. AUBERTINE MOORE, Toastmistress.

The Composite Delta Gamma Girl. - - Response from Sigma.

The Delta Gamma Boys. - - - - Response from Chi.

The Delta Gamma Girl in Practical Life. - Response from Eta.

Our Baby, Kappa. - - - - Response from Alpha.

"Auf Wiedersehn." - - - - Response from Omega.

The toasts were an important part of Conventions. Here is the program of toasts presented in 1889.

...MENU...

Macedonian Fruit
Frogs' Legs on Toast, Tartar Sauce
Olives   Salted Almonds
Deviled Lobster
Filet Mignon a la Richelieu
Cauliflower Hollandaise
Sorbet en Surprise
Spring Chicken a la Maryland
Pomme de Terre   Petis Pois
Stuffed Tomatoes a la Waldorf
Wafers
Glace Fantastique
Petite Fours
Fromage Variee   Crackers
Bon Bons
Cafe   Demi   Tasse

...TOASTS...

Toastmistress, Elizabeth Wing, Kappa Theta.

Delta Gamma, Juanita Williams. Lambda.
"One of the few, the immortal names
That were not born to die."

Without Anchor, Edna Polk, Kappa Theta.
"The union of souls is an anchor in storms."

Delta Gamma Hymns, Agnes Merrill, Omega.
"Blest be the tie that binds."

Zeitgeist. Helen Louise Brown, Chi.
"Thro' the ages one increasing purpose runs,
And the thoughts of men are widen'd with the process of the suns."

Song—*Vive la Delta G.*

Skeleton Key, Rhoda Gooch, Sigma.
"The time has come." the walrus said,
"To talk of many things,
Of shoes and ships and sealing wax,
Of cabbage and of kings."

Toujours la Femme, Jeanette Ostrander, Psi.
"I think it was a Persian king
Who used to say, that evermore
In human life, each evil thing
Comes of the sex that men adore."

Golden Age, Grace Snitseler, Xi.
"Yet, ah! that Spring should vanish with the rose;
That Youth's sweet scented manuscript should close."

Song—*Banquet Song, Edith Abbott, 1901.*

Auf Wiedersehen, Alice Joiner, Upsilon.
"Good night, good night:
parting is such sweet sorrow
That I shall say—good night,
till it be a tomorrow."

...BANQUET SONG...
[Tune—' Old Lang Syne.'']

To Delta Gamma, firm and true
And strong the ties that bind
Our hearts in mystic love and trust
For days o' lang syne.

CHORUS.

Time ne'er can steal our love for thee
Our dearest friends are thine.
To Delta Gamma ever sing
For day's o' lang syne.

Tho' we may wander far apart
In that long after time,
Our sweetest thoughts will be of thee
And days o' lang syne.—Cho.

And as we part in sorrow now,
We pledge our hearts to thee.
To Delta Gamma ever loved
And clear in memory.

The 1901 Convention Banquet Program.

Delta Gamma Conventions

1	1881	Oxford, Mississippi	24	1928	Coronado, California
2	1883	Akron, Ohio	25	1930	Asheville, North Carolina
3	1885	Madison, Wisconsin	26	1932	Victoria, British Columbia
4	1887	Cleveland, Ohio	27	1934	Green Lake, Wisconsin
5	1888	Evanston, Illinois	28	1936	Lake Placid, New York
6	1889	Madison, Wisconsin	29	1938	Colorado Springs, Colorado
7	1891	Ann Arbor, Michigan	30	1940	Mackinac Island, Michigan
8	1893	Akron, Ohio	31	1942	Chicago, Illinois
9	1895	Minneapolis, Minnesota	32	1946	Pasadena, California
10	1897	Ithaca, New York	33	1948	Swampscott, Massachusetts
11	1899	Albion, Michigan	34	1950	Banff, Alberta
12	1901	Lincoln, Nebraska	35	1952	White Sulphur Springs, West Virginia
13	1903	Madison, Wisconsin			
14	1905	Evanston, Illinois	36	1954	Sun Valley, Idaho
15	1907	Boulder, Colorado	37	1956	Quebec, Quebec
16	1909	Ann Arbor, Michigan	38	1958	Miami Beach, Florida
17	1911	Waupaca, Wisconsin	39	1960	Estes Park, Colorado
18	1913	Niagara Falls, Ontario	40	1962	Mackinac Island, Michigan
19	1915	Berkeley, California	41	1964	Miami Beach, Florida
20	1919	Christmas Lake, Minnesota	42	1966	Portland, Oregon
21	1922	Spring Lake, New Jersey	43	1968	Dallas, Texas
22	1924	Estes Park, Colorado	44	1970	Lake of the Ozarks, Missouri
23	1926	Mackinac Island, Michigan	45	1972	Los Angeles, California

The Delta Gamma gavel, used at each Convention, was presented by Blanche Garten to the Fraternity in 1905. Both the gavel and the crest on its case, presented by Miss Garten in 1924, were made from wood from the Lewis School.

CONVENTION PHOTOGRAPH, EVANSTON, 1905.

Advertising helped finance Anchora in the early days.
This was a matter for Convention discussion.

THE AUTO RIDE
GIVEN BY THE
DENVER
ASSOCIATION
OF
DELTA GAMMA
A FEW OF THE
MACHINES
READY TO START

THE
GRAND COUNCIL
IS READY
FOR THE RIDE

A parade was part of the 1907 Convention's welcome to Boulder, and the sight of so many automobiles (at that time a rare occurrence) made the city well aware of Delta Gamma's presence.

Convention, 1909, in Ann Arbor, Michigan. A moment never forgotten by those who attended was the arrival of the two Founders and the appearance of George Banta as well.

THE GRAND COUNCIL

ROSE F. SMITH, Grand President   RUTH ROSHALT, Grand Secretary

GRACE ABBOTT, Editor of Anchora

MARGARETHE SHEPPARD, Grand Treasurer

MARY ROSEMOND, Grand Vice-President

January, 1908
Anchora

The Delta Gamma Crest, designed by Denver artist, Leota Woy, Φ-Colorado, was accepted by the 1909 Convention.

MISS LEOTA WOY

Leota Woy, Φ-Colorado, who designed Delta Gamma's crest was an artist of note in Denver, having been chosen to design Colorado's exhibit at the 1893 Columbian Exposition. She also created the cover (right) for this special issue of the Denver Times. (Photos courtesy Denver Public Library, located there by Alpha Gamma Delta editor, Mickey Maker.)

The Denver Times

Festival Edition 1898

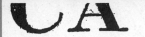

THURSDAY, JUNE 29, 1911

DELTA GAMMA CONVENTION

ALL OF THE LEADING COLLEGES REPRESENTED

225 Young Ladies at First Summer Session—Iowa University and Leland-St. Jr. Chapters Hosts

The National meeting of the Delta Gamma Fraternity is in session at the Grand View Hotel, Chain o' Lakes and the attendance is about 225, exceeding that of any previous meeting.

This is their first summer meeting and it is proving a most enjoyable and profitable one. The former gatherings have been held during the college year and in a college town and Waupaca is indebted to Miss Mae Browne of Rhinelander for bringing the convention to the Chain o' Lakes.

All the sessions both business and social are being held in the Amusement hall. The business sessions are devoted exclusively to the work of the fraternity and reports of the several chapters and the social sessions consist of music and dancing.

The lakes and walks afford inviting pass time for the young ladies when a leisure hour permits. The Chapters who are giving the convention are Tau University of Iowa, which is represented by Miss Helen Reaver of Des Moines, Ia., and Upsilon of Lelan Stanford, Jr. University represented by Miss Mae Browne of Rhinelander.

The officers are: Pres., Mrs. Chas. R. Carpenter, Racine; Vice Pres., Mary Rosemond, Des Moines, Ia.; Sec., M. Agnes Burton, Detroit, Mich.; Treas., Marguerite B. Lake, Forrest Hill, Md.; Editor of Anchora, Ethel M. Tukey, Omaha, Neb.

Twenty-eight of the leading colleges and universities of the United States are represented as follows: The Collegiate Chapters represented are:

Eta—Buchtel college, Akron, Ohio.
Omega—University of Wisconsin, Madison.
Lambda—University of Minnesota, Minneapolis.
Sigma—Northwestern University, Evanston, Ill.
Zeta—Albion College, Albion, Md.
Chi — Cornell University, Ithaca, N. Y.

1911

Tuesday, June 27

8 p. m.—Jolly-up, Amusement Hall.

Wednesday, June 28

8:30 a. m.—Convention Session.
1:30 p. m.—Convention Session.
Evening—Initiation.

Thursday, June 29

8:30 a. m.—Convention Session.
1:30 p. m.—Convention Session.
Evening—Boat Parade.

Friday, June 30

8:30 a. m.—Convention Session.
1:30 p. m.—Convention Session.
7:30 p. m.—Banquet.

Boats may be had at any time Wednesday, Thursday or Friday by getting boat checks from the office.

Launch rides around the Lakes, 25c.

Look Out For Poison Ivy

Hours For Meals

Breakfast—7 to 9 a. m.
Dinner—12 to 1:30 p. m.
Supper—6 to 7:30 p. m.

Capsule program, 1911—and do look out for poison ivy!

The Green Lake, Wis., paper featured the Delta Gamma 1911 Convention on its front page.

After their initial trip in 1909, Mrs. Leonard and Mrs. Dodd were enthusiastic Conventioners.

Certificate of Delta Gamma Membership Fraternity

This is to certify that   has been initiated into Delta Gamma in   chapter, on   day of   A.D., 1   and is entitled to all the rights, privileges and immunities of the fraternity.

In witness whereof we hereunto set our hands and cause the seal of the fraternity to be affixed this   day of   A.D., 1

President *Ada May Brown*

Secretary

A Membership Certificate of this period is printed on parchment and is somewhat smaller than today's version which has been in use since the thirties. This, too, was a matter of Convention business.

The Charm of Electric Table-Cooking

"Dainty menus cooked on glowing coils."

So easy—so quick—and withal so inexpensive.

No wonder electric cooking on the table is the delight of womankind. Think of the cool cleanliness, the dainty convenience, the wide range of usefulness, the appetizing results. It is easy to see why every woman—housewife and bachelor maid, mother and daughter, hostess and guest—is enthusiastic in praise of the

G-E Radiant Grill

It boils, toasts, fries, stews and broils. Always ready, taking its electricity from any lamp socket, the G-E Grill operates for only two or three cents a meal.

It is as attractive as a chafing dish and of much wider usefulness. Besides the hinged grid, it is supplied with interchangeable stewing, boiling and frying pans, removable grill-rack and the attaching cord and plugs.

Electric shops, hardware stores or any lighting company can supply you.

Send for our handsome book, "Electric Heating and Cooking"—64 pages with many beautiful illustrations in color, explaining the helpfulness and economy of electricity in the home. Write for it today.

The Guarantee of Excellence on Goods Electrical

General Electric Company
The World's Largest Electrical Manufacturer

(Dept. 39)   3763   Schenectady, N. Y.

DELTA GAMMA COOK BOOK

Compiled and published for the benefit of the

NATIONAL SCHOLARSHIP FUND

By

LAMBDA NU CHAPTER
Minneapolis, Minnesota

1912

Press of
HAHN & HARMON COMPANY
Minneapolis

The first Delta Gamma Cook Book (this is the title page) appeared in 1912 after a campaign for contributions at the 1911 Convention.

SCHEDULE OF SPECIAL TRAIN

Our train will be Personally Conducted on the entire trip from Chicago by a Passenger Department Representative. It will be elegantly equipped and one of the handsomest trains ever assembled. The equipment will include a dynamo baggage car (from which the train will be brilliantly lighted), standard drawing room and compartment, steel sleeping cars, observation library car, and dining car; serving meals a la carte.

Every possible effort will be made by the Railroads to make this one of the most comfortable and enjoyable trips ever undertaken by the Delta Gamma Fraternity.

Lv Chicago	5.30 pm	Tuesday,	July 27th	Burlington Route
Ar Omaha	7.30 am	Wednesday,	28th	"
Lv Omaha	11.30 am	"	28th	"
Ar Lincoln	1.00 pm	"	28th	"
Lv Lincoln	6.00 pm	"	28th	"
Ar Denver	7.00 am	Thursday,	29th	"
Lv Denver	11.00 am	"	29th	D. & R. G.
Ar Colorado Springs	1.30 pm	"	29th	"
Lv Colorado Springs	8.00 am	Friday	30th	"
Ar Glenwood	7.30 pm	"	30th	"
Lv Glenwood	9.00 pm	"	30th	"
Ar Salt Lake	11.00 am	Saturday,	31st	"
Lv Salt Lake	10.00 am	Sunday,	August, 1st	Western Pacific
Ar Oakland	2.30 pm	Monday,	2nd	"
Ar Berkeley	3.30 pm	"	2nd	"

TRAVEL ARRANGEMENTS.

For the convenience of our members, headquarters in Chicago will be made at the Rest Rooms on the main floor of the General Office Building of the Burlington Railroad, 547 West Jackson Boulevard, one block south and one block west of the Union Depot.

Cards of introduction will be issued to delegates by the railroad company to Burlington, D. & R. G. and Western Pacific, representatives on the coast and intermediate points which will assure special attention and assistance in getting desirable return reservations.

Suit cases and small hand bags will be taken into the cars; trunks will be carried in a special baggage car, provided for them, and will be accessible at all times throughout the trip.

Mail and telegrams should be sent to our party in care of Delta Gamma Fraternity's Special Train as per schedule.

2

ITINERARY.

Tuesday, July 27th.

Our special train will leave at 5:30 P. M. from the Union Passenger Station, Chicago (Canal and Adams Streets). An excellent opportunity will be given during the early evening for a view of Chicago's western suburbs and the beautiful farming communities of Western Illinois. Dinner will be ready shortly after the train leaves Chicago. All meals will be served on the a la carte plan.

Wednesday, July 28th.

Our train will leave Pacific Junction about 6:30 in the morning and for eighteen miles to the northward it will run parallel to and at intervals close along the bank of the Missouri River. After passing through Council Bluffs Missouri River is crossed on a massive double track bridge and Omaha is reached at 7:30 A. M. Here our party will be entertained at breakfast by the Omaha Delta Gammas.

After a three hours' stay, our train is due to leave Omaha at 11:30 A. M. and arrive in Lincoln at 1:00 P. M. where a similar program has been arranged for, the members of our local chapter. Leaving Lincoln at 6:00 P. M. the night will be spent traversing the prairie country of Western Nebraska and Eastern Colorado.

Thursday, July 29th.

Our train will arrive in Denver at 7:00 A. M. Breakfast will be served immediately upon our arrival, after which we will take automobiles, reserved for our exclusive use, for a sight-seeing tour of business and residence districts of Denver. The trip will include a visit to the State Capitol and the United States mint, and a number of the most interesting parks and driveways, in all including about eighteen miles.

Leaving Denver at 11:00 A. M. after some very delightful hours spent in passing parallel to and in full view of the snow covered Rocky Mountains, prominent among which are several well known mountains, such as Pike's Peak, our train is due at Colorado Springs at 1:30 P. M., where our cars will be conveniently parked near the Antlers Hotel, convenient for our use during our sojourn here.

An interesting afternoon will be spent in and around Colorado Springs and Manitou, including several of the most delightful side trips.

Friday, July 30th.

Everybody should arrange to retire early Thursday night and respond to the first call in the morning, which will be at 3:00 A. M. Arrangements have been made to take the famous Crystal Park automobile trip over the substantially constructed

3

Pages from the booklet sent to those who would be part of the "houseparty special" train en route to the 1915 Convention in Berkeley.

Monday, August 2:

8:00 p. m.—Informal Reception at Delta Gamma, Kappa Kappa and Pi Beta Phi Houses, Channing Way.

Tuesday, August 3:

9:00 a. m.—Business Session, Twentieth Century Club House.
1:30 p. m.—Business Session, Twentieth Century Club House.
4:00 p. m.—Tea served at Delta Gamma House.
8:00 p. m.—Stunt Night, Twentieth Century Club House.

Wednesday, August 4:

9:00 a. m.—Business Session, Twentieth Century Club House.
1:00 p. m.—Trip to Stanford. Take 1:10 Key Route or 1:12 S. P. Special Train leaves 3rd and Townsend, S. F., 2:35 p. m.
Evening: Initiation at Stanford by Upsilon Chapter.

Thursday, August 5:

9:00 a. m.—Business Session, Twentieth Century Club House.

1:30 p. m.—Business Session, Twentieth Century Club House.
4:00 p. m.—Tea served at Delta Gamma House.
4:30 p. m.—Automobile Sight Seeing Trip.
8:00 p. m.—Pan-Hellenic Session and Reception to Grand Officers at Twentieth Century Club House.

Friday, August 6:

9:00 a. m.—Business Session, Twentieth Century Club.
1:30 p. m.—Business Session, Twentieth Century Club.
4:00 p. m.—Tea served at Delta Gamma House.
7:00 p. m.—Banquet, Hotel Oakland. Special cars leave corner of College and Channing at 6:00 p. m.

Saturday, August 7:

Delta Gamma Day at Exposition.
Take Direct Ferry. Train leaves Telegraph and Bancroft at 9:50 a. m., or Berkeley Station at 10:00 a. m.
12:00 p. m.—Luncheon at Japan Beautiful, 50 cents per plate.

In capsule form, came the program for the 1915 Convention at Berkeley's Twentieth Century Club. Conventioners set policies which guided Delta Gamma activity for years to come.

Bi-Annual ΔΓ National Convention Fiftieth Anniversary
Estes Park 1924

A spectacular Golden Jubilee was the 1924 Convention at Estes Park. It remains today recorded as one of Delta Gamma's largest Conventions.

Delta Gamma
Fiftieth Birthday
Convention

June 23-28
1924

Burlington
Route

STANLEY HOTEL
ESTES PARK, COLO.

ANCHOR LINE

NUMBER 1   CORONADO, CALIFORNIA, THURSDAY, JUNE 28, 1928   PRICE, 10 CENTS

"And Why to Bed?"

MRS. PEPYS PRIVATE LINE.

Did arrive this day at Coronado, and did find all in a flurry and hub-dub because of the great comings to and goings fro of a vast number of females of all ages, stages, and variations of pulchritude, but for the most part of such comeliness and youth that I was impelled to withdraw myself into a corner to be sure that I had not fallen by mischance into a gathering for the choosing of that damsel to be known as Miss America. But then I did reflect upon that which had caused me to hurry thither, being no more than a remark of my son's as to what queer clothes they wore in the olden days, and I did agree till I did find the volume upon which he did make his observances to be no more than a class book of the year 1913. If youth is to be acquired by contact, surely I could come to no better place than this, and can find plenty of association with friends and cronies of my vintage, should I tire of too much effervescence.

Was no sooner established in my room with a great view of ocean wave and sand and azure sky, than in did come Polly Pert, whom I had not seen since she did go trailing down the aisle at her graduation with a wad of gum in her mouth, because she averred that she was so excited that she would be sure to chew her tongue. Remained a few minutes to save my face and to unpack my new evening gown which is of silver cloth and crimson sash which doth become me well, and thence to various rooms where there was much laughing and gabbing, and I did fall upon many friends of other years, in especial Nina Goodnow Belcher, whom I did know when I did suck upon a peppermint stick and roll the hoop of the gay nineties, and was pleased to find her risen to such high esteem in the fraternity and no whit diminished in the charm with which my youthful fancies had endowed her.

Tonight did attend the reception to our National Council, and did find all to be most human, albeit having their names so oft in the publick prints, I was afeard lest they be haughty because of their position and provoke hushed tones and some obeisance. After that didst go from room to

(Continued on Page Four)

CONVENTION OPENS

"So this is California—where then, are all the Indians?"

To the Delta Gammas—

GRAND PRESIDENT URGES GENERAL ATTENDANCE

Attending the first session of Convention is considered the most important event of Thursday. Nancy B. Woollett urges every Delta Gamma to be in the ballroom at 10 A. M. sharp. Florence Bingham, Chi, will deliver the address of welcome for Province Seven, while Mrs. Woollett will respond.

Who Claims Highest Delta Gamma I. Q.?

You have tried out the puzzlers on travel, history, science and baseball. Now take a swing at your fraternity questionnaire. Contest open to all those attending Convention. Sharpen your pencils and your wits and write to win. See page four for full details of contest.

Cheer! Cheer! The Gang's All Here!

June 28th has arrived! Convention has opened, and we are gathered together for the twenty-fourth time in Delta Gamma History. We have come from far and near, we are meeting old friends and making new ones, and we are all happy together. In our cordial welcome to each one of you we ask you to "Come Join the Band" and help make the spirit of this Convention one of outward friendliness. Please remember that introductions are unnecessary; we are all Delta Gammas gathered here for a common purpose. To absorb all that will be offered us at this meeting we must talk with as many as we possibly can, exchange new ideas, elaborate on old ones and collect new ones. What we are able to carry home to the unfortunates, who could not come, depends on just how much we put into this Convention ourselves. So it devolves on each one of us to "carry on," and with the spirit of friendliness the keynote of Convention, to make this the outstanding Convention of Delta Gamma history.

MAE BROWNE TOMPKINS,
Permanent Convention Chairman.

Gay Theatricals Feature First Program Tonight

With a brilliant array of events scheduled for almost every hour of the six days of Delta Gamma's twenty-fourth Convention, delegates and visiting members arrived several hundred strong yesterday afternoon when registration and its attendant duties claimed everyone. Reunions were the chief order of the day, culminating in that best reunion, last night's reception to the national officers, Mrs. W. C. Fankhauser having arranged all details.

Today's morning session scheduled for 10 will claim every visiting member in addition to official delegates, Mrs. Woollett having asked that every Delta Gamma present at Convention attend. Afternoon session will claim many again, followed by an informal alumnae session, but playtime will begin at 8:30 tonight, when Gamma will present "High Hat" and Alpha Pi stage the intriguing "Superstition."

Events scheduled for the remainder of Convention are as follows:

Friday, June 29.
9:00 A. M.—Morning Session.
1:30 P. M.—Afternoon Session.
8:30 P. M.—"Open Barriers," by Alpha Nu.

Saturday, June 30.
9:00 A. M.—Morning Session.
1:30 P. M.—Alumnae Session.
8:30 P. M.—Student Tour Review, by Alpha Sigma.

Sunday, July 1.
Drives, morning and afternoon. All conventionites to be guests of Province Seven on one drive.
8:30 P. M.—Initiation.

Monday, July 2.
9:00 A. M.—Morning Session.
1:30 P. M.—Afternoon Session.
7:00 P. M.—Banquet.
"Something Spanish" by Upsilon.

All alumnae are urged to attend the alumnae conference, 3:30-4:00 today. This will be followed by a joint meeting with the active members, 4:30-5:00.

Answers to Contest may be left at Room 5 or dropped in Contest Box in the lobby.

Telegrams reached two members of Council the morning after their arrival at Coronado. One read "Rainy and warm," the other "Lovely and cool." We recommend that Mr. Woollett and Dr. Gradle get to-gether in Chicago and make their stories agree.

We think that Indiana will have to offer special inducements to Mrs. Erlbacher; she seems to like our state.

More guests arriving so Mrs. Hawley will be prepared to answer questions about the dog.

Delta Gamma Air Mail

NUMBER 2   ASHEVILLE, NORTH CAROLINA, WEDNESDAY, JUNE 25, 1930   PRICE, 10 CENTS

Hostesses At Reception

Alpha Rho Are Reception Hostesses

In a setting befitting the sea-loving daughters of Delta Gamma, Alpha Rho Chapter was hostess at the welcoming reception last evening. Invitations in the form of gob caps brought the guests arrayed in charming summer gowns to a ship. The main floor of Grove Park Inn had been transformed into a steamer with all its accoutrements. Only by gazing through the port holes or by walking the decks could one realize that the ship was stationary and anchored to a mountain side.

About eight-thirty o'clock the guests embarked for an evening of entertainment and getting acquainted. To while away the hours on board, dancing was an attraction for many. In addition, various features were presented for the pleasure of the guests by the hostesses who were distinguished by their gob uniforms One of these was a dance, the Sailor's Hornpipe.

In the receiving line were the Founders of Delta Gamma, the National Council, and the Secretaries: Mrs. Joseph Halstead, the Misses Donna Amsden and Marguerite Winant, Mrs. H. S. Gradle, Mrs. Edward Hawley, the Misses Pauline Schmid, Adelaide Miller, Pearl McDonnell, Jessie Fitzpatrick, Mrs. Mark Hamer, Mrs. W. T. Belcher, and Mrs. L. E. Schuessler.

Mortar Board, Alpha Rho
  Margaret Rinehart, 1930
  Martha Brashares, 1931

Phi Beta Kappa
  Helen Beetham, 1930

President W. S. G. A.
  Margaret Rinehart
  These girls will not be able to be present at convention though.

Beauty
  Eileen Christensen, 1933
  "Miss Rocky River," Ohio

A Treat In Store Thursday Night

Not only can you view the mountain from your hotel window and smell the pungent pine odor blown in by the cool mountain breezes, but you will have the opportunity at Thursday evening at nine o'clock in the hotel lobby of seeing the real mountains in action.

This treat, a part of Province II's entertainment will consist of a program under the direction of Mr. Bascom Lamar Lunsford of Asheville, better known as the "Minstrel of the Appalachians." The songs, many of them dating back to English and Scotch ballads, were gathered on Mr. Lunsford's roaming through the mountains as school teacher, fruit tree expert, political stunt speaker, and bee enthusiast. He plays the fiddle, banjo, guitar, is a college graduate and a lawyer of renown, but owes his popularity to his musicianship.

The group of people who accompany him and help him in the folk dances will be dressed in their picturesque mountan clothing.

Don't miss the wholesome view of real mountain life.

Delta Beta Gets D. G. Charter

In the report of the Ritual committee, it was announced that Delta Gamma had voted a charter to Delta Beta of the University of Arkansas. Delta Beta was founded in December, 1925, with the express purpose of petitioning Delta Gamma and today it stands on a par with the national fraternities on the campus. In scholarship Delta Beta is the highest on the campus and has been the highest in the institution since it has been organized.

The installation of our forty-fifth chapter will take place in the fall when the Alpha Omega Chapter of Delta Gamma is installed.

National Officers

After wracking my stupid brain for hours and after asking all the national officers, one after the other for suggestions for editorials, the thought suddenly struck me—what could be more interesting to everyone or a more fruitful topic than these same national officers.

I am not going to recite for you their various virtues. You all know them well. Besides these dear ladies have to live with us for four whole days and open-mouthed awe would no doubt become somewhat tiresome to them soon. If any of their works are overlooked, then, you know why.

I am, however, going to tell you what they have meant to me. For some few years I have heard of Lulu, Donna, Alice, Mary N. and Marguerite. Yet today I met them for the first time. They have all been so cordial and so willing to help me (even if they do call me "one of those horrid people") that I feel that they are not merely exalted beings who sit in state on our misdeeds and sign our certificates of membership but that they are real human beings.

To rule and make that governing welcome takes tact, untiring patience and above all understanding. They seem to have all of that and more. They are cordial and personal in their contacts so that when once they have been encountered, they are no longer imaginary orges but people just like ourselves. In fact, Mrs. F. B. Culbertson confided to me that she is really the stupidest person alive and that she really doesn't know anything.

I hope that everyone at convention can have some contacts with some of our national officers and committee chairmen and know them too.

---o---

Ruth Bryan Owen Gets New Honor

Perhaps as illustrious a Delta Gamma as there is anywhere is Ruth Bryan Owen. We feel like shouting her from the house tops. Following is a clipping contributed from Washington which informs us that "to those who have it shall be given."

WASHINGTON, June 21.— (A. P.)—Representative Ruth Bryan Owen of Florida has been appointed one of the American delegates to the inter-parliamentary union to meet in London July 16 to 26.

She is the first woman ever to represent the United States at this gathering of the parliaments of the world. She will sail July 6 and return July 30.

Mrs. Dodd and Mrs. Leonard Arrive

At 2:40 Tuesday afternoon Mrs. Dodd and Mrs. Leonard, two of our three founders, arrived at Grove Park Inn. Mrs. Hawley had given us the information that they could not be here so their arrival was a delightful surprise and a real thrill.

To think that the girls who conceived the ideals which founded our now widespread organization can be here to view their handiwork and that all of us to whom for years their names have been words of magic, can have the wonderful privilege of seeing them and having them with us here at the Grove Park Inn for three whole days!

Mrs. Leonard and Mrs. Dodd we are sincerely glad and proud that you have come all the way to Asheville to the 1930 Convention.

Let us say to you that we hope your trip will be delightful and that we can make you realize the love and honor we bear you. May we see you at many more conventions. The memory of this one will always be more wonderful for your having been here.

---o---

Southern Hospitality

Coming from north, east and west are gathered unto our gathering a throng of miscreants and whatnot. They descend upon us like the Assyrians. Being loving and peace-abiding souls, we welcome them into our arms with love and thanksgiving. And they say unto us "What is this southern hospitality of which we have heard so much? I crave a mint julep!"

Coming into Asheville (don't let me hear anyone say "Land of the Sky" again) we are coming into the home of southern hospitality. Not only at the Grove Park Inn where we have all been welcomed so grandly, where our every wish seems to be transferred by mental telepathy (and it doesn't all go on the bill either) but all over Asheville, we are treated in a manner entirely fitting with our romantic, and we feared idealistic, notion of what southern hospitality means.

It is an attitude that seems to pervade the city as well as the Inn. We hope the south doesn't think us a group of cutthroats and savages, but we find here a spirit of—of—well of hospitality, welcome and friendliness which we miss elsewhere.

It will be necessary for us to tear ourselves away in order that the other cities of the United States may be inhabited, else we are afraid that we might remain indefinitely—the sunny south has won our hearts so.

Ruth Billow, H-Akron, who was herself blind, and her appeal, written in Braille, and read by her to the 1936 Convention, did much to establish Sight Conservation and Aid to the Blind as the Fraternity Project. A Memorial Fellowship bears her name.

A wartime Convention which met strictly for business was held at the Edgewater Beach Hotel, Chicago, in 1942. Here is this streamlined Convention as it appeared in session.

A truly gala affair was the 1946 Convention in Pasadena, one of Delta Gamma's largest conclaves to date. The California color which characterized the social side of Convention is evident here.

The historical pageant in 1948 was part of the Diamond Jubilee celebration.

The Council badge was presented to incoming officers for the first time at Banff in 1950. The five emeralds, appended on a scroll at the base of the anchor, represent the then five member Council.

The Executive Secretary and the new Council at Banff—Miss Abernethy, Mrs. Forman, Mrs. Wildasin, Mrs. Byars, Mrs. Banker, and Mrs. Preston. Since the Foundation had been voted into being at this Convention, this was its first Board of Directors.

A collegiate representative for Council addresses the Convention banquet—E. J. Holt, from the University of Miami.

Workshops have been a major item on recent Convention programs. This was 1962 at Mackinac.

1958 guest speaker was George Banta, Jr., who received a plaque declaring the 1957-58 George Banta Memorial Fellowship in recognition of the part the latter played in Delta Gamma expansion to the north. This date also commemorated a half century that the Banta Company had printed the Anchora.

Lena Ellington, ΑΨ-Mississippi, daughter of Anna Boyd Ellington, was an honored guest at the 1964 Convention and receives cream colored roses from President Maisie Groves.

Jackie Martin's spectacular Convention exhibits were an important part of the background in 1964.

A Cavalcade of Conventions climaxed the 1966 program.

Popular 1970 Convention speaker was Dr. Frederick D. Kershner, Columbia University professor and Delta Tau Delta scholarship supervisor.

Awards have been a big part of recent Conventions.

close in December, 1908, when her resignation was accepted by Grand Council. The charge that the number of women students at Mt. Union was not adequate to support a chapter of Delta Gamma, especially with another rival in the field, was result of an investigation by Grand Council of conditions at Mt. Union. An examination of the catalog of the college for the six years prior to this time gave the following figures: Number of women students—1901, 22; 1902, 15; 1903, 20; 1904, 25; 1905, 36; 1906, 36. Alpha had always been most careful to fulfill all constitutional requirements of the fraternity and deserves all honor for the maintenance of its chapter under adverse conditions.

And so another chapter joined the roll of extinct chapters. Sometimes this list seems alarmingly long to Delta Gammas of recent years. Blanche Garten recorded this in covering the situation: "In considering the number of extinct chapters of Delta Gamma we must realize that those of the South were chartered before we ever became a bona fide national college fraternity and should not be considered unless apart from the others. Those of the North whose charters were withdrawn or who returned them were installed in colleges where fraternities were not encouraged or coeducation never became strong and chapters could not thrive. When collegiate work for women became established on a firmer basis, fraternities had more to guide them in choosing new fields. In every case, except that of Alpha, either about the time Delta Gamma withdrew a charter or soon after, the other women's fraternities in the field, withdrew and at that time only those fraternities which are ranked as the oldest, were in existence. In examining the chapter roll of some of the strongest among men's fraternities, we find many extinct chapters which were withdrawn probably because of similar reason."

Anti-coeducation movement

Even as late as this, anti-coeducation movement was active at the University of Wisconsin, and the lead article in the November, 1908 *Anchora* covers it thoroughly. The author comments, "The portion of the public interested in such matters has been surprised that at the University of Wisconsin, hitherto supposed to be entirely satisfied with coeducation, and anti-woman movement should arise enlisting an influential part of the faculty, including the president." Needless to say this movement was defeated.

Adelphi College

In May, 1908, Council traveled East with three-fold purpose: to hold its annual meeting with Rho chapter at Syracuse, to visit Chi chapter at Cornell, and to install Omicron chapter at Adelphi College, then located in Brooklyn. Delta Gamma's high standards and ultraconservative expansion policy had appealed to a group at Adelphi which in 1905 was collecting material about the various nationals. With Chi Upsilon's (New York alumnæ) aid they petitioned—and campaigned—and eventually received a charter.

National Panhellenic Congress

September was once more Intersorority Conference time, and September 10-12 twelve sorority representatives met in Chicago, Delta Gamma's delegate being Margarethe Shepard. It was at this meeting that the organization changed its name to National Panhellenic Congress.

Sixteenth Convention
1909—Ann Arbor, Michigan

For the second time Xi was scheduled to entertain Convention—Delta Gamma's Sixteenth, April 13-15, 1909. Rose Smith again presided; meetings were held at Carpenter Hall. Pre-Convention correspondence reflects the considerable concern over growing expense to the hostess chapter. After this convention, several chapters shared the obligations of hostess to convention.

Convention business

- **Membership requirements** were an important topic and standards were raised for eligibility.
- **A crest** had been designed by Leota Woy, Phi-Colorado, was presented and accepted by Convention.
- **A chapter library** was urged by Council, containing bound volumes of *Anchora*, Constitutions, fraternity manuals, and other volumes of fraternity interest as well as books for general use. It also recommended a chapter history record book in which to compile individual chapter history.
- **The season for Convention** was discussed at length, and it was finally decided that the summer was most feasible. The next Convention date, hostesses, and place were to be left in the hands of Council. Because of increased expense, it was decided to have two chapters entertain instead of one.

Who's Who

After completing her great contribution to Fraternity archives—the Honor Roll and Who's Who in Delta Gamma—Lambda (Ruth Rosholt) resigned as secretary. These volumes, which recorded the achievements of outstanding members, contained the classification and data of those Delta Gammas in special lines of work or study. Miss Rosholt had also made as complete as possible the records and archives of Delta Gamma's earlier days.

The Founders return—

There was about this 1909 Convention in Ann Arbor a certain magic of all the years which had gone before, for present were two of Delta Gamma's founders, Mary Comfort Leonard and Eva Webb Dodd. Blanche Garten writes, "No

Imogene Hand Carpenter, Ω-Wisconsin, President 1909-11, presided at Convention with an awe-inspiring dignity that was never forgotten by 1911 Conventioners.

one can quite appreciate the intense excitement of the few of us who were seated on the platform during that first session and anxiously waiting for the two Southern ladies to appear, especially escorted to convention upon their arrival in Ann Arbor. They were led to the platform and introduced while Convention arose and the hall resounded for many minutes with peals of applause. These two dear gentle women were quite overcome. The bigness of us, the surprise to see over two hundred happy enthusiastic girls and women honoring them, two of the three women who as young girls had created the little club which had become such a wonder to them, was too much, they were very silent for some time. Only as they sat in sessions or talked to groups that always crowded around them during our playtimes, plying them with question after question of those first days, only did time make them understand Delta Gamma and we who composed it."

George Banta present, too

Though Council had renewed contact with the founders several years before—through Miss Garten—this was their first real view of the strong organization of 1909. Quite naturally they *were* overcome! The Convention presented them with badges—for they shyly related having given their pins, the H, to their sweethearts who afterwards became their husbands. The pins were lost, and these were their first anchors.

George Banta was in Ann Arbor, too, and

again Convention eagerly heard his reminiscences of the period in which he figured so prominently. For the first time, Delta Gamma's history became a real thing to Conventioners; it is no wonder that the intense enthusiasm of this Convention is felt even half a century later through those who have eagerly contributed to this history and who are still enthusiastically attending Conventions.

Anchora scope broadened

During this period the *Anchora* had grown and prospered under the direction of Grace Abbott, K-Nebraska. Broader subjects were featured, and editorial pages were interesting because of the touch of her personal interests, her work at that time in the League for the Proetction of Immigrants. This work increasing forced her to resign just after this Convention, and Kappa elected Ethel Tukey to the office of editor. Once more the editorship was in capable and loving hands.

University of Missouri

Several weeks after the Ann Arbor Convention was adjourned Mu chapter was installed at the University of Missouri. This group of petitioners had formed the year before under the close watch of Missouri's dean of women as part of a movement to reform the sorority system as it then existed in Columbia. Kappa Kappa Gamma and Pi Beta Phi had been annual rivals for a number of years and could only take a few girls each year though the enrollment of the university was growing steadily. There was an obvious need for more Greek-letter groups. Finally in the spring of 1909 Kappa Alpha Theta granted a charter to the only local sorority on campus. The Delta Gamma petitioners had maintained secrecy throughout the investigation in January and until word came in April that their charter had been granted by Convention. The speed of the granting of the charter—not usual for Delta Gamma—was probably due to careful guidance and aid by the dean of women and several faculty members and the obvious need for another group in an institution of high standing.

Council meets in Akron

Grand Council was Eta's guest for its May, 1910, meeting. A charter was granted the Milwaukee alumnæ as Omega Sigma. Earlier the Los Angeles alumnæ had been chartered as Gamma Upsilon. During this Convention interim all chapters of the Fraternity were visited by one or more members of Council.

Ohio State University

Encouraged by two members of Council who visited Columbus in the spring of 1910, a group at Ohio State (organized fall, 1909) formally petitioned in fall, 1910. Success was theirs and Epsilon chapter was installed March 17, 1911. The opening of a women's dormitory in

1908 had greatly increased the out-of-town enrollment in Columbus, and there was an obvious need for more groups to compete with those which had been concentrating on local girls. The group organized itself well before its final petition was submitted—and it remained sub rosa as there was already another local on campus. Even the official investigation was conducted secretly and the secret kept until the telegram arrived in February, 1911, announcing that the charter had been granted.

During this spring excitement was mounting in all Delta Gamma quarters, for we were entering a new Convention era. For the first time a resort Convention was planned, an innovation in itself but really only an omen of a new era in other ways.

II—*A resort Convention and more expansion*

A new era

The Seventeenth Delta Gamma Convention was destined to be a record breaking success. The enthusiasm of the 1909 meeting was still in the air, there were to be two hostess chapters (Tau and Upsilon) instead of one, the Wisconsin lakes were an enticing spot for a summertime Convention. So no one seemed surprised when chapter delegations of twenty and more arrived at Chain O'Lakes, Waupaca, Wisconsin, June 28-30, 1911. Imogene Hand Carpenter, Ω-Wisconsin, Grand President, held the historic gavel. For the first time visitors paid their own expenses; delegates and officers, only, were guests of the entertaining chapters.

University of Idaho

Without ado two charters were granted in the West—to petitioners at the University of Idaho and the University of Montana. At Moscow, Idaho, Beta Sigma had been organized as a local in 1900 and petitioned in 1907. In 1909 she was inspected and received some encouragement from the 1909 Convention. This spurred the Beta Sigmas on to greater effort and the 1911 Convention rewarded them with the charter. They were installed in the fall following Convention.

University of Montana

At Missoula, Montana, four girls had banded together as Sigma Tau Gamma in the fall of 1908 with the definite aim of petitioning a national group, and very shortly narrowing this generality to one, Delta Gamma. Their petition brought an inspection tour by Agnes Burton, Ξ-Michigan, and Ethel Tukey, K-Nebraska, Secretary and Editor respectively, in the spring of 1909—the pair inspecting Idaho at the same time. They had been, during this time, rushing successfully against Kappa Kappa Gamma and Kappa Alpha Theta. The 1911 Convention granted the charter and Pi chapter was installed just a week before Nu.

Conservatism wanes

Delta Gamma's ultraconservative spirit had fallen away, and the Fraternity appreciated the fact that the young colleges of the West would soon be larger and stronger. Instead of delaying and later going in after the other fraternities were well established, it was far wiser to enter when Delta Gamma could choose its material. Swarthmore was again under consideration and the University of Toronto and the University of Oregon were petitioning.

First philanthropic project

Another milestone in Delta Gamma activity, for it was at this Convention that Delta Gamma's first philanthropy came into being—the realization of a plan set forth so many years ago by those active Delta Gammas in Tehuacana, Texas. Scholarship Loan Chairman, Ruth Rosholt, had made a thorough investigation of fellowships and scholarships in the collegiate alumnæ and fraternities where they supported funds. She made a full report. She also had collected suggestions from the Fraternity as to methods of raising a fund. Convention decided to take two hundred dollars from the treasury, and each year fifty cents from every initiation fee and fifty cents from the annual dues of each member. This provided for a constant revenue—though not large, it would be a start. The conditions of granting the scholarships were to be decided when enough money was raised to be used for this purpose, the Fraternity to decide through a Convention.

Fifty years later a delegate to this 1911 Convention—Marguerite Williams from the newly installed Epsilon chapter—recalled a great campaign for contributions of recipes to be compiled in a Delta Gamma Cook Book, another enterprise whose profits would enlarge the Scholarship fund.

Founder present again

Once more Convention enjoyed the inspiration of the presence of Founder Eva Webb Dodd and of the Delta Gamma who had guarded our early possessions so well through the years in Mississippi, Minnie Wohlleben Carter. Mrs. Carter brought with her many of Psi's treasures including the old book of records. Mr. Banta was there, too, and though he and Mrs. Carter had never met, they recalled incidents and friends in common who had helped promote the interests of Delta Gamma both in the South and in the North. As they spoke together many facts were recalled which had been forgotten in the thirty years.

Anchora presents directory

The *Anchora* at this Convention presented a directory which had been compiled by Rho under the direction of Frances Huntley Truair and another edition of the *Songbook* which had been edited by Chi.

This Chain O' Lakes Convention was an out-of-doors meeting and was a great play day; its great success established without question the summer Convention tradition.

Council meets in Omaha

The following spring Grand Council went to Omaha as guests of Kappa Alpha association for Council meeting. They also visited Lincoln as guests of Kappa and Kappa Theta association.

Swarthmore College

This spring of 1912, too, Alpha Beta chapter was installed at Swarthmore College. This was an invincible group, for it had first petitioned and been refused in 1905, again petitioned and refused again in 1908, and in 1911 tried again. When no word came from the 1911 Convention, the Beta Sigmas—as they called themselves—were almost certain that for the third time the answer was "No." However, the Psi Phis (Philadelphia alumnæ) had joined the campaign and in the fall of 1911 there was an official investigation.

Again a discouraging silence until finally in April, 1912, word finally came that the chapter would be installed. The day was May 17.

More alumnæ chapters

Two alumnæ chapters were established in 1913—Theta Sigma at Evansville, Indiana, and Alpha Theta at Indianapolis—both in time to be represented at Convention.

Eighteenth Convention
1913—Niagara Falls, Ontario

This was Delta Gamma's Eighteenth Convention, and for the first time delegates and guests would travel across the United States Border into Canada to Niagara Falls, Ontario, June 26-28, 1913.

There was a special reason for this: a charter had been granted to a petitioning group at the University of Toronto, and the chapter was to be installed at the Convention, another first. Psi and Theta were hostesses at the Clifton Hotel; Ada May Brown, Ω-Wisconsin, President, called these meetings to order.

University of Toronto

The Toronto local which was to receive its charter—the only one ever to be chartered at Convention—was organized by a group of underclassmen in 1907. Its competitors Kappa Alpha Theta and Alpha Phi and another local which

Ada May Brown, Ω-Wisconsin, President 1911-15, presided at Delta Gamma's first Canadian Convention in 1913 and installed Delta Gamma's first Canadian chapter.

became Pi Beta Phi that year, doubted that it could hold its own; they were proved wrong in an incredibly short period of time, and Sigma Beta Pi did succeed. With the long planning that goes into an installation in these days, we smile when we learn that the local did not receive word that their charter—long since petitioned for —was to be granted at all until the night before installation was to take place. Their historian reported later that telephones were busy most of the night rounding up members to take the boat to Niagara Falls for initiation and installation the next evening. Rho chapter conducted the initiation service, and Alpha Gamma was officially present at Convention.

Alumnæ panhellenic affairs

The topics for discussion at this Convention were of broader interests and generally under the supervision of well-known alumnæ. Particular attention was given to alumnæ and intersorority affairs. Ruth Raymond, X-Cornell, reported that she and the President had attended the " 'first real Panhellenic' meeting in Chicago" "first real," she says, because both men and women attended. Representatives from 55 fraternities had been present.

- **High school sorority** existence was being discouraged by every means known to Panhellenic, and in support of this movement, Delta Gamma ruled that no more girls who had been members of a high school sorority could be initiated. This ruling would go into effect in the fall of 1915 and would apply only to girls who had joined high school sororities after this rule was passed.

- **Engraving of each pin** with the owner's name and the name of her chapter before delivery was to be a universal practice and it would be the responsibility of the secretary of each chapter to see that this was carried out.

- **Official jeweler** authorized in 1913 was Ambrose Kent & Sons of Toronto, this at the request of the newly installed Canadian chapter.

Cook Book is profitable

The Scholarship Fund had been in existence for two years and emphasis at this Convention was on the ways and means of providing the necessary amounts of money. A Cook Book compiled by the Minneapolis alumnæ had been sold in several places and had been able to provide $500 profit already with $400 more due shortly. This was directed by Lillian Smith Burwell, Λ-Minnesota. Convention decided that Delta Gamma pins which were found and could not be identified should be sold to other Delta Gammas and the proceeds turned over to the Scholarship Fund.

Miss Brown continues in office

Beta chapter was elected president, but at the Convention banquet she resigned in favor of the re-election of Miss Brown, an arrangement which met the sincere approval of convention.

More than fifty years later, as the 1966 history was going to press, Pearl McDonnell, B-Washington, came to Convention and reminisced about this incident. It was she who had been her chapter's choice to represent Beta as president of Delta Gamma. She recalled considerable discussion over the decision that Beta should decline the presidency altogether. They felt that they were so far away from any other chapter that they were too remote geographically to offer Delta Gamma the sort of leadership she needed at this time.

As it happened, Pearl McDonnell would be offered the presidency again thirteen years later, and again she would decline. This was 1926, however, and will be covered in proper sequence in this narrative.

University of Oregon

Lambda Rho had been established at the University of Oregon in 1909, and in the fall of that year the thirteen girls who were charter members decided to petition Delta Gamma. Several other locals had previously tried for Delta Gamma and failed, so Lambda Rho had decided incentive. The investigation took place and by August following the Canadian Convention all the affirmative votes had been received. Alpha Delta chapter was duly installed on October 17.

Washington University

Council met with Iota at Champaign, Illinois, April 22-27, 1914, and from this meeting they traveled on to St. Louis to install another chapter—Alpha Epsilon at Washington University. In 1909 when the girls dormitory on the campus was new several clubs were formed, but the Shrine of the Mystic Seven was the only one which lasted. Since they were dubbed "The Shriners" they changed their name to Kleo and began to think about petitioning one of the nationals. The brother of one of the girls, a Beta Theta Pi, suggested Delta Gamma, and so the petition was begun. In the interim between this first petition and the granting of the charter in 1914, Kleo received offers from others, but they remained firm in their desire for a Delta Gamma charter.

And there were undoubtedly some Delta Gammas that spring who wrote to the United States Superintendent of Documents to secure a first edition copy of a volume which has since been reprinted to 28,000,000 copies. This was Infant Care, *the work of Mary Mills West, Λ-Minnesota, who had edited the* Anchora *from 1888-91, married and mothered five children, and then entered upon this new literary endeavor.*

12 — A complete history in history making times

War years

The Delta Gamma Orphanage in Marchienne, Belgium, whose maintenance was later assumed by the town of Marchienne.

In January, 1915, Blanche Garten made another great contribution to Delta Gamma. The *Anchora* of that month became a history, a detailed record of Delta Gamma's early years, a piece of the finest sort of original research. Miss Garten lived in Lincoln, Nebraska, near the then *Anchora* editor, Ethel Tukey, and this provided an excellent working combination to turn out this monumental work.

It had been nearly fifteen years since Blanche Garten had begun to renew contact between the fraternity and the separated fragment in Mississippi, and through these years her search for facts and mementoes continued relentlessly. She corresponded with the two living founders, Mrs. Leonard and Mrs. Dodd, as well as with Lillie Wohlleben Hudson, Minnie Wohlleben Carter, Kate Miller Harper (sister of Corinne Miller), all of the Mother Chapter, with Carrie Hawk Walcott, H-Akron; Cornelia Wadhams Beardslee, Θ-Adelbert; Carrie Shimp Goss, Λ-Mount Union; Aurora Fiske Zueblin Σ-Northwestern, and Mr. George Banta. Even with this background information she is hesitant to submit the history as a perfect piece. For the first time complete lists of all who have served as fraternity officers was in print as well as lists of Convention delegates, historical records of all alumnæ and collegiate chapters, as well as a great deal of other statistical data.

Nineteenth Convention
1915—Berkeley, California

If this January *Anchora* in the year 1915 took its readers into Delta Gamma's past, the next issue—April—skyrocketed them into the present and future with its enthusiastic enticements for convention goers. The 1915 Convention was to be held at the Twentieth Century Club House, Berkeley, California, with Beta and Gamma chapters as hostesses. The dates were August 3-6. An all day excursion to the Panama-Pacific International Exposition in San Francisco was scheduled as well as numerous other exciting events.

Special train "house party"

The special train was dubbed a "house party," and with stopovers planned en route to make the trip take six days out of Chicago, this indeed it was. The train stopped in Omaha long enough for the delegates to be the guests of the Omaha alumnæ for breakfast at the Happy Hollow Country Club. The same day the Special travelers were luncheon guests at the Commercial Club in Lincoln. The next morning Denver Delta Gammas were hostesses at breakfast and then the train went on to Colorado Springs where it parked for over night so that the Delta Gammas aboard could see the various attractions there. At Glenwood Springs, Colorado, the traveling Conventioners were greeted with a box of flowers and a letter from the sorority women living there —who had planned a gala evening, but had to cancel their plans because of the lateness of the train. Another stop in Salt Lake City allowed for sightseeing and swimming there, and then on to the Coast to be officially assembled for Convention. In these days Council, rather than going ahead to meet prior to Convention, traveled with other Conventioners on the Special, holding meetings on the train.

Once more George Banta addressed the Convention, discussing the question of expansion and the various anti-fraternity legislation movements in several states. He recommended to the assembled delegates wider diffusion of membership and more careful consideration of the type of institution we enter.

Convention action

- **Council members** were to be elected from the general membership of the Fraternity, no chapter to have more than one officer at a time. Former Council members were to be organized into an advisory group with a definite program of advancement for the Fraternity. Long after 1915 this Convention is referred to as another important milestone in long-range planning, using woman-power to its fullest, a time when important goals were set and an organization inspired to travel toward them.
- **Scholarship requirements** were set up, stating that Freshmen must complete successfully a semester's work before being initiated.
- **Province government** was discussed, and a committee was appointed to present a plan for provinces within the Fraternity.
- **A recognition pin**, to be used nationally, would be the crest.

Lawrence College

The petition of Theta Gamma Delta at Lawrence College, Appleton, Wisconsin, was accepted at this Convention, and Alpha Zeta chapter officially joined the chapter roll in Appleton, September 11, 1915. It had been a surprisingly easy road to a charter for this group; having been established as a local in 1903, the girls did not seriously try to secure a Delta Gamma chapter until the spring of 1915. Through interested Delta Gammas in Appleton, Omega's approval was gained, an official inspection was made, a formal petition sent to Council—and Convention voted its approval. Mr. George Banta, who had shown interest in Theta Gamma Delta from the first—his home in Menasha being only five miles from the Lawrence campus—addressed the installation banquet.

And just as it seemed that Delta Gamma must have grown too large for much inter-chapter assistance of a direct sort we find the Xi Zeta (Detroit) alumnæ reporting in their chapter letter the campaign to collect tinfoil to aid Iota chapter's fund for a new house. The Detroit Delta Gammas had so recently aided in building a comfortable home for Xi in Ann Arbor, and now they felt great satisfaction in extending their interest to Illinois.

Ex-officers organized

The 1915 Convention had voted to organize the ex-officers of the Fraternity so that they might furnish experienced aid to the organization. The Council meeting in the spring of 1916 appointed Ethel Tukey Korsmeyer chairman of this group, and after these officers had been circularized the following committees were appointed: one to investigate the initiation of the alumnæ of charter groups, another to look into a means of holding the interest of alumnæ, another to consider alumnæ dues, one to consider the question of supply chaperones, another to consider the expansion question, and another to consider the possibility of colonization.

The increasing part the fraternities were taking in community and even national affairs was reflected in the report that the secretary (Leulah Judson Hawley, Λ-Minnesota, Secretary-Editor) and five delegates from Delta Gamma were asked to attend and participate in the sessions of the Second World Court Congress which was held at Carnegie Hall, New York, May 2-4, 1916.

Council endorses one jeweler

Council met May 26-29, 1916, in Evanston, Illinois, and among other things decided to adopt Newman as sole, exclusive jeweler for the Fraternity. This contract it was agreed should hold until the 1917 Convention.

Banta official NPC printer

The Fourteenth National Panhellenic was held in 1916 and George Banta was appointed official printer for the Congress which meant that in the future *Banta's Greek Exchange* would contain regular reports of NPC matters. It was agreed, too, that from this date the Panhellenic conventions would be held biennially rather than annually. In June, 1915, the following notice had appeared in *Anchora*:

> After January, 1916, no girl who becomes a member of an organization bearing a Greek name, and called a fraternity or sorority, shall be eligible to a National Panhellenic Fraternity. This is exclusive of Junior College and Professional fraternities.

Whitman College

Gamma Kappa at Whitman College, Walla Walla, Washington, had been organized in 1903. When fraternities were approved by the Board of Overseers, members applied for a Delta Gamma charter. In 1914 the group had its official inspection, and then sent Marguerite Hunt to Berkeley to the 1915 Convention where general sentiment, she later reported, was in favor of a chapter. So after the usual official procedure and subsequent approval, the group became Alpha Eta chapter of Delta Gamma on September 30, 1916.

University of North Dakota

Simultaneous with the efforts of the Whitman would-be Delta Gammas was similar activity at the University of North Dakota. Kappa Alpha Theta and Alpha Phi had been installed in 1911, before the 1910-11 school year ended. Two rushees of these groups felt that a third organization was needed on the campus and, with the dean's approval, formed Beta Gamma Psi on December 14, 1911. At first the group wasn't interested in national affiliation, but as rushing against two nationals became difficult, correspondence opened with Delta Gamma. This was the spring of 1913. Interest in Delta Gamma had come through Mary Alice Bates, ϒ-Stanford, who was visiting her brother, a U-ND student. In 1916 the group bought a home and the news of acceptance from Delta Gamma followed shortly. December 16, 1916, Alpha Theta of Delta Gamma was installed in Grand Forks, North Dakota.

World War I

The presence of one Canadian chapter—Alpha Gamma at Toronto—on our roll had made all Delta Gammas feel something even more than the strong sympathetic interest in the Allied cause which prevailed in the United States in these first years of World War I. Since the first days of the War, Anchora pages carried much to reflect the feelings of the Canadians: "(War) is a strange and unaccustomed occupation for a people so in love with peace, so far removed from the militaristic influences of Europe, and so busy with their own development as to have little time to worry over wars and rumors of wars. . ." This made us early conscious of our opportunities for War Work, and by the time the United States entered the war, Delta Gamma was well at work for the Allies.

During the course of the war one chapter was to have the opportunity to make a unique contribution of its own to the allied effort. This was Zeta, occupying Delta Gamma's first house at Albion, a lodge. Late in the war when the flu epidemic struck not only the United States and Canada but around the world, additional hospital space was needed in the Albion area. The Delta Gamma lodge was offered by Zeta chapter and accepted as a temporary hospital, another "first" for Zeta's home.

Delta Gamma War Record

Delta Gamma's wartime philanthropic activity, its scope and significance, is a proud page in the Fraternity's historical record. The size of the task and the achievement are mute evidence of the strength and capability of Delta Gamma less than fifty years after its simple founding in a Mississippi girls' school. As has been recorded—*

"Almost immediately after the United States had entered the World War, President Wilson

* *An Historical Sketch of the Delta Gamma Fraternity, 1934, and Delta Gamma History, 1945.*

Jessie McGilvray Treat, ϒ-Stanford, President 1915-19, guided the Fraternity through World War I years during which Delta Gamma not only produced an enviable war record but also strengthened her own internal organization.

requested that all organizations contemplating conventions postpone them to lessen the railroad congestion and to save expense. The Delta Gamma convention of 1917 was therefore deferred and the Council suggested that $1,000 of the unused convention fund be appropriated for war relief work of some sort. The condition of little children in the occupied territory of Belgium made a direct appeal. This first gift of $1,000 was made through the Belgian Ambassador at Washington, Baron de Cartier, and was applied directly to a hospital in Scheveningen, Holland, where was established the home 'des Petits Orphelins de la Guerre.'

"All sorts of schemes were resorted to in the raising of funds for the Delta Gamma war work. The Fraternity had been carefully circularized by Blanche Garten's committee in the drive for the Scholarship Fund and so was awake to the idea of sharing and giving. Bridge parties, theatre parties, moving pictures, rummage sales, food sales and numerous other ways of raising money were employed to swell the fund. A plan suggested by Mrs. Lillian Burwell of Lambda, who was well known to all through the Lambda Cook Book sales for the Scholarship Fund, was greeted with enthusiasm. She suggested we raise a 'mile of dimes,' having figured that it would amount to $8,976. It was hoped that the amount would exceed this and reach the $10,000 mark. The country was divided into seven districts with capable captains over each division. These most efficient captians were Josephine Beedy, Υ-Stanford; Alice Owsley Vose, Σ-Northwestern; Elizabeth Brown Thayer, Φ-Colorado; Ethel Tukey Korsmeyer and Sara Schwab Deutsch, K-Nebraska; Agnes Merrill Scott, Ω-Wisconsin; Mabel Tichenor, Θ-Indiana, and Pearl McDonnell, B-Washington. The first year with the aid of the 'mile of dimes' $13,416.73, exclusive of the $1,000 voted by Council, was raised.

"During this year Delta Gamma acquired what came to be known as The Delta Gamma House at Ossendrecht, Holland, a seaside home for destitute and ailing children. Here they were restored to health and whenever possible returned to their families. Lives of many were saved. Delta Gamma sent $8,000 the first year, with an additional Christmas Greeting of $500.

"In June, 1918, Delta Gamma extended her activities to the home town of Baron de Cartier, at Marchienne, here again to care for Belgian children. A sum of $7,300 was sent to Marchienne, including a $500 Christmas gift for shoes and clothing, and Delta Gamma decided to continue if possible through the following year, 1919.

"Our membership at the time of the War was about 5,000 and the results showed an almost unanimous participation in the fund raised for this war work among the children of the stricken district of Belgium. Many of our members served in France, Canada, and the United States as nurses, Red Cross workers, canteen workers, interpreters, reconstruction aides, as well as in political and social work of various kinds.

"The National Fraternity invested $10,892 in Liberty Bonds and War Savings Stamps. Practically all chapters made similar investments and hundreds of individual members likewise. Many adopted war orphans for the period of need, and many chapters gave liberally to Y.M.C.A. and Y.W.C.A., Red Cross and war relief drives. The Los Angeles Delta Gammas, under the direction of Mrs. Jessburg and Miss Ashley, made badges of the Allied colors and raised $2,400 toward the War Relief Fund.

"November, 1918, brought the Armistice, but as an aftermath of the War the need for funds still continued and another sum, $13,684.19 was raised. The enthusiasm of our National President, Jessie Treat, and our War Work Chairman, Jessie Kingery, was shared by all Delta Gammas, with the result that $28,300.91 was collected for our war relief work. Enough money was supplied to establish a permanent orphanage in Marchienne to which the name Delta Gamma Orphanage has been given although the town of Marchienne has assumed the future care of this institution.

"The King and Queen of Belgium conferred the decoration of the 'Order of Elizabeth' upon Jessie Roberson Kingery in recognition of her accomplishment for Belgium through the Delta Gamma Fraternity.

"Beside the relief work done in Belgium, $1,000 was used for the education and restoration to health of an Armenian girl, Miriam, eighteen years old, who had been adopted by Mr. and Mrs. Ernest Riggs. Mrs. Riggs was Alice Shephard of Rho chapter. They were teaching and working in Armenia at the time of the War and the money was spent under their jurisdiction. Miriam was restored to health and trained for kindergarten work.

"In addition to her district chairmen, Mrs. Kingery had a very able and helpful committee associated with her all through this war work, Cecil Mill Holmes, Vera Allison Huntington and Margaret Wheeler Willard. Practically every penny raised was made available for relief work because the expense of collection was largely assumed by those actively engaged in the undertaking.

"Here in brief are the war relief fund figures:

In 1918 Delta Gamma raised . . .	$13,416.72
In 1919 Delta Gamma raised . . .	13,684.19
Donated from 1917 Contingent Fund	1,000.00
Accumulated interest	200.00
Total	$28,300.91

Of this amount $16,800 was actually used in war relief work, leaving a balance of $11,500.91.

"(Detailed figures for districts may be found in the Convention Report of 1919.)

"From the above balance sums were taken for the further education of Miriam Riggs and her sisters, who had been rescued from the Turks by American Relief Workers in Turkey and Armenia. Delta Gamma felt that education was quite as needed as food and clothing. All money used for Armenian relief was dispensed by Mr. and Mrs. Riggs.

"Although Delta Gamma's original idea for a scholarship loan fund to assist needy members in finishing their college course had never been lost sight of, it had been overshadowed by the demands of the World War but grew but slowly during this period and only through the regular sums set aside for it. So when the need of a war relief fund no longer existed, the balance left in that fund was added to the scholarship fund, thus bringing us back to our purely educational project. The war years doubtless left us the richer by this period of effort. Service and friendship, dominant in the idealism of our Founders, had been definitely manifested as well as a willingness to share and help. We had been given an opportunity to enlarge our sphere of usefulness. On returning with renewed effort to our scholarship fund project, we found Mrs. Dodd one of the first to respond to the furtherance of this purpose by a generous donation to the Endowment Fund."

In spite
of war—

Award from
Belgian Government
to Jessie Roberson Kingery
for War Work

Though all minds were first occupied with the War, Fraternity activity continued at a steady pace. Constitutional revision that would have taken place at a 1917 Convention had been carried on by mail, and the vote of the chapters was reported by Council: the first important change, the establishment of province government; second, the provision that members attending institutions where there are chapters of Delta Gamma shall be accepted as affiliates simply by virtue of their membership in Delta Gamma; third, that a lump sum shall be required of each member upon initiation which shall cover the cost of her badge, membership certificate, constitution, Anchora subscription and Scholarship Fund tax.

War time Council busy

Council met to review these matters and other wartime measures October 20-22, 1917. An auditing committee composed of members of three chapters residing in Rochester, New York, was to be appointed which should examine the books and papers of the Treasurer upon the transfer of office from the present officer to the incoming officer and which shall be authorized to destroy papers which are of no value.

J. F. Newman was to be retained as exclusive jeweler, but Mr. Balfour of the L. J. Balfour Company was asked to submit further samples of badges and to report at the next meeting. The minutes of this Council meeting—since many of its actions would have normally taken place at Convention—were printed in pamphlet form for distribution among interested members.

First province secretaries

The establishment of province government provided for the appointment of Delta Gamma's first province secretaries that year. These new officers were to provide the link between an in-

creasingly busy Council and the individual chapters, the close personal touch, supervision and guidance, now impossible for national officers to continue themselves.

Council reports in Anchora

Council reported fully to Anchora readers during the war years. In the January, 1918, issue of the magazine, with the fraternity in its third year without a Convention, the Council members felt keenly the need to maintain close contact between officers and general membership which would be lost if the War long prevented the holding of a Convention. Thus, a full report of the October Council meeting to the membership. This meeting had been officially announced to all collegiate and alumnæ groups well in advance of its scheduled time so that all who wished to could present business of any kind to Council in session.

The Council meeting report in January told in full of Delta Gamma's war work, reported on the renewal of exclusive contract with the J. F. Newman Company, reviewed the Panhellenic Congress which had met in October, too. To encourage the holding of Council meetings of the different Panhellenic groups in conjunction with the National Panhellenic Congress, the Edgewater Beach Hotel in Chicago had offered special rates. This is one of the first times this plan is recorded, but it has in the years since become the usual custom wherever NPC is in session.

On transfers

It is interesting that during this same year that such a wide welcome is to be given any and all affiliates, a "delicate matter" of a transfer arose which called for a special notice in the Anchora. "We believe that no member of the fraternity would ask to be received by a distant chapter without having satisfactory credentials or references, and we suggest, in view of this present imposture, that each member carry with her her membership certificate, or make her identity clear in some other way without putting her hostesses to the embarrassment of questioning her." This evidently was a matter troubling all Panhellenic groups, and in the case of Delta Gamma, led later to the transfer of credentials through the Province Secretary's hands.

University of Oklahoma

At the University of Oklahoma a local, Phi Chi, had organized during the winter, 1915-16. Soon the group had one aim in mind: petitioning Delta Gamma for a charter. Two Delta Gammas living nearby did the official investigation and heartily approved the group. Alpha Iota of Delta Gamma was installed in Norman, Oklahoma, on June 4, 1918. This group had had its own house since the fall of 1917 and had been helped in their efforts toward a Delta Gamma chapter by a number of Delta Gammas already living in the area.

Twentieth Convention
1919—Christmas Lake, Minn.

The long hoped for Armistice came on November 11, 1918, and almost immediately the Convention wheels were oiled and began once more to turn with plans and program focused on Christmas Lake, Minnesota, June 24-27, 1919.

This was Delta Gamma's Twentieth Convention; business sessions were held at The Radisson Inn, and Jessie McGilvray Treat presided. Lambda and Mu chapters were hostesses.

Delta Gamma's first meeting since before the War was naturally an enthusiastic one. There was a great deal of business to dispose of, and the social program was a busy one. For the first time province secretaries were official members of Convention.

- **Incorporation** had once more been investigated, and a committee appointed for this purpose in 1915 reported that it was impossible at this time except in each individual state —which didn't seem practical. It was likewise impossible to copyright the pin as a national fraternity emblem. Many years later when incorporation took place it was in one state only, Ohio, where the international headquarters was located.
- **The plain badge** only was to be worn by a Delta Gamma initiate.
- *Banta's Greek Exchange* subscription would be required of each chapter.
- **Colonization** in a desired locality, rather than waiting for a petitioning group, was explored.
- **One official jeweler** would supply pins, a practice begun in the interim since 1915 Convention and deemed most satisfactory.
- **A triennium**, rather than a biennium, for Conventions would be an experiment, and the next Convention was scheduled for 1922. Delta

Gamma's War Work was reported in full, and it was at this time decided to dispose of the $11,500 remaining in the War Fund, partly by establishing the Orphanage at Marchienne and partly for Miriam Riggs' education.

Investigate new project

Inspired by their own successful altruistic work during the World War, Delta Gammas began at once to fill this gap in their post-war activity by establishing a Committee for Social Service Work which would explore this field and provide a social service project for the Fraternity. This group was to be headed by Jessie Roberson Kingery who had led Delta Gamma in its various war projects.

Colonization idea investigated

The possibilities of colonization rather than waiting for a petitioning group in a desired locality were explored.

Rushing continued to receive the concerned attention of not only Delta Gammas but all fraternity women. The need for a definite form of rushing reform was brought before the membership in a message on the opening pages of the April, 1920, *Anchora* from the President, Gertrude Bradley Wilbur. She says, "In some cases the objectionable summer rushing has actually been extended over the entire four years of high school course with periodical entertainments for high school girls."

Triennium makes work heavy

The 1919 Convention had voted to experiment with a triennium rather than the biennial Convention which had been the custom before the war. The next Convention had been scheduled for 1922, so for three years Council's burden of work was, as during the war, a heavy one.

Council assembled March 27, 1920, at the Edgewater Beach Hotel in Chicago for its meeting. Once again the matter of fraternity jewelers came up for considerable discussion. The historian was to enter into correspondence with jewelers to receive bids on an exclusive contract.

Financing chapter houses

This Council also discussed the possibility of helping chapters finance chapter houses. The next year a request is recorded from Epsilon for a loan of $500 from the scholarship fund. They were duly informed that this was impossible, but, from the house fund, they were granted a loan.

Washburn College

In 1920 Alpha Kappa was added to the chapter roll. Kappa Kappa Chi had organized at Washburn College, Topeka, Kansas, in 1910 with the early intent of proving themselves to the extent that they would some day become a chapter of Delta Gamma. In 1917 a petition had been refused, but during 1919-20 a mighty campaign paved the way for the local's acceptance and subsequent installation on June 9, 1920 as Alpha Kappa of Delta Gamma.

Advancement of Scholarship

By the fall of 1920 the Social Service Committee had changed its name to the Committee for the Advancement of Scholarship. As an editorial in *Anchora* states, "If Delta Gamma is to accomplish the aims of which we talk, she must first of all stand back of the colleges in their efforts to train and educate the students who come to them for education."

Drake University

April, 1921, added another chapter to Delta Gamma's roll, Alpha Lambda at Drake University, Des Moines, Iowa. A local, Iota Alpha Omega, had been founded in 1906, and Delta Gamma was long considered the group's choice if and when the University would permit nationals to enter the campus. This time came in February, 1920, when, under the sponsorship of Mary Rosemond, T-Iowa, Iota Alpha Omega petitioned Delta Gamma. Two other locals were simultaneously petitioning Kappa Kappa Gamma and Kappa Alpha Theta, and all three were to be installed, according to the University, March 15, 1921. The other two locals were accepted by their choice of national immediately, but Delta Gamma's voice was not heard until March 23. Installation date for the three was postponed until April 15, when Chi Omega, too, decided to install a chapter at Drake.

Anchora—
A life subscription

Again at the Edgewater Beach Council met; this was June 15, 1921. It was decided that each initiate should be required to take out a life subscription to *Anchora* at $20. This was, of course, preliminary to that action taken a year later at the 1922 Convention which provided for a life subscription as part of the initiation fee. The editor was stiffening her campaign for a sound operating base for the magazine.

At this time the office of historian was moved to "central office." The minutes record, "It is understood that the Central Office is to do the work formerly done by the historian. The Secretary-Editor is to keep the records of the historian and to summarize them for Convention."

Uniform pledge book

A uniform pledge book was adopted to be used by all chapters in which must be written the names of the pledges at the time of formal pledging.

Endowment fund campaign

Even before the 1922 Convention, plans were formulated for the gigantic Birthday Fund raising campaign to be culminated at the Golden Jubilee Convention in 1924. Jessie Roberson

Gertrude Bradley Wilbur, Σ-Northwestern, Delta Gamma's post-war President 1919-22, served during a period when many milestones were passed in Fraternity annals.

Kingery had been appointed chairman of the campaign for this large Scholarship Endowment Fund.

Also before the 1922 Convention, the chapter roll was again lengthened by the addition of three chapters—Alpha Mu, Beloit College, Beloit, Wisconsin; Alpha Nu, University of Southern California, Los Angeles; and Alpha Xi, West Virginia University at Morgantown.

Beloit College

At Beloit the local Theta Pi Gamma had existed since 1896, the first sorority on campus. Theta Pi first petitioned Delta Gamma in 1916, starting a succession of visits and inspections from fraternity officers. Perseverance characterized these would-be Delta Gammas, for it was not until 1922 that Alpha Mu chapter became official. In June, 1923, Alpha Mu was granted permission to initiate into Delta Gamma all those members of Theta Pi Gamma who cared to return to Beloit for the ceremony. At this time more than seventy members became Delta Gammas, and in this same year Alpha Mu's lodge was built, the first sorority house at Beloit.

University of Southern California

Another long-time local was Beta Pi at the University of Southern California, having been established in 1902, five years after Delta Gamma had withdrawn her first SC chapter, Delta. In 1909 the group became owners of their first house, "The Pines." By the early twenties, California's potential for the future was apparent, and the Fraternity welcomed the opportunity to re-establish itself on the Southern California campus. And so Alpha Nu chapter was installed, too, in 1922.

West Virginia University

Early 1922 was a busy time for Delta Gamma with three new chapters, in scattered parts of the country. On February 18 thirty-one members of Delta Sigma Sigma, were installed as Alpha Xi chapter in Morgantown, West Virginia. This group had first written to Council in August, 1920, requesting permission to petition Delta Gamma.

Delegates receive advances

Council met March 23, 1922, again at the Edgewater Beach. It was decided to advance Convention delegates the amount necessary for expenses to come to Convention.

By this time the *Anchora* had tried and found agreeable its change in schedule, the former April and June issues now appearing in March and May.

Twenty-first Convention
Spring Lake, New Jersey

The Fraternity had accepted the invitation of Alpha Beta, Rho and Omicron chapters for an Eastern Convention, and the Twenty-first was held at The Essex and Sussex, Spring Lake, New Jersey, June 26-30, 1922. Gertrude Bradley Wilbur, Σ-Northwestern, presided. Mrs. Leonard and Mrs. Dodd were special guests.

The November, 1922, *Anchora* carried such a complete review of this Convention—devoting the entire issue to it—that much of the sparkle and enthusiasm at Spring Lake are passed along to the reader more than thirty years later. For the first time, too, informal snapshots of a wide variety of Convention activities appeared as part of *Anchora* coverage.

For the first time the Milwaukee Activities Award was presented—the winner, Alpha Mu chapter which had been installed only a few months before Convention. A musical comedy skit, "Isn't it Just Too Splendid," by Alpha Beta chapter brought forth rave notices from Convention goers and was much in demand as a rushing skit later.

Convention action

- Life subscription to *Anchora* ($20.00) was to be included in the initiation fee. This was part of a plan submitted by Secretary-Editor Leulah Judson Hawley—the beginning of the present day system whereby the *Anchora* is operated (non-profit) solely on the interest from investments from the fund built up by these life subscriptions.
- This *Anchora* Endowment Fund was to be invested in chapter house mortgages and securities. The farsighted Editor knew that she would be for a time operating in the red (on financing by the fraternity's General Fund), but through the long range figuring and planning, she knew that within the succeeding ten-year period the life subscription fund would build to something quite sizeable, and that within this time the *Anchora* would be running in the black.
- Charters would be granted with a 95% vote of the collegiate chapters and 90% of the alumnæ chapters rather than the unanimous vote previously required.
- Province meetings were for the first time part of the Convention program, and it was suggested that province conferences be held in the years between Conventions.
- A biennium was deemed much preferable to the triennium tried for this Convention. The next Convention, then, would take place in 1924.
- An alumnæ representative was added to Council, an office which later developed into Second Vice-President. Irene Jenner Erlbacher, Θ-Indiana, was the first to hold this office, and she plunged into alumnæ activity with a force that was felt throughout all provinces.

The Golden Jubilee—
Birthday Fund

Probably the greatest inspiration to Conventioners at Spring Lake was Jessie Roberson Kingery's report to those assembled on the progress of the Birthday Fund which Council had set up with 1924's Golden Jubilee as its goal for $50,000 for a Scholarship Endowment Fund. The fact that it was a very real and going thing and was well on its way to success made an impression on those present as did the realization that Delta Gamma was now a big and serious business. The Convention had indeed been successful in one of its chief aims, to ignite the enthusiasm for a giant final push toward its fiftieth birthday goal. The tremendous success of the campaign during the next two years was best evidence of the accomplishment of this 1922 Convention.

Plans for alumnæ organization

By January, 1923, the new Alumnæ Representative to Council came forth on *Anchora* pages with an ambitious plan for alumnæ organization. Even at this date she pointed out that organization itself is simple; the real need was for a purpose for the organization of alumnæ. During her term of office Irene Erlbacher is heard to repeat this thought many times—and yet it was fourteen years before a definite Fraternity project came into being to provide this purpose for alumnæ. At this time, however, the Birthday Fund was certainly a gigantic job which united alumnæ effort.

Mrs. Erlbacher's success in organization could be noted in less than six months when five new alumnæ chapters and ten new associations had been added to the roll. And even at this time the Alumnæ officer recommended the breaking down of large city groups into sectional ones—"in such congested districts as New York, Chicago, Los Angeles and San Francisco," she says, "this would be a better working plan."

Miami University (Ohio)

In Convention, 1922, notes in the *Anchora* there is some comment on Ohioans campaigning for the installation of a chapter at Miami University, Oxford, Ohio. On February 3, 1923, this came to pass and Alpha Omicron chapter was installed. Its charter members had organized in 1920 as Beta Phi Sigma for the express purpose of petitioning Delta Gamma. The famed Miami triad, Beta Theta Pi, Phi Delta Theta and Sigma Chi, aided in the installation of Alpha Omicron, the formal initiation taking place at the Sigma Chi house.

Organization of funds

When Council met March 19, 1923, at the Edgewater Beach it was agreed that Mrs. Hawley consult with a Minneapolis bank as to investments and the possibility of their taking the matter over for Delta Gamma. Since the war there had been a growing feeling of disorganization in the matter of various funds.

State Alumnæ Chairmen
Endorsement of pledges

Alumnæ organization was to be attempted through state chairmen. The growing role of the alumna was evident in another way. Council adopted a policy that no girl could be pledged to any chapter of Delta Gamma until she had received the endorsement of one graduate alumna of the fraternity. The high school scholastic record was also to be investigated and found to be above a C average.

First Province Conferences

Province Conferences had been established by the vote of Convention at Spring Lake, and their trial run was in spring and early summer, 1923. The *Anchora* carried a complete report of Province III's first Conference, April 13-15, at Madison, Wisconsin, and Province II's at Indianapolis, June 25-27. The then petitioning group at Butler had a part in the latter by entertaining the entire Province group for an evening lawn party at the home of the University president. The two reports echo a combination of grave business and varied and constant social activity, and they obviously set a pleasant and profitable precedent.

University of Arizona

During this same spring Delta Gamma granted another charter, this time to a local called Alpha Gamma at the University of Arizona. Alpha Gamma had been organized in 1920 with the idea of petitioning some national. By the time a chapter house had been located in 1921 the group had decided that Delta Gamma was it's goal. During the school year 1921-22 contact was made with Delta Gamma's Council and an inspector was sent. Her high recommendation brought permission to petition formally. Before the official petition was sent, however, the group carried on a contact campaign, data going out from time to time to each Delta Gamma chapter. Having paved its own way, Alpha Gamma received word in March, 1923, that it would be Alpha Pi of Delta Gamma, and the chapter was installed in October, 1923.

The fiftieth anniversary

This school year, 1923-24, which had begun with the installation of Alpha Pi chapter was one of fierce activity on the part of Delta Gammas everywhere. It was not just an ordinary Convention year but one in which the Fraternity would celebrate its Fiftieth Birthday. Though Christmas, 1923, was the actual fiftieth anniversary, the big event was to be celebrated officially in June, 1924, at Estes Park, Colorado, at Delta Gamma's Twenty-second Convention. The chief goal was, of course, the Scholarship Endowment Fund of $50,000, by this time nearly over the top. Money making schemes were numerous and varied, and the final success of the campaign is mute evidence of the fact that every Delta Gamma had a part in building this important endowment fund.

A Panhellenic House

In Chicago again Council met March 19-22, 1924. The campaign had begun for the Panhellenic House which was to materialize as Beekman Tower in New York. Delta Gamma guaranteed $1,000 toward the project, $100 to be paid at once.

It was voted that the Treasurer was to receive a salary of $250 per year.

Again the alumnæ were part of the discussion, and it was decided to send an Alumnæ Bulletin, as a letter of information, to all alumnæ chapters.

Ohio Wesleyan University

During this same spring another chapter was added to the roll, Alpha Rho at Ohio Wesleyan University, Delaware, Ohio. For ten years, Phi Omega Phi, a local group existed on this campus before it became Alpha Rho at Delta Gamma. It had been disbanded in 1913 as were all locals at Wesleyan, but in 1920 it was reorganized and four years later, after the usual petitioning and subsequent suspense awaiting approval, it was installed as a Delta Gamma chapter.

14 — Birthday Fund and anniversary celebration are overwhelming success

Golden Jubilee

Jessie Roberson Kingery, Υ-Stanford, who directed the Delta Gamma Scholarship Endowment Campaign—the Birthday Fund—watched its glorious climax at the 1924 Convention.

In Hollywood terminology, Delta Gamma's Twenty-second Convention was a colossal affair.

The Fraternity was celebrating its Golden Jubilee, and a capacity crowd was on hand at Estes Park, Colorado, June 23-28, 1924—the register contained more than 600 names, even today listed as one of Delta Gamma's largest Conventions.

The Birthday Fund, with Mrs. Kingery's spirit of inspiration and enthusiasm behind it, had skyrocketed beyond all expectations, and it was a total of $57,000 which was presented to the Fraternity. To be properly impressed with both this total and the number in attendance at Convention, consider the fact that the total living membership at this time was only 8,000. In fact, one can't help wondering if the large attendance cannot in some part be attributed to the fact that here was the climax of a project in which everyone had had a part, for it had been no small task to raise this sum which measured percentagewise more than seven dollars per member.

Council suggest changes

Council was in session for two days prior to the opening of Convention concentrating largely on heated discussions of the possible separation of the office of Secretary and that of Editor. Hinged to this was the possibility of a secretary to be available to the President and Vice-President who could do work of a confidential nature —an executive secretary. Along with these changes it was voted to revoke the Scholarship Fund Chairman from Council and also the Alumnæ Representative, the duties of the latter being taken over by the Vice-President. In the final session of this Council meeting, however, it was decided that with such great diversity of opinion on these changes in office, all action would be postponed until the Spring, 1925, Council meeting.

Convention action

When Convention assembled the following was enacted:

- **A reserve fund,** as Council had suggested, was set aside (the original goal of the Birthday Fund) intact for investment in chapter house loans, providing interest to be used for scholarship loans.
- **Three fellowships** of $500 each were to be created (from the amount raised over the goal of $50,000 for the scholarship fund). These would honor each of the three founders and would be awarded to graduate Delta Gammas whose graduate work would bring scholastic distinction to themselves and to Delta Gamma.
- **The Delta Gamma Home** in Marchienne, Belgium, would received $1,000 (also to be taken from this scholarship fund surplus). The remainder of the surplus was to be set aside as an emergency fund, the interest to be used for the special assistance of any member in need.

Nancy Brown Woollett, Φ-Colorado, was born the same month and year as Delta Gamma and seems to have been imbued with a special Delta Gamma spirit, for her contributions have been many and varied. She served as president 1922-28 and later as chairman of the 1934 History committee, chairman of the Memorial House Fund Committee, on the 1945 History committee, and even for a short time as housemother in the Memorial House at Ole Miss.

• **Financing Conventions** had been a growing problem, and Convention adopted a plan by which a per capita tax of $1.00 per annum be asked of each alumna as a contribution to the Convention Fund. The collection of this would be made by alumnæ chapters and associations. Each of the alumnæ chapters would also be taxed $10 per year for the Convention Fund.

• **A National Convention Chairman** should be appointed by Council to serve four years. Her duty should be to supervise and manage Conventions. Appointed to serve in this capacity was Mae Brown Tompkins, Upsilon-Stanford, neice of former President Ada May Brown. Mrs. Tompkins remained Convention Chairman until 1934.

• *The Anchora's* official pronunciation should be with the accent on the first syllable. And how often, more than forty years later, do the Executive Offices and Council receive requests to clarify the correct pronunciation of this word!

Campaign for central office

This 1924 Convention marked the beginning of a campaign for a Centralized Office—a dream which took 16 years to materialize as the business office we know today in Columbus, Ohio. At this time volunteer workers in Minneapolis were assisting Mrs. Hawley in maintaining files, keeping up with the never-ending stream of address changes and handling various other office details. This arrangement continued until the office of Secretary-Editor was finally split in 1932. Mrs. Hawley, in whose home this office was housed, retained the editorship, and the work of the secretary went to a new officer at that time.

It was President Woollett who, throughout her term of office, constantly promoted the establishment of a real Central Office, a dream she knew in a few years would become a necessity. The post-Convention Council meeting in 1924 did authorize a "permanent executive secretary to serve for the next two years,"—to be appointed and equipped by the President, salaried by the Treasury. It was also agreed that at the next Council meeting a permanent plan would be presented and the financing of this executive secretary be placed in the hands of the Finance Committee. There is, however, no record of these plans coming to pass at this time.

Alumnæ expansion

The work of the Alumnæ Representative had progressed during the infancy of the office at an admirable rate. Twenty-four alumnæ chapters had been in existence to be listed in the Convention 1924 Messenger, and by Convention time Mrs. Erlbacher was able to report 34. The number of alumnæ associations had risen from 17 in 1922 to 29 as of Convention at Estes Park.

On the other hand—the collegiate level—twenty-four campuses were discouraged in their interest in acquiring an active chapter of Delta Gamma. Among them—Arkansas, Chicago, Carnegie Tech, DePauw, Buffalo, Gettysburg, Howard, Hunter, Illinois Wesleyan, Knox, Kansas, Kentucky, Mississippi, New York University, Pennsylvania, Utah, Kansas State, Washington State, Wittenberg, Waukesha, Tulsa, Susquehanna, Middlebury and Manitoba. Within the next two years other applications were added to this list: Alabama, Arkansas again, Buena Vista College, Buffalo once more, Chattanooga, James Millikin, Drexel, Florida State College for Women, Georgetown, Kansas State and Kansas, Knox, Kentucky, Louisville, Millsaps, Maine, Miami at Coral Gables, Mississippi, National University Law School, Sophie Newcomb, Ohio University, Purdue, Rochester, Rollins, Simpson, Vermont and Wyoming.

Distinguished Service Medal

At this Convention Delta Gamma for the first time presented to a member its first medallion for distinguished service to the fraternity. This went—can't you guess?—to Jessie Roberson Kingery who had so ably directed the Birthday Fund Campaign. It was a special medal, not to be duplicated in size or mounting, designed by the famed medallion sculptor, Julio Kilyeni. Seven inches in diameter, it included some of the ideas and symbolism of Delta Gamma and was executed in bronze.

A box for the gavel

Another significant presentation was made in 1924 at Estes Park. Blanche Garten who had twenty years earlier opened Delta Gamma's paths into its past and had in 1905 presented the fraternity with its historic gavel came once more in 1924 with a gift of historic value to her Fraternity. After the gavel had been carved from the wood taken from Lewis School, there had been left over a small piece for which, at the time, Miss Garten had been able to find no use. Though she could see no reason for keeping it, keep it she did, and for this Fiftieth Anniversary convention she had had carved a replica of the Delta Gamma crest and had it placed on beautiful polished wood box which would be the resting place for the gavel between Conventions.

Finance committee formed

Nancy Brown Woollett, Φ-Colorado, who presided over this Golden Jubilee had been elected to the Fraternity Presidency at the 1922 Convention. She, like presidents before and since, possessed special qualities of leadership and special abilities which appeared at this time to be another special gift for Delta Gamma particularly at this point in Fraternity history. Mrs. Woollett's business training led her to require the most precise of business methods in handling Fraternity funds, and so she was responsible for the organization of the Finance Committee. As Mrs. Hawley reported at the 1926 Convention, "It was upon her insistence that all securities belonging to the Fraternity were placed for safekeeping in the hands of the strongest and largest banking house in the country outside of New York City. . . . She has made a real contribution to the Fraternity in working out the details connected with the administration of its funds. The Secretary-Editor, more than any other member of Council, is in position to know and to understand what Mrs. Woollett's presidency has meant to Delta Gamma. And in those things that pertain to personality, as well as to business matters, her touch has been firm, constant and wise and effective. One can feel the jump forward which has been made while she was at the helm."

On women's place—

In compiling the Delta Gamma story—or that of any of the other Panhellenic groups—we are curiously conscious of another story which weaves itself as a part of the Fraternity fabric. It is not only the evolution of Delta Gamma on the campus and in the community, her growth nationally or internationally, but it is the story, too, of the growth of women in the world since the sheltered 'seventies. During the first score years of Delta Gamma's existence the college woman was only beginning to discover herself as a coed, and in the nineties she began to analyze this position while others scrutinized. The college alumna is taking her place in the community, too, not only as teacher which had been an accepted occupation for some time, but as missionary, physician, librarian, nurse and a variety of other semi-professional vocations.

The century turned and with it woman-kind discovered herself a new force in the world— and Anchora contributors joined the cavalcade with such pieces as "The College Woman and Equal Suffrage" and "The Relation of Home Economics to Other College Studies." More dubious writers asked, "Is the All-Around Girl Ideal?"

With the next decade and World War I Delta Gammas proved themselves an organized force doing good not only at home but abroad. During post-war days a reprint of an essay by Chi Omega's Mary Love Collins, "College Women and the Day" again reflected college women and the times. During this entire period however, we find creeping into the Anchora in greater numbers articles pointing with specific pride to one Delta Gamma's achievements in one field or another, rather than articles of general pertinence. Ruth Bryan Owen's name had made news for some time, and Hazel Whitaker Vandenberg, who had been Delta Gamma's Vice-President from 1919-1922, had had a busy career before her marriage to Publisher Vandenberg, Senator from Michigan 1928-51.

University of California at Los Angeles

In the fall following the Estes Park Convention, a Delta Gamma charter was granted to a group on the Los Angeles campus of the University of California, UCLA. Delta Phi, a local, had been organized in 1919, one of nine Greek-letter locals. In the summer of 1923 Delta Phi filed a formal petition for a Delta Gamma charter. She had already assumed the responsibility of a house under her own management, raised her scholarship from ninth to second place on campus and was represented in virtually all of the student campus organizations. After due inspection the petition was accepted and Delta Phi became Alpha Sigma of Delta Gamma on November 18, 1924.

Financing Anchora

During the fall, too, the President, Vice-President, and Secretary-Editor (the Finance Committee) met at President Woollett's home in Evanston, Illinois, to wind up a number of Convention matters which needed attention. The auditor had made a study of the financial problems of the *Anchora* and found that the $1.00 per year subscription rate did not cover the cost of publication and he suggested an increase of .50 per annum. It was agreed that this could not be settled until Convention met again, but the President, in her report of this meeting in the *Anchora*, remarks that a large number of alumnæ subscriptions would help make up this deficit for the intervening period. The matter of concentrating all Delta Gamma funds in the hands of a dependable trust company was discussed. The Finance committee interviewed a trust officer of Chicago's largest bank, and a plan was worked out whereby this company would, for a nominal cost, relieve the Fraternity officers of the responsibility of handling all of Delta Gamma's funds, except *Anchora* accounts which would remain in Minneapolis.

NPC, 1925

Panhellenic met once more, and though very little that was new developed, the March, 1925, *Anchora* carried a full review of the current and past work of National Panhellenic Congress and a history of the fraternity system in the United States.

A custodian of securities

Council met April 6-9, 1925, at the Edgewater Beach Hotel in Chicago. It was at this time that the Continental and Commercial Bank of Chicago, Ill., was officially appointed custodian of securities and the depository for the national funds of Delta Gamma, excluding *Anchora* funds which remained in Minneapolis. This was according to the plan worked out in the fall by the Finance Committee. This Council session also devoted a great deal of time to the scholarship developments—matter concerning awarding them, etc., as well as to certain changes in ritual equipment made under the administration of Blanche Garten in this office.

Loans for houses

In its financial disucussions the Council decided that in the case of loans to chapter houses the amount loaned be determined, of course, on the merits of each case, but the sum of $5,000 be considered an approximate limit. Loans were to be made at 6%.

It was decided that the Secretary-Editor's salary be $2,500 to include office rent, until the 1926 Convention.

Butler University

Two months after this Council meeting another chapter was added to the Delta Gamma roll, Alpha Tau at Butler University, Indianapolis, Indiana. Sigma Delta, a local, had organized in 1922 with two-fold purpose: to perfect an organization which should be recognized for its high ideals of scholarship, democracy and wom-

anhood, and second, to petition Delta Gamma for a charter. From the beginning the group worked closely with Theta Alpha, the Indianapolis alumnæ chapter. Through this connection, encouragement was given by Council from the beginning, and the Convention of 1924 gave the group further encouragement so that in September, 1924, the petition was officially submitted to Council. In November word came that the petition had been accepted, but the installation did not take place until June 15, 1925.

"Delta Gamma System" for bookkeeping

Three years had now elapsed since the inauguration of the Delta Gamma bookkeeping system. Already it had attracted considerable Panhellenic attention with even an offer or two for "royalty" on its use. Council preferred, however, to freely advise and assist in establishing it for any desirous group, to keep it known in the fraternity world as the "Delta Gamma System." In *Anchora*, November, 1925, the fraternity auditor, Thomas Wallace, viewed the system and its successes during its infancy. Its first strong point had been, of course, that it was specifically designed to be used efficiently by persons totally inexperienced and with no training in bookkeeping. The establishment of the system had made it possible for the national officers to be furnished with accurate information as to the financial situation of each chapter, and even in this short time a number of opportunities had been offered to correct unfavorable situations. Mr. Wallace concludes from this early survey, "Delta Gamma, being the pioneer of Panhellenic fraternities to install a uniform bookkeeping system, has ample cause for satisfaction in taking this initial step; and no small amount of credit for its success is due to the many treasurers who have earnestly and faithfully endeavored to discharge their duties."

Should undergraduates smoke?

Council met once more at the Edgewater Beach, March 15-18, 1926. By now the total of the scholarship fund had reached $61,500. There was considerable discussion of the growing smoking habit among undergraduates—a habit generally disapproved by Council. In fact, articles appeared in the *Anchora* from time to time discussing the unhealthfulness of the habit, one by Los Angeles physician Dr. Lillian Ray Titcomb, Υ-Stanford. A general feeling against smoking by undergraduates was also officially registered by this Council meeting.

Council suggests revisions

Council decided at this meeting to recommend to the Revisions Committee for the coming Convention that Council once more be reduced to five members. It was also to be recommended that the full life subscription be paid at the time of initiation rather than on the installment plan.

15— Delta Gamma returns to Oxford

Forward motion only

Mrs. Dodd and Mrs. Leonard at Mackinac

Once more a Convention year. Delta Gamma's Twenty-Third Convention assembled at Mackinac Island, Michigan, June 29-July 2, 1926. Once more Nancy Brown Woollett held the gavel. Two founders were present, Mrs. Leonard and Mrs. Dodd—inspired to plead the cause of the University of Mississippi to be considered for a Delta Gamma chapter. The story is told that after entering this plea they retired to their rooms to pray while Convention decided the fate of the petitioners at Ole Miss.

After considerable discussion on the matter, especially of conditions on the Mississippi campus, it was agreed that at the earliest possible time, whenever the group organization of the petitioners was satisfactory, a chapter should be placed at Ole Miss. Much concern over the situation had stemmed from the political factors present. In 1912 an anti-fraternity bill had been passed in the state which had been repealed only in January, 1926. Tri Delta and Chi Omega organized immediately, and Professor French had written Alice Perry Gradle of the fine group petitioning Delta Gamma. When she waited a day or two to reply, he wired her, "Delta Gamma does not hurry. Do this time."

Convention action

The chief actions of this Convention were as follows:

- **Council** was reduced from seven to five members, the official group to be composed of President, First Vice-President (directing collegiate affairs, Second Vice-President (directing alumnæ affairs), Treasurer, and Secretary-Editor. The installation officer and chairman of the Scholarship Advancement Committee, having completed special tasks, were dropped from Council. Blanche Garten had been installation officer and had set up the new ritual equipment and had completed its distribution to all chapters. Jessie Roberson Kingery had completed the raising of the scholarship endowment fund and its uses had been pigeon-holed and were growing from contributions and producing, from investments, a good income.

- **Scholarship Loan Committee** was the new name of the Scholarship Advancement Committee, now to be a standing committee of the Fraternity which would process applications for loans. Marguerite Winant, O-Adelphi, was appointed chairman.
- Identification of alumnæ groups would hereafter be by location rather than Greek letter.

Alumnæ organization

The report of the alumnæ representative, Mrs. Erlbacher, was lengthy, including detailed analysis of what organization had taken place in each state as well as a topic discussion: I. Relation of active and alumnæ chapters within the province. II. How can a closer cooperation be brought about between the large and small chapters in the same community? III. Relations of an alumnæ group with a local active chapter. IV. Alumnæ recommendations of rushees.

Elections

Pearl McDonnell, B-Washington, who had been Chairman of Province Secretaries, had been nominated for the Presidency for the next four years, but when her name was presented she "in a very beautiful way withdrew her name in favor of that of Mrs. Woollett on the ground that Mrs. Woollett's policies, which had been of so much benefit to Delta Gamma could be carried on best by her if she could be persuaded to continue. Mrs. Woollett's name was then presented and was received with great applause," and she was unanimously elected, with the agreement that, at her request, she serve for only two years more.

Southern Methodist University

In the fall of this convention year Delta Gamma welcomed a new chapter, Alpha Upsilon installed October 16 in Dallas, Texas. This was the culmination of ten years of effort in this direction on the part of Lambda Rho, a local at Southern Methodist University. The group had organized as a secret social society originally. The need for fraternity was felt in the fall of 1921 and the group reorganized under the name Rannau. Acknowledged that year by the campus, Rannau was once more reorganized, this time by Panhellenic in the fall of 1922, and became Lambda Rho. In December that year it received official Delta Gamma inspection, but action was deferred and another inspection took place in January, 1926. Later that spring, the group received its acceptance as a potential Delta Gamma chapter.

Jessie Roberson Kingery dies

It was a sad note which echoed through the January, 1927, *Anchora*, for this issue carried to Delta Gammas the news of the death of Jessie Roberson Kingery, she who had inspired the $50,000 Birthday Fund and then directed a smashingly successful campaign to raise this and nearly $10,000 more. There are eulogies from personal friends and the Fraternity as a whole, and there was a proposition from the Boulder alumnæ of a Jessie Roberson Kingery loan fund, already begun in Colorado. Eventually, this took form as a project in Colorado, and the Fraternity, too, memorialized Mrs. Kingery with a Jessie Roberson Kingery Fellowship, similar to those established at the 1924 Convention.

Council meeting, April, 1927

Council met once more at the Edgewater Beach Hotel, opening its sessions there April 27, 1927, and covering a considerable amount of routine business.

University of Mississippi

The Founders had prayed for the return of Delta Gamma to Oxford, Mississippi; the Mackinac, 1926, Convention had voted it so, and in May, 1927, Alpha Psi chapter was installed at the University of Mississippi. The old Wohlleben home—the site of Delta Gamma's first Convention—listened once more as there Minnie Wohlleben Carter administered the pledge service to the petitioning group. On May 21, President Nancy Brown Woollett, Vice-President Donna Amsden, ϒ-Stanford, and six girls from Washington University installed Alpha Psi. Second Vice-President Erlbacher and Province Secretary Hamer were there, too. Later the Secretary-Editor, Leulah Judson Hawley, visited for in the same *Anchora* which reviews the installation she writes about the Lewis School. Finding it for sale during her first visit in Oxford she enthusiastically suggests the hope that through contributions from members, Delta Gamma may purchase the house as a possible chapter house for Alpha Psi as well as for a Fraternity memorial. This campaign went well for a time, but eventually it was deemed impractical.

Hazing discouraged

Council met March 9, 1928, at The Georgian Hotel, Evanston, Illinois, to dispense with the usual accumulation of business. Two resolutions are of particular interest: "That chapters be requested to treat pledges with especial consideration and courtesy for a period prior to initiation, and that at no time shall there be any pre-initiation razzing of pledges or any requirements which are menial or undignified," and

"That the chapters be requested to abolish the practice of calling attention publicly to the failures or mannerisms of pledges or members, that corrections must be made courteously and gently in private."

Twenty-fourth Convention
1928—Coronado, California

The prologue to the 1928 Convention which was to be held at the Hotel del Coronado, Coronado, California June 28-July 2, 1928, was a real California campaign. *Anchora* pages were devoted at length to books one should read before going, the history of California, things to see, to do, and so on, a much more lavish tourist lure than had previously been included to build up Convention attendance.

Pre-Convention
Council discusses NPC

Unlike the earlier California Convention when Council joined the six-day "Special house party" en route to Convention, Council arrived early at the del Coronado for its pre-Convention conference. These five moved to recommend to the incoming Council that at the next NPC, Delta Gamma be represented by the President as delegate with the outgoing President as alternate and a province secretary as second alternate. Nancy Brown Woollett was the first Delta Gamma to serve as delegate over a period of several NPC's, and the carry-over of one delegate had been beneficial to everyone concerned. Many of the other groups had been served by the same delegate for a period of many years. This suggestion was accepted when the new Council met following Convention.

To this Council was also reported a unanimous vote on the petition of a group at the University of British Columbia and plans were made for installation early in the fall.

Alumnæ project urged

Once more May Brown Tompkins served as Convention chairman, and for the last time Nancy Brown Woollett presided. In her presidential address Mrs. Woollett expressed her fervent hope that Convention would not adjourn until plans were formulated for a worthwhile alumnæ altruistic project. Mrs. Erlbacher, she continued, had brought into actual existence a real alumnæ organization, one to be turned over to her successor to capitalize on its potentialities. This dream, like Mrs. Woollett's dream of a real Central Office, did not come about for another decade.

Day of flapper discussed

Mrs. Woollett, too, considered gravely the day at hand, the day of the flapper as we now recall it, "Seeking some new field of personal adventure is as old as human life. There seems to be a broadcasting of behavior laxity and indifference, we are all in a certain sense modernists, else we are swept aside, no one of us would return to the good old days and weave and spin in lieu of the thought and action of today. Progress and civilization—do they mean a laxity of behavior? Are we carried away as with a tidal wave? Has this freedom of thought and action that some of our young women have sought really brought the longed-for freedom to them? Has it not rather brought or created a sort of hysteria and unrest? The urge for excitement, pleasure, popularity, amusement, all somewhat disguised as freedom, must be carefully watched and managed lest we find ourselves far from the mark of real attainment and accept as camouflage for real freedom and truth."

Negotiations with high school sorority, Delta Gamma

One of the most interesting reports of the Convention was made by the Secretary-Editor:

"There is very little history as such to be reported to this convention, with the exception perhaps, of that connected with the high-school sorority which for the past many years has borne the name of Delta Gamma. In 1915 negotiations to come to an understanding with that high-school group failed utterly and we were forced to admit ourselves defeated since the courts promised us no redress under the law, and the officers of the sorority refused to meet us or to acknowledge our letters. During the intervening 13 years the high-school sorority has added many chapters to its roll, figured unpleasantly in many so-called society columns and caused pain and humiliation to several of our chapters who could not understand why we were not protected from what seemed to them an outrage to Delta Gamma. By a very fortunate circumstance the whole matter has been settled and there is now no longer a high-school sorority bearing the name of Delta Gamma.

"It may be of interest to you to know the circumstances which led to this settlement.

Balfour takes our side

"Two years ago the L. G. Balfour Co. was made one of our official jewellers. Mr. Balfour suggested to all fraternities for whom he makes pins that steps be taken to register their names as a trademark, for he had been informed that whereas a copy-right had been shown to have no legality the registered trade-mark complied with all requirements. In our correspondence with the patent attorney in Washington it developed that since the name Delta Gamma was not used exclusively by us our name could not be registered. Just at that moment a confusion arose in the Balfour orders which revealed the fact that Balfour was official jeweller for the high-school sorority called Delta Gamma as well as for us. The

only alternative seemed to be to cancel our Balfour contract, which Mr. Balfour was loath to accept. He, therefore, offered to use such influence as he felt he had with the high-school sorority in an attempt to have them change their name. The officers of today had inherited traditions of hostility and were unwilling at first even to discuss the subject. Finally, however, they were won over and promised to bring the matter before their convention. The convention voted 73 to 3 against any change of name and the situation looked hopeless. At this point the Balfour Co. won permission to address the convention from the floor. They offered to exchange the old pins for new ones bearing a new name, to present the sorority with a cash payment of $500, and to make several other concessions. The outcome was a settlement on the basis of change of name and for us the incident closed. Mr. Balfour was able to do for us what we could not hope to do for ourselves, in relieving us of this mortification and removing the obstacle in the way of the registration of our name. Upon the earnest solicitation of the Secretary-Editor the Finance Committee voted to make good to Mr. Balfour the $500 paid out by him in cash. It has seemed to her only fair and honorable to make this repayment, since Mr. Balfour accomplished what we could not do. Had we gone to court and lost—as we should have—the cost would have been far greater. Had we not repaid this sum we should always have been embarrassed by our obligation to the Balfour Company.

"With the settlement of this controversy the registering of the Trade-Mark (our name) went forward and is now an established fact. We are henceforward protected from the use of our name by any unauthroized persons or groups."

Oxford House

This Convention, acting on the inspiration and urging of Mrs. Hawley, resolved "That the appropriation of funds be authorized for the purchase of the Oxford House upon joint recommendation of the Oxford House Committee, the Council Finance Committee and the Second Vice-President." More of the development of this later in these annals. . . .

Elections

Mary MacHarg Halstead, Σ-Northwestern, was elected to the presidency of the Fraternity at the final session of this Convention, and Marguerite Winant, O-Adelphi, who had distinguished herself both as chairman of the Scholarship Loan Committee and in the part she played in the campaign for the New York Panhellenic House, replaced Irene Erlbacher as Second Vice-President.

Vigorous alumnæ program

During Mrs. Erlbacher's energetic term of office (first as Alumnæ Representative and then, by change of name, Second Vice-President) state alumnæ chairman had been put to work, not only to keep track of Delta Gammas in each state, to collect convention taxes, report changes of addresses if and when they received them, but also to invigorate Delta Gamma in each individual state. Of these state chairmen one of the most farseeing and enthusiastic was Audrey Wilder, Z-Albion, who started in Michigan what might be among Delta Gamma's first State Days. They began in 1926 as inter-city luncheons when one in Lansing attracted 60 Delta Gammas and within a two year period six had been held. One reported in Albion, March 17, 1928, tells of 94 present to hear speakers from the represented cities in the state and from the two active chapters.

Indeed, the two retiring Council members, Nancy Woollett and Irene Erlbacher, had left affairs in an admirable state when their files were handed over to their successors.

16 — Politics, a pledge manual, project

Busy years

Fall, 1928, was busy for everyone.

This was an election year in the United States, and other Delta Gammas were engrossed in political achievement. When the ballot count was complete after the first Tuesday in November, Herbert Hoover had been elected and to Washington with him went Delta Gamma's First Vice-President Donna Amsden as his secretary, while Mrs. Hoover's secretary was Ruth Fesler, Ψ-Stanford. Ruth Bryan Owen was elected to the House of Representatives from Florida's 650-mile long Fourth District, and Hazel Whitaker Vandenberg's husband, Arthur Vandenberg, became freshman Senator from Michigan. Madge Lee Vincent's husband was to be Congressman from Iowa.

University of British Columbia

On September 7, following the California Convention, Alpha Phi chapter was installed at the University of British Columbia, becoming the 43rd on the Delta Gamma chapter roll and the second in Canada. The local which was to become Alpha Phi chapter had been organized as Theta Epsilon in 1919. After going her own way for several years, she became conscious of the advantages of becoming international, and Delta Gamma soon became her goal.

Panhellenic House opened

That fall of 1928, too, marked the opening of the Panhellenic House in New York. Opening day was October 1. Carrying Delta Gamma's responsibilities with distinction through the organi-zation, sale of stock and construction period had been Marguerite Winant. Miss Winant had served on the board of trustees and was chairman of furnishing for this gigantic undertaking. She was to be Vice-President of the Panhellenic House Association, Inc., from the time of its organization in 1927 until March, 1955, when she was elected President.

Pledge manuals for actives and province meets for alumnæ

Pledge manuals were compiled and issued to the chapters for the first time during this school year, and at the same time, Marguerite Winant, the new Second Vice-President, was offering the alumnæ something new, a plan for alumnæ sessions at the province conferences which would take place in the spring. She describes this as a "departure from our regular procedure" and evidently it was met with enthusiasm, for it was continued as a matter of course.

During this busy fall the finance committee met at Mrs. Woollett's home in Evanston. Most attention at this meeting was given to the deficit from the 1928 Convention, and the amount, it was decided, should be made up from the General Fund.

Council discusses expansion and other things

Council met once more at the Edgewater Beach Hotel in Chicago, opening their sessions there on March 19, 1929. Expansion consideration took a large part of conference time. It was decided that a committee of three should be appointed to compile a history of Delta Gamma, and Lambda Nu (Minneapolis alumnæ) were to be requested to compile a manual of fraternity information. Council also decided that if the Oxford house could be purchased for $6,000 or less that the deal should be closed. It was at this meeting that the chapter budget committee was set up, for it was decided that chapter house budgeting needed much closer supervision than it was getting. This committee was to operate in conjunction with Mr. Wallace.

Need for fraternity project

The feeling of need of a definite large-scale fraternity project was growing steadily. In the November, 1929, *Anchora:* "The interest on the part of our alumnæ in national projects and organization is steadily increasing," and in the same issue Second Vice-President Marguerite Winant said in a message to alumnæ, "There have been requests from many of our alumnæ for a national alumnæ project. This will be presented to the alumnæ at Convention. I feel that from the splendid work of so many of our alumnæ groups there should come suggestions for a national alumnæ work that will be worthy of our alumnæ organizations."

Even at this point, seven years before the project connected with the blind actually materialized, an article appeared in the January 1930 *Anchora,* "Not All Blind" by Marion Kappes, Σ-Northwestern. This was about the plight of blind children and what could be done for them and it was followed by a contribution from the Cleveland alumnæ chapter, "Report on Discussion of Work for the Blind." This is a complete discussion containing a definite outline of possible contributions, time-wise and money-wise, which Delta Gamma alumnæ could make, this list including twenty points. "We may give brains, or time, or money. Surely this is opportunity for those who feel that service is some part of the privilege of being a Delta Gamma." A strong appeal, this, for a Delta Gamma blind project—

However, Sight Conservation and Aid to the Blind, as a project, was not destined to take shape at this time, for the committee appointed at the 1928 Convention, the Alumnæ Project Committee, reported to Council a month after this article appeared. The opinion of the committee was that it was the duty of everyone in even a small way to promote international good feeling, and, therefore, that Delta Gamma's project should be biennial Foreign Fellowship of $1,500 to go to a Delta Gamma senior or graduate who "is seriously interested in study abroad and the result of whose work would reflect honor on the fraternity."

Alumnæ discussion

In March, 1930, Council once more assembled at the Edgewater Beach Hotel in Chicago. It was decided to issue leaflets of instruction to alumnæ.

Mary MacHarg Halstead, Σ-Northwestern, became President at the 1928 Convention, having served as her chapter's delegate to Convention. She was President until 1932.

From time to time differences had arisen over alumnæ members of petitioning groups who, for some reason, were not initiated at the installation. This was settled by a blanket resolution at this Council meeting: That alumnæ members of installed groups be initiated up to one year after installation.

The formal report from the alumnæ Project Committee was received at this time, and it was decided that the fellowship fund was to be raised by a $20 assessment on each alumnæ chapter every two years.

Oxford House plan dropped

Council also recommended that Convention vote to drop the Oxford House plan and return the money to its contributors. This project had been dropped after Mrs. Woollett and a contractor had inspected the house from top to bottom and discovered that to put it in shape for chapter use would require almost complete rebuilding. By this time, too, the owners, hoping to profit by the tremendous desire of Delta Gamma to own the house had raised their asking price outrageously. Consequently it was decided to leave the Lewis School building as it was, just a landmark on the shady street which leads to the gates of the University of Mississippi.

Twenty-fifth Convention
1930—Asheville, North Carolina

Convention time was approaching and though

the nation was already knee-deep in the depression, lures to conventioners were as enthusiastic as ever. This Twenty-fifth Convention was held at the Grove Park Inn, Asheville, North Carolina, June 24-28, 1930. Special guests were Mrs. Leonard and Mrs. Dodd and Lillie Wohlleben Hudson who had presided over Delta Gamma's second Convention.

When Mary MacHarg Halstead had been nominated and elected at the 1928 Convention it was a trifle of a surprise as her name had not been mentioned previously (as many others had) in connection with anything other than purely local Delta Gamma activity. Oddly enough, her President's address, which opened this 1930 Convention, reflects just that: an almost wide-eyed amazement at the great Fraternity organization at whose helm she stood.

Pennsylvania State College

The ritual chairman, First Vice-President Donna Amsden, reported the installation of Alpha Chi chapter at Pennsylvania State College, State College, Pennsylvania, just a month before Convention—May 17, 1930. Miss Amsden says, "For four years the members of La Camaraderie have worked for a Delta Gamma charter, and May 17, 1930, was the culmination of this period of untiring effort. . . . The eagerness with which Delta Gammas in the East welcomed the new chapter is attested to by the fact that there were one hundred and three present at the initiation and installation banquet."

A central office report

Even at this date the Secretary-Editor refers to her operation simply as Central Office. She reported to the Asheville assemblage: "Delta Gamma is in step with the more progressive of Greek Letter groups in our emphasis on a centralization in one office wherein permanent records are filed which shall be available to the historian of future days as well as of the present. More and more as a definite and conscious business system is being formulated, the work of administering our large fraternity is done by committees, so to speak, presided over by one or another of the members of Council.

"It is possible, probably, only to those who work year after year in the central office quite to grasp the advance in business conduct of our organization. For as needs have appeared means have been devised to meet and dispose of them efficiently. But it is not only through experience that progress has been made. In the past very few years a better understanding between fraternities has led to an interchange of ideas and a definite lending of assistance as between groups. This give and take has been of great benefit to all fraternities. It is possible for us today to take a deep breath, look about us and estimate our position with respect to our own internal operations as well as toward other similar groups."

Anchora self-supporting

Since Mrs. Hawley became editor in 1915, she had worked and hoped for the day when the Anchora endowment fund would produce enough income to make the magazine completely self-supporting. This goal was reached during the 1928-30 period and was happily reported by Auditor Thomas Wallace to this Convention.

Convention Fund

The Convention fund—after several years of trial and deficit—was thus defined: The Convention Fund shall consist of:

(1) An annual tax of three dollars ($3) from each member of a collegiate chapter.
(2) Twenty dollars ($20) annually from each alumnæ chapter.
(3) One dollar ($1) annually from each member of an alumnæ chapter.
(4) The sum of three dollars ($3) from the initiation fee of each member of the Fraternity, this sum to be reserved for the expenses of active and alumnæ delegates.

The possibility of this being insufficient was also reckoned with by providing that in this case the general fraternity treasury could contribute, so long as not more than two-thirds of the money in the treasury be appropriated for this purpose.

House Budget Committee

The House Budget Committee, only three months old, reported for the first time at this Convention. The importance of budgeting had become urgent as depression days darkened the immediate future of college financing. In the recent boom of campus building, it is sometimes a little hard to remember the early thirties when wings of dormitories were shuttered and locked because there was no one to occupy them.

Possibly it was because of this depression gloom which had settled over the country as a whole that the November Anchora, devoted almost entirely to Convention, reflects a particularly happy time in Asheville.

Candlelighting Service

It was at this Convention that the now traditional Candlelighting service was presented for the first time, by its originators of Eta chapter. In the search for ideas to make the Convention banquet carry a feeling of the Old South and to commemorate the southern origin of Delta Gamma, the banquet committee, Eta and the Akron alumnæ, developed the idea of the candlelighting service and asked Ruth Smith See, Ξ-Michigan, to write it.

Elections

As Convention closed, Florence Cornell Bingham, X-Cornell, who was one of the first Delta Gamma daughters (her mother had been an early member of Chi) to be initiated, replaced Donna Amsden as First Vice-President, and

Hazel Brown, AB-Swarthmore, succeeded Alice Perry Gradle as Treasurer.

University of Arkansas

Plans had been made at Convention for another fall installation; Delta Beta, a local at the University of Arkansas, was to become Alpha Omega chapter on October 11, 1930. Proximity to Mississippi made it possible for the two living founders Mrs. Dodd and Mrs. Leonard to be present in Fayetteville, Arkansas, on that October day—in fact the only installation they were ever able to attend together. Delta Beta had been organized in 1925 with its aim Delta Gamma, and one organizer of this original local traveled with her husband and small baby all the way from California to be present at the installation of Alpha Omega chapter.

News of the day

The January 1931 Anchora, which featured the Arkansas installation, noted, too, a list drawn up by a news syndicate of the 50 most outstanding women in the United States. The editor, Mrs. Hawley, pointed with pride to two Delta Gammas on this roll of distinction, Grace Abbott, K-Nebraska, head of the Children's Bureau of the Department of Labor, and Ada Louise Comstock, Λ-Minnesota, president of Radcliffe College.

And at this time, when cost of living was of utmost importance, the Anchora also carried a review of "Comparative Costs of the Dormitory and Fraternity House."

McGill University

Another installation was held during this 1930-31 school year—February 21, 1931, Beta Alpha chapter at McGill University, Montreal, Quebec. The installation was held in conjunction with Province I Conference so that it was indeed an impressive affair by its size alone. The C.D. club had been organized in 1926 for purely social purposes, one of the first such clubs on campus. Others formed similar clubs and rushing went along lines similar to Panhellenic groups on other campuses. Finally the weakening resistance at McGill was crushed and the C.D.'s petitioned Delta Gamma. To raise their initiation fee, the C.D. club held a Thousand Dollar Ball at the then famous Venetian Gardens in Montreal. It was both successful and memorable.

To divide Secretary-Editor office

Council had met just prior to the Montreal installation—February 15-17 at the home of Second Vice-President Marguerite Winant in New York City.

While expansion accounted for a great deal of business, one important decision was made—that "the offices of Secretary and Editor be divided so that the editor shall be appointed by Council and shall be ex officio member of Council with no voting power." This, of course, would have to be presented to the 1932 Convention.

Alpha Psi charter held in abeyance

It had been only a single college generation, four years, since with happy tears and high hopes Delta Gamma had returned to its birthplace with the installation of Alpha Psi chapter at the University of Mississippi. And then in the spring of 1931 the May Anchora issues a sad report:

"Due to conditions existing at the U. of M. and the fact that so few members of Alpha Psi will return in September, 1931, Council has agreed to allow us to hold in abeyance our charter and all Delta Gamma properties until such time as Ole Miss again holds 'A' grade rating and conditions are favorable for the functioning of Alpha Psi."

And from an editorial in the same issue. "It saddens one to think that an institution so rich in tradition, so eager to preserve the best, so full of promise for the future should have become the plaything of a political machine, but inasmuch as this has taken place, and many unfortunate changes have been made at Mississippi, the Association of American Universities has found cause to remove the University of Mississippi from its list of Grade A institutions.

"This action on the part of the political powers in Mississippi, followed by the announcment of the Association of American Universities, has placed Delta Gamma in an equivocal situation, from which she has been extricated by the wisdom and inspiration of her members resident in Mississippi.

"Upon petition of Alpha Psi and the Oxford Alumnæ, Council has agreed to allow the charter to be held temporarily in abeyance until such time as Mississippi shall regain her scholastic prestige in the educational world. When that time arrives the fraternity will stand wholeheartedly back of Alpha Psi in her re-establishment.

"To the end that the Delta Gamma tradition in Mississippi shall not suffer, a conscious effort should be made on the part of Delta Gamma chapters to seek out for members Mississippi girls who attend their institutions, for in this way the Mississippi chapter can be kept alive for the present and a foundation be built up for the future."

University of Alberta

Another Canadian chapter was entered on the chapter roll in 1931: Beta Beta at the University of Alberta in Edmonton, Alberta, installed on May 9. Phi Gamma, a local, had been in existence for a few years and through six Delta Gamma alumnæ in Edmonton petitioned Delta Gamma. Two tours of inspection were made by Mrs. Halstead and Mrs. Bingham and the charter was granted very quickly, for Delta Gamma was to be the first NPC group to organize and it seemed a promising field.

Again in the fall of 1931 Council convened at the home of Marguerite Winant in New York

City.

University of Utah

Two more chapters in the West were added to the role during this school year, both in the spring of 1932. Gamma Sigma, a local at the University of Utah, had organized in 1920, and since that time had been seeking a Delta Gamma charter. During the twelve intervening years they were aided and encouraged by Delta Gamma alumnæ living in Salt Lake City, and finally the week end of May 6-8 saw their dreams realized, and Gamma Sigma became Beta Gamma chapter of Delta Gamma.

Colorado College

This was actually part of a twin installation, for the following weekend the Minerva Society at Colorado College, Colorado Springs, Colorado, became Beta Delta of Delta Gamma. Minerva had existed at Colorado College for forty years and held an outstanding position on the campus and of course had by this time a large and strong group of loyal alumnæ. Delta Gamma was the first to grant a charter on the Colorado College campus, but within a few weeks follow-ing the Beta Delta installation, Kappa Kappa Gamma, Kappa Alpha Theta and Gamma Phi Beta granted charters, too. May 14 was installation day.

New editorial duties

The 1932 Convention was to be held at the Empress Hotel, Victoria, British Columbia, and from January until May, *Anchoras* were stuffed with lures to Convention-goers. Again it is a little hard to remember that historians recall this as the "depths of the depression."

Council met en route to this Convention at the Banff Springs Hotel at Banff, Alberta, and joined the Convention special at Lake Louise. Mrs. Halstead called this officers' meeting to order on June 22. A new pledge manual was urged and it was finally decided that the Publications Chairman (one of the new duties of the *Anchora* editor) should direct its preparation, selecting her own committee to do so. A special committee was also to be appointed to draw up a model chapter constitution. Council also voted at this time to rescind an earlier decision that the outgoing President be alternate NPC delegate.

Personalities of this period—

Mae Brown Tompkins, Υ-Stanford, niece of former President Ada May Brown, served as Delta Gamma's permanent Convention Chairman for ten years.

Leulah Judson Hawley, Λ-Minnesota, was Anchora Editor from 1915 until her death in 1934 (Secretary-Editor, 1915-32) and operated the first centralized office. It was she who worked endlessly to put Anchora on a self-supporting basis, a job in which she succeeded. A Memorial Fellowship is named for her.

17 — Planning pays well in these times

Depression days

The Anchora of Delta Gamma

VOL. XLVIII, NO. 2

THE ANCHORA OF DELTA GAMMA

JANUARY, 1932

January, 1932

As Conventions go, Delta Gamma's Twenty-Sixth was a short one. It was in session for only three days, June 28-30, at the Empress Hotel, Victoria, British Columbia.

On scanning the minutes of that Tuesday, Wednesday and Thursday in 1932, one gets the impression of a much longer business session than the calendar would indicate. It is evident from President Halstead's opening words that, since many disapproved of the frivolity of sorority conventions in days of such financial stress, the most must be made of Convention time.

Change in organization

There was to be a major change in organization. Mrs. Halstead outlined this in her address:

"We are looking forward to some changes in our organization, but we plan to guard jealously the principles upon which that organization rests. Our policy in the past has included the development of a sufficient centralization to ensure efficiency and a certain uniformity while allowing a liberty of action to our chapters that maintains their development as strong individual units. Your Council is in no sense greedy of power and feels convinced that this line of action promises a maximum of strength to the fraternity as a whole.

"The change that we contemplate, the division of the office of our Secretary-Editor, seems at present opportune. The combination of the two offices that was practical at the time when Mrs. Hawley assumed it would, without subsequent growth in size and in organization, be difficult for a new officer to handle. Mrs. Hawley has developed her methods with the growth of the demands upon her, and her intelligent and unremitting service has earned our warmest gratitude. While she gives up the office of Secretary, she is to retain energy and foresight that our journal (be kept) on its present secure financial basis, and we look eagerly forward to the *Anchora* that shall represent the result of her undivided effort."

This change was officially put into the Constitution two days later. With it came, quite naturally, an avalanche of minor changes concerning various duties of these two offices. One imagines that the Constitution and By-Laws Revisions committee for this convention, faced with this multitude of changes, deemed it advisable—and surely no more trouble—to go over the entire Constitution and By-Laws and attend to improvements in phrasing and clarification of wording. By the major change that started this large revision in 1932, the Secretary would continue to be an elected member of Council and the editor would be appointed by Council and serve as an ex officio member of the official body with no voting power. The Constitution outlined her duties thus:

"The *Anchora* shall be managed by the editor. The editor shall be responsible for the editing and publishing of all official publications of the fraternity. She shall be Treasurer of the *Anchora* Endowment Fund. She shall be a member of the Fraternity Finance Committee and shall attend the regular meetings of Council. She shall be Chairman of the Publication Committee." Much of this official activity was set up with Mrs. Hawley's particular ability and longstanding Fraternity background in mind, for it was she who would now devote her entire time to Fraternity affairs.

The splitting of the office of Secretary-Editor caused Delta Gamma to regress in one respect. This split caused the separation of the day to day business of the fraternity operation—that is, the Editor was to maintain the fraternty files and all material connected with the *Anchora*, but the secretary would handle the other records (address files, etc.) and supplies. This broke up the centralization for which Nancy Woollett had campaigned and certainly brought an end to the Central Office which Mrs. Hawley had had in operation for ten years or more. Fraternity officers—and probably members, too—didn't view it in this way, however, for they had never officially, by act of Convention, set up a Delta Gamma Central Office. This was not to happen for another ten years. Mrs. Hawley's already well-organized business center for Delta Gamma, like Topsy, had "just growed."

It is "The Anchora"

One "minor" change in Constitution wording which was voted piece by piece at this Convention is worth noting at this time. Throughout this history we have used our present day terminology and when referring to the magazine called it *The Anchora*. Up to 1932, however, the "the" was never included; it was just *Anchora*. By Convention vote this was changed throughout the Constitution and By-laws and "the" was inserted in front of *Anchora* each time it was mentioned.

A Founders' portrait

Portraits of the three founders (photographic reproduction of an 1874 daguerreotype of the trio) were presented to the four Canadian chapters and after Convention were mailed to each chapter in the United States. This difference in manner of presentation was, of course, because of customs restrictions since this Convention was in session in Canada.

Attention to pledges

When the chairman of Province Secretaries, Pearl McDonnell, reported, she commented, "The active chapters should be complimented on the elimination of 'rough week.' A girl should go into the chapter with the love and respect for every member of the chapter, and not with hatred for the girl who has 'razzed' her and made life miserable for her. Since the dropping of 'rough week' initiates have had an entirely different attitude." She also reported the compilation of a pledge manual, the one then in use (Delta Gamma's first) being a temporary thing. The pledge manual then in use had grown out of the fact that a few years before the Fraternity had returned to the practice of an annual Fraternity examination, an idea which had been dropped during the mid-twenties. This office received considerable attention at this time, for many people thought that the Chairman of Province Secretaries should be a member of Council. But the added expense this would bring about caused much hesitation—these being depression days of course heightened this feeling. A year later when Miss McDonnell resigned, having served admirably in the office for ten years, the chairmanship of the Province Secretaries was added to the duties of the Fraternity Secretary.

Expansion

Expansion, as usual, demanded a great deal of attention. Though applications had been received from 28 campuses during the preceding two year period only two charters had been granted—Beta Gamma at Utah and Beta Delta at Colorado College, and these had been in active files for some time. After listing the 28 colleges the Expansion Chairman commented, "Most of these applications have been discouraged by the Expansion Committee, either because the institutions did not come up to our standard or because

we felt that the neighboring chapters would not welcome the petition. In certain instances, somewhat promising groups have been discouraged by our $1,000 installation fee—a sum which looms large in these difficult times, but which barely covers the cost of installing a new chapter."

Elections, 1932

Marguerite Winant, O-Adelphi, whose wisdom and ability in fraternity affairs were well known not only to Delta Gammas but to those who had worked with her on the New York Panhellenic House, was elected President of the Fraternity as this Convention closed. The first Canadian to hold a Council position was to be A. E. Marie Parkes, AΓ-Toronto, who became Second Vice-President, and Alice Perry Gradle, Ξ-Michigan, who had already served as First Vice-President, became Secretary as this office was made separate from that of Editor.

Special exhibit

The hostess chapters' members had dressed dolls in costumes representing periods in the history of Canada. These dolls were part of the Convention banquet decoration. When Convention was over, the Fraternity presented the dolls in an attractive glass case to the Parliament Building, Victoria, B.C., for a permanent exhibit.

Council meeting, Fall, 1932

For the first time in many years there was no chapter installation scheduled for the early fall following a Convention. Council, however, scheduled a fall meeting, October 24-26, at the Edgewater Beach Hotel in Chicago.

Installation fee reduced

One item for discussion was the $1,000 installation fee, and it was decided that this should be reduced at the discretion of the First Vice-President, if the field warranted reduction.

It was decided again to defer any further action in regard to an Alumnæ Project and the alumnæ chapters were to be notified of this action.

Installment initiation fee

It was also decided that, because of the current financial crisis, initiation could take place with the payment of a minimum of $10, the remainder of the initiation fee to be paid in agreed installments.

Preferential bid system and pledge quotas

Council met again in the spring, and the Finance Committee convened, too, at the Panhellenic House in New York. Most of the business of the latter was confined to routine financial affairs, but this group also found it in its power to accept the offer of Jean Rathburn Faulkner, K-Nebraska, Province Secretary, to collect and

Marguerite Dawson Winant, O-Adelphi, already had a record of distinguished service behind her when she became President of the Fraternity in 1932, serving until 1940. During her term (1928-32) as Second Vice-President she had suffered an attack of polio, accomplishing a miraculous recovery from the paralysis which followed.

compile material for a rushing pamphlet. This occurrence in 1933 was particularly timely, for the fall of that year marked the beginning of the preferential bidding system as we know it today. As Marguerite Winant reported to the 1934 Convention, "—a pledge quota system was tried for the first time in the fall of 1933, and then only on five campuses. Comments of Deans and College Panhellenic officers, confirmed that neither the quota system nor the Illinois Temporary Emergency Plans attained the hoped for goal—balanced distribution of available material—each group of normal size. The five campuses are University of Maine, Montana State, University of North Dakota, Ohio Wesleyan University and University of Illinois."

The Depression

Though the depression had been with us for several years, it was during 1933 that the *Anchora* first made one conscious of its presence. The paper stock on which the *Anchora* was printed had been a high gloss enamel, but the March, 1933, issue—and subsequent ones—are printed on a less costly, though good quality, paper. An issue later in the year carried an article by the Fraternity auditor, Thomas M. Wallace, "Delta Gamma and the Depression." Mr. Wallace commented at that time, "While business in general has been declining, Delta

Gamma funds have been growing." Officers mentioned, too, in reports at conventions within the next few years that this fact, this weathering of dire financial stress with no indebtedness and no loss of chapters, is certainly evidence of the basic solidarity of the Fraternity and the entire Greek-letter world.

Student Loans

One final depression note—during the 1932-34 biennium, more than $14,000 was granted in student loans, usually amounts between $50 and $100, enough to enable a girl to complete school during this period of universal financial stress.

Sororities leave Swarthmore

When Council met again in the fall of 1933, it was time once more to talk about another Convention. There was much talk, too, of the election which was to take place on December 12 on the Swarthmore College campus which was to decide the fate of sororities there. The outcome was alarming to many, for the sorority women themselves voted the Greek-letter groups off campus, and by 1934 our Alpha Beta chapter was no more. The chapter was, however, represented at the Convention that year.

Two deaths sadden 1934

Two deaths saddened the early months of 1934. On January 28, Founder Eva Webb Dodd passed away at her home in Kosciusko, Mississippi. Her lifelong friend Mary Comfort Leonard was with her constantly throughout the last weeks of her illness. Mrs. Leonard wrote of her friend after her death, "This friendship of so many years is rare, yet it is ours." Mrs. Dodd had attended many conventions and was well loved by Delta Gammas everywhere and her passing was deeply mourned.

In May an *Anchora* was scheduled to feature the Golden Jubilee of the Delta Gamma magazine. Editors and editorial memories were featured, and a special feature lauded the vision and accomplishments of Leulah Judson Hawley. This issue was for the most part compiled by the editor's sister, Edna Judson Wilde who had been on her Central Office staff for many years, and in writing of her sister she begins, "As our present editor, Leulah Judson Hawley has been gravely ill for some time, though now well on the road to recovery, it is not possible for her to write her own memories, so we two, who are acting as her assistants temporarily, will give a brief statement of what has taken place in her nineteen years of editorship, merely adding a few facts to Mrs. Woollett's words of high appreciation."

Even before this issue of the magazine was in the hands of its readers—in April—Mrs. Hawley's recovery was suddenly halted. Death came even as the presses were rolling out these words of tribute to her years in office. It was characteristic of Mrs. Hawley to die "with her boots on." Her vision and persistence in reaching her goal had made the *Anchora* the self-supporting organ it is today; her ability had produced a magazine of editorial excellence, one which kept step with the times not only in editorial content but in layout which reflected the immediacy of today. Her contributions, too, to the office of secretary had been innumerable, not the least of this the Central Office which she had maintained for so many years in her own home.

18— With bad times nearly behind us—

Today good— tomorrow better

AN HISTORICAL SKETCH OF THE DELTA GAMMA FRATERNITY

1874-1934

Delta Gamma had weathered the worst of the bad times smoothly. Those who thought about this knew that this was due largely to the vision and planning with which the Fraternity was endowed by officers who had served ten and fifteen years before. Now, however, they looked upon the fact calmly and in a matter-of-fact manner. Today was good, tomorrow would be better; in fact, today was the time to begin to work on tomorrow.

Twenty-seventh Convention
1934—Green Lake, Wisconsin

At 2:45 p.m. on Monday, June 25, 1934, Marguerite Winant rapped her Delta Gamma gavel and spoke:

"Sixty years ago, Eva Webb Dodd, Mary Comfort Leonard and Anna Boyd Ellington founded the Delta Gamma Fraternity. Throughout these sixty years Delta Gamma has progressed because of the high ideals set forth by her three Founders. At this time we of Delta Gamma with love and reverence dedicate to our Founders this our Twenty-seventh Convention and our Sixtieth Anniversary of Delta Gamma's birth. In a spirit of deep appreciation for what our Founders have given to us, I do hereby declare the Twenty-seventh Convention of The Delta Gamma Fraternity now in session."

Thus the Twenty-Seventh Convention of the Delta Gamma Fraternity opened at the Lawsonia Country Club Hotel, Green Lake, Wisconsin. It remained in session for four days, June 25-29.

Banta's last Convention

The Convention received a pleasant surprise with the unannounced arrival of George Banta, its only male member. He was accompanied by his son George Banta, Jr., then president of Phi Delta Theta. For the last time Delta Gammas listened attentively to Mr. Banta's recollections of the Fraternity's early days. He died September 23, 1935.

An Historical Sketch—

At this Convention the chairman of the History Committee, Nancy Brown Woollett, announced the presentation at that time of "An Historical Sketch of the Delta Gamma Fraternity, 1874-1934." This was a sixtieth birthday edition, and the committee presented it knowing its incompleteness and hoping that work could continue, using this as an outline, for a really comprehensive historical work. It was dedicated to the recently deceased member of the committee, Leulah Judson Hawley. Also at this time another Delta Gamma Memorial Fellowship was set up in Mrs. Hawley's honor.

The Dawson legacy

Convention, 1934, received, too, the announcement of a legacy to the Fraternity from Olive Ione Dawson in memory of her two sisters who were members of Phi chapter. The original legacy had been for $20,000 but financial conditions had reduced it to about $16,000.

Expansion quiet

Expansion was considerably quieter than usual —only 14 applications having been received since 1932. The depression gravely influenced this, of course, and by the same token the expansion chairman, Florence Cornell Bingham, felt Delta Gammas, too, were not in favor of undue expansion at this time. This conclusion she had drawn from the episode which had occurred in connection with the petition of Ero Alphian at Michigan State College. A most favorable account of the campus and the local had been presented at the 1932 Convention and shortly after this the approval of the Province was gained. When, however, it was put to a general vote, the "no's" were such that Mrs. Bingham felt it was not only a vote against the proposed Michigan State College chapter but against expansion in general at that time. It had been so assumed that, with the Province's affirmative vote, the general vote would be "yes," that this resounding negative decision was extremely embarrassing not only the the Ero Alphian group itself but to Delta Gammas in the area. Another expansion episode reflected the unfavorable feeling of the times at this Convention. Dalhousie University in Nova Scotia had been granted a petition, and then, because of financial reverses in Eastern Canada, decided at the last minute to withdraw its petition, even though it had already been accepted. Fortunately, both of these occurrences are exceptions to Delta Gamma's expansion records.

Other Convention action

- **Editor's duties** were reduced sharply. A new editor would be appointed soon, one who, in spite of ability, could not be endowed with Mrs. Hawley's nineteen years of experience in Fraternity affairs. In fact, it was probably that no one would care to take on the staggering number of tasks Mrs. Hawley had assumed through the years. The Constitution now stated: "The *Anchora* shall be edited by the editor who shall be responsible for its publication and such other editorial duties as may be assigned by Council."
- **Province Secretaries** would now be under the direction of the First Vice-President. Previously, the Secretary had handled this area of activity, but the change seemed logical since the First Vice-President was in charge of collegiate affairs.

Elections

Three officers were re-elected and re-installed at the close of this Convention: Florence Cornell Bingham, First Vice-President; Alice Perry Gradle, Secretary, and Hazel Brown, Treasurer.

New editor appointed

A few months after Convention a new editor was appointed by Council. She was Alta Gwinn Saunders, I-Illinois, of the English department at the University of Illinois, suggested by her own Iota chapter of which she had been a charter member. Their predictions were well founded that she would be able to assume the office smoothly and carry on easily the editorial excellence of the magazine.

Mrs. Saunders felt strongly that college trained women deserved a magazine as timely and thought-provoking and with as high literary standards as any other periodical that they might receive. Thus, the *Anchora* gained a new kind of maturity.

These first years of the editorship of Alta Gwinn Saunders certainly marked an intensified consciousness of Delta Gammas who were leaders in their chosen fields. The November, 1935, issue salutes educational administrators—leading off with an article by Ada Louise Comstock, Λ-Minnesota, president of Radcliffe College, and followed by an impressive series of articles by and about an equally impressive group of Delta Gamma administrators and educators.

Another issue features librarians; another, entertainers; another, members of the professions, and so on. This series of *Anchoras* in itself crystallizes the position women have achieved during the existence of fraternities for women. Another innovation had appeared in the *Anchora* during 1935-36—the Manuscripts section which carried reprints and condensations of works of Delta Gamma writers.

Province Secretary instruction

During the years since 1917 when the office had come into being, the province secretaries had more than proved their worth as the necessary link in administration between the Council and chapter officers. By 1934 the membership had nearly tripled that of 1917; there were seven provinces instead of five. Everyone was busier, and an informal word-of-mouth training when files passed along from one province secretary to her successor no longer sufficed. During the 1935-36 school year, First Vice-President Florence Bingham introduced a more tangible training program. Instructions for Province Secretaries were compiled, and, in addition, all province secretaries were assembled for a two-day training school. At the same time, Mrs. Bingham was preparing—and issued after the 1936 Convention —a handbook for guidance for chapter officers, alumnæ advisers and house chaperones.

A new Pledge Manual

In January, 1936, came the official announcement of Delta Gamma's new pledge manual—for the first time a really sizeable volume to be placed in the hands of fraternity pledges and including a well-planned training program to be administered by the chapter pledge mistress. This volume had been compiled by First Vice-President Florence Cornell Bingham.

American University

In the spring of 1936—March 21—Beta Epsilon chapter was added to the role, at American University, Washington, D.C. The group had been organized as Epsilon Kappa in 1929 and during the years preceding installation had established itself as a campus leader.

Political interests

Naturally, increasing interest during 1936 was focused on a Kansas Delta Gamma, Theo Cobb Landon, AK-Washburn, whose husband was the Republican candidate for President that year.

Twenty-eighth Convention
1936—Lake Placid, New York

This was a Convention year, too, and a symphonic theme had been chosen for the conclave. The Lake Placid Club, Lake Placid, New York, was the site which had been chosen for this Twenty-Eighth Convention, June 22-25, 1936.

Two new Fraternity standing committees had been created and were present for the first time at this Convention: Membership (handling rushing) and Mothers' Clubs. Mothers' Clubs had been in existence in a number of cites and towns where chapters were located for many years, but for the first time they were recognized nationally and a program was set up for their organization.

Delta Gamma Project

The biggest thing to come from the 1936 Convention had the traditionally small beginning. The Delta Gamma Project, Sight Conservation and Aid to the Blind, was born of a suggestion made in an alumnæ workshop session. The idea, of course, did not hop into the mind of the delegate at that moment in the Convention workshop—it was an idea which had been growing in the minds of the members of a number of alumnæ groups for some time. It had almost come into being on several other more auspicious occasions—which possibly makes it more a real *fraternity* project: the fact that it came from the minds and hearts of the membership itself and was not pressed upon the alumnæ by an official group appointed by or a part of Council.

In the minutes of the Alumnæ Workshop it appears like this:

"The discussion revealed that most alumnæ favored an altruistic project. It was moved, seconded and passed that the alumnæ *go on record as desiring an altruistic project.*

"A motion that a committee be appointed to consult with Council about these suggestions and report back to the delegates was passed. This motion was amended to read that a preliminary report by the Committee be submitted by September 1 and that there be a final vote of Chapters by October 15.

"Miss Winant appointed this Committee which was to report back to the alumnæ session: Chairman, Mrs. Shriver, Baltimore; Mrs. Fuller, Berkeley; Mrs. Tucker, Akron; Miss Adams, Chicago; Mrs. Firstbrook, Toronto.

"At a later session the following report was submitted by the Committee above:

"'After much thought and careful consideration the Committee voted to present as a National Delta Gamma project—*Aiding the Blind.* We would like to suggest that as a possible name *The Delta Gamma Foundation for the Blind* might be a good one.

"'The Committee felt that with a title as broad as this, each chapter could decide for itself whether it wanted to contribute to a general fund for an endowment of the Seeing Eye Fund or locally by providing talking books, Reader's Digest, etc.

"'The Committee felt that perhaps each chapter could have a part in both phases. Over a period of years we might branch out in several directions, that is why with a general name such as this we might even eventually associate ourselves with the American Association for the Blind.

"'We would like to suggest that each delegate take back to her chapter the suggestion that in making their choices they must try and consider both the administration of the money and the advertising value to Delta Gamma of the phase of the project which they select.'

"The report of the Committee was accepted."

A discussion on the founding on an altruistic project for Delta Gamma had been introduced by Mrs. Tucker of Akron. Suggestions for projects included aid to the Central Institute for the Deaf, an enlarged scholarship fund, aiding the Warm Springs foundations, etc.; but the list was sparked by its number one speaker—Ruth Billow, H-Akron, herself blind, who read her appeal which she had previously typed in Braille.

When this digest of the alumnæ sessions was read on the floor of Convention, Elizabeth Weintz, Θ-Indiana, Province II's secretary, moved that the action taken by the alumnæ to present "Work for the Blind" as a suggested project to the alumnæ chapters by October 15 be approved. This was seconded and carried, and, as we all know, the Project was gladly accepted by the alumnæ during the following year.

In March, 1937, the first real Project committee was appointed by Council; Jane Hawk Schuessler, Γ-California, was its chairman. At this time chairmen were appointed in each province to work as the members of Mrs. Schuessler's committee. The same issue of the *Anchora* which carried the first Project Chairman's first messsage to the Fraternity also included an article "Dogs against Darkness," a piece about the work of Seeing Eye Dogs.

Elections, 1936

Marguerite Winant, President for the past four years, was re-elected to this office for the next four. Emma Sperry Robertson, Φ-Colorado, was elected Second Vice-President, and Edith Taylor Smith, AB-Swarthmore, was elected Treasurer to complete the remaining two years of Hazel H.

(Continued on page 145)

Delta Gamma
Panorama

a Fraternity in action
a Foundation at work

A History of Delta Gamma is the story of an organization founded on sound principles and the high ideals that only youth can envision and seek. This pictorial section is a bird's eye view of that organization in this decade.

on the

campus

scenes of the decade:
tomorrow's history

*this room contains
the records of more than 75,000
women who are Delta Gammas . . .
but their real record
is written*

in the

community

RECOGNITION OF ACHIEVEMENT

A PROJECT WELL DONE

ROSE AWARD TO AN EXECUTIVE

COMMUNITY SUPPORT FROM JUNIOR GROUPS

A VARIETY
OF TALENTS

NEW INTERESTS
THROUGH THE FOUNDATION

CONTINUING EDUCATION

PERSONAL SERVICES
THROUGH PROJECT
ACTIVITY

A LIFETIME MEMBERSHIP

through the years

Council

is a continuing thing, expanding its program-ming, listening to its collegians, encouraging its alumnæ, providing the core of an organ-ization to keep its lifetime membership a worth-while thing. . . .

No one has estimated the number of hours each Council member contrib-utes, without financial reward, to ex-pedite the progress of the Fraternity. Council meets semi-annually to handle routine business. Often this includes special sessions to listen to the sugges-tions of field secretaries and Collegiate Representatives to Council.

Field secretaries are trained in Executive Offices each August.

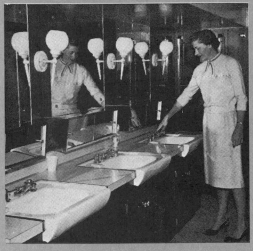

Each Council member directs an area of Fraternity activity—here the Housing Director inspects.

Keeping alert to new programming techniques—these two have a practical conference with Fran Stevenson of Communications and Information on visual aids.

Council members are frequently Founders Day speakers—here President Kathryn Gary during her years as First Vice-President (second from right).

First, each is a woman and exercises her womanly talents —Mrs. Moorman, chairman of Guest House remodeling, trained as a dietitian tries the Guest House kitchen.

a central office since 1942

1942: A BEGINNING

1949: ROOM FOR EXPANSION

1955: MOVE TO THE SUBURBS

1965: A GUEST HOUSE

1967: TWENTY-FIFTH ANNIVERSARY

1961: A PERMANENT HEADQUARTERS

Executive Offices

3250 Riverside Drive
Columbus, Ohio 43221

Roberta Abernethy, who had been First Vice-President for three years, became Executive Secretary when the office opened in 1942. She had been its guiding spirit for thirty years when she retired in 1972, having overseen expansion of space and of office responsibilities, having directed the construction of the Executive Offices building and ten years later the burning of its mortgage, and having served as president of the Panhellenic Central Office Executives.

Mortgage burning: January 7, 1972

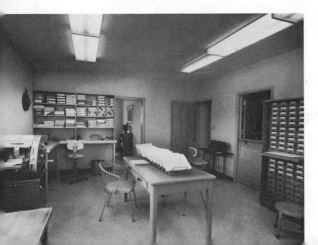

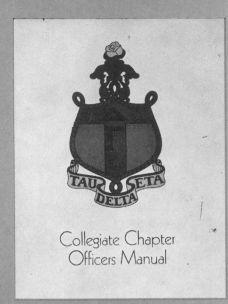

Collegiate Chapter
Officers Manual

Officers Training was offered more than forty years ago, but from the biennial Officers Training School of the 'fifties, the Leadership School evolved.

The program for the first Leadership School to include collegiate presidents.

Leadership School

Convention interim training for officers and collegiate presidents

*Delta Gamma
Officers' Training School
and
Collegiate Presidents Leadership School
June 17-23, 1963
Ohio State University Campus
Delta Gamma Executive Offices
Columbus, Ohio*

Delta Gamma operations were discussed, demonstrated, and displayed at sessions at the Executive Offices, conducted here by President Groves with Miss Abernethy looking on.

Facilities of Ohio State University and the Executive Offices are used for the school.

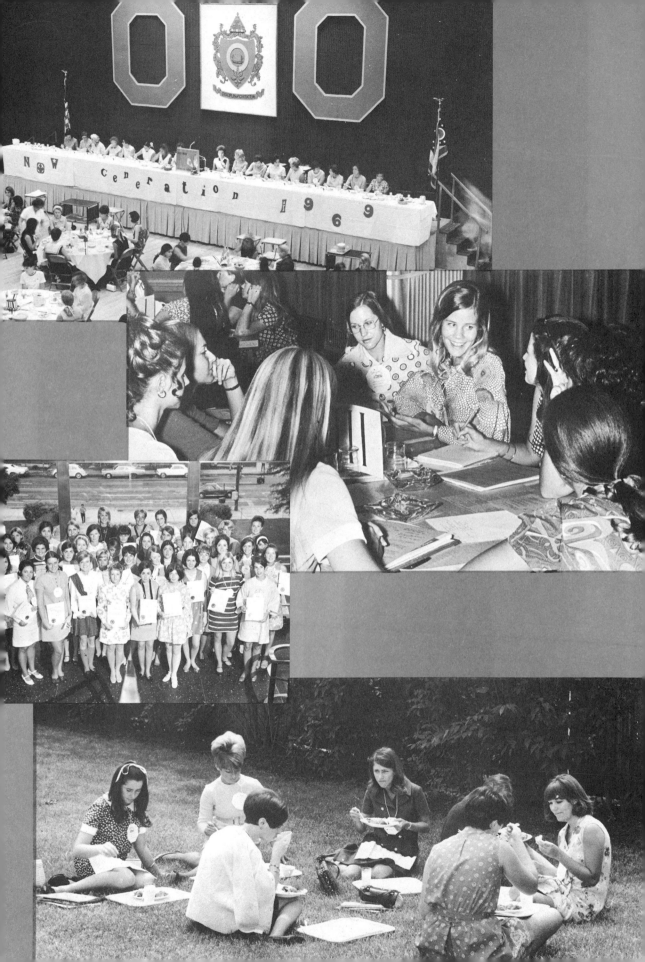

Delta Gamma
Foundation

is the organization which
is the channel for the
philanthropic projects
of the Delta Gamma
Fraternity:

- Grants and Loans in education, through which at least 12 in fellowships and scholarships are offered annually and more than $150,000 in loans has been granted since 1910.

- The Project, Sight Conservation and Aid to the Blind, the area in which alumnæ and collegians across two nations not only contributed financially but participate personally with total accomplishments reaching more than $6,000,000 and 100,000 hours clocked annually.

- International Education, a plan adopted after World War II whereby an international guest may live with a chapter for a year, with both guest and hostesses gaining in knowledge, 1945-1973.

When National Society for Prevention of Blindness holds its annual meeting, Delta Gamma is well represented, with NSPB board members, state presidents and executive directors.

Gifts of equipment and service aid the blind and partially sighted wherever Delta Gamma has a chapter or association in the United States or Canada.

"In these days of Foundations dealing in the millions of dollars, through my lifetime membership in Delta Gamma I have my own Foundation to which I may not only contribute financially but in which I may participate to the extent I choose."

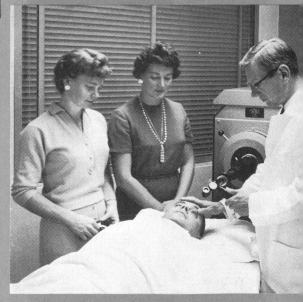

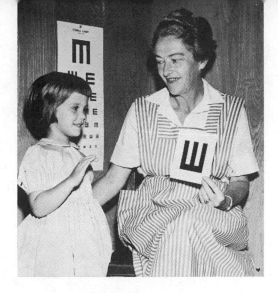

THE LARGEST area of Foundation participation is pre-school vision screening.

THE LARGEST single Foundation donation was the 1965 bequest of Margaret Price, Σ-Northwestern, $218,372.21.

THE ONLY Fraternity-wide ways and means project is The Delta Gamma Cook Book, launched at Convention 1966.

THE LARGEST continuing local ways and means project is the St. Louis Christmas Tree Lot.

THE OLDEST AND LARGEST locally sponsored institution for the blind is the Blind Childrens Center in Los Angeles.

THE
DELTA
GAMMA
COOK BOOK

SHINING LIGHT
XMAS TREE LOT
BENEFIT DELTA GAMMA ALUMNAE
NURSERY SCHOOL FOR BLIND TOTS

The Archives

*mementoes of the past
provide living
history—a section of
Executive Offices*

Dedication
Delta Gamma Archives
June 22, 1965

Brown's term of office. Hazel Brown under press of professional duties had submitted her resignation to take effect at the close of convention.

Fraternity examinations

After the 1936 Convention, a change was made in the traditional (or so it seemed) Fraternity Examinations, and in the vernacular of the day it was known as "a new deal." Instead of the annual examination for all members, it was now to be a pledge examination to be taken a few weeks prior to initiation, with panel discussions to be carried on once a month by the active chapter, covering the subjects which had previously come into the Fraternity Examinations.

Delta Gamma Dream Girl

And since at Convention a desire for a Delta Gamma sweetheart song had been registered, Alpha Kappa presented via the *Anchora* its "Delta Gamma Dream Girl" which has since become officially Delta Gamma's sweetheart song. It had been written by Ralph Stowell, an Alpha Delta (a Washburn local) for Vera Grace Rickenbocker, who was at that time president of Alpha Kappa chapter. Vera and Ralph later married and went to live in Horton, Kansas, according to this report in early 1937.

A Texas Judge

Not long after this Convention a story appeared in the Anchora *featuring Texas' first woman judge—Sarah Tilghman Hughes, Ψ-Goucher.*

19 — Pleasant and prosperous progress

The pre-war years

These were the pleasant and prosperous pre-war years, the years economists gleefully turn to and knowingly call normal. We had come—though not without a struggle—out of that worst of all depressions. The world seemed to be at peace, and security seemed to smile like the warm spring sun.

The themes for banquets, and conventions and conferences were pleasant platitudes like love and friendship and sisterhood—none of the serious and specific issues we later liked to face when we met together. Indeed, things seemed—even in reading our records these years later—not to move at all. On the contrary, however, move they did. Delta Gamma's progress, like the days at hand, was steady and settled. The future was bright, times were good, and plans could be made. Nothing needed to be attacked with a sense of urgency, and yet wheels turned rapidly because the road was smooth.

Return to Oxford

Founders' Day, 1937, had a special significance, for once more Delta Gamma was in the process of returning to Oxford, Mississippi, her home town. Because Alpha Psi's charter had

been held in abeyance for six years, too many classes had come and gone for any holdover of membership. It was, therefore, necessary once more to colonize. In the fall of 1936 three transfers from Ohio Wesleyan, under the direction of Province Secretary Dorothy Wildasin, had arrived in Oxford to take their part in the University of Mississippi's 1936 rushing season. Nine Ole Miss girls were pledged, and with the three transfers to inspire and assist, the colony was on its way.

The actual reinstatement of the charter did not take place until February, 1938, when a four-fold commemoration took place: The memorial services at the graves and the marking of the graves of two Founders; the official opening of Alpha Psi's new home, the Delta Gamma Memorial House; the initiation of Alpha Psi's pledge class, and the reinstatement of the Alpha Psi charter.

Memorial House

The campaign for funds for the Memorial House had been going on for some time, and now an assemblage of Delta Gamma officialdom arrived to view the finished product. Former

President Nancy Brown Woollett had worked long hours directing first the campaign for funds to build the house and then the actual construction, and wrote of the pillared colonial home: "Planned by Miss Ruth Darville, and furnished throughout by Miss Marguerite Dawson Winant, who is a licensed interior decorator, assisted by Mrs. James Madden and Miss Darville—it is all one's heart can desire in beauty and comfort."

At the time the Memorial House was constructed, all women at the University lived in the dormitory system. Consequently the house was designed to accommodate only a few—at first only officers, then seniors, and then as other groups were allowed to live in their houses (previously used only for meetings), and chapters grew, it became necessary for Delta Gamma to enlarge the Memorial House. Originally the Memorial House was to serve not only as a home for the Ole Miss chapter but also to represent Delta Gamma's contribution to the educational, social and cultural life of the University. It was to serve as a center for University activity where lectures, informal musicals and concerts, and meetings could be held and guests could be entertained. Former President Nancy Brown Woollett was the Memorial House hostess during the first year it was open and directed the beginning of this program.

In the March, 1938, *Anchora* "A House in Oxford Town—Alpha Psi's New Home," by Adeline Erlbacher,* Θ-Indiana, who had transferred to Ole Miss in 1937, is the number one feature—leading off in an issue that features outstanding Delta Gamma homes across the nation.

Delta Gamma treasures given to Miss Winant

During one of Miss Winant's trips to Oxford in 1937, she paid a visit to Minnie Wohlleben Carter, then very ill. To Miss Winant she entrusted the most cherished possessions of the Mother Chapter, the original minute book, the strongbox, and a great deal of correspondence. These things she had kept safe since 1889, and now she was ready to turn them over to the Fraternity. Miss Winant promised Mrs. Carter that these treasures would be kept in her posession until Delta Gamma had a place for them. This she did, sending them to Central Office soon after it was established.

Denison University

In the fall of 1937 on the Denison University campus in Granville, Ohio, a situation developed in which Delta Gamma would soon be playing a major role. When rushing was over, it was discovered that a large proportion of desirable girls had not been pledged. This was because of a

* Adeline Erlbacher was following her Delta Gamma mother's pioneering footsteps, for she was the daughter of the spirited alumnæ organizer of the twenties, Second Vice-President Irene Erlbacher.

sharp increase in the women's enrollment who had been rushed under a quota system set up the year before. Actively conscious of the high percentage of girls pledged at Denison each year, the college Panhellenic, desiring to keep up this high average, decided to invite another strong national to the campus immediately. Two Delta Gammas on the faculty—Helen Badenoch, Σ-Northwestern, and Helen Barr, Ω-Wisconsin, were largely responsible for the fact that the choice was Delta Gamma. Province Secretary Dorothy Knight Wildasin, AO-Miami, inspected the campus, approval of Denison as a field for expansion came quickly, and Council acted rapidly. Mrs. Wildasin directed the formation of the colony in November, 1937, and on May 13, 1938, Beta Zeta chapter of Delta Gamma was officially installed.

University of Texas

During 1938 another colonization project was in progress. The University of Texas had had its first inspection in November, 1937, and in February, 1938, First Vice-President Bingham arrived to find that the alumnæ in Austin had lined things up so that they were in complete readiness for an actual beginning of a colony. Mrs. Bingham talked to six girls who had been selected as a possible nucleus for a colony, and they subsequently became just that. In May, Mrs. Bingham returned and formally pledged fourteen members of the colony that was to become Beta Eta chapter. A successful rush season that fall furthered the colony's success, and on April 21, 1939, they were officially installed as Beta Eta chapter.

Who's Who

> The *Anchora* reprinted during 1938 from the Who's Who, *1937 edition, the Delta Gammas listed there: Grace Abbott,* Κ-Nebraska; *Ada Louise Comstock,* Λ-Minnesota; *Gratia Countryman,* Λ-Minnesota; *Dorothy Gardiner,* Φ-Colorado; *Alberta Pierson Hannum,* E-Ohio State, *and Gertrude Tressel Rider Harpham,* Λ-Mt. Union.

Twenty-ninth Convention 1938—Colorado Springs, Colorado

June 21-25, 1938, Delta Gammas assembled for the Twenty-Ninth Convention at The Broadmoor Hotel, Colorado Springs, Colorado. Beryl Barnett, AI-Oklahoma, former Province Secretary, was Convention chairman, and President Marguerite Winant, of course, held the gavel.

Guest of honor and keynote speaker was Ruth Bryan Rohde, Κ-Nebraska, who was presented with a diamond Delta Gamma badge for distinguished service.

Another Fellowship

A new Memorial Fellowship was created, this a $500 award to be known as the Corinne Miller Fellowship for Fraternity Service, honoring that energetic member of the mother chapter who had designed the Delta Gamma anchor and who was responsible for the first expansion.

Model chapter house

Ruth Darville, X-Cornell, Chairman of House Financing, reviewed "The Model Chapter House,"—a report that is still model in application to ideal fraternity accommodations.

This Convention was unique in that no Constitutional revisions were presented. Mary Longbrake Harshman, Λ-Minnesota, chairman of the revisions committee, reported that suggested revisions received by the Committee on June 1 of that year had been too lengthy to prepare within three weeks before this Twenty-Ninth Convention. She, therefore, moved that all revisions be postponed and referred to the Thirtieth Convention in 1940. This was agreeable to all concerned.

"Dignified publicity"

A publicity chairman reported under the title "Dignified Publicity"—a seemingly reticent approach, but in essence much like our present aggressive public relations program.

Balfour Contract

It was decided that L. G. Balfour would remain the one official jeweller of the Fraternity for the period 1938-40. This exclusive agreement had been entered into and announced to the membership and other fraternity jewellers the year before.

Elections, 1938

Elections at the close of this Colorado Convention included: First Vice-President Mary Myer Tobin, E-Ohio State, of Columbus, Ohio; Secretary, Dorothy Brown Holland, K-Nebraska, of Lincoln, Nebraska, and Treasurer, reelected, Edith Taylor Smith, AB-Swarthmore, of Philadelphia.

A new songbook

A new Convention exhibit was one of music—song books—from twenty-three panhellenic groups. A Delta Gamma song contest was on the program, too, with the first prize going to Alpha Kappa for "Delta Gamma Dream Girl." Second prize was Beta Delta's "All the Little Ships Go Sailing," and honorable mention, Beta Gamma's "Won't You Be a Delta G," and Alpha Chi's "Happy Hours."

Beekman Tower for the Fair

Anchoras *during 1938-39 were announcing Beekman Tower as fraternity headquarters during the New York World's Fair. During this same year a future article spotlighted Merry Hull (Gladys Whitcomb Geisman, AP-Ohio Wesleyan) who had revolutionized the glove-making industry with her "finger free glove."*

Los Angeles Nursey School for Visually Handicapped Children

On October 3, 1938, the Los Angeles Nursery School for Visually Handicapped Children, under the auspices of Delta Gammas in Southern California, was officially opened.

By January, 1930, the Fraternity Project was firmly enough established to warrant a special section in the *Anchora*. Under this heading—Fraternity Project—articles began to appear, not only of what Delta Gammas were doing, but also informative pieces like one in May, 1939, "The History of Braille."

Council resignations

In the spring of 1939 two resignations from Council took place—Dorothy Brown Holland who had served as Secretary, and Mary Myer Tobin who had been elected First Vice-President at the 1938 Convention. Alice Perry Gradle who had already served as First Vice-President, Secretary, and Treasurer of Delta Gamma, was appointed Secretary to serve until the 1940 Convention of which she was already chairman.

To fill the First Vice-President's office after Mrs. Tobin's resignation, Council appointed Roberta Abernethy, E-Ohio State, who until a few months before had been Secretary of the College of Arts and Sciences at Ohio State.

Duke University

The new First Vice-President's first duties included three installations in fairly rapid succession, considering Delta Gamma's pace during the preceding years. These groups had not been haphazardly chosen and installed as suddenly as this seems, but had been carefully groomed for some time for the Delta Gamma charters they were about to receive. Beta Eta, already reviewed, was the first for Miss Abernethy during that busy year. Then in June, 1939, Beta Theta chapter was installed at Duke University. Delta Chi had been organized the year before—February, 1938—and the 26 members who had in the intervening months been working toward this Delta Gamma charter were all destined to be initiated at this installation.

Gettysburg College

Beta Lambda chapter was installed October 7, 1939, at Gettysburg College, Gettysburg, Pennsylvania. The local from which this chapter was born had been organized in 1916 and was known as Beta Lambda, and so instead of becoming Beta Iota as they would have in the normal succession of the chapter roll, the group was allowed to skip a few letters and become Beta Lambda chapter of Delta Gamma.

NPC biennium—DGs very much present

At NPC's biennium in the fall of 1939 at the Greenbrier, White Sulphur Springs, W.Va., Delta Gamma was very much in evidence on the program, with Hazel Whitaker Vandenberg as banquet speaker and Jackie Martin, P-Syracuse, professional photographer, as speaker of the editors' banquet. Alta Gwinn Saunders was chairman that year of the editors' banquet.

Who's Who

Delta Gamma found a number of its members listed in Who's Who *that year—Elsie Singmaster, X-Cornell; Margaret Cammack Smith, Λ-Minnesota; Hallie Paxson Winsbrough, Δ-Fulton Synodical College; Margaret Shove Morriss, Ψ-Goucher; Lois Kimball Rosenberry, Υ-Stanford; Dr. Alice E. Gipson and Ruth Gipson Plowhead, both N-Idaho, and a group whose names have already been mentioned and had appeared previously. Interest in each issue of the* Anchora *in Delta Gammas with careers was shown, and in the January, 1940, issue, those with particularly colorful jobs were featured—starting with a résumé of the activities of screen star Brenda Joyce.*

Purdue University

Another Indiana chapter was added to Delta Gamma's roll on February 17, 1940, when Pedalion at Purdue University at West Lafayette became Beta Iota of Delta Gamma. Delta Gamma was the eighth national to be installed on the Purdue campus and as Pedalion the group had already established its reputation there. Pedalion had been organized three years before from a group of "unorganized girls" who were led by Jean Soehner, a transfer from Butler and Alpha Tau chapter.

The Anchora's *first reflection of the World War which had begun the fall before in Europe came in the May, 1940, issue with "London in War Time" by Eleanor Walker, ΑΛ-Drake.*

Thirtieth Convention
1940—Mackinac Island, Michigan

The Thirtieth Convention, June 23-29, 1940, at Grand Hotel, Mackinac Island, Michigan, was destined to be the last time Delta Gammas "convene normally" until World War II had been brought to an end. Naturally with the four Canadian chapters already "at war," a Delta Gamma War Project was discussed. It was finally resolved that local chapters would work locally with community Red Cross programs. Gifts from Convention of $100 each were sent to the American Red Cross and the Canadian Red Cross. Alice Perry Gradle was Convention Chairman with Province III chapters hostesses.

Marguerite Winant presided once more. Her keynote, "Friendship," inspired these words as Convention opened, "If fraternities accomplish nothing else in the world than creating and cementing of sincere friendliness among their members, their existence would be justified." She had, during her eight years as President of Delta

Gamma, visited every collegiate chapter and nearly all the alumnæ chapters.

The new First Vice-President Roberta Abernethy reported an increased interest in housemothers or chaperones of our chapter houses and their opportunity to influence the lives of our members. Their duties included personnel work, institutional management, hostess and chaperone. Miss Abernethy was preparing a manual of instructions for them. She also reported the progress through recent years of the Membership Committee in its contact with collegiate chapters and alumnæ.

Once more, a Central Office was considered, but no action taken.

A revised pledge service was submitted and accepted. The fraternity was to be officially registered as The Delta Gamma Fraternity.

Grace Abbott Fellowship

This Convention voted a $1,000 fellowship honoring Grace Abbott, K-Nebraska, former Chief of the U.S. Children's Bureau in Washington. Miss Abbott had died in 1939. A committee composed of Hazel Whitaker Vandenberg, Ξ-Michigan; Joy Webster Bowerman, K-Nebraska; Ruth Bryan Rohde, K-Nebraska; and Blanche Garten, K-Nebraska, was appointed to raise this amount and to award the scholarship during 1941-42 to a woman graduate of an American college or university, who had had experience in public social service, and who would submit an approved plan for a year of professional study with the object of returning to public welfare service.

Two DG deans speak

Adele Chomeau Starbird, ΑΕ-Washington University, Dean of Women at Washington University, addressed the Convention on the need of understanding and cooperation of the Fraternity and college administrations and their responsibility as good citizens. Dean Audrey Kenyon Wilder, Z-Albion, of Ohio Northern University also spoke.

The project committee reported considerable progress during its short existence, and noted especially the work of Southern California Delta Gammas in uniting efforts of various alumnæ groups to establish the Los Angeles Nursery School for Visually Handicapped Children.

Elections, 1940

Elected to office in the last session were: President, Florence Cornell Bingham, X-Cornell, who from 1930-38 had served as First Vice-President; and Second Vice-President, Jean Gooch Teall, Γ-California. Roberta Abernethy was elected to fill out the term of First Vice-President to which she had been appointed by Council when Mary Myer Tobin resigned, and Dorothy Knight Wildasin, ΑΟ-Miami, was to fill the office of Secretary for the remaining two years of the current term.

Mary Comfort Leonard

The last of the three Founders, Mary Comfort Leonard, died on August 4, 1940. She, of course, had been in longer contact with the Fraternity than the others, and was well known and loved by Delta Gammas everywhere. She was the only one of the original trio who had lived to see Alpha Psi reinstated for the last time at Ole Miss and the beautiful memorial house opened there. She, too, had had the pleasure of assisting in the initiation of her own granddaughter, Bettye Leonard, and later seeing her married in the Memorial House to John Long.

Project committee in one location

In 1940 a new project committee took office with Lois Robinson Richter, Λ-Minnesota, as chairman. Instead of members of the committee representing each province and resulting in a cumbersome by-mail transaction of committee business, the entire committee was to be located in a single city—in this case, Minneapolis-St. Paul. When, after a four-year term, the Council appointed a new chairman, it would be a city which would be appointed to provide chairman and committee.

Founders' portraits

Once more, on April 18, 1941, Delta Gammas' attention was focused on the Memorial House in Oxford, Mississippi, where the memory of the three Founders was being honored. The reason for the pilgrimage to Ole Miss at this time by officers and other representatives of 21,000 living Delta Gammas was the unveiling of portraits of the three founders. These had been painted by a well-known portraitist, Helen Humphreys Law-

rence, Λ-Minnesota, from a tintype of the three taken when they were students at Lewis School. At this time, too, the Delta Gamma pilgrims went on to Kosciusko to place a third tablet on a grave, this time, of course, on the final resting place of Mary Comfort Leonard.

University of Kansas

Another chapter was added on April 26, 1941 —Beta Kappa at the University of Kansas in Lawrence. This was one of the cases of colonization which had been thoroughly discussed and approved at the 1936 Convention at Lake Placid. Delta Gamma was the first national to be introduced on the Kansas campus in 24 years. Lacking housing, this new chapter experienced an exciting moment at its installation banquet when word was phoned that a beautiful pillared colonial home was theirs. This residence (designed as a fraternity house) became available when the charter of one of the campus fraternities was removed.

Manuscripts—Julia McCune

With the November, 1941, *Anchora*, Julia McCune, Z-Albion, took over the editing of the Manuscripts section in the *Anchora*, a post which she handled admirably until her resignation in 1962. Sarah Trousdale Mallory, N-Idaho, had pioneered this section under Editor Saunders and had reintroduced the literary endeavors of members to fraternity journalism. These articles and poems had been a major part of the sorority and fraternity magazines in their early days, but had been more or less dropped as other fraternity activity and achievements crowded out space for anything else.

Florence Cornell Bingham, X-Cornell, President 1940-47, served the Fraternity admirably as its World War II President. She received the Order of the Rose for distinguished work in the field of Education, and a Memorial Fellowship carries her name.

World War II

In the years since World War II, people seem to enjoy shuddering together comparing a specific bit of reminiscence: "What were *you* doing when you heard about Pearl Harbor?" Delta Gamma, though already its Canadian chapters were much involved in the war in Europe, was probably not unlike most United States citizens—going along from day to day, doing as much as its allied sympathies indicated that it should, but still planning a large Convention on the West Coast for June, 1942.

Council meeting was, in fact, in session on that December 7 in New York. Then, of course, came the news of the disastrous Japanese attack and, like everyone else, Delta Gamma changed those plans. Even the January *Anchora* had gone to press with stories of the glorious Thirty-first Convention to be held at the Hotel Del Monte on the Monterey Peninsula in California.

Convention "at war"

By March the entire outlook of the magazine had changed and a different sort of Convention was scheduled. The March *Anchora* featured Canadian Delta Gammas already at war—and in uniform. A news story reprinted from the Detroit *News* was included reporting "no word" from newswoman Gwen Dew, Z-Albion, who was assumed to be a prisoner of the Japs in Hong Kong, a fact later confirmed. President Bingham's editorial was "Meeting the Challenge."

Thirty-first Convention
1942—Chicago, Illinois

No blurbs attracted *Anchora* readers to the forthcoming Convention. Council merely announced that the Thirty-first Convention of the Delta Gamma Fraternity would be in session at the Edgewater Beach Hotel, Chicago, June 25-29, 1942—business only.

This first Convention ever held with the United States at war was in every sense a wartime Convention. President Bingham, reports the

1945 *History,* justified Council's decision to call the 1942 Convention because of the urgent need of guidance for the collegiate chapters' in this emergency. The President's address closed on a high note of courage and faith, and it was not only the keynote of the work for the following Convention days, but of the three war years to come.

Workshops were geared to war schedules in which we were all involved, and the revisions to Constitution and By-laws were made to expedite Fraternity functions through the war years.

Fraternity Project

The Fraternity Project played an important part in this Convention, Chairman Lois Richter giving splendid reports of current project activity. The Committee recommended that a Delta Gamma War Project be a part of "Our own Fraternity Project, 'Aiding the Blind'; that it be carried forward locally as needed; that a fund be provided by the 1942 Convention as a nucleus for war work to be known as the Delta Gamma War-Blind and War Emergency Fund and to be increased by voluntary contributions by individual members and chapters and associations and to be administered by the project committee and Council, and built up as a reserve pending a need during or after the war. It was further recommended that a sum of $1,500 be appropriated from the Alumnæ Service Fund to establish this War Fund." This motion was made and accepted by the Convention. It was discovered, however, that federal legislation for the war blind made the use of such a fund doubtful. As local needs arose, however, local Delta Gamma groups were on hand to assist as requested.

It was at this wartime Convention that the Project became By-Law XVIII: "The Fraternity shall carry on the Fraternity Project of Sight Conservation and Aid to the Blind.

"The general committee shall act as a clearing house for information, shall direct Fraternity publicity on the Project and shall receive reports from local groups. Each local group shall decide upon and finance its own Project work.

"Any group may send money to the treasury of the Fraternity to be allocated to the Fraternity Project Fund. Such money may be spent on any phase of the Project recommended by the committee and approved by Council."

New Song Book

A new edition of *Delta Gamma Songs*, edited by Marian Neil Giger, ΑΔ-Oregon, was introduced at this Convention, and the seemingly 24-hour-a-day business sessions for collegiates was interrupted long enough to entertain midshipmen from the Naval Training School at Abbott Hall at a dinner dance.

Elections, 1942

The Nominating Committee listed this slate: Dorothy Glenn Holsinger, I-Illinois, First Vice-President; Edith Taylor Smith again for Treasurer; and Dorothy Knight Wildasin, ΑΟ-Miami, to continue as Secretary. This slate of officers was accepted unanimously by the Convention.

Central Office

Probably the most important action of this 1942 Convention was that it made a Central Office, in true office form, a reality. Roberta Abernethy, who had completed her term as First Vice-President became Delta Gamma's first Executive Secretary, returned to Columbus with, no doubt, mixed emotions on the subject. She had a gigantic task before her. Well-schooled and experienced in the type of work which was the best sort of background for what was at hand, she knew that in normal times the organization of a national headquarters was no small job. And now even the procurement of a typewriter or filing cabinet brought shaking heads and "There's a war on, you know." By September 1, however, mid packing boxes and cartons (everyone was delighted to ship their long-accumulated files to Columbus to be stowed away in this new office), the new Executive Secretary and one assistant, Jean Pierce, E-Ohio State, were officially in business. A report some months later in the *Anchora* claimed that what actually put the office in business was the arrival of 52,000 membership and geographic cards from the Secretary and fifteen cartons of financial records from the Treasurer.

Even before Council could meet again it was seen that the space allotted for a Central Office was too small, and Council approved by correspondence the enlarging of quarters within the limits of the budget set up for that purpose.

House rules adopted

Before this 1942 Convention Council had met at the Edgewater Beach. (Most business concerned the Convention at hand.) The First Vice-President had offered a set of house rules to be used by chapters living in their house; this was accepted by Council.

Wartime planning

Council met following the Convention, too, taking care of business which had accumulated as a result of Convention. The new Central Office was an added project, and, of course, the possibility of this being the last Convention for some time because of the war touched every aspect of Fraternity business.

During the expansion projects of the past few years transfer students had been used with considerable success in aiding new colonies. An outstanding example of this was, of course, the reinstatement of a chapter at Ole Miss. The assistance they offered new groups was quickly seen to have equal possibilities with older groups, which, for some reason, needed this special sort of adviser. These transfers were students, living and eating with the chapter, not—as in the case of the alumnæ advisory board—just attending chapter meetings. At this post-Convention Council meeting a program to use these transfers to the fullest extent during the war was set up. Special assistance was worked out for new groups needing aid in rushing.

Council correspondence during November, 1942, indicates that much business still surrounded the newly opened Central Office. It was natural that details which no one had thought of at the post-Convention Council meeting should arise.

President's reports

These were the bleak years of the war when it seemed to go on and on and on, and we were all in some way part of it. Council had shouldered the complete responsibility of fraternity government "for the Duration." No Convention was in sight. Through *Anchora* editorials, Florence Bingham's warmth and clarity of expression made every member a part of all that Delta Gamma was doing—even though only these five officers, with the Editor and Executive Secretary, were attending to the actions themselves. Now, reading back over these bits of history makes one feel that Florence Bingham's reports were one of her great contributions to her Fraternity.

Bowling Green State University

Another chapter was added on November 6, 1943, when Skol, a twenty-year-old local at Bowling Green State University, Bowling Green, Ohio, became Beta Mu chapter. Council met following installation in Toledo for three days.

Office duties expand

The duties of Central Office continued to expand. This Council meeting decided: "Council approved of the Central Office sending out all reports instead of the chairmen. The chairmen are to send the material to be sent out to the Central Office." And another notation: "council will approve any changes made by the Treasurer and Executive Secretary in bookkeeping." Central Office was rapidly becoming the capitol of Delta Gamma.

An alumnæ manual to be gotten out by Mrs. Teall and a financial manual to be compiled by Mrs. Smith were both authorized.

Carnegie Institute of Technology

Council met again early the following year—January 29-February 3—in Pittsburgh in connection with their attendance at the installation of a chapter at Carnegie Institute of Technology. This was the installation of a local—Gamma Phi Sigma—which had petitioned Delta Gamma when all the locals at Carnegie Tech were given official sanction to join national fraternities.

Field secretaries—a beginning

Though no formal program involving field secretaries had yet come about, it was at this Council meeting that such a program had its beginning. At this time Council made provision for a member of the Central Office staff, Jean Pierce, E-Ohio State, to visit a collegiate chapter to aid with chapter problems. This was to be one of many such trips for Jean, who was later followed by other members of the Office staff—Delta Gamma's first field secretaries.

Wartime on campus

During these days WACs and WAVEs, and members of all the other US and Canadian branches of service for women dotted Anchora pages along with a larger than usual number of Mortar Boards and Phi Beta Kappas. (More of the latter, naturally, for with fewer social distractions, college women directed greater attention to studies and taking over campus offices usually held by men. Many were accelerating their classwork and qualifying for graduation in much less time than the usual four-year period.)

As might be expected, the war had by now topsy-turvied the entire academic world. Rushing was indeed a new and gigantic problem. With fraternity houses closing for the duration, the college officials seized these vacant residences gladly to house the greater influx of women on campuses. Thus, three and four times as many women as usual were entering college and rush lists were longer and longer. Fields for expansion which had been closed for ten or more years because of lack of sufficient increase in female enrollment were beginning to welcome new sororities with enthusiasm. Wheels were beginning to turn toward what was to become one of the greatest expansion periods in the history of the American fraternity system.

D-Day—in Columbus

Then, June, 1944. Instead of Delta Gamma attention being focused on another fabulous Convention spot, eyes were on maps of Normandie and the islands of the South Pacific and ears were attentive to the radio. As Helen Russell Byars, M-Missouri, then Province V Secretary, wrote, "The problems of Delta Gamma had, however, been intensified rather than diminished by the exigencies of the war, and in lieu of Convention Council called the province secretaries to a five-day conference and training school in Columbus, Ohio, June 6-11." Most of us will remember June 6 quite well—D-day and the invasion of Europe, so long awaited.

Council met at the same time, and to the background of news broadcasts laid plans to publish Delta Gamma's History in January's *Anchora*. Reports were made by members of Council, the Editor, the Executive Secretary, and the ten province secretaries. Much of this Council meeting was devoted to special sessions with province secretaries who reported on their various chapters and received instructions.

Anchoras, as we look back on these war issues, were a mirror view of women and the war. The November, 1944, issue carried a story about Dean Audrey Wilder, Z-Albion, of Bowling Green State University and her summertime factory job; a wedding in England of a Delta Gamma whose future husband had first spotted her anchor when she went to work for the US Foreign Service in London; Washington and the war; the launching of the Liberty Ship SS John Goucher which had been christened by Ensign Janet Miller, Ψ-Goucher, granddaughter of John Goucher—this was a typical issue along with its reports of Delta Gammas recently enlisted in women's branches of the armed forces.

Farewell at Stanford

This issue carried, too, a farewell to one of Delta Gamma's oldest Western chapters—Upsilon of Stanford University. The Stanford administration had been hostile to fraternities for some time and had laid down a number of restrictions to housing and membership which had meant that, as Stanford's women's enrollment increased, its sorority membership remained static. This had caused anti-fraternity feeling to sift from administration down to the growing number of nonaffiliated women. The obvious solution—to allow more Greek groups to enter the campus (there were only nine sororities at the time)—was denied. The dean of women regarded the sororities simply as units for housing and when the University adopted absolute control over the housing of women, the end of their existence was in sight. Finally the board of trustees acted to deprive women's fraternities on the campus of active status, and the nine NPC groups which could no longer pledge turned in their charters. Within a few years, of course, the remaining members had been graduated.

The 1945 History

January, 1945, was something special in the way of *Anchoras*. It was the History issue, dedicated to long-time fraternity officer, Alice Perry Gradle, who had died in October, 1944. The chairman of the 1945 Delta Gamma *History* was former President Nancy Woollett; it was edited by Alta Gwinn Saunders and among the contributors to this complete review of Delta Gamma's past were President Bingham; Mrs. Gradle; Edna Nowland, T-Iowa, chairman of student loan; Lois Robinson Richter, Λ-Minnesota, project chairman; Nancy Lamb Orr, T-Iowa, historian; and Roberta Abernethy.

A new Project chairman was appointed during the year with Rochester, New York, the committee's home and Irene Howell Forman, AK-Washburn, chairman.

War's end in sight

With the end of the war in sight by the spring of 1945, chapters—inspired first by Delta Gammas in Minneapolis—were supporting the appointment of Ruth Bryan Rohde as delegate to represent United States women to the international peace conference.

When the United Nations Conference opened in San Francisco there were a number of Delta Gammas present as official delegates to study international organization. Three prominent ones were Mrs. Rohde; Delta Gamma's president, Mrs. Bingham, and Hazel Whitaker Vandenberg. The November Anchora covered not only their activities but the part the San Francisco alumnæ in the area had played in entertaining for the trio during their stay there. During the conference Mrs. Vandenberg launched the Victory Ship New World Victory.

Newly appointed officers came to Central Office early in the summer for a training school.

Field secretaries and publications

June 28, 1945, found Council assembled at Bigwin Inn at Ontario for meeting. Now field secretaries were very much part of the collegiate program—a growing necessity with the expansion that was taking place during the year and the few years to come. Four field secretaries were authorized at this meeting, all to be directed by the Executive Secretary.

A large number of publications were discussed —the recently published songbook, the *History*, a pledge manual, pledge mistress' manual, treasurer's manual, housemother's manual, president's manual, house corporation booklet, house rules, Mothers Club publicity, *Alumnæ News Letter*, a foreign letter, rushing manual, procedure for installations and so on. The songbook and history issue of the *Anchora* were already in the hands of the membership, and the pledge manual was merely to be revised. All others were in production and to appear during the coming year.

21—*All expansion records are broken*—

The post-war period

Delta Gamma President Florence Cornell Bingham was a special delegate to the United Nations 1945 San Francisco conference and here addresses a session.

In August the war ended and we were catapulted into a new era. Gas could be bought with abandon and nylons would be on the market again soon. Colleges heaved a sigh of relief and began to relax tight wartime schedules—realizing, however, that in reality their problems were only beginning. Housing—all kinds, any kind, some of which had been the property of women during the war—would have to be converted for the surge of veterans campus-ward on the GI Bill. With war-postponed weddings taking place rapidly, apartments—GI villages, would have to be found, too, for many honeymoons were to begin on the nation's college and university campuses.

College women who had been freshmen during the middle of and late in the war were suddenly plunged into a completely different sort of campus life, and those whose degrees had come a little earlier just before all this excitement began were longing to be back—so along with the tremendous increase in undergraduate registrations, there was a proportionate increase in the heretofore forgotten segment of the student body, those in graduate school.

Increased enrollments of women during the war meant that many colleges were again applying to the NPC groups for chapters. At the same time, government aid during and after the war had enabled many campuses to provide facilities that increased their standing, and Delta Gamma was looking around at schools she had snubbed as "not meeting our standards" in former years. During the first post-war years Delta Gamma broke all her own expansion records.

George Washington University

In the fall after the end of the war, there was a twin installation in Washington, D.C.—Beta Rho chapter at George Washington University and Beta Sigma at the University of Maryland in suburban College Park. The Themians, a local at George Washington, had been interested in Delta Gamma by Idaho transfer, Flavia Lee, N-Idaho, and the way was smoothed by the University president's wife, Dorothy Betts Marvin, AΠ-Arizona. After an official inspection of the two year old group in April, 1945, plans were formulated for a fall installation.

University of Maryland

Simultaneously, other Washington Delta Gammas were stirring up a little activity on the University of Maryland campus ten miles away. Beta Sigma was colonized so it was more than "a little activity," and included a real rushing period and series of interviews with prospective sorority women until a nucleus was selected late in June. A house was ready for rushing and moving into in September, and Beta Sigma was officially installed along with Beta Rho during the week of October 5, 1945—Beta Rho installed October 6 and Beta Sigma, October 12.

Council meets—Fall, 1945

Council met again between these installations in Washington D.C. With plans already under way for Delta Gamma's first post-war Convention, much discussion was on this gigantic task.

Willamette University

A month later, November 10, Council representatives traveled west for another installation—Beta Pi, Willamette University, Salem, Oregon. Beta Pi was the installation of the local, Delta Phi, as a Delta Gamma chapter. Delta Phi had been organized in 1920, the second women's group on campus, and had its own house in 1928.

Michigan State College

January 5, 1946, was a day on which another chapter was added to the roll—Beta Xi, Michigan State College, East Lansing, Michigan. This was another case of colonization and field secretary assistance.

University of Miami

An expansion chairman with less spirit and vigor than Secretary Dorothy Knight Wildasin couldn't have kept up with the crowded installation schedule during 1945-46. No sooner had the Michigan State chapter been sent officially on its way than attention must turn to Florida and the University of Miami at Coral Gables. Eight girls were pledged in the spring of 1945 to form the nucleus of this Beta Tau colony and in the fall Field Secretary (another from Central Office) Mary Jeanne Barricklow Bohannon, E-Ohio State, arrived to assist with rushing and preparing the group for installation in February.

Transfer aid approved

With installation bringing Council members together frequently, Council meetings were likewise frequent. This speeded the pace of business which would otherwise have been handled by mail. After the Michigan State installation Council assembled at Dearborn Inn, Dearborn, Michigan. A month later they were in session in Miami during the Beta Tau installation. Council approved the following setup for transfers who would be assisting with colonies or new chapters: 1. Pay tuition. 2. Pay over and above room and board they have been paying on the other campus. 3. Pay one round trip to new campus.

University of Pennsylvania

The spring season was a time for even more installations involving cross-country hops. April 6-7 Beta Phi was installed at the University of Pennsylvania in Philadelphia. This was another colonization with assistance from a field secretary and three transfers. Again in connection with this installation Council met.

Oregon State College and Washington State College

Three weeks later April 26-28, another colony was installed as Beta Upsilon at Oregon State College, Corvallis, Oregon. Jean Pierce, field secretary, and Central Office veteran, assisted this group and then traveled on to Pullman, Washington, and another colony—the embryo Beta Omega chapter at Washington State College—was installed on October 30.

International Education

With the end of the war Delta Gamma's international education project was set in motion. This venture into international education was headed by Irma Twining Madden, Θ-Indiana, and during the 1945-46 school year Alpha Delta, Beta Kappa, Lambda, Beta Mu, Beta and Phi all had foreign student guests. Alpha Zeta, having no house, made it a Panhellenic project. Alpha Omicron assisted in the support of a Polish girl; Beta Epsilon entertained a Finnish girl and pledged three Icelandic girls.

Thirty-second Convention
1946—Pasadena, California

The March, 1946, *Anchora* opened enthusiastic pages with this headline: "Delta Gamma will hold its long-postponed Convention this summer!" The place for this Thirty-second was to be the Hotel Huntington, Pasadena, California, and the dates July 10-15. Margaret Tindall Pyle, AΣ-UCLA, was the chairman for this which was one of Delta Gamma's largest Conventions to date—the guest book including some 700 names, over eight hundred attending the Convention banquet.

Prior to this Convention another five-day officers' training school was held at the Alpha Nu chapter house in Los Angeles.

Colorful and festive these California hostesses made this Convention with a continuous social whirl during all non-business moments on the crowded schedule. The various alumnæ and collegiate groups in the area were hostesses at these affairs which included a spectacular water ballet and a dance, luncheons, teas, receptions, and a "Stuntcapade," at which the Convention song contest winners were honored—Harriet Harlow, BK-Kansas, taking first place with DG *Dreams*.

Again a Delta Gamma Convention entertained the officers of other NPC groups at a Panhellenic session.

Businesswise this Thirty-second Convention accomplished much, too. The Project Scholarship Fund was set up, sending our Fraternity Project into a new field of accomplishment.

The Constitution and By-laws were amended to recognize the Central Office and Executive Secretary officially. Though both had been voted into existence at the 1942 Convention, they did not become part of Delta Gamma law until 1946.

Reporting for the first time at a Convention were the International Education committee and a field secretary.

Elections, 1946

Elected to office at the closing session of the Convention were Florence Bingham once more as President and Helen Russell Byars, M-Missouri, Second Vice-President.

University of Denver

At the model initiation at this Convention three members of the group soon to be chartered at the University of Denver were initiated. They returned to their campus in the fall, and on September 27 Beta Chi chapter was installed and the rest of the members of the colony were initiated.

Colonization: Tennessee, Alabama, Tulsa, Texas Western

Meanwhile, colonization was beginning at several points through the South and Southwest. The University of Alabama and the University of Tennessee, The Texas College of Mines (later to become Texas Western College) and Tulsa University—all were scenes of much Delta Gamma activity as colonies were formed. Beta Psi at Alabama, Gamma Alpha at Tennessee, and Gamma Beta at Tulsa, all had their start in 1946 and were installed during 1947, while Gamma Gamma at Texas Mines was installed in 1948. The latter was a local group which petitioned Delta Gamma. Field secretaries were assigned to aid all of these groups during their early days.

Province Alumnæ Chairmen

Following the installation of Beta Psi at the University of Alabama February 8, Council went to nearby Birmingham and the Hotel Tutwiler for a meeting. Mrs. Byars presented for the first time her plan for a Province Alumnæ Chairman organization and a stepped up alumnæ program. Council approved and voted that she could present any part of her program to the alumnæ as soon as she wished.

Mrs. Bingham resigns

At the close of this meeting Mrs. Bingham presented her resignation as President of the Fraternity. Later, at a Council meeting held in conjunction with the installation of Gamma Beta at Tulsa, March 22, Treasurer Edith Taylor Smith was appointed to the Presidency by Council to serve until the 1948 Convention.

May 12-16 Council met again this time in connection with the installation in Knoxville, Tennessee, of a chapter at the University of Tennessee. The Council went to nearby Gatlinburg's New Gatlinburg Inn for its meeting.

Treasurer appointed

Margaret Smallpage Banker, Σ-Northwestern, former Province Secretary, was appointed Treasurer in Mrs. Smith's place to serve, too, until the 1948 Convention. She assumed her duties as Treasurer on May 14 during this meeting. Again the discussion centered around expansion and a forthcoming Convention.

Again, early in the summer a training school for newly appointed officers was held in Central Office.

Louisiana State University

The fall of 1947 saw more busy colonization under way. A group was being formed at Louisiana State University, Baton Rouge, aided by a field secretary. This was to become Gamma Zeta chapter when it was installed in March, 1948.

Montana State College

At Montana State College a group of six had signified their desire to become a Delta Gamma colony and were, after official inspection, pledged by Pi chapter at the University of Montana. Montana State was to be Gamma Delta chapter after its installation January 31, 1948.

NPC Biennium

National Panhellenic met in 1947, and Delta

Gamma's Council held its meeting once more in conjunction with Panhellenic sessions—November 15-21. The program for Convention was approved.

Three weeks later Council met again at Kent during the installation of the chapter there.

Kent State University

At Kent State University, Kent, Ohio, education groups had turned in charters in order to petition NPC groups and Delta Gamma's Gamma Epsilon chapter was installed early in December, 1947. This was the last time a change of this sort could take place for in November, 1947, when National Panhellenic convened, it was agreed to begin proceedings to open NPC to education, Catholic and Jewish sororities. Eleven groups of these were admitted to associate membership at that time and in two years became full members.

San Jose State College

On the West Coast at San Jose State College, San Jose, California, another local whose petition to Delta Gamma had been accepted was awaiting its charter. Gamma Eta chapter was thus installed during the early spring of 1948.

Alumnæ Expansion

While collegiate expansion had been occupying the front pages, the alumnæ organization was undergoing expansion of its own. Helen Russell Byars had presented her program to the alumnæ and had, with Council approval, appointed the first contingent of Province Alumnæ Chairmen. Though the program itself had to become part of the Constitution and By-laws at the forthcoming Convention, it was by no means "unconstitutional" in this first year. Council is given the power to appoint chairmen and to bring them to Convention—thus, the title chosen for this group of officers. That even their earliest operations were paying off was obvious in the steady increase in organized alumnæ groups. Led and inspired by Second Vice-President Byars, the PACs were keeping alumnæ activity in line with wide collegiate expansion.

All of this was reported by Mrs. Byars when Council met in Columbus at Central Office, March 25-April 1, 1948. This Council session also decided that an aggressive public relations program should replace the current publicity setup.

22 — Joy with sadness, and business as usual

Diamond Jubilee

It was a glorious Diamond Jubilee which had been planned by the charming and capable Thirty-third Convention chairman, Irene Howell Forman, AK-Washburn, at the New Ocean House, Swampscott, Massachusetts, June 22-28, 1948. The gaiety of the occasion seemed dimmed from the beginning, however, for a number of highly controversial constitutional changes were to face the delegates as well as an unprecedented three-way candidacy for the remainder of the current term of office of President. And then, when Council convened a few days before Convention was scheduled to open, the gala spirit of the affair received a final blow. Word came suddenly that *Anchora* Editor Alta Gwinn Saunders, I-Illinois, had been killed in a plane crash en route to the Convention.

Editor's death severe loss

This was a loss felt keenly by Delta Gamma, and spontaneously Conventioners felt the desire to act immediately to memorialize an outstanding and well-loved member. Alta Gwinn Saunders, in what seemed to be an editorial tradition, had persued a career in which she had made her name well-known. She had been editor of the *Anchora* since 1934 and during this time had become head of the business English department at the University of Illinois. She was the author of a number of business English texts, widely used on the college level.

Memorial to Editor

Throughout Convention members and entire province delegations made trips to the platform to make monetary donations to a Memorial Fund and to eulogize Mrs. Saunders. One of the first such donations was a bag of silver dollars from the West's Province XII.

There was much discussion as to just what this memorial should be and finally a committee was appointed to make arrangements at its own discretion. Retiring First Vice-President and fellow member of Mrs. Saunders' own Iota chapter, Dorothy Glenn Holsinger, was made Chairman of the group.

Political Interest

As frequently happens during Delta Gamma Conventions, one of the U.S. political party Conventions was in progress simultaneously— the Republicans were meeting in Philadelphia where a Delta Gamma husband, Arthur Vandenberg, was being offered the candidacy for President which he turned down because of Mrs. Vandenberg's health and probably his own, too. This Republican Convention kept Hazel Whitaker Vandenberg from joining the Delta Gamma conclave at Swampscott, but because the Democrats would not meet until several weeks later another of the nation's political leaders, Ruth Bryan Rohde, could be there and was the banquet speaker.

Pageant

However, a full and complete Convention program had been planned including an elaborate historical pageant depicting in song and costume the history of the Fraternity. This had been written and produced by Jane Cowell, AX-Penn State. Each chapter, to celebrate this diamond jubilee, had dressed a doll depicting the formal dress at the time the chapter was installed. For the first time, a formal Memorial Service, honoring members who had passed from us during the two year interim was held at the first evening meeting. This service had been written by Jane Cowell also.

Possible among the best remembered points of this Convention was the New Ocean House cuisine—and some delegates claimed at the close of the Convention to have gained ten pounds during the six-day session. Also well remembered by many was the "Virus X," a twenty-four hour flu which vacated many delegates' seats on the floor of Convention each day.

Province Alumnæ Chairmen official

It was at this 1948 Convention that the Province Alumnæ Chairmen were first formally introduced and a Constitutional provision cleared the way for the continuation of the "operation alumnæ" which had begun the preceding year. A by-law covering and earmarking the various Fraternity funds was also enacted.

International Education guest

One of the International Education guests was present and was presented at one of the evening meetings of this Convention. The appearance of this charming and colorful guest, who had been initiated by her hostess chapter, Beta Mu, completely sold the program to the many who had had no contact with it previously.

Convention decisions

- **Consecutive terms** would be limited to two for each Council office. It was decided that this should go into effect at the close of this Convention to allow several of the candidates for office in 1948 to remain on the slate.
- **A public relations program** was to be set up by the Fraternity. This decision was made after delegates had listened to the report of Jean Speiser, K-Nebraska, a professional in this field. A PR program would replace what had formerly only covered publicity.

Elections, 1948

When the election, which had been one of the controversial issues of the Convention, was over, Edith Taylor Smith had, by an overwhelming majority, been returned to the office of President to fill out the remaining two years of the term to which Council had appointed her. Dorothy Knight Wildasin, who had been Secretary of the Fraternity since 1940, was elected First Vice-President, and Irene Howell Forman, now well known as Project chairman and Chairman of this Diamond Jubilee Convention, was made Secretary. Margaret Smallpage Banker, appointed in 1947 to fill out Mrs. Smith's term as Treasurer, was elected to her own term in this office.

Fall, 1948, Council meeting

The Homestead, Hot Springs, Virginia, was the scene of the fall Council meeting—November 7-13. For some time Second Vice-President Byars had been noting the progress of junior alumnæ groups, but this Council decided that for the time being they would remain affiliated with senior groups in the cities in which they were located. A great many policies were considered and formulated at this Council meeting, and the entire Collegiate program was reviewed and its future weighed.

University of Florida

In April, 1949, Gamma Theta chapter was installed at the University of Florida, Gainesville, Florida. The University had, until 1947, been a men's school, and women were enrolled at Florida State College for Women at Tallahassee. At this time both schools were made coeducational and sororities entered at Gainesville while the fraternities established themselves in Tallahassee. Delta Gamma colonized in the fall of 1948 with three transfers and a field secretary, followed second semester by six transfers and another field secretary to assist the new group.

June, 1949, Council meeting

Once more, in June, 1949, Council met in Co-

Edith Taylor Smith, AB-Swarthmore, President of Delta Gamma 1947-50, had served the Fraternity as its Treasurer since 1936. An untiring student of college and fraternity affairs, she contributed much during her fourteen years on Council.

lumbus, Ohio, this time at the Epsilon chapter house which was vacant between Spring and Summer Quarters. Unlike the hotel meetings Council had held for many years, this time the official group was able to direct its own kitchen and housekeeping, and possibly this return to chapter house living added a collegiate viewpoint to their decisions.

At any rate, it made it possible to entertain and meet with officials of Delta Gamma and other fraternity officials in the area during its meetings. Council was even fortunate in meeting with a representative group of active chapter presidents, for half a dozen "collegiate chiefs" from a widespread group of chapters for 1949-50 happened to be Columbus residents. Though a cook was hired to prepare luncheon and dinner each day, members of the Central Office staff volunteered their services, each taking a day during Council meeting to fix her own breakfast specialty for the official group. This Council session opened on June 12, the day after the officers had assembled to attend the 25th anniversary of Alpha Rho chapter in nearby Delaware, Ohio. The meeting closed on June 15.

Publications department in Office

At this meeting a new publications department was set up as part of the Central Office. This section of the office would house an editor who would handle all Delta Gamma publications, the

list headed, of course, by the *Anchora*. Since Mrs. Saunder's death, the magazine had been rotated among a group of guest editors: the November issue, completely prepared earlier by Mrs. Saunders, was produced by her secretary and Miss Abernethy; the January issue, by Miss Abernethy assisted by Central Office; March, Frances Holyoke McCoy, K-Nebraska, of Milwaukee, and May, Joan Murchison, M-Missouri, of New York. The permanent editor appointed by Council at this time was Frances Lewis,* Z-Albion, who had spent the preceding two years as field secretary for Delta Gamma, after a number of years of editorial experience and, in particular, magazine training. Her work was to be directed by the Public Relations Committee.

Council badge adopted

It was voted that an official Council badge be adopted for Fraternity officers, to be presented upon their election to office. All former officers would be entitled to purchase one of these official anchors, and future incoming officers would be presented with them at the time they took office.

Fall, 1949, Council meeting—NPC

Council met again in the fall of 1949 in conjunction with National Panhellenic meeting at Skytop Lodge, Skytop, Pennsylvania. It was at this time Delta Gamma became a member of the Executive Committee of NPC. Edith Smith as President and NPC delegate became NPC Treasurer.

Memorial Fellowship

The Grace Abbott Memorial Fellowship committee presented a recommendation for Council approval that the Grace Abbott fellowship be discontinued after the 1949-50 award had been made. Council voted to place this proposal on the agenda for Convention vote along with the further recommendation that this fellowship be replaced by another Delta Gamma Memorial Fellowship to be offered annually. The Grace Abbott Fellowship had been a part of Delta Gamma's philanthropic program since 1940.

Magazine agency

Mr. George Whitney, representing the Fraternity's investment counsel, Scudder, Stevens and Clark of Philadelphia, met with Council at Skytop, reviewing the Fraternity's current investments.

The possibility of a Delta Gamma magazine subscription agency had been suggested by the Westchester alumnæ and it was voted that they be asked to submit a detailed plan which, if ac-

* Six months after taking office the Editor was married and is better known to the membership as Frances Lewis Stevenson, a name which frequently confused pledges taking their initiation exam, who in listing the fraternity officers often included: Editor—Mrs. Robert Louis Stevenson.

cepted, would be headed by a member of that alumnæ chapter.

Finance meeting

March 13-17, 1950, the Finance Committee, with the Executive Secretary, met at the French Lick Springs Hotel, French Lick, Indiana. This meeting covered business largely dealing with housing and with the financial aspects of the Convention coming in June. It was at this time a change was made in the set-up of the Finance Committee: "Because so many of the decisions to be made by the Finance Committee involve policies and all policies are voted on by members of Council, it seemed logical that the Finance Committee be composed of all members of Council. It seemed logical too that the Treasurer be made the chairman of the committee."

Honor fifty-year members

Founders Day in 1950 was of special significance for Delta Gammas who had been members for fifty years or more. At this time the Golden Certificates were presented for the first time to these members so that all who had been initiated from the founding until 1900 were honored. In succeeding years fifty-year members from initiation groups of 1901 and so on received the certificate.

De Pauw University

Another 1949 installation took place December 3, DePauw University, Greencastle, Indiana. A colony of 39 members was formed in the spring to be aided until the end of the school year by two field secretaries. The local alumnæ had the housing problem solved by the time school opened and rushing began in the fall, and another field secretary was on the scene until installation took place in December.

Alumnæ program

During the three years since the Province Alumnæ Chairmen had been installed in office in 1947, the entire alumnæ program had plunged full speed ahead. By January, 1950, Second Vice-President Helen Byars was able to report 59 new alumnæ groups, including both new chapters and associations, in less than three years.

Post-war building boom

After wartime restrictions were lifted in 1945, all Panhellenic groups entered upon mammoth building programs. Treasurer Margaret Banker reported to the fraternity five years after the war's end, "To help in launching a building project, the fraternity housing committee, with the aid of the consultant architect, has prepared a house planning guide, stating minimum requirements and giving general suggestions for building the most efficient and attractive house at the most reasonable expenditure. The fraternity architect is now designing a model house which, it

is hoped, may be adaptable for various localities. In all cases, the major responsibility falls on the local house corporation and the success of all present building projects is due to strong alumnæ support."

University of California at Santa Barbara

Gamma Kappa chapter was installed in Santa Barbara, California, on January 28, 1950. Chi Delta Chi, a local on the University of California campus at Santa Barbara, had petitioned Delta Gamma, having organized 10 years before.

Alta Gwinn Saunders Memorial

The Alta Gwinn Saunders Memorial which had been authorized by the 1948 Convention was awarded in the spring of 1950. The committee, headed by former First Vice-President Dorothy Glenn Holsinger, had allocated $100 ($1,300 in all) to each province which would be awarded to the person in each province who wrote the best chapter history.

Thirty-fourth Convention
1950—Banff, Alberta

Under the direction of Convention Chairman Helen Mahan Hill, AI-Oklahoma, the public relations committee whose enthusiasm had been growing since its installation as a part of Delta Gamma operation late in 1948, threw itself into the preparations for the Thirty-fourth Convention. For this event members were eagerly looking forward to the remote and impressive background of the Canadian Rockies, for the Banff Springs Hotel, Banff, Alberta, was to be the site, June 25-30, 1950, the dates.

The hostess area, the Northwest, had gone all out to bring a little of their own areas to Convention. This they accomplished, but not without a few Customs problems. The eve of Convention found the Executive Secretary at the Calgary Customs House assuring the Inspector that each and every one of the Idaho potatoes which had been transported across the border would be baked and eaten in Canada! From potatoes she continued to Washington state apples and a motley assortment of other Convention supplies which had been shipped by enthusiastic (and successful) hostesses.

Summary of two years

Edith Smith who was completing her term of office as President summarized the previous two years in her President's report:

"Aims and goals were set high as befits Delta Gamma.

"In general they can be summarized as: greater stress on scholarship, standards, and service; expansion of alumnæ organization, development of new fields of endeavor and the strengthening of old ones. . . . The over-all picture does show a steady progress forward in every department and phase of Delta Gamma activities.

"The following steps under advisement at the last Convention have been taken:

"1. A consulting architect has been retained.

"2. A housing committee with the chairman not a member of Council was set up under the supervision of the Treasurer.

"3. The armed forces committee was created, and has made remarkable progress.

"4. The dolls exhibited at the last Convention have been brought into the Central Office as a permanent collection.

"In the field of reorganization the fiscal year was changed from May 31 to June 30 to make it possible to include all items in the year in which they were due or payable.

"Policies have been brought up to date and tabulated to become a matter of record.

"Central Office was expanded to take care of the editor's office."

Workshops and business

Well-planned workshops were a big part of this Convention and the minutes recorded some important actions on the floor of Convention:

• **Incorporation** was to be acted upon for the Delta Gamma Fraternity. This action which had seemed of such little importance to accomplish 50 years before would finally come to pass.

• **The Delta Gamma Foundation** was to be formed. This was an especially important move as it grouped all of Delta Gamma's philanthropic activity in one spot. It also provided a recipient for donations, memorials, and bequests for this important work.

• **A Delta Gamma Magazine Agency** was set up, This had proved a good source of revenue for philanthropies for other groups, and so Delta Gamma followed other footsteps.

• **A Delta Gamma Memorial Fellowship would replace the Grace Abbott Fellowship** which was being terminated after ten years of annual awards. The Memorial Fellowship would be awarded annually, and the first grant would be named to honor Hazel Whitaker Vandenberg who had died a month before Convention opened.

• **A Public Relations program** was an important part of this Convention. For the first time the Editor reported not only for the *Anchora* but for the publications division of Central Office of which *Anchora* had become a part.

Fraternities exit at Goucher

Another chapter was gone from the chapter roll when school opened in September, 1950. Goucher College had for several years been in a gigantic construction program, building an entirely new campus outside its old hometown Baltimore, in suburban Towson. When construction began, the college officials had made it known that when the campus moved from downtown Baltimore to new quarters, no provision would be made for fraternities. So as school closed in

June, Psi chapter was no more, though its delegate was recognized as an official member of the Convention at Banff.

Elections, 1950

At the last business session the following officers were installed: President, Helen Russell Byars, M-Missouri, who had successfully served a term as Second Vice-President, and Second Vice-President, Helen Million Preston, Ξ-Michigan, who had been one of the Fraternity's first PACs.

Council meeting, Fall, 1950

Council met at the Greenbrier, White Sulphur Springs, West Virginia, October 25-30, 1950. This choice of spot for Council meeting at this time was with an eye on the site for the 1952 Convention.

At this Greenbrier meeting Mavis Mann, AΞ-West Virginia, former PAC, was appointed Delta Gamma's delegate to NPC. In the past Delta Gamma's president had served as delegate, but generally it was felt that the office of President had become too time-consuming to handle the delegate's office as well. This was particularly true since Delta Gamma was now on the NPC executive committee and during 1953-55 would serve as Chairman of National Panhellenic.

The songbook committee was to be asked to have a new songbook ready for the next Convention.

It was also decided that a life subscription to the *Anchora* for those initiated before 1922, when the life subscription became part of the initiation fee, be reduced to $5.00.

Delta Gamma incorporated, Foundation formed

Council met at Central Office April 1-4, 1951. It was at this meeting that, with the assistance of Fraternity Attorney George Chamblin, Delta Gamma was incorporated and the Delta Gamma Foundation formed. This work had been started by R. T. Boehm (husband of Charlotte Drake Boehm, E-Ohio State) who was called into the Navy at the outbreak of the Korean action and was replaced by Mr. Chamblin. An agreement was formed with Mr. Weber, fraternity architect, whereby he was to supervise the enlarging of the Memorial House in Oxford.

Graduate Counselors

At this Council meeting a Graduate Counselors program was approved. Through this, program awards were to be made to Delta Gammas, outstanding in their campus and chapter work, to do graduate work on certain campuses where collegiate chapters of Delta Gamma needed some special type of assistance from an experienced member. Usually these awards were made to attract these graduate students to campuses where Delta Gamma had recently established a chapter. Undergraduate transfer scholarships of a similar nature were also to be offered as they had been for some time "to Delta Gammas still in college who would like to spend a year on a different campus and work with a new chapter."

Fresno State College

Another chapter was installed May 5, 1951, in Fresno, California, at Fresno State College—this being Gamma Lambda. When the college was opened to national groups, California Delta Gammas aided in the petitioning of Omega Xi Omicron for a Delta Gamma charter.

Florida State University

When Florida State College for Women in Tallahassee had become co-educational, it had also changed its name to Florida State University. With the added male student enrollment, new facilities were added to the University and women's enrollment increased, too. Delta Gamma was invited at this time to colonize, and so in the spring, 1951, the project began. A colony was formed and it was installed as a chapter September 19, 1951.

23 — The Foundation

Delta Gamma
at work

The year 1951-52 was declared by President Helen Byars to be devoted to the theme "Delta Gamma at Work," coming to its climax at the 1952 Convention. Not only were *Anchora* readers made conscious of this theme throughout the four issues that year, but a special booklet was issued, entitled, *Delta Gamma at Work*. This reviewed Delta Gamma's philanthropic activities through the years in scholarship, war work, the project and other fields of endeavor.

Anchora reading during the year was geared to what makes Delta Gamma's wheels go around, the November issue sketching, among other things, the work of Delta Gamma's professional assistants: Thomas M. Wallace, the Collegiate chapter accountant; George Chamblin, Delta Gamma's attorney; George F. Whitney, investment counsel representing Scudder, Stevens and Clark; Bertram Weber, architect, and Felix R. Konkle, fraternity accountant, who died shortly after this review was presented.

NPC biennium, 1951

Once more an NPC biennium was the time for a Delta Gamma Council meeting this time at the Williamsburg Lodge, Williamsburg, Virginia, December 2-7, 1951. This was the NPC biennium held in conjunction with the 150th anniversary of the founding of the first Greek letter fraternity, Phi Beta Kappa, which had had its start in Williamsburg in 1776.

The resignation of Mavis Mann as NPC delegate was received and the President, Mrs. Byars, was appointed to the office. She was to resign her office as President in order to serve as Delta Gamma's delegate to National Panhellenic, but to hold both offices until Convention could elect her successor the next summer.

Secretary Forman presented a Delta Gamma Expansion Guide which was approved by Council.

Delta Gamma, through its years of work in the field of Sight Conservation and Aid to the Blind, had established itself as an active aid to effort in this field. In 1951, Delta Gamma was recognized by the National Society for the Prevention of Blindness with the following resolution: "Whereas the Delta Gamma fraternity, through its scholarship program of grants and loans, has played an important part in the preparation of special workers for the field of sight conservation since 1945, and whereas the Delta Gamma fraternity is rendering effective service in stimulating public interest and enlightment in relation to the subject of eye health and protection, be it resolved that the Board of Directors of the National Society for the Prevention of Blindness convey its warm commendation and appreciation to the Delta Gamma fraternity for these valuable contributions to the movement to prevent needless loss of sight."

Order of the Rose

In the spring of 1952 another special Delta Gamma award was created—The Order of The Delta Gamma Rose. This was to be presented to

Helen Russell Byars, M-Missouri, who as Second Vice-President had initiated the PAC program, was President of Delta Gamma 1950-52 when she resigned to become the Fraternity's Panhellenic delegate, and Chairman of NPC 1953-55.

members who, through their outstanding achievements in their chosen fields of endeavor, had brought honor and distinction to themselves and to the fraternity. These presentations were to be made at Founders Day or Conventions.

For the first presentation of the Order of the Rose the following Delta Gammas were approved by Council: Lillian Ray Titcomb, M.D., Υ-Stanford; Virginia Sale Wren, I-Illinois; Ruth Bryan Rohde, Κ-Nebraska; Edith Abbott, Κ-Nebraska; Ada Comstock Notestein, Γ-Minnesota; Margaret S. Morris, Ψ-Goucher; Inez Robb, Ν-Idaho; Adele Starbird, ΑΕ-Washington University.

Book of Remembrance

At this time, too, the Book of Remembrance was presented to provide a living record of those who had contributed to the Foundation in memory of a friend or relative as well as a record of those they had so memorialized.

New publications

A new edition of the Delta Gamma songbook appeared in time for the 1952 Convention. It had been compiled and edited by Irene Blades, Θ-Indiana. Simultaneously, the Housing chairman and Treasurer Margaret Banker had compiled a new housing manual which, entitled *The DG House,* was presented at the 1952 Convention.

When Council met preceding the Greenbrier Convention all of the Fraternity's policies, coming under each Fraternity officer's realm of jurisdiction, were scrutinized carefully and approved in their final form.

Thirty-fifth Convention
1952—White Sulphur Springs, W.Va.

The Greenbrier, White Sulphur Springs, West Virginia, was a perfect setting of beauty and dignity for the Thirty-fifth Convention, one that was indeed to climax the year that had been dedicated to "Delta Gamma at Work." Each detail had painstakingly been taken care of by a Convention chairman from California, Margaret Richardson Hay, Υ-Stanford. Peggy Hay had visited the Greenbrier the fall before and from then until Convention time worked strictly by mail with her assistant chairman in the hostess Provinces III, IV, and V.

Project film produced .

The film "Visibility Unlimited," which had been compiled by the Detroit Project committee from contributed lengths of film from Delta Gamma groups throughout the United States and Canada, had its premier at the Greenbrier. Exhibits of all phases of Delta Gamma work were admirably displayed. The reports of Delta Gamma's standing committee chairmen were organized as round table discussions, groups appearing on the platform with the officer under whom the committee operated.

Convention speakers

During these panel discussions the fraternity attorney, George Chamblin, and investment counsel, George Whitney, reported in person to the Convention.

Two special Convention guest speakers were Grace Bok Holmes, representative of UNESCO, who reviewed the work of the United Nations division for which she worked, and Virginia Rowe Holmes, Χ-Cornell, of the Williamsburg Restoration. The post-Convention tour, which many were scheduled to take, was to go to Washington and Williamsburg, and so her discussion of the restoration was particularly timely. Mrs. Holmes directs the hostesses at the colonial capital.

President reports

President Byars in her report to the 1952 Convention stated:

"The following instructions were given by the 1950 Convention of Delta Gamma which was held at Banff, Canada:

1. Incorporate the Delta Gamma Fraternity, Incorporated and the Delta Gamma Foundation, Incorporated.
2. Institute the research and compilation of Delta Gamma History and transfer a surplus of $1,044.44 from the Alta Gwinn Saunders Memorial Fund for the further-

ance of this work.

3. Prepare and forward to Senator Arthur Vandenberg a Resolution honoring Hazel Whitaker Vandenberg who passed away shortly before the 1950 Convention.
4. Institute the research and compilation of a motion picture film depicting the activities of Delta Gammas everywhere in connection with charitable programs.
5. Set up a Central Magazine Agency to handle subscriptions secured by local groups or individual members, and set up a Memorial Fellowship to be awarded by the Grants and Loans Committee each year in memory of an outstanding Delta Gamma, using a part of the proceeds from the Magazine Agency sales for this purpose.

"It is with pleasure that I inform this Convention that all of the foregoing commissions have been executed by Council.

Mrs. Byars also reported:

Publications activity

"During the past two years much time and effort has been devoted to the preparation of Manuals and Booklets of Information. The following is a list of these publications:

Council Manual of Information and Fraternity
    Policies
Housing Manual
Expansion Pamphlet
Public Relations Booklet of "Know-How"
Delta Gamma Song Book
Delta Gamma At Work Booklet

Memorial Room

Also included in President Byars report:

"Since the 1950 Convention your council has been responsible for the building, or the remodeling of thirteen collegiate chapter houses. One of these was the remodeling and enlargement of the Delta Gamma Memorial House at Oxford, Mississippi, which is also the home of the Alpha Psi chapter. The membership will be interested to know that one of the rooms in the new building contains original flooring, wood trim, and fireplace taken from the Old Lewis School for girls where Delta Gamma was founded in 1873."

Convention awards

The awards were also a big part of this Convention with particular emphasis on scholastic achievement of chapters during the past two years.

For the first time the Fraternity award to the outstanding Delta Gamma active chapter was presented. This award is based on all phases of chapter life, campus, community and intra-chapter activities and relationships, and the relationship with the national organization. The award in 1952 was presented to Alpha Epsilon chapter at Washington University.

No changes were made in the Constitution and By-laws.

Election, 1952

Since Mrs. Byars had resigned as President the preceding fall in order to become Delta Gamma's NPC delegate, the remainder of her term had to be filled. Council veteran, Dorothy Knight Wildasin, who had already served as both Secretary and First Vice-President, was elected to this office. Margaret Richardson Hay, Υ-Stanford, was elected First Vice-President; Irene Forman was re-elected Secretary, and Helen Bradford Anderson, M-Missouri, became Treasurer of the Fraternity as this 1952 Convention closed.

Council came again to Central Office for its meeting November 9-15, 1952. Once more, though this was not a history-making session, many routine affairs of the Fraternity were covered and much business transacted and discussed.

Council meets, Spring, 1953
Presidents' pins

Looking over the site of the 1954 Convention was the reason for Council selecting Sun Valley, Idaho, as the spot for its meeting April 21-28, 1953.

Council decided to have Balfour produce a large badge, similar to the early Delta Gamma badges, for chapters to purchase as president's pins. Many old chapters were already possessors of the large, old pins which had been given to them by an early member of the chapter, and many of the new chapters were anxious to have a similar badge for their own president to wear.

Office building fund

Possible expansion for Central Office was discussed and a building fund for this purpose was to be set up.

The revisions to the Constitution which should be taken up at the next Convention were covered by Council.

A "Delta Gamma Serenade," which was written by the father of a Denison Delta Gamma, P. A. Losch of Pittsburgh, Pa., father of Barbara Losch, BZ-Denison, appeared in record form. Later in the year prizes were awarded to top salesmakers in collegiate and alumnæ chapters. Proceeds from sales went to the Foundation.

Anchora schedule revised

During 1953 the Anchora schedule was rearranged, this the first time in nearly fifty years. Instead of four issues to be distributed during the school year, the schedule was changed so that the quarterly issues appear seasonally: Spring, Summer, Fall and Winter.

Project growing

In reading these Anchoras of the early 1950's, one can see and feel the growing vistas of Delta Gammas in their work for and with the blind. Such headlines as "The Miracle of the Welcome Home for the Blind," "Kansas City has a Nursery School for the Blind," "A Class for Blind

Dorothy Knight Wildasin, AO-Miami, President 1952-54, contributed sixteen years of outstanding service as Province Secretary, Secretary, and First Vice-President, before she was elected to Delta Gamma's highest office. She has since been President of the Ohio Society for Prevention of Blindness.

Children," "Snack bars with blind operators," "Visual screening the Long Island way," "The Eyes of Texas—" and so on—these are indicative of the intense activity of Delta Gammas in project work. During these recent years, too, the project section is the official organ of the project committee known as "Visibility Unlimited," a section which expands to 16 pages in sight-saving green ink, in the summer issue of alternate years.

With the Fall *Anchora* now appearing just as schools open in September, this issue is geared to the collegiate membership, an overall picture of Delta Gammas on campus as the rushing season opens.

After the Labor Day Miss America contest in Atlantic City in 1953, Delta Gamma eyes followed with interest the travels by and awards made to an attractive blond Miss America from Pennsylvania. She was Evelyn Ay, BΦ-Pennsylvania. The following year with Evvy looking, on, another Delta Gamma won the Miss America talent contest—Barbara Quinlan, E-Ohio State.

North Texas State College

Gamma Nu of Delta Gamma was installed at North Texas State College, Denton, Texas, on November 22, 1953. For many years the members of Phi Gamma Kappa local sorority had hoped to someday affiliate with a national sorority. In 1952 the administration of the college announced that national sororities could come onto the campus. In due course, Phi Gamma Kappa petitioned Delta Gamma and the petition was accepted.

Delta Gamma becomes Chairman of NPC

When National Panhellenic Conference met in November, 1953, in Pasadena it was an event of special significance to Delta Gamma. At this time Helen Russell Byars assumed the chairmanship of National Panhellenic.

Council met again along with Panhellenic at the Huntington Hotel, Pasadena, California, Council being in session there, November 8-14 following the NPC meetings.

Texas Technological College

Texas was in the installation news again during 1953-54 with Gamma Xi chapter being installed at Texas Technological College, Lubbock, on March 6. This group had been colonized in October, 1953, and had been prepared for installation by a field secretary. Members of the colony for the first time wore a colony pin instead of the official pledge pin as colony members had previously.

Council meets Spring, 1954

Council met again in the spring at Dearborn Inn, Dearborn, Michigan, April 7-11, 1954, with a large amount of business concerning the Convention to be held in June. With Convention Chairman Marcia Connell Strickland, Ξ-Michigan, living nearby, it enabled her to be part of this discussion. The Editor, Frances Lewis Stevenson, Z-Albion, was also present for part of the session. It was at this time that she presented her resignation which would take place sometime during the following year as soon as a successor had been selected.

Indiana State Teachers College

At Indiana State Teacher's College, Terre Haute, Indiana, Gamma Omicron chapter was installed May 15, 1954. Gamma Gamma local had petitioned and was installed as Delta Gamma's 80th chapter.

IRAC organized

At the pre-Convention Council meeting at Sun Valley, Mrs. Byars reported on the reorganization and aims of the Interfraternity Research and Advisory Council.

Thirty-sixth Convention 1954—Sun Valley, Idaho

"Sun Valley is Fun Valley," was the Convention come-on gimick which opened the January, 1954 *Anchora* and when Convention assembled June 25-29 at Sun Valley, Idaho, it was, in truth, "Fun Valley." Convention chairman Marcia Connell Strickland, Ξ-Michigan, had used the gay informality of the famed ski resort's summer scene as the perfect background for Delta Gamma's Thirty-sixth meeting. On the pond in front of the Sun Valley Lodge a huge gleaming styrofoam anchor floated throughout the Convention. Alumnæ were housed in the Lodge, collegiates in the Challenger Inn, and meetings were held in the Opera House between. Delta Gammas were spilling over the tiny Sun Valley "village."

Nominating committee

This 1954 Convention decided that hereafter the Fraternity Nominating Committee should be elected rather than appointed by Council. The set-up was to provide for definite regional representation, and it was put into effect at Sun Valley so that at that time the 1956 Nominating Committee was elected.

Expansion policies outlined

Secretary Forman, who was also expansion chairman, set before Convention the summary of Expansion policies of the Fraternity.

1. To grant charters to petitioning or to colonized groups as Council and Convention decide is wise for the growth and strength of Delta Gamma and in accordance with the Fraternity Bylaws.
2. To grant charters in colleges meeting the highest standards of accrediting of the respective regional accrediting associations of the United States and southeastern and southwestern Canada.
3. To consider the academic prestige of the institution as an important factor in granting charters.
4. To give serious consideration to the financial stability and educational trends of the institution, in so far as possible.
5. To give serious consideration to the spirit of the institution as to whether or not it is favorable for fraternities.
6. That expansion chairman, during the early phases of an investigation, contact the nearby organized groups for their reactions before definite steps are taken for an official investigation.
7. To investigate fields which would add to the strength of Delta Gamma. That we not wait for an approach from the school or nearby alumnæ. That college campuses should be studied periodically, records and fields kept up to date and contacts with colleges kept alive.
8. That special consideration be given to an institution which gives special attention to the program of women and also to the recognition of women and women students in all departments, including evaluation according to the following points: are women represented on the Board of Trustees or similar body; is there a trained Dean of Women; is she a member of the policy-forming group; are women properly represented and recognized on the faculty; are scholarships, fellowships, and assistantships, etc., equally available to women; and are facilities of special interest to women given equal consideration in the institutional budget.

9. To give special attention to establishing chapters in the South, East, and New England, and to arouse alumnæ interest in these sections in advance of installation.
10. To give preference to the petitioning method on campuses recently opened to NPC groups if there are locals there.
11. To give preference to the colonization method on campuses where NPC groups have been established for many years.
12. To install new collegiate chapters in sections where the nearby collegiate and alumnæ members are enthusiastic about having another chapter and/or where it is advisable to have more chapters in order to maintain strength or to add strength where Delta Gamma is not represented.
13. That an investigating committee be composed of not less than three nor more than five members, including at least one Council officer, one province officer and one nearby Delta Gamma alumna. (At least two chapters must be represented.)
14. To give particular attention to the development of fields approved by Convention vote.
15. To install an average of not more than two new collegiate chapters each year.
16. To keep an open mind, in view of changing programs in higher education, on entering formerly specialized institutions.

Resolutions

Though a number of minor revisions were made in the Constitution and By-laws at this time, a resolution was adopted that a committee, appointed by Council, should be authorized to present a general revision to the 1956 Convention. It was added that this committee should work with Mrs. Gano Senter (parliamentarian for 1952, 1954 and now scheduled for 1956 Convention) to iron out parliamentary difficulties in the present Constitution and By-laws.

Another resolution asked "That the Council, at the next spring meeting, shall appoint a National Panhellenic delegate, to serve from the close of the NPC Biennium held in November, 1955, until our next Convention in 1956—at which time our revised Bylaws should provide for election and term of office and duties of our NPC delegate."

President's words

Through the years growing emphasis on alumnæ activity has developed in the fraternity world in general. In her presidential address, President Wildasin emphasized the responsibilities that each alumna member of the Fraternity should assume. Her address closed with what has become a much-quoted statement:

College campuses and American and Canadian communities need women whose feet are on the ground but whose eyes are on the stars, women who are doers and dreamers, women who are realists and idealists, women who live by the Golden Rule and give to the world kindness, understanding and tolerance. As Delta Gamma continues to grow in power and beneficence and as the immortal principles of our Founders take root in the fertile soil of our hearts and minds, we must remember that she who wears the golden anchor must wear it with pride and cherish its ideals but likewise she must deserve to wear it.

Outstanding chapters

At Sun Valley the Fraternity award to the outstanding chapter of the Fraternity was made. It was received by Alpha Nu chapter with Epsilon as runner-up and Kappa, Pi, Phi, and Alpha Upsilon following for honorable mention.

Delta Gamma Foundation

The Delta Gamma Foundation, which had been voted by the 1950 Convention and organized in 1951, presented a summary of its activities and its future. Mrs. Wildasin reported as follows:

"Delta Gamma's Foundation was incorporated in 1951 to provide a means by which Delta Gammas might act in concert with each other in the furtherance of exclusively charitable, scientific, literary, and educational objectives.

"At present the work of the Foundation includes our project program, Sight Conservation and Aid to the Blind, which was started in 1936, student loan funds which date back to 1909, fellowships since 1924 and our international education program begun in 1945.

"We have proceeded with caution and will continue in such a manner so that the most good can be realized from our Foundation funds. Council has been studying the organization plan of the Foundation and within the next two years we expect a definite plan of operation to be presented to the members and that by the 1956 Convention we should be ready to make additions to the constitution of the Foundation as might be needed and that by that time bylaws of operations should be ready.

"The Foundation is beginning to be known by our members and that must come before much is known to the outside world. Several of our chapters have made use of the Foundation in handling tax expense benefits for themselves—that by giving the money to the Foundation they have been exempt from admissions tax and in that way the total amount they have earned has gone to Delta Gamma rather than part of it to taxes.

"Funds for the Foundation can be provided by the following methods:

1. Allocations and gifts from the Delta Gamma Fraternity.

2. Outright gifts from Delta Gamma alumnæ, Delta Gamma collegiates and from non-members.

3. Book of Remembrance.

4. Living Trusts. It is sometimes advantageous to the donor to establish a trust by gift rather than by will. A living Trust is often attractive because the donor has the privilege of seeing his beneficiaries at work.

5. Wills.

6. Life Insurance Trusts. Excellent uses of life insurance to establish a charitable trust for Delta Gamma Foundation as beneficiary can be suggested by its underwriters.

"Gifts to Delta Gamma Foundation will be considered as charitable gifts and will be deductible as such for income tax purposes. Bequests by will also will afford advantages in the reduction of estate, inheritance and succession taxes.

"Contributions to the Foundation to date total $16,454.99 including the income from the magazine agency.

"At present the Foundation activities are directed by Council. The members of Council will continue to direct its function until the activities get more extensive and the services of a director will become essential for promoting and supervising the activities of the Foundation.

Elections, 1954

At the close of Convention the following were installed as new officers: President, Helen Million Preston, Ξ-Michigan, who had just completed a term of office as Second Vice-President; Second Vice-President, Virginia Ungemach Brown, Φ-Colorado, and Secretary, Nancy Harris Cooper, ΑΣ-UCLA.

Shortly after Convention Virginia Brown was forced to resign her office by doctor's orders, and Carolyn Boli Stanton, ΑΥ-SMU, who had served the Fraternity in several capacities, was appointed Second Vice-President and was installed in November. She would serve until the 1956 Convention.

Council—Fall, 1954

In Miami Beach, Florida, November 13-17, Council met at the Roney Plaza Hotel, again to look over the possibilities of Miami Beach hotels for future Conventions. As a result of this visit the 1958 Conclave was scheduled for the newly constructed Hotel Fountainbleau in Miami Beach.

Contributions to NSPB, Foundation for Blind

Contributions of $100 each were voted to the American Foundation for the Blind and the National Society for the Prevention of Blindness, a practice which had begun several years before and has continued.

Anchora guest editors

A series of guest editors for the *Anchora* were

set up at this meeting with the possibility of one being chosen as the new permanent editor. Fran Stevenson was editing her last regular issue which would appear the following month as Winter, 1954, and would edit the Delta Gamma History which would appear as the Winter, 1955 issue of the magazine. For Spring, 1955, the editor would be Aubrey Hamilton Leonard, Γ-California; for Summer, 1955, Jean Hartman Culp, Σ-Northwestern, and for Fall, 1955, Edith Murphy Sackett, ΑΛ-Drake. Fran Stevenson, who was to take over the Public Relations chairmanship, was to represent Delta Gamma at the NPC editors' conference in November, and would edit the Delta Gamma History.

Council—Spring, 1955

In the spring of 1955—April 18-22—Council met at The Shamrock Hotel in Houston, Texas.

The requirement that chapters buy fraternity jewelry, badges and metal products only from the Balfour Company was reaffirmed.

Plans for new Office

The plans for a new location for Central Office were well under way by this time and it was agreed that Mrs. Preston and Mrs. Anderson would work with the Executive Secretary on the decorating. The building in which Delta Gamma was to move was to be located in Columbus' northwest suburban area and was being constructed with office space designed for Delta Gamma's use for a probable period of five years. At the end of this time it was planned by Council that Delta Gamma would build its own permanent headquarters.

Officers Training School

The officer training school plan was revived, and for a week during June, 1955, the Iota chapter house was taken over for a training school for Province Secretaries, Province Alumnæ Chairmen, field secretaries, and standing committee chairmen working under the First Vice-President and Second Vice-President. These two officers conducted the school with the assistance of the Treasurer and the Executive Secretary.

Delta Gamma presides at National Panhellenic

In November, 1955, Delta Gamma's official attention was turned to The Greenbrier, White Sulphur Springs, West Virginia, and the National Panhellenic biennium there. Helen Russell Byars, as Delta Gamma's delegate, was serving as chairman of this meeting, which was indeed a memorable affair. Other Delta Gamma Council members, the Executive Secretary and Editor, were among the hostesses for the conclave. The Executive Secretary, Roberta Abernethy, was elected president of the Central Office Executives conference, which meets as a part of Panhellenic.

Roanoke College

Before going to the Greenbrier, Council had met in Roanoke both for its official Council meeting and to attend the installation of Gamma Pi chapter at Roanoke College, Salem, Virginia. This group had petitioned Delta Gamma when the campus opened itself to national sororities. This was to be one of several installations during the 1955-56 school year, others scheduled at Wittenberg College, Springfield, Ohio, where colonization had taken place in the fall; at Texas Christian University, Fort Worth, Texas, and at the University of Houston, Houston, Texas, where a local had petitioned when the campus opened to nationals.

Helen Million Preston, Ξ-Michigan, as she appeared in 1954 when she became President, an office she held until 1962. She had served four years as Second Vice-President. Her mother, a charter member of Xi chapter—Helen Lovell Million—had before her contributed years of service to Delta Gamma, and her daughter Betty, was later initiated at Wittenberg.

The Central Office moved to a new suburban location in Columbus.

24 — Agitation and expansion

Growth all ways

Officers Training Schools developed and grew during this period—eventually to evolve into a Leadership School which included collegiate presidents.

During these years another wave of anti-fraternity agitation had alerted the organized Fraternity world. Frequently, college administrative groups have in this decade called upon the Greek-letter groups on their own campuses to open their Constitutions and show that no clauses restricting membership by race, creed, or color were included. In many cases these governing groups on campus have demanded that, if such clauses were present, they be removed by a certain date. When President Helen Preston replied to such a request, she carefully outlined Delta Gamma's philosophy of membership as well as the fact that no restrictive clauses were present in the Delta Gamma Constitution.

Expansion

Though generous news space is always given to agitation against fraternities, the overwhelming number of requests for consideration of campuses for expansion is never mentioned, and seldom are the statistics displayed beyond the confines of NPC. The Expansion Chairman was receiving (and continues to receive) a steady flow of such requests from campuses in all areas. She must be acutely conscious of campus trends and both perceptive and knowledgeable in each situation, for many times it is necessary to act quickly. Though we continue to approve a number of potential fields at each Convention, many times a campus not even considered at one Convention may within a period of months become such a promising spot for a chapter that approval action must be completed by mail.

Wittenberg College

Thus, the 1955-56 school year was an active one in this area of activity. In the fall of 1955 Delta Gamma had assembled alumnæ and collegians in the Springfield, Ohio, neighborhood to aid in colonizing at Wittenberg College, a field which had been heartily approved at the 1954 Convention. With these "imported" rush teams, Delta Gamma would take its place to enter rush with the already established groups. Jean Shade Sheahan, E-Ohio State, former field secretary, spent three weeks in Springfield to coordinate this effort, and with the enthusiastic support of all members in this Delta Gamma-populated part of Ohio, Delta Gamma pledged her quota. The colony began its preparation for installation under the direction of Field Secretary Marilyn Monahan, Alpha Gamma-Toronto, and became a chapter on March 10, 1956.

University of Houston

Simultaneously, another group was being readied for a 1956 installation. Pi Lambda Chi, a local since 1940 at the University of Houston, had petitioned Delta Gamma and been accepted by the necessary vote of the surrounding chapters. Convention had previously approved the University of Houston for expansion. The chapter was installed.

Two other campuses in the South were in the process of opening doors to Greek groups, Texas Christian University and Emory University, but since the chapters were not installed until later, their stories will appear in proper sequence.

Central Office moves

In December, 1955, Central Office had reversed its usual activities and was giving as well as receiving a change of address, its own move from its original downtown location to an outlying area of Columbus, a new office building at 1820 Northwest Boulevard. In the words of the release issued at the time, "Keeping pace with the modern business world, Central Office has relocated in the Columbus suburbs." Though the new office was still within the city limits of Columbus, it was only so by half a block and was to all intents and purposes, suburban.

It was certain that Delta Gamma was part of a widespread trend in the mid-'fifties of the decentralization of business areas of our cities. Fraternity officers, in arranging a five-year lease on the new office, felt that this would provide a period in which to view the advantages or disadvantages of an outlying location for a permanent Delta Gamma headquarters building.

Anchora comments on the new Central Office continued, "The location must be convenient for staff as well as visitors, have access to bus service and ample parking area, be pleasant, too, with moderate rent befitting a non-profit organization."

Facilities included offices for Executive Secretary, Editor and other permanent staff members as well as a large work room for assembly of mailings, machinery involved in preparation of out-going material, and handling of mailing lists, space for membership files and records, area for bookkeeper with provision for accountant service and storage space. Some display area was also provided for the beginnings of the developing archives.

The decor preserved a business-like atmosphere against a background of femininity. This had been an era of pink in decorating, and the "blues" were just beginning to be "in," so it was an obvious time for Delta Gamma to use its own colors to best advantage. The reception room, Executive Secretary's and Editor's offices which were one unit, stayed with the blue shades; the workroom was pink, and what a lot of comment was caused by those pink files! Everyone loved them! The large black and white tile squares of the workroom area reflected another decorating twist of the times. To complete the bronze, pink, and blue theme, the individual offices surrounding the workroom were in greens (effecting the bronze).

Council Meeting—Spring, 1956

When Council met March 14-21, at the Netherlands Plaza Hotel in Cincinnati, it was natural that a large amount of time was given to plans for the forthcoming Convention. Another item which occupied many Council hours during this period was housing. Requests for housing funds were numerous, and it was necessary to schedule these—a few each year—for several years in advance.

Fraternity Fellowship established

With the Grants and Loans committee located during this period in Columbus where it had the opportunity to work closely with the office, this was a period of expansion in this area. It had been decided to add two senior scholarships of $250 each to be awarded annually, beginning in 1957, and in addition, Council decided at this meeting to create an annual Fraternity Honorary Fellowship of $500 which would be awarded to a Delta Gamma for graduate study in the field of her choice. This would be named for an outstanding Delta Gamma. This fellowship differed from the Memorial Fellowship in both the fact that it honored, by name, a living member and also that the Memorial Fellowship could be awarded to a non-member and was restricted to second-year graduate study, currently in social service. Also in the Grants and Loans area, it was decided that sophomores would be eligible for short-term emergency loans, previously allowed only for upperclassmen.

Honors recognition

Honors recognition was emphasized at this time, too, and fraternity recognition certificates were to be mailed to each collegiate member who was accorded membership in Phi Beta Kappa, Sigma Xi, Phi Kappa Phi, and Mortar Board, or who was graduated Summa Cum Laude, Magna Cum Laude or Cum Laude.

Delta Gamma songs recorded

Council, just prior to this Spring, 1956, meeting, had accepted the offer of Mercury Record Corporation to record some Delta Gamma songs in a proposed album.

Thirty-seventh Convention
1956—Quebec, Quebec

Once more it was a year for Convention in Canada, and the dates circled on the calendar were June 26-July 1, 1956, the place to be Chateau Frontenac, Quebec, for Delta Gamma's Thirty-seventh Convention. Marian Hill Keenan, Omega-Wisconsin, of New Rochelle, N.Y., was chairman.

During the spring prior to this Convention and at the Convention itself much concern was evidenced by officers over the rising costs of the Convention to members of the Fraternity. Treasurer Helen Bradford Anderson had written in the spring issue of Anchora that nearly 600 Delta Gammas would probably attend the Convention at Quebec and that the cost to the Fraternity would reach $70,000. (Delta Gamma was —and still is—the only women's fraternity to pay both hotel and transportation costs for all delegates.) Registration fee had been raised to $25, and the fact was emphasized that each officer would pay this personally, not as an expense account item. At the Convention itself President Helen Preston repeated this concern over rising costs and stated that Council was requesting the approval of Convention to bill each chapter seventy-five cents per member each year to replace the present Convention hostess tax plan which formerly had taxed Delta Gammas in the hostess states $3.00 each. Because of the fact that so few hotels in the resort areas are large enough to hold Delta Gamma Conventions, it had become almost impossible to make the hostess states the location for the Convention.

Convention Special

For the last time a Convention Special Train was scheduled, but only for the 25-hour run from Chicago to Quebec, with stops for passengers in Detroit and Toronto and another stop in Montreal where arrivals from New York and the South would converge with the Special. Mixers and hostesses made the most of the short time on board so that it was a festive group which detrained in Quebec for Convention.

The French flavor of the city was emphasized in the social planning for Convention, and with Chateau Frontenac menus printed in French a standard item, it wasn't difficult to make the most of what this bilingual city offered. It was a Convention to be remembered for its gaiety, for the interesting background provided by Quebec, and by the smoothly running program.

Because this Convention was so close to the East coast there was considerable promotion for European or Around-the-World tours following Convention. Former Delta Gamma President, Florence Cornell Bingham, did a recollection of her years of travel in the spring *Anchora* to promote an Around-the-World tour which she was sponsoring as a Delta Gamma tour. At the same time, Joan Murchison, M-Missouri, with Pan-American Airways, was promoting a European tour following Convention. There is no record of their success, but many Delta Gammas did enjoy trips to the Gaspe Peninsula, Nova Scotia, and nearby portions of the St. Lawrence following the meetings at Chateau Frontenac.

Housing

Officers emphasized to delegates the tremendous chapter expansion during this period and the resulting requests for housing funds. It was announced that this housing assistance from the Fraternity was being granted on a priority basis —first come, first served. However, commitments to new chapters which have few alumnæ and no equity must be considered before requests from old and well-established chapters. The Central Office Building Fund, established on a purely surplus and salvage basis, would in no way take money which might otherwise be allocated to a chapter needing housing. At least 25%

of the surplus in the Fraternity account each year would be turned over to the Central Office Building Fund.

Initiation

The 1956 Convention viewed for the first time a revised initiation ceremony which had been recently completed by the Rituals Committee.

Foundation

A Foundation Director had been appointed and was for the first time a member of Convention; she was Marcia Connell Strickland, Xi-Michigan, a person well known in many phases of Delta Gamma activity. Approved during this year had been an operating budget for the Foundation, to cover expenses incurred by the three Foundation committees in handling their duties plus the new Grants and Loans awards. The amount of $1,000 had been set aside for the International Education committee to use at its own discretion to assist chapters having foreign guests and an item to meet unexpected emergencies. This fund was to be reviewed annually by Council in its capacity as the Board of Directors of the Delta Gamma Foundation. At the suggestion of the International Education committee, Council had approved a policy that the collegiate chapter's sponsorship of an International Education student be limited to one year for any one student.

Roberta Abernethy Fellowship

A focal point of this Convention was the expansion being made in the Grants and Loans area of the Foundation. Convention was indeed a logical spot to announce not only the fact that the new $500 Honorary Fellowship would be awarded but also the very fitting choice of honoree for its first appearance. The 1957-58 Honorary Fellowship would bear the name of Delta Gamma's beloved Executive Secretary, the Roberta Abernethy Honorary Fellowship. An interesting sidelight to Grants and Loans at this Convention—though it hadn't been planned that way —was that the Memorial Fellowship for 1956-57 was awarded to a Quebec province resident, Doris Frazer of Dundee. This had been announced just as Convention opened.

1956 Elections

The office of Panhellenic Delegate, as a member of Council, was finally created at this Convention, and with remarkable dispatch considering the hours and even years of debate which had ensued previously. Elected to this new office was Dorothy Glenn Holsinger, I-Illinois, who had served as First Vice-President from 1942-48.

Re-elected First Vice-President for a 1956-60 term was Margaret Richardson Hay, and the Secretary's position, also up for election in 1956, was filled by Laura Bertram Dillon, Z-Albion, of Birmingham, Mich. Re-elected Treasurer was Helen Bradford Anderson.

Carolyn Boli Stanton has resigned from the Second Vice-Presidency at this time, and Maisie Clugston Groves, AΦ-British Columbia, of Vancouver, B.C., was elected to fill this unexpired term.

Rose Award at Convention

For the first time at a Convention a Rose Award presentation was made. Former President, Helen Russell Byars, received this honor having just completed a term as president of another international organization, National Panhellenic Conference.

Workshops

Considerable attention was given at this Convention to collegiate and alumnæ workshops, with each group having an attractively printed program in addition to the usual official Convention program.

Emphasis, too, was placed on youth, and in her Convention address, "Think Delta Gamma," President Helen Preston said, "Youth brings to us a constant examination of the value of our ideals and the testing of our procedures. They keep us alumnæ young in spirit and understanding. As each generation finds inspiration and satisfaction from ideals and friendships of Delta Gamma, we feel more and more convinced that what we have is GOOD."

Anchora

Anchora Editor Frances Lewis Stevenson "had been resigning" over a nearly two-year period (and was listed in this 1956 Convention program under her new title, Public Relations chairman). Following the large task of producing the 1955 Delta Gamma history, she had continued to edit two more issues of the magazine, spring and summer, 1956. In June, 1956, her third child was born and to cover Convention and edit a fall issue, Aubrey Hamilton Leonard once more appeared on the masthead as guest editor. By September, 1956, however, Nancy Gregory, Sigma-Northwestern, had been duly appointed Delta Gamma editor and was installed in the Central Office publications department. Nancy, daughter of Nancy Hyde Gregory, also of Sigma chapter, very capably directed Delta Gamma publications for the next four years.

Anniversaries

Delta Gamma had reached an era when its oldest living chapters were celebrating their diamond jubilees. Eta was, of course, the first to reach its seventy-fifth year, in 1954, and by 1956 it was Omega's turn with Lambda and Sigma the following year and Zeta in 1958, all products of Delta Gamma's first decade expansion. Fiftieth anniversaries were becoming more numerous, too, and, oddly enough, seemed to draw larger numbers of chapter members than the seventy-fifth celebrations. We contemplate the possible reason being that when a chapter is celebrating 50 years, there are still charter members living

and others who worked hard during early struggles whose enthusiasm for this cause for celebration is contagious enough to insure success.

Foundation stimulates activity

The formation of the Delta Gamma Foundation in 1951 had stimulated not only the project and provided a channel for all the philanthropic activities of the Fraternity, but it had also instigated new vigor in other areas. Under Grants and Loans we have already viewed considerable activity. Besides this, one fellowship, which had been in existence for a number of years, had not been awarded simply because after the initial announcement, publicity of its existence had been dropped. Thus, possible applicants were unaware of its existence. The Alice Perry Gradle Fellowship, established by the 1946 Convention with the stipulation that the winner be a member of the Fraternity, was re-announced in *Anchora* and awarded for the 1956-57 school year.

Pre-school vision screening was rapidly becoming a favorite project of alumnæ chapters. Not only did members find this to be a highly worthwhile service activity (as one remarked, "You aren't selling anything or sitting in a meeting, but you're at work every minute of the time you are on an assignment"), but it was turning out to be an expanding interest which was attracting members who had not been particularly active.

Texas Christian University

In February, 1956, Delta Gamma and Pi Beta Phi had simultaneously colonized on the Texas Christian University campus in Ft. Worth, Texas, joining the eight other NPC groups which had been established at TCU the year before. Nine had been pledged at that time, and 42 more were added during fall rush. The original nine became the charter members of Gamma Tau chapter when it was installed on September 29.

Council Meeting—Fall, 1956

Sites for Council meetings are frequently chosen to give the officers a chance to look over a possible Convention area. Thus, the Council traveled to the Bedford Springs Hotel, Bedford, Pa., for its semi-annual meeting October 29-November 3. This location also made it convenient for Mr. George Whitney, representative of our Investment Council, Scudder, Stevens and Clark of Philadelphia, to meet with Council.

The Hungarian cause

Once more during this fall of 1956, Delta Gammas across the continent expressed spontaneously the desire "to help." This was the time of the Hungarian uprising against the Communist regime after which the defeated Hungarians were in dire need of aid. Contributions for this purpose were coming to Council, so contact was made with Christine Lambacher, an International Student guest who had been initiated by Gamma Lambda *chapter in 1955, and it was she who disbursed the $500 check sent by Council for Hungarian relief.*

Carolyn Stanton dies

Shortly after Council meeting closed, the entire Fraternity was saddened by the sudden death of Carolyn Boli Stanton, who, at the June Convention, had stepped out of the office of Second Vice-President. One of Carolyn's last official acts had been in connection with the installation of Delta Gamma's newest chapter in Ft. Worth.

Overseas expansion

With many military installations still in Europe and the Far East, and with many businesses operating on an international scale, Delta Gamma appointed a new Overseas Expansion chairman. This was Sylvia Sweetman Sunderlin, Π-Montana, whose husband was Deputy Director of the National Science Foundation. Though many members live out of the country, most of them are fairly transient—on assignments, military or civilian, of only a few years' duration—and consequently, most organization is through Panhellenic rather than individual groups.

Rushing is Your Business

The summer, 1957, issue of *Anchora* launched a special pull-out section at the center of the issue, "Rushing is Your Business," sixteen pages of instructions and a directory of collegiate rush chairmen, advisers, state and city recommendations chairmen. This was designed to encourage member participation in rush throughout the Fraternity, and it was to become a regular summer *Anchora* section.

Increased alumnæ activity

Rushing was only one area which alumnæ were encouraged to make their business. To co-ordinate all alumnæ activity the Second Vice-President, Maisie Groves, had launched a program aimed to aid internal organization. She issued a PAC and Alumnæ Presidents Manual and later pointed up the varied alumnæ program with the reorganization of alumnæ *Anchora* reports.

Council Meeting—Spring, 1957

The spring Council meeting was destined to be colorful in a quite unexpected way. While meeting March 22-31 at the famed Mark Hopkins Hotel in San Francisco, members noted that the pictures on the wall and the lamps were beginning to sway. Yes, it was an earthquake, (sharp, rolling and jolting) and later in the week when officers attended Gamma chapter's fiftieth anniversary, they heard local Delta Gammas comment that it was really an appropriate moment for this to occur. For more than fifty years before it had been the well-remembered tragic earthquake and fire in San Francisco which had helped delay Gamma's installation until 1907 in the first place. Even the local press, in covering the anniversary, took note of this fact!

Chapter audits

In view of subsequent events, one piece of business at this meeting is especially worth note: it was agreed that starting with September, 1957, the monthly financial report of each chapter would be sent to Central Office to be checked for mathematical and clerical errors by a person employed for this purpose. The reports will no longer be sent to the Province Secretaries, and it was further agreed to take the books of a selected twelve to fifteen chapters into Central Office for audit this summer. This action at the spring, 1957, Council meeting was the beginning of what was to become the Collegiate Auditing division of the office.

At the same time, in dealing with chapter finance, a set of revisions in the Code of Regulations for House Corporations was approved.

Foundation

One session of Council meeting is set apart as a meeting of the Board of Directors of the Delta Gamma Foundation, since personnel of the two bodies is the same. At this meeting it was agreed that the term of office for the Foundation director should be for four years, and that Washington, D.C., be the next city to be asked to take the responsibility of the Project committee, as the Oklahoma City committee was about to complete its four-year term.

Memorial House addition

Once more Alpha Psi chapter at the University of Mississippi was campaigning for funds for an addition to the Memorial House in which the chapter lives. In 1937 when plans were made to build this house, sororities at Ole Miss met in lodges. We were given special permission to house a limited number of girls (officers of the chapter) so that the house could be used as guest quarters for official visitors to the University, a facility Ole Miss sorely lacked at the time. When even these few Delta Gammas moved into their Memorial House it was natural that other groups on campus should desire the same privilege, and with World War II this desire turned into a necessity with so many demands for women's housing on all campuses. In due course, all Ole Miss chapters were living in their houses, and twice during the 'fifties a wing was added to the Memorial House.

Officers Training School

An important event occurred June 25-July 1, 1957, when an Officers Training School was held at the Omega chapter house at Madison, Wisconsin. Officers training schools had been held from time to time since World War I, but the approach taken at this time was of a permanent, regularly occurring school, not one to meet a particular situation or to tide over a period (such a war) when a Convention could not be held. With Council as the faculty and province officers and fraternity chairmen as students, it was a week of intensive training in the policies, rules, regulations and ways of Delta Gamma. This was to become an increasingly important biennial event, and by 1961 would expand to include three days of sessions for collegiate chapter presidents. At this School, it was natural that the Madison alumnæ had a part in entertaining the participants during their stay.

University of Wichita

The University of Wichita had opened its doors to national fraternities, and the local petitioning Delta Gamma had been pledged on June 8, the group traveling to the University of Oklahoma for the ceremony conducted by Alpha Iota chapter. The petitioning group accepted by Delta Gamma was Alpha Tau Sigma, the oldest local on the campus, founded in 1909. Alpha Tau Sigma had a long history of prominence on campus, consistently winning honors in scholarship, activities, and leadership. Each of the five women's groups owned its lodge, and Alpha Tau Sigma had pioneered by building the first lodge on property reserved by the University for sorority housing. The chapter was installed February 1, 1958.

Pledge Manual

A new pledge manual was to appear in 1957, and a fraternity-wide competition was held for a cover design. The judging was done by the Pledge Training committee headed by Ruth Canary Turpin, AN-Southern California. The winning cover was that of Patsy Tubb, AI-Oklahoma.

Panhellenic Biennium

The thirty-fifth session of the National Panhellenic Conference convened November 4-8 at the French Lick Sheraton Hotel, French Lick, Indiana. Dorothy Holsinger was Delta Gamma's delegate with the President and First Vice-President as alternatives. Roberta Abernethy at this session was president of the Association of Central Office Executives meeting in conjunction with NPC. Nancy Gregory attended her first session of the NPC Editors' Association.

The Conference passed as a binding agreement for all college Panhellenics the Declaration of Freedom and a Statement of Rights designed to express the intent of members of NPC to defend their rights of free association as private organizations.

The NPC Secretary reported the addition of 68 new chapters and 69,500 new members to NPC groups within the preceding biennium. She also reported the past ten years had seen a fifty per cent increase in the number of chapters over the number in 1947, a fact which certainly belied the rumor that NPC sororities were on the way out. It was predicted (and it came to pass) that by 1960 NPC membership would reach 1,000,000. Very graphically it was reported that

a new chapter of some NPC group was installed every ten days!

Communism and agitation

For at least 75 years fraternities had faced and met the challenges of anti-fraternity agitation from whatever quarter it appeared. Politics was not new as an agent of anti-fraternity activity, but during the 'fifties it became intensified with the alleged infiltration of communism into all areas of American life. Acutely interested in combat with this vicious creature were President Helen Preston and Editor Nancy Gregory who, together, directed many *Anchora* pages toward this effort. This included a wide variety of reprints from such authorities as the FBI's J. Edgar Hoover to inspired pieces of collegiate members. The reaction—when reaction came—was vehemently in favor of or as violently against using *Anchora* pages in this way. By the early 'sixties it became evident that rather than to sponsor a debate on the subject, it would be more profitable for the *Anchora* to reflect the positive force of the fraternity on campus and in the community.

In years to come when Delta Gamma historians peruse these particular pages, it is hoped that they will be able to smile at yet another *Anchora* reflection of signs and spirit of the times. For since 1884 when the *Anchora* was born, it is not only the pictorial matter ("were skirts really that short?—or long; did we really wear our hair like that?") that has served as this mirror of "how things were," but the topics for review and discussion, too.

The times

And bound with these pages, which were accused of having political overtones, were others which reflected other phases of everyday existence. When the International Education chairman, Cornelia Powell Draves, reported that 36,000 foreign students had studied in the United States during the past school year and reviewed Delta Gamma's part in this movement, she was not only stating a fact but was reflecting what would be called a trend. When another story told of Pop McHale (a Delta Gamma husband) who had coached at the University of Arizona since 1914 when 300 students were enrolled, it was not only Pop McHale's story but a mirror of the phenomenal growth of the Southwest during those fifty years. When an art gallery opened at Starr Commonwealth for Boys was named in memory of Ruth Bryan Owen Rohde, the Anchora carried the story because Mrs. Rohde had been an outstanding Delta Gamma. Her life, and her "firsts" as a woman, were another kind of pioneering which both the United States and Canada, it has been said, are now growing old enough to revere. It is certain that even in the Anchora what we report today as news tomorrow is a trend.

25—Creating new order from within

Policies and PR

75 years
of continuous publication
1884-1959

When National Panhellenic closed its 1957 session at French Lick, officers who attended went on to Chicago for the fall Council meeting, November 10-15 at the Drake Hotel.

Public Relations for the Fraternity had traveled far from the days when it meant just a little more than furthering publicity, and now keeping members informed was recognized as an item of considerable importance on the PR program. With the Public Relations committee located in Columbus form 1956-58, it was able to work closely with the publications department of Central Office which was of advantage in this area. A pocket-size brochure for issue to all members with the fall billing had been created by the Public Relations committee in 1957 and was duly admired by Council at this meeting: "When You're Talking Delta Gamma." Soon after the Council session closed, another facet of this program appeared with the addition (first time, Winter, 1957) to *Anchora* of a regular Foundation section, "Design for Giving." Prior to this time, Foundation activity had been featured with a special section which appeared at intervals.

The symbol designed for the Foundation at this time by Nancy Gregory was registered as The official trademark of the Foundation. During the next year, 1958, a two-color booklet entitled "Design for Giving" was issued on the Foundation's behalf.

Also in the publications area at this time was the production of a Social Log (1957) and a Pledge Trainer's Manual (1959).

Policies and procedures

The withdrawal of a chapter of Delta Gamma is not, fortunately, an every day occurrence, but the need for a formal procedure to be followed, should this situation arise, had been felt for some time. So this was an item on the agenda which was completed and approved at this Council session.

Fraternity policies had been in the process of review and study by Council members for some time, and in 1957 a revised single volume of Fraternity Policies was issued. The background of this edition, which is a companion piece to the Fraternity Constitution, covered many years.

The Constitution of Delta Gamma is the product of Convention action, and only a Convention assembled may make changes in the Constitution. Fraternity Policies, on the other hand, are the result of Council action. For many years these actions were recorded only in Council minutes—though some were the basis of directives issued to the chapters or membership. During the late 'forties the Secretary and Executive Secretary (Dorothy Wildasin and Roberta Abernethy) worked together to record these policies as they existed at that time and organized them under proper departmental headings. In 1949 these were approved by Council and distributed, by subject matter, to the proper officers' notebooks.

It was in 1957, then, after considerable scrutiny, that these policies were once more reviewed and approved as a single volume. On the basis of these two Fraternity documents, the Policies and Constitution, directives, regulations, and procedures are developed to be used by the chapters and individuals. Some flexibility is given to province officers and chairmen in dealing with regulations and directives, but Policies must be followed unless exceptions are made by Council action. The issue of this book of policies clarified these procedures for the chapters. Subsequent Council meetings could (and did) make changes in some of these policies; these changes were, of course, published and distributed to the chapters to be inserted in the book of Policies.

One evident outcome was natural. The mechanics of change—of being certain that each change issued by Council had been recorded in each copy of the Policies—was cumbersome and not always accomplished. This was a problem which was not conquered until the Officers Manuals were published during 1965, a matter which will be covered in due course in this history.

Arizona State University

Delta Gamma's eighty-fifth chapter was installed in the spring of 1958 in time to be represented at Convention. This was Gamma Phi at Arizona State College (soon to be University), Tempe, Arizona. Delta Gamma and Alpha Phi had been invited simultaneously to the campus and colonized in February, Margaret Richardson Hay directing the operation for Delta Gamma. This colony was also trained for installation by Shirley Kubik, and the charter was granted on May 10.

Keeping informed

With efforts geared during these days to keeping the widely scattered membership informed, the summer issue of *Anchora*, appearing just prior to the opening of Convention, had been planned accordingly. The issue opened with President Helen Preston's summary of Council's work during the past biennium. This special presidential report in print closely paralleled her president's address in person to open Convention. The only sad note present was the report of the withdrawal of Beta Phi chapter at the University of Pennsylvania where it was felt that there was not enough material to supply the number of chapters on campus.

This pre-Convention issue also carries several other timely items, one being the second appearance of the rush pull-out section in the center of the issue. Second is a timely editorial by Secretary Laura Bertram Dillon, a salute to alumnæ initiates and a review of the concept of initiating alumnæ at chapter installations in areas where a collegiate group would obviously need alumnæ support beyond what is already present in the community.

Council Meeting—Spring, 1958

As usual this had been a busy pre-Convention spring. Council had met March 18-25 at The Antlers Hotel, Colorado Springs, Colorado, with an eye toward the possibility of a Colorado Convention.

Collegiate auditing in Central Office was rapidly developing, and a monthly audit under the Delta Gamma Fraternity Bookkeeping System in Central Office was formally approved at this time. This had been presented to Council by the Collegiate Finance chairman.

The Second Vice-President, Maisie Clugston Groves, reported some foreign organization activity through her Overseas Expansion chairman. It was noted that Lucia Frier McKenzie was chairman of the Tokyo alumnæ group which was planning a Founders' Day observance, an event also being planned by Delta Gammas in London.

Thirty-eighth Convention
1958—Miami Beach, Florida

"Sojourn in the Sun" it was called, and the sun did shine on Delta Gamma's Thirty-eighth Convention, June 19-24, at the Americana Hotel in Miami Beach, Florida. Plans and preparations had been monumental, and each detail seemed to mesh perfectly and properly. With a colorful background and plenty of Delta Gammas in the immediate area, the basic insurance for a successful Convention was present from the start. Virginia Leudemann Terry, O-Adelphi, of Miami was the chairman.

Persistence of business over pleasure in Florida was not so surprising to Conventioners as it was to the incredulous members of the Americana staff and between-season vacationers at the hotel. It was clear to everyone that it was a working Convention, truly fulfilling its purpose. President Helen Million Preston keynoted the 1958 Convention in her address to the assembly by elaborating on the working theme, "Delta Gamma Privileges and Responsibilities." She stated that "in these times of great disturbance we have a responsibility to our members and through us to society . . . It is not clearly in our minds what are our ideals of behavior, to reaffirm them, and to be adamant in upholding them and to require equal respect and observance of them from those who would call us friend. . . . A sense of responsibility is the thing that gives us our greatest strength, that sense of responsibility which comes from deep and sincere friendships among our members, based upon love, understanding, loyalty, and giving and receiving the best that is within us."

Special guests were an important part of this Convention. Mr. George Banta, Jr., President of the George Banta Company, Inc., publishers of the *Anchora* for fifty years, was present to speak and to accept a framed citation on behalf of his company. It announced the Fraternity's $1,500 Memorial Fellowship for 1957-58, named for his father who was Delta Gamma's only male member. The citation was presented this year in recognition of Delta Gamma's long association with the company. Mr. Banta charmed his audience with early reminiscences of his father and his association with Delta Gamma, and a discussion of the fraternity system. (This address is reprinted in the Fall, 1958 *Anchora*.)

The Delta Gamma Foundation, at its general meeting, had as its guest, Mr. Donald J. Shenk, executive vice-president of the Institute of International Education which administers the exchange program through which Delta Gamma receives its International Education guests.

A third guest was the banquet speaker, a Delta Gamma who had received the Order of the Rose at an earlier date. She was Oleda Shrottky, AZ-Lawrence, national consultant for the Girl Scouts of America, who titled her address, "What It Means to Belong."

Model initiation is a part of each Convention program, but in 1958 the ceremony had a rather special aspect. The two initiates were Dianne Hay, daughter of First Vice-President Margaret Richardson Hay, and Pennie Pittman, daughter of Eugenia Van Cleve Pittman, AΔ-Oregon, and a member of what is probably the largest Delta Gamma family, numbering at this time more than forty Delta Gammas in its ramifications. They were initiated as members of TH-San Jose.

Collegiate Representatives

Generally conceded to be the most significant piece of business transacted was the election of two collegiate representatives for Council, one from chapters living in their houses and the second from chapters having lodges or rooms for fraternity activities. The first collegians elected to this position were Barbara Wallenfang, BΨ-Alabama, from a chapter living in its house, and Sue Daugherty, AP-Ohio Wesleyan, from a chapter with a lodge. Sue's mother was also a delegate to this Convention as chairman of the Foundation's Grants and Loans Committee.

Convention action

- National Panhellenic Delegate, since 1956 an ex-officio member of Council, is now a full member of Council and as such will assume added responsibilities. This brings the number on Council to six. The delegate would assume her duties from date of election, not from next NPC biennium as previously voted.
- Fifty-year members would be excused from paying annual dues.
- Senior scholarship allocations would be increased from $500 to $1,500, thus allowing for six senior scholarships beginning the following year.

Elections

Delegates voted almost unanimous approval of the candidates presented by the nominating committee for the three Council positions open for election. President Helen Preston and Second Vice-President Maisie Groves were re-elected to serve four-year terms in their present offices. First Vice-President Margaret Richardson Hay would succeed Dorothy Glenn Holsinger as the National Panhellenic Conference Delegate at the close of the 1959 NPC biennium. Elected to the 1958-60 Nominating committee were Eleanor Smith Slaughter, Province IV Secretary; Kathryn Maple Roberts, Province I Secretary; Agnes Beach, Province XV Alumnæ Chairman; Helen Russell Byars, former Fraternity President, and Mary Brundage Crawford, K-Nebraska, former president of the Omaha alumnæ.

Expansion

The meeting devoted to expansion is one delegates find exciting, and this 1958 Convention heard Laura Bertram Dillon, Secretary and Expansion chairman, announce that in accordance with 1956 Convention approval, an invitation from Long Beach State College (California) had been accepted and Delta Gamma would colonize in the fall of 1958. She then recommended seven possible fields for expansion, all of which were approved, giving Council authority to proceed with colonization providing favorable conditions exist. They were: Emory University, Mississippi Southern College, Colorado State University, Wake Forest College, Hanover College, Lake

Forest College and St. Lawrence University.

Delta Gammas in the Southeast had gone all-out to entertain Conventioners, and a wide variety of fun was present at all times at this "Sojourn in the Sun."

Current Events

Convention reports from officers and committees are always an interesting supplement to the Convention minutes, and this year is no exception.

The Rush committee reported that during the last two years every Province Secretary was with one or more chapters during rush and some officers of the Fraternity also participated in this program—the beginning of the rush counseling which would materialize within a few years. This, too, included the encouraging of a rush school before formal rush opened. The chairman calls the year 1957-58 the Asiatic Flu year (which it surely was!) as most campuses were riddled with this illness.

Public Relations was another committee which had been active. Not only had "When You're Talking Delta Gamma" and other publications appeared, but the PR committee and Central Office had put out a new set of posters issued to replace the project posters which had been released in 1951. This new series contained three, Design for Giving (Foundation), Design for Campus Living (Collegiate programming), and Design for Alumnæ Living (alumnæ activities).

Project

Through these years we have watched constantly widening areas of activity for chapters with the Project, Sight Conservation and Aid to the Blind. As state organizations of the National Society for Prevention of Blindness were coming into existence, there were an increasing number of Delta Gammas participating and attending annual national meetings of the NSPB. Not only are a number of state and county officers of NSPB Delta Gammas, but also a number of the state executive directors and national officers and board members.

Long Beach State College

As had been reported at Convention, colonization was to take place at Long Beach State College in the fall. It would be Gamma Chi chapter, and to colonize, Delta Gamma elected to enter rush in competition with the already established groups on the campus. Under the direction of First Vice-President Peggy Hay, Delta Gammas in this area turned out with usual California enthusiasm to help with rush and colonization. The chapter was installed on March 7, 1959, with Alpha Sigma officiating at initiation.

Panhellenic

After a decade of debate concerning the status of the Panhellenic delegate seemed settled at Convention, it was with both grief and shock that the Fraternity learned of the death of NPC

Delegate Dorothy Glenn Holsinger in October, 1958. To fill the interim until the close of the 1959 NPC Biennium when the First Vice-President, Margaret Richardson Hay, had been elected to begin her term as delegate, Council appointed Ruth Canary Turpin, AN-Southern California. Ruth Turpin had been Fraternity Pledge Training chairman since 1955. Since the 1959-60 Memorial Fellowship had already been named to honor Edith Abbott, Council decided to name the 1960-61 Fellowship in Mrs. Holsinger's memory.

Council Meeting—Fall, 1958

The appointment of an interim NPC delegate was only one of the many items of business covered by Council when it met November 5-12 at the Waldorf-Astoria Hotel in New York.

Collegiate Representatives to Council

For the first time a day was reserved for listening to the recommendations of the collegiate representatives who had thoroughly surveyed their chapters before presenting their ideas to Council. Several of the innovations advocated by the collegiate representatives were immediately adopted, and it is interesting to note (from the present vantage point more than 15 year later) that all of the suggestions of these first two collegiate representatives have since been put into practice.

When the plan for this collegiate representation was first devised, it had been thought that two more would be appointed during the alternate years between Conventions. However, at the suggestion of Barbara and Sue, Council agreed at this time to postpone appointment of succeeding collegiate representatives until the 1960 Convention when they would again be elected. It was also agreed that the current representatives would not, as previously thought, attend the spring 1959 Council meeting as well as fall, 1958. Unless something vital arose, the collegiate delegates said that they preferred not to attend because of their very busy spring schedules.

This Council session also declared an end to attempts toward any overseas alumnæ organization because of the transient qualitities of overseas Delta Gamma populations.

Emory University

In September, 1953, women were admitted for the first time to Emory University, Atlanta, Georgia. Seventy women enrolled in the College of Arts and Sciences and 65 more in the School of Nursing. By June 1, 1955, Dean Nina Rusk reported that the total undergraduate women's enrollment had reached 400 in all schools. The newly admitted women lost no time in organizing clubs in anticipation of the day when national sororities would also be admitted to Emory. They had such provacative names as Anchora Club, Kite Club, P. M. Club, Adelpheans

and so on. The Anchora club wore gold pins like those assigned by Delta Gamma to colonies and was a member of the Inter-Club Council which would one day become Panhellenic. By 1956 there were 11 "colonies" of NPC groups at Emory when the board of trustees announced that these groups could petition "their" nationals when they had fulfilled University requirements —first being a chartered Emory club for two years. The Anchora Club had qualified for all requirements by 1958 and was installed as Gamma Psi chapter of Delta Gamma on May 9, 1959.

Council Meeting—Spring, 1959

Council assembled in St. Louis at the Park Plaza Hotel, March 10-16, for its semi-annual meeting.

A great amount of Fraternity business was transacted and a day set aside for a session with the Delta Gamma Recommendations chairman, Kay Blankenship Lemmer, M-Missouri, to cover changes in this area. Council approved the new recommendation form presented at this time.

Gamma Gamma chapter withdrawn

At this Council meeting it was voted to withdraw Gamma Gamma chapter at Texas Western University. This was a sad conclusion, brought about by the realization that the campus did not provide enough material from which to draw— considering the number of groups on campus.

Thomas M. Wallace

In the spring of 1959 Delta Gamma was also paying tribute to Thomas M. Wallace, Delta Gamma auditor for 36 years, on the occasion of his retirement. He had drawn up the Fraternity's first uniform system of collegiate bookkeeping in 1922. Delta Gamma became the first women's fraternity to operate under this system and was rapidly followed by many of the other Panhellenic groups. So from his initial contact with Delta Gamma through Secretary-Editor Leulah Judson Hawley (both living in Minneapolis), Thomas M. Wallace had become known as "The Fraternity Auditor."

Naturally, Mr. Wallace's retirement had been one of the major factors in setting up a Delta Gamma Collegiate Finances Chairman and the resulting move to Central Office of the monthly audit of chapter books.

The times—and the Foundation

Once more in the spring, 1959, Anchora we are conscious of times with a story by Betty Lyster, BX-Denver, who had gone to the Univeristy of Alaska as Dean of Women. Told with true pioneer spirit, Dean Lyster's story was the story of a new state, for it was also 1959 when Alaska achieved this status.

Possibly as timely as Alaska is the cover of the Foundation's "Design for Giving" section of An-
...
(Continued on page 192)

A history of
Delta Gamma
is the story
of women . . .

during the last century—
* *Their acceptance as something*
more than adequate academic
competitors in the world
of coeducation . . .

* *through the years of expanding*
curriculum to stretch beyond
the classics, explore the sciences . . .

* *emergence into public life,*
proof of their worth during two
World Wars . . . the days of the flapper
with new freedoms and a multitude
of new career horizons . . .

* *and today new worlds of growth*
and service on campus
and in the community, and even a return
to the campus through
continuing education . . .

An Anchora index *from a year early in this century reflects the thinking of the times.*

The growing desire to serve during the first World War . . .

On the back lawn of the Delta Gamma orphanage children are tended by members of the staff. After the war the orphanage was turned over to the town of Marchienne for maintenance and administration.

New career horizons opened for women during the first quarter of the century and continued to expand—a few shown here

Grace Abbott, K-Nebraska, Editor 1905-09, was well known in the field of social service, having served as Chief of the Children's Bureau in the Department of Labor. The 1940 Convention established a Fellowship in Social Service in her memory which was granted annually for ten years.

Educator—Ada Louise Comstock, Λ-Minnesota, became president of Radcliffe College and also served as AAUW president.

Judge—in the courts of Pennsylvania, Hazel Brown, AB-Swarthmore, was for a time Treasurer of Delta Gamma.

Diversified writing careers—Miriam Clark Potter, Λ-Minnesota, right, children's fiction, and Phyllis Battelle, AP-Ohio Wesleyan, left, columnist interviewing Helen Keller.

Women "with heads for business" were on the scene, too—evidenced here in the fraternity building programs of the period

Beekman Tower, the Panhellenic House in New York, was opened in the fall of 1928.

Omega chapter house, University of Wisconsin

Among the Delta Gamma houses of the period—

Sigma chapter house, Northwestern University

*Another World War,
1939-45, found women
catapulted into a new
life—on campus and in
the community*

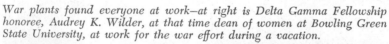

Campus at war—this was taken at war's end,
a few veterans back, service men still on
campus, and the post office still an important
stop for the girls.

War plants found everyone at work—at right is Delta Gamma Fellowship
honoree, Audrey K. Wilder, at that time dean of women at Bowling Green
State University, at work for the war effort during a vacation.

Shipyards were busy day and night, and many names honored outstanding women of the day—this is the "Grace Abbott," for Delta Gamma's well-known social worker.

And women went to war for the first time in their own branches of the service. Columnist Inez Robb, Delta Gamma Rose award winner in correspondent's uniform, is at her typewriter, North Africa, 1943.

*And after
World War II
further
recognition ...*

Further service for Belgian relief was given by Delta Gamma during World War II. This award was made to the Fraternity, represented by Central Office in Columbus, Ohio, which handled the relief work for the Fraternity.

Further recognition for Delta Gamma war relief was presented to Hazel Whitaker Vandenberg as the Fraternity's representative in Washington. The wife of Michigan's Senator Vandenberg had contributed years of service to Delta Gamma and was memorialized by a Fellowship bearing her name.

This triumvirate of Delta Gammas frequently formed front page news during the 'thirties and 'forties, and so it was not surprising that they should be among the United States representatives at the 1945 San Francisco Conference, the organizational meeting of the United Nations. Left to right, they are Florence Cornell Bingham, Delta Gamma president 1940-47; Hazel Whitaker Vandenberg, and Ruth Bryan Rohde.

And greater responsibility

Ruth Bryan Owen Rohde, K-Nebraska, received a special award at the 1938 Convention at which she was guest speaker. Mrs. Rohde, who as Minister to Denmark was the nation's first woman in such a high diplomatic post, later received the Order of the Rose.

When National Panhellenic met at The Greenbrier, White Sulphur Springs, W.Va., in November, 1955, this was an official view of the conference taken over the shoulders of the presiding officers. Chairman Byars is at the rostrum and other Delta Gamma delegates (alternates) are at the extreme left of the visitors section behind the delegates.

*Importance on campus
an established fact . . .*

During the 'sixties the presence of college panhellenic presidents and advisers provided a weekend of special programming at National Panhellenic Conference benniums. At the 1969 meeting in Miami Beach, Delta Gamma was represented by this group which includes two panhellenic advisers, Delta Gamma's official NPC delegation, and the collegians.

*Never underestimate
the power of women—
united in a single cause*

*And what better example than the famed Blind
Childrens Center in Los Angeles which opened
in 1938 as the Southern California Delta Gammas'
part in the newly accepted (1936) fraternity philanthropic project.*

*The Order of the Rose—Dr. Lillian Ray Titcomb, Υ-
Stanford, (right) receives her award. Dr. Titcomb was
founder of the Los Angeles Nursery School for Visually Handicapped Children, now known as the Blind Childrens Center.*

*The Blind Childrens Center of Los Angeles, formerly the Los Angeles Nursery School for Visually Handi-
capped Children, receives its support from Delta Gammas in Southern California and their friends.*

Her Majesty Queen Elizabeth II, accompanied by His Royal Highness the Prince Philip, Duke of Edinborough, in 1957, visited the Supreme Allied Commander in Europe, General Lauris Norstad and Mrs. Norstad (Isabelle Jenkins, A Δ-Oregon).

In public affairs—
on their own
or as husband's aide—

Margaret Aitken, AΓ-Toronto, was another recipient of the Order of the Rose for distinguished work in the field of journalism, for she has been considered the First Lady of the Canadian Press. Lord Beaverbrook's niece, she was in 1953 elected to the Canadian parliament, holding here her certificate of election.

When President Nixon appointed Patricia Reilly Hitt, AN-USC, Assistant Secretary in the Department of Health, Education, and Welfare, she became the highest ranking woman in his first administration. Delta Gamma recognized her achievement with the Order of the Delta Gamma Rose, presented by President Marcia Strickland at the 1970 Convention.

A historic photo—Judge Sarah Tilghman Hughes, Ψ-Goucher, administers the Oath of Office to President Lyndon B. Johnson in the Presidential plane in Dallas minutes after the death of President Kennedy.

*Recognition for
special abilities*

Once president of Beta Mu chapter at Bowling Green, Eva Marie Saint pursued her dream of an acting career, winning an Academy Award in 1954 for her role in On the Waterfront.

Charming the public as Miss America 1969, Judi Ford returned to school at the end of her reign to be pledged and initiated by Iota chapter at the University of Illinois.

Among Delta Gamma's more prolific authors are
Amanda M. Ellis, BΔ-Colorado College, above,
and Alberta Pierson Hannum, E-Ohio State. Both
are recipients of the Fraternity's Order of the Rose.

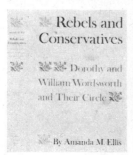

chora. Here are outlined the various methods of giving to the Delta Gamma Foundation—cash, real estate, gifts in trust, life insurance, bequests, gifts designated by chapters and associations and in honor of deceased members. In an era when we seem surrounded by foundations and their good works, Delta Gammas have this opportunity to participate in their own Foundation, not only financially, but personally, too.

Officers Training School

Once more an Officers Training School was in session—June 19-23 at the new Xi chapter house in Ann Arbor, Michigan. Forty-six officers covered all areas of collegiate programming, fraternity operation, Foundation, and alumnæ activity. Again, this was indeed a work session, with "classes" scheduled from 10 a.m. until 10 p.m. each day. Council held a special meeting in conjunction with the School to handle necessary Fraternity business.

Council Meeting—Fall, 1959

New Orleans was the site of the Council meeting scheduled for November 1-8, 1959, at the Roosevelt Hotel. A southern location had been chosen to accommodate Council members who also had to attend National Panhellenic Conference whose sessions opened on November 9 in Boca Raton, Florida. Editor Nancy Gregory arrived in New Orleans in time to spend a day with Council covering a great amount of *Anchora* and other publications business before going on, too, to Boca Raton.

As is usually the case at the fall Council meeting preceding a Convention, a sizeable amount of time was given to plans for the meetings scheduled in June in Colorado.

Officers who went on to Boca Raton for NPC were Delegate Ruth Turpin and her alternates, President Helen Preston and First Vice-President (NPC Delegate-elect) Peggy Hay, as well as Robert Abernethy who was meeting with the Central Office Executives and Editor Nancy Gregory with the NPC Editors' Association.

Anchora is 75

Seventy-five years of continuous publication were observed by *Anchora* with a special issue for winter, 1959. The *Anchora* had, as we know, been the second sorority publication to come into existence, Kappa Kappa Gamma *Key* predating it by two years.

College of the Pacific

Delta Gamma was this year to be the first NPC member to enter the College of the Pacific when the 101-year-old local, Epsilon Lambda Sigma, petitioned to become a chapter. Since this local had been know as "Epsilon" for a century, Delta Gamma skipped a few letters in the Greek alphabetical order of chapters to allow the new chapter to be Delta Epsilon as it had requested. The College of the Pacific (now University of the Pacific) is the oldest college in California, having been chartered in 1851. The local sorority formally became a colony on October 4, 1959, and was installed on December 4 with 61 collegiate members and 10 alumnæ initiated.

Council Meeting—Spring, 1960

Once more a busy pre-convention spring, and when Council met March 12-18, 1960, at the Georgian Towers, Vancouver, B.C., much attention was given to the program of the forthcoming Convention.

Nominating Committee

For the first time the Nominating Committee, set up by Constitutional amendment in 1958, had submitted for Council approval a number of suggestions for procedures for implementing the nominations process. Of these several were accepted: that Council appoint a chairman of the newly elected committee at Convention, that the committee then meet before the close of Convention, and that Council furnish complete information about the offices to be filled (qualifications, in addition to the obvious ones, which would be helpful to one holding a particular office).

At this Council meeting a clarification was also made in the line of authority in the case of a chapter (or member) having a problem, complaint or a need for information:

1. A request for a report and recommendation should be sent to the Fraternity Chairman responsible for the particular area of work. The Chairman will then refer the matter to the Province officer concerned, not to the group involved.

2. The Province officer will investigate and report back to the Chairman.

3. The Chairman will report to the Council officer to whom she is responsible, who will in turn refer it to Council if necessary.

4. If it is a minor situation, the Province officer will resolve it immediately and report to the chairman who, in turn, will report to the Council officer.

5. If a matter is once reported to Council for action, Council will follow through to its completion.

Building plans for office

By this spring of 1960 Council knew that the day was nearing when the Fraternity would be able to move forward in the building of a headquarters. Miss Abernethy reported that a piece of property in which she thought they might be interested had become available, and it was decided that Mrs. Dillon and Mrs. Anderson should come to Columbus as soon as possible to investigate this. Plans for the building were also discussed.

Thirty-ninth Convention
1960—Estes Park, Colorado

Delta Gamma's Thirty-ninth Convention was scheduled for June 25-30 at the Stanley Hotel,

Estes Park, Colorado. Colorado Delta Gammas who were on various Convention committees (under the direction of Chairman Jeanne Catlett Strong, Phi-Colorado) knew that they had a long-time reputation to live up to (1907, 1924, 1938) in providing the "spectacular" expected of another Colorado Convention. And this they accomplished. However, through no fault of theirs, the Convention was a near comedy of errors, but one which seemed to inspire delegates and visitors to greater heights of accomplishments and amusements.

Turning to Editor Nancy Gregory's hilarious account of the opening of Convention,

"The Stanley Hotel, nestled in a lush mountain valley, surrounded in all sides by the towering peaks of the Rocky Mountains, lists among its assets an 'atmosphere of friendly informality.'"

This fact was witnessed by 446 Delta Gammas and a large number of the world's most renowned scientists.

"Consider this situation at the Stanley: The Society of Nuclear Medicine, which arrived 700 strong on June 22, was scheduled to depart sometime on the 25th. The Delta Gamma Fraternity was scheduled to arrive sometime on the 25th. The Rocky Mountains were in full glory; the weather was delightful, and the hotel code says you can't evict a guest unelss he sets fire to his room.

"This, in short, means that the ΔΓ's arrived faster than the scientists departed. Yes, there was a little friendly competition for rooms the evening of the 25th; and in compliance with the hotel code, sixty to eighty Delta Gammas bowed to the atomic experts who decided to stay, and with luggage in hand they took their places in line for the Stanley station wagon, which has a capacity of five guests with luggage plus driver." The station wagon deposited these frustrated Delta Gammas at nearby motels.

"Add to this general confusion the fact that the switchboard operator was new and inexperienced and cut off more than she connected; that the fur which flew the night of the 25th so unnerved the room clerks it took them three days to figure out which guests were in which rooms, and in fact, at least two days to figure out which rooms were occupied.

"However, contrary to what the logical conclusion should be, the 1960 Convention will go down on record as one of the most successful of meetings—(a credit to the chairman and her assistants), and all but the most sensitive and demanding delegate had the time of her life at the Stanley. The situations which seemed to lead to the darkest depression and despair were the very things which raised the spirits of the crowd and which eventually led to almost gay anticipation of inconvenience."

Convention visitors and 270 delegates divided their time between four general meetings and five collegiate and alumnæ workshop sessions, and a number of special meetings and events.

Elections

Unanimous approval was accorded the nominating committee selections for Council positions up for election this year: Elizabeth Coffinberry Kloppenburg, Γ-California, of Seattle, First Vice-President; Kathryn Maple Roberts, ΔH-Whitman, of Boston, to complete two years of Maisie Groves' term (she had resigned as of this Convention) as Second Vice-President; Ruth Canary Turpin, ΔN-Southern California, of Pasadena, Secretary, and Marjorie Reeves Van Ness, Θ-Indiana, Treasurer.

Elected to the nominating committee for 1962 were Maisie Clugston Groves, ΔΦ-British Columbia, Chairman; Jean Falconer Chase, K-Nebraska; Harriet Harrison McIntyre, ΔΨ-Mississippi; Fay Hamilton Jones, Υ-Stanford, and Jane Teagarden Brutsche, ΔΥ-Southern Methodist.

For the second time two Collegiate Representatives to Council were elected, Carolyn Kloppenburg, B-Washington (daughter of the new First Vice-President), from chapters living in houses, and Peggy Flowers, ΓA-Tennessee, from chapters in lodges or rooms.

Convention action

- **Chapter newsletters** to all alumnæ of the chapter are no longer required.
- **Nominating Committee vacancies** shall be filled by Council appointment.
- **The Fraternity Seal** shall be hereafter included, by picture, in the Constitution.
- **Notification of Founders Day** need not be sent by each chapter to each of its living alumnæ, as in the past.
- **Delta Gamma Foundation** may purchase property or invest in first mortgages up to fifty per cent of the Foundation assets, providing thirty per cent of the assets remain liquid.

Resolutions and Recommendations

Among the resolutions and recommendations were the following:

1. A check for $100 be sent from Foundation funds to the American Federation for the Blind, the National Society for Prevention of Blindness, and the Canadian National Institute for the Blind. (This is a customary Convention procedure.)

2. An independent House Loan Commission, composed of seven commissioners to be elected at the 1962 Convention, should be established to handle the sale and promotion of Delta Gamma Youth Bonds.

3. The Delta Gamma fraternity go on record as opposed to summer rush in accordance with the opinion registered by NPC, realizing there are a few scattered areas in which it is carried on and that we must participate in these places in order to maintain our competitive position—but that we may agitate for elimination of this practice in the future.

Advisers attend

For the first time, collegiate chapters had been invited to send (at chapter expense) their advisory board chairmen to Convention where Advisers Chairman, Eleanor Smith Slaughter, conducted workshops for the fifty advisers who came.

Guest speakers

Among the guest speakers to appear at Convention were Mr. Stanley T. Wallbank, president of Phi Gamma Delta; Mr. Francis S. Van Derbur, president of the Interfraternity Research and Advisory Council, and the Foundation guest, Mr. Rexford G. Moon, director of the college scholarship service, College Entrance Examination Board. Banquet speaker was Dr. Clara A. Hardin, Phi-Colorado, executive director of the American Nurses Association, who also that evening received the Order of the Rose. Attendance at the banquet was swelled to 520 by the arrival of Delta Gammas living in the area.

St. Lawrence University

After 73 years absence, Delta Gamma was returning to St. Lawrence University, Canton, New York, with the installation of Gamma Omega chapter. Delta Gamma had established its first Upsilon chapter there in the early 'eighties and then, for lack of enough fraternity material, had withdrawn in 1887. Obviously, after nearly three-quarters of a century, there were no remnants—nor alumnæ—of that early chapter. At the time of the colonization in May, 1960, however, A. K. Peters, St. Lawrence librarian commented "It is apparent that the Delta Gammas enjoyed full recognition. They occupied a chapter room in the old college where their meetings were held on Thursday evenings in full secrecy. They participated in campus events, and contributed to the cultural advancement of the community by sponsoring concerts and lectures." Gamma Omega chapter was installed on December 3, 1960, when 20 collegiates and six alumnæ were initiated. One of the latter was Virginia Smith Boyce, who, as a member of the national staff of the National Society for Prevention of Blindness, had worked closely with Delta Gamma for many years in this area of the Delta Gamma Project.

Recognition certificates

As 1960 came to a close, Executive Secretary Roberta Abernethy reported that 246 certificates of recognition that year had been mailed to Delta Gammas in the following categories: Phi Beta Kappa, 42; Phi Kappa Phi, 6; Mortar Board, 85; summa cum laude, 21; magna cum laude, 6, and cum laude, 85.

Nancy Gregory resigns

The winter, 1960, issue of *Anchora* brought another announcement: the resignation of Nancy Gregory as editor of Central Office's publications department. Once more the search began for a replacement to follow Nancy's four years of creative guidance to all Delta Gamma publications, chiefly, of course, the *Anchora*. For the spring issue, four former publications associates were called upon to combine efforts: Aubrey Hamilton Leonard, a former guest editor, as managing editor; Frances Lewis Stevenson, former editor, handling the Design for Giving section, and Sharon Ruh Manhart, former field secretary and editorial assistant, editing the chapter reports.

International Education grants

Through this period the International Education program had grown and needs as it developed were more clearly defined. Alumnæ groups were being urged to take their part in this Foundation project by providing grants to aid collegiate chapters to help finance their campus guests during their stay. Fairfield County alumnæ chapter, which had been close to this project since its beginning, was the first to take this opportunity and named its grant in honor of one of its members. (All International Education committees are located in the New York-New Jersey area to facilitate work with the National Institute of International Education and to make it possible to give guests a personal greeting in New York before sending them on their respective ways to hostess chapters.)

Youth Bonds

A committee had been appointed following the 1958 Convention to study the possibility of selling Delta Gamma Youth Bonds to add to the funds available for chapter house loans. This plan was deemed feasible by the investigating committee, and early in 1960 a House Loan Committee met in Central Office to plan for actual sale of Youth Bonds. Four members of the House Loan Committee were at Convention and launched the sale with enthusiasm and a gay promotional theme, "Have Your Cake and Eat It Too." The Bonds were sold in denominations of $100 and would draw four per cent interest at the end of 10 years and could be redeemed at face value at any time during that period. Though the committee had been aware of the controls most states maintained over the sale of stocks and bonds, and it had been known that each sale would have to be cleared through its particular state, after a few months of selling, it was felt that these intricacies and the red tape involved made it impractical to continue the sale of these bonds.

Election methods

At the request of a Convention resolution, President Helen Preston appointed a committee to investigate fraternity election methods, including the work of the Nominating Committee. During the 'fifties, election methods had been the subject of much official and unofficial discussion and Convention debate, and this committee was formed to do a thorough investigation which might bring about a solution to the problems. Chairman of this committee was Irene Howell Forman, ΔK-Washburn, former Fraternity Secretary. Other members included Nancy Harris Cooper, ΑΣ-UCLA, also a former Fraternity Secretary; Marcia Connell Strickland, Ξ-Michigan, Director of the Delta Gamma Foundation; Mildred Moyer Baynard, former PAC, and Mary Frances Cornell Grubbs, Θ-Indiana, another former PAC and current Province Secretary. Each had had Nominating Committee experience. The results of their canvassing and deliberations would be brought to the 1962 Convention.

Chapter reports

At the 1960 Convention, Editor Nancy Gregory had presented in an alumnæ workshop a plan for a new presentation of individual chapter news—hoping to solve the problem of ever-lengthening pages of chapter letters. With alumnæ approval, this plan was adopted and launched during the 1960-61 year. It was a sectioning of alumnæ activities: programs, alumnæ work with collegians, ways and means, Panhellenic, service, and names in the news, an arrangement destined to be followed with growing success for a number of years to come.

Council Meeting—Fall, 1960

Council traveled to Minneapolis and the Curtis Hotel to meet November 10-18, 1960. The three new Council members had plunged with enthusiasm into their jobs, and Kay Roberts, the newly elected Second Vice-President, presented a long range plan for alumnæ programming development. This emphasized, among other things, the relationship of the alumnæ and collegiate chapter, when both were in a single city, and in this area Mrs. Roberts was working closely with First Vice-President Elizabeth Kloppenburg.

In recent months several disastrous fires had occurred in fraternity houses, and a requirement for Delta Gamma chapter house fire drills was initiated by this Council. The necessity for fire prevention and preparedness was largely brought about by the increased size of chapter houses which demanded such uniform regulations.

This meeting in Minneapolis enabled the Grants and Loans chairman, Elinor Andrews, to be present for a session with Council. The Dawson Loan Fund was discussed in some depth, and it was decided that the limitations imposed in this bequest could be eased to the extent that individual loans could be raised from $100 to $500 and sons, as well as sisters and daughters of Delta Gammas would be eligible.

"Go ahead" for the office

And possibly the most important action—at least with most tangible results—of this Council meeting was the instruction to the Executive Secretary to proceed as planned with the construction of a new Delta Gamma headquarters building.

Since 1955, when Central Office had joined a national trend of businesses moving to outlying areas of cities, the suburban location had proved entirely satisfactory, and a search for a perfect construction site had been narrowed to this suburban area. The spot had been found, a wooded lot opposite the park on the banks of the Scioto River. In a residential area, it had been tailor-zoned by Upper Arlington commissioners to Delta Gamma needs, an office of a non-profit organization. Later these limitations were expanded so that we were able to rent second floor office space to other business offices. Being on U.S. Route 33, this location was easily accessible, not only for out-of-town visitors but for employees living in other parts of the city.

And so in April, 1961, President Helen Preston and Treasurer Marjorie Van Ness were in Columbus, and Architect-Contractor George Stegmiller furnished a gold shovel tied with bronze, pink, and blue ribbon for Mrs. Preston to officially break ground for the new building. In spite of April on the calendar, it was a spadeful of snow which the President turned in her official act.

Council Meeting—Spring, 1961

Following a visit to the Kansas City Nursery School for the Blind, Council opened its Spring, 1961, meeting on April 7 at the Muehlebach Hotel. This session in Kansas City closed on April 13. Primary attention was divided between plans for another Officers Training School scheduled for June and the more immediate decisions in connection with proposed color schemes and furniture for the under-construction central office building.

Goals for Delta Gamma

Goals for the Fraternity and in respect to individual Council offices were discussed with special consideration given to the following items:

1. Promotion of Fraternity Education through better and more extensive use of Anchora and materials and programs already developed.

2. Stressing in our Scholarship Program good attitudes on study and learning, rather than putting too much emphasis on competitive grade position.

3. Improvement in internal public relations— such as better communications, clearer and more definite instructions, ways of insuring new appointees having complete understanding, not only the duties but the dates of the term of office, etc.

4. Maintaining good position in NPC by continuing strong representation, cooperating with other groups in increasing NPC effectiveness and influence.

Resolutions presented at Convention had been under discussion for some time, stemming from the feeling that those which demanded Convention action might better be presented prior to Convention. Council considered this matter again at this meeting and agreed that while it would still be permissible to present resolutions at Convention, it would be requested that as many as possible be submitted in writing prior to Convention—by March 10, in the case of the next (1962) Convention.

Appointed officers' terms

Appointments of province officers and committee chairman, had, for some time, been made in the year between Conventions and in time for appointees to attend the Officers Training School. Terms were for two years with the possibility of reappointment for one additional two-year term. This system was working well—though, of course, cases did arise when replacement was necessary at other times. For the first time, however, at this Council meeting in an odd-numbered year an entire schedule of appointments and reappointments is contained in the minutes.

University of New Mexico

A month after Council meeting, May 20, 1961, Delta Alpha chapter was installed at the University of New Mexico. Delta Gamma had colonized in February by pledging 25 girls, the eighth NPC group to enter the campus.

Officers Training School

Fayetteville, Arkansas, the spacious Alpha Omega chapter house, was the scene of the 1961 Officers Training School, another successful session of learning and listening for the Fraternity's appointed officers.

Editor Pro Tem

By fall, 1961, Fran Stevenson was back at the editor's desk on a part time basis and bearing the title "editor pro tem," an arrangement that would continue until mid-1963 when she once more resumed the full direction of the Publications Department as Editor.

Council Meeting—Fall, 1961

Three Council members (Mesdames Preston, Hay, and Van Ness) and the Executive Secretary (Miss Abernethy) took a "busman's holiday" and traveled to Hawaii for a fall vacation prior to the Council meeting in Los Angeles. So it is presumed that it was with some degree of gaiety that they arrived for the opening Council session on November 3—gaiety which possibly had been worn down just a little when the meeting adjourned on the tenth.

Dawson Loan use expanded

An entire new program was set up for the Dawson Loan Fund so that its use could be further encouraged by the Grants and Loans Committee. At the same time, the graduate counselor and transfer scholarship program was removed from the jurisdiction of Grants and Loans and placed under a special chairman who could work closely with the First Vice-President.

National Panhellenic Conference

Following Council meeting the NPC delegate (Mrs. Hay) and her two alternates (Mrs. Preston and Mrs. Kloppenburg) and the Executive Secretary traveled to Chandler, Arizona, for the National Panhellenic Conference biennium in session from November 13-18. The editor pro tem, Fran Stevenson, represented Delta Gamma at the Editors' Association meetings. It was at the Editors' session that considerable action was apparent, for this traditionally close-knit and active group (often accused of having "more fun that anyone else at Panhellenic") presented a recommendation to the Panhellenic Conference proposing a public relations program to be investigated and entered into by NPC. It should be recorded here that in spite of its enthusiastic send-off, the program was later doomed to an early death. It was duly investigated by a committee of editors and a presentation made to a special Panhellenic group later by a public relations firm. At this time (April, 1962) this particular program was voted not acceptable to the NPC delegates assembled.

University of Kentucky

As the new building, which Council had designated officially as the Delta Gamma Executive Offices, neared completion, two dates were being circled on the 1962 calendar. The Executive Offices were to be dedicated on March 10, and the week before, March 3, Council members would assemble in Lexington at the University of Kentucky for the installation of Delta Beta chapter. Delta Beta had been colonized during the fall and had been prepared for installation by Field Secretary Nancy Weigle, ΓΦ-Arizona State. A heavy snow nearly stranded Council in Lexington following the official chartering of Delta Beta, but after a day or two delay, the group went on to Columbus for Council meeting at Executive Offices which would precede the dedication the following Saturday.

Council Meeting—Spring, 1962

The snow in Lexington resulted in the Spring, 1962 Council meeting officially opening at the Downtowner Motel, Lexington, Kentucky, taking a break, resuming and concluding at the Executive Offices in Columbus, Ohio, covering the period March 5-10. This may be the only "in transit" Council meeting in recent history. Officers could, of course, look back to the pre-Convention, 1915, meeting when Council met officially on the special train en route to Berkeley and Convention!

A large part of this meeting was devoted to a review of the Constitutional amendments which would be presented at this 1962 Convention.

Other routine business was handled with dispatch, and officers took advantage of being in the Office to work with their own particular departments there. The focal point of the week, however, was the dedication of the building (which the staff had occupied December 1, 1961) on Saturday.

26 — Beauty with purpose proves productive

Executive Offices

And so at 10 a.m. on Saturday, March 10, 1962, nearly 100 persons assembled at 3250 Riverside Drive, Columbus, Ohio, for the dedication of the Delta Gamma Executive Offices. After a week which appeared to be winter's last stand, the day was one that truly promised that spring was only days away. Inside the building spring had already come—with the many floral greetings from well-wishers for the future success of the Delta Gamma Fraternity and Foundation.

Presiding at the dedication and the festivities which followed throughout the day (more than 700 Delta Gammas and guests toured the building that day) was President Helen Preston. The invocation was given by the Rev. Herbert W. Veler, president of the Ohio Synod of the Lutheran Church, whose daughters, Lois Ann and Ruth Ellen, were members of Gamma Rho chapter at Wittenberg University.

Officially welcoming Delta Gamma to Upper Arlington, the suburban community in which the new building is located, was Mayor Warren C. Armstrong, who, coincidentally, is a Delta Gamma husband (of Virginia Bing Armstrong, AP-Ohio Wesleyan) and father (of Ann, AP-Ohio Wesleyan, and Susan, AO-Miami).

President Preston reviewed the years of Delta Gamma history which led to the opening of a central office in Columbus in 1942 and graphically illustrated the further growth of the Fraternity during the past twenty years. She then introduced all of the people who had had a part in financing, building, decorating and landscaping the building, receiving the key officially from the Architect-Builder, George Stegmiller. She in turn, presented the key and its accompanying responsibilities to the Executive Secretary.

Delta Gammas throughout Central Ohio had various parts in the dedication and the open house which progressed throughout that March 10. More than 50 chapters were represented in this participation.

The Offices

"The Delta Gamma Executive Offices are, without question, impressive as a thing of beauty, but a tour tells best their true worth in efficiency. Even the color scheme—the red and white of the foyer, conference room and exucutive secretary's office and the light blues and lavenders of the operation areas—are part of this picture in providing not only a background of beauty but one of lightness and brightness conducive to the best production."

Thus reported the summer issue of *Anchora* in covering this important step by the Fraternity. At the time of dedication the local press also had words to say:

"Any time a lady can get two for the price of one, she'll take it," wrote Jenice Jordan, women's writer for the Columbus *Dispatch*. "So naturally, that's what the women of Delta Gamma got in the function of formal rooms at their new headquarters.

"They also acquired some decorating ideas that could do any private home proud. Take the reception center for example. It's planned for use either as a meeting place or an entertaining area.

"At one end of the room a dining table is located where it will give separateness for large scale conferences or form a good traffic pattern for serving buffet refreshments.

"Grouped around the fireplace is a sofa flanked by red velvet love seats making an ideal conversation center for committee meetings or casual visiting at teas.

"The sofa is covered in a Williamsburg print which repeats the pattern of wallpaper in the foyer," also red and white.

"That way, for especially large gatherings, the two rooms can be thrown together and decoratively as well as practically speaking seem as one.

"For easy service, a dinette-kitchenette opens directly off the main conference room. But it's more than a kitchen.

"Its work center is on one wall so it can be closed off with a white folding door. Then the dining area becomes another spot for small meetings."

Miss Jordan's glowing description continues with decorative details, better shown in accompanying pictures. And, that the prophesied adaptability of all portions of the building came to pass is now a matter of record. All manner of meetings have been held in the conference room while smaller groups frequently convene in the kitchenette. Council has met, field secretaries have been trained, the Ohio Society for Prevention of Blindness has convened, and countless Fraternity committees have circled—all around the large dining table in the conference room.

In 1962, when the Executive Offices were dedicated, it could not be imagined that another year would find the editorial-financial wing as outgrown as a child's last year's coat. In 1962, the entire second floor was rented to other businesses, but by 1964 when the largest of these areas became vacant, the editorial offices would be expanding to this araa. All of this, however, seemed far off on March 10, 1962.

Officers meeting

Scheduling of meetings at the Executive Offices began the moment it opened, but the first large-scale officers meeting occurred a month after dedication when Council and Fraternity chairmen came to Columbus to meet in a pre-Convention session.

Special Issue

The summer issue of *Anchora* was a special one in several ways. The cover was a four-color one, the first in *Anchora* history, a picture of the new Executive Offices taken during the glory of the first week in May. The dedication was, of course, featured, and the issue included other special timely features. It had been decided that the 7-page directory of all officers (Council, Chairmen, Provinces, Foundation, chapter and association) was too space-consuming to appear each issue. For the first time a full directory appeared with the usual center pull-out section for rush. Thus, like the 'phone book, the annual

"yellow pages" would be the Fraternity directory. The other three issues would then carry only Council, Fraternity, Foundation and Province Chairmen, a total of two and one-half pages, with a regular In Memoriam section appearing (for ease in finding) in the remaining half page of this area.

Fortieth Convention
1962—Mackinac Island, Michigan

Once more, Delta Gamma was "Going Back to Mackinac" for a Convention, this one July 1-7, 1962, at the Grand Hotel which had been the site of Delta Gamma Conventions in 1926 and 1940. Both this popular spot and the issues before this Convention found the Grand Hotel turned into "world's largest Delta Gamma house," bulging at the seams with 541 members in attendance.

Laura Bertram Dillon, Z-Albion, Fraternity Secretary 1956-60, was Convention chairman, but due to a shoulder injury prior to Convention, the on-the-spot chairmanship was taken over by her charming assistant chairmen, Patty Buter Taylor, Z-Albion, and Eleanor Oakley Cameron, AO-Miami.

The national holidays of two nations were observed with proper festivities during the course of Convention, Canada's Dominion Day on July 1, and the United States' Fourth of July three days later.

The long porch of the Grand Hotel is famous, and it is difficult to remember a Convention where natural surroundings—the beautifully green island in the circling blue Great Lakes water —exerted more power in soothing and refreshing meeting-wearied Conventioners. If the issues became warm, the porch was cool, and it is safe to say that its clear air was an important part of the 1962 Convention.

Louise Brown Christianson, Λ-Minnesota, was Constitution Chairman, and it was her duty to present the lengthy Constitutional changes. To assist in untangling the often knotty accompanying problems, Fraternity Attorney George Chamblin of Columbus attended several sessions. When the voting concluded—

- **A Third Vice-President** had been added to Council, her duties being to direct the group of chairmen who have charge of Fraternity programs.
- **Terms for Council members** would be reduced from four to two years. A Council member could serve no more than three terms in the same office and no more than six consecutive terms on Council, with the exception of the Panhellenic delegate, who, having served six terms on Council, could serve three consecutive terms as NPC delegate, providing her total terms in that office did not exceed six. (If this seems complex, much of it was simplified by the limitations voted at the 1964 Convention!)
- **Nominating committee** selection was revised so that each of the five members would be elected

by the area each represents, rather than the five area representatives being elected by the Convention as a whole.

Alpha Mu suspension

The delegate from Alpha Mu chapter, though present at Mackinac, was not seated at Convention* because the chapter had been suspended on June 30 following the 60-day probationary period. During the following months, Alpha Mu was encouraged to rebuild its position, but no action was initiated by the local group to reestablish itself and regain Delta Gamma status. By June, 1965, no Delta Gamma collegians remained on the Beloit campus, and Council then completed the formal withdrawal procedure.

Workshops

Once more in 1962 advisers were a part of the Convention, and their workshops as well as those of alumnæ and collegiate delegates were an important part of the program. An always popular workshop for conventioners are the early morning parliamentary procedure workshops conducted by the Convention Parliamentarian who for a number of years during this period was Mrs. Gano Senter of Denver.

Elections

For the first time in eight years Delta Gamma would have a new President. Maisie Clugston Groves, of Vancouver, who had served as Second Vice-President 1956-60, was elected to this office, thus becoming the first Canadian President in the history of the Fraternity. Re-elected Second Vice-President on the new two-year term basis was Kathryn Maple Roberts of Boston. In the newly created office of Third Vice-President would be Marcia Connell Strickland of Bloomfield Hills, Michigan, who had already served the Fraternity in a number of offices, most recently Director of the Delta Gamma Foundation. Margaret Richardson Hay was re-elected Panhellenic Conference Delegate for another two years.

Elected to the 1964 nominating committee were Janet Lau Sullivan, Province I Alumnæ Chairman; Mildred Moyer Baynard, past Province Alumnæ Chairman; Gloria Schnaiter Blake, Fraternity Rush Chairman; Betty Beach Norris, Province X Alumnæ Chairman, and Lucia Frier McKenzie, B-Washington, San Francisco delegate to Convention.

The two Collegiate Representatives for Council would be Sally Myers, AII-Arizona, from chapters living in houses, and Lois Haegley, AX-Penn State, from chapters not living in houses.

* It is not unusual for a chapter not to be seated at Convention due to disciplinary probation invoked by Council. With sufficient improvement in the delinquent areas of chapter activity, probation is ended. Occasionally, when this involved payment of unpaid bills, which can be taken care of immediately, the delegate may be seated later in the same Convention.

Maisie Clugston Groves, AΦ-British Columbia, who served as president 1962-66, was the first Canadian to be elected President of the Fraternity. She had previously served as Second Vice-President, directing alumnæ affairs 1956-60. She presided at Delta Gamma's first Presidents' Leadership School.

Manuscripts

Always an interesting section of Anchora has been Manuscripts, edited since 1940 by Julia McCune, Z-Albion, for whom the current 1962-63 Fraternity Fellowship was named. Rarely in all years in this position did this Manuscripts editor, with a truly fantastic memory for names, miss anything published by a Delta Gamma. Sometimes the authors' names were more generally familiar than others, and this was true in the fall, 1962 issue when Columnist Inez Robb's Don't Just Stand There was reviewed along with The Heritage by Ellen Bromfield Geld, daughter of Louis Bromfield.

Council Meeting—Fall, 1962

With an eye to a future Convention, Council met in Portland, Oregon, at the Sheraton-Portland Hotel, October 24-31.

During the summer the resignation of Secretary Ruth Turpin had been received by Council with great regret. Serious illness caused this very active Council member to discontinue her service in office.

The first duty of Council in session at this fall meeting was to appoint a Secretary, and their logical choice was Margery Sommers Hammill, AM-Beloit, who had served as Housing Chairman for several years. As Secretary, she would also serve as Expansion Chairman (as was customary), and it was decided that she might continue, too, as Director of Housing. During the coming year several of the Standing Committee chairmanships were discontinued, and a Council member added the directorship of a particular area to her duties.

Mrs. Groves presented for Council approval (which it received) a formal statement reflecting the philosophy of membership as outlined in the Constitution of the Fraternity. This was to serve as a base upon which we could not only stand in cases where policies concerning membership were questioned by university committees, but it would also aid in plotting a course of direction for a difficult transitional period on college and university campuses.

A new feature in Fraternity education was planned by this Council: The province leadership conferences were to be discontinued and all newly elected collegiate presidents would meet in June, 1963, for a Presidents Leadership School, probably in Columbus to make use of the new Executive Offices.

Editorial Board

Upon the Editor's and Executive Secretary's recommendation, an Editorial Board was to be formed to act as an advisory body to the publications department.

Since Marcia Strickland had been elected to Council, it was necessary to appoint a new Director for the Foundation. This was Fay Hamilton Jones, Υ-Stanford, who had been serving as Project Chairman.

Housing

Fraternity housing during this era is, like the country in general, described in one word—boom! The spring issue (1963) of Anchora is once more a housing issue with Director of Housing Margery Hammill doing a question/answer feature on the housing picture and then a series of stories and pictures of what is new in housing among Delta Gamma chapters.

Council Meeting—Spring, 1963

Council had selected Washington, D.C.'s new International Inn for its spring Council meeting, with the idea that this would be the site for the 1964 Convention. As it turned out, Convention was not held in Washington, but Council did meet there March 27-April 1, 1963.

During the week in Washington the two collegiate representatives for Council met with the officers for two days, offering as usual a number of very sound suggestions.

Since the establishment of the enlarged office facilities and staff, it was decided to transfer the custodian responsibility for all Fraternity stocks and bonds from Philadelphia to Columbus.

For many years it had been a Delta Gamma policy that a member who was married secretly was expelled. In fact, this was among the oldest policies on record. At this Council meeting it was voted to rescind this policy as well as several others concerning married students as chapter officers.

Much time was devoted to the planning of the first Presidents Leadership School which was to be combined with Officers Training School in June in Columbus.

Public Relations Consultant

During the officers' stay in Washington, several had met with Jackie Martin, P-Syracuse, Rose Award recipient, currently operating her own Public Relations office. After discussing the entire field of Delta Gamma public relations with her, it was decided to employ her services for the Fraternity for the coming year, starting with her attendance at the School in Columbus.

OTS-PLS

The written record of this period is a little reminiscent of the New Deal in its lavish use of initials. It was natural that Officers Training School-Presidents Leadership School should become OTS-PLS—attended by PAC's and PS's, among others!

Its coverage in the fall issue of Anchora, the first public relations project supervised by Jackie Martin, indicates to some extent its complete success.

Dormitory facilities at Ohio State University were used for housing, and most meetings were held on campus in Pomerene Hall. University buses transported presidents and officers the four miles to the Executive Offices for a tour of the building and a half-day session there.

Person to person communication between Fraternity officers and collegiate chapter presidents which this School made possible was possibly one of its most valuable results. Collegiate endorsement of the high goals outlined in Fraternity programming was heard on all sides, and it is interesting to note that the most quoted discussions during the school were Standards and Scholarship.

One chairman wrote following the School, ". . . However, more than all of these things, I am proud of the road Council has staked out for the future: The road of rediscovering—reinterpreting —and plainly stating the standards and principles in which we believe.

"Council's basic philosophy as so beautifully presented by Mrs. Groves is a summation of Council's first obligation to the Fraternity—*to understand its nature, and to ploy the course for is development.* This philosophy clearly states that Delta Gamma's progress is not something that can be directed by outside influences—but it must come from within and that Council has summoned the will and the means for taking the initiative."

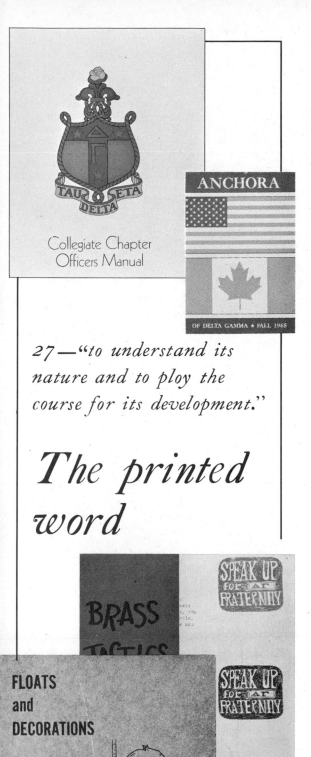

27—"to understand its nature and to ploy the course for its development."

The printed word

FLOATS
and
DECORATIONS

When Council traveled to Dallas, Texas, for its fall meeting, November 18-23, it could not anticipate those few minutes on the afternoon of November 22 when Dallas, tragically, became the most important city in the world. It was their last afternoon in Dallas, and during the luncheon break several had chosen to shop while others watched the parade honoring President Kennedy and his wife who were visiting the city. While none were eyewitnesses when the President was felled by an assassin's bullet, the Council minutes record, "It should be noted that the memory of Council's last afternoon in Dallas, November 22, 1963, will never be erased."

Back in Columbus the editor was finishing the final proof stage of the winter *Anchora* and had on her desk the first contributions for the spring issue. Among the latter was a note from a Dallas Delta Gamma concerning a feature planned for spring about a famed Texas member, a Rose Award winner, Judge Sarah Tilghman Hughes, Ψ-Goucher. The note, from Patricia Weiss Barron, I-Illinois, commented that her interview with Judge Hughes had been delayed until the following Monday because the local Democrats were so involved with all the activities surrounding President Kennedy's Friday arrival.

Minutes after the President was shot, it was Judge Hughes who was sped to the airport to swear into the highest office in the land Lyndon Baines Johnson. It was natural, then, to hold the *Anchora* for the Judge Hughes story including the only picture taken of this historic moment. It might be noted, too, that Mrs. Barron's interview was further delayed, for "the following Monday" Judge Hughes was one of the many mourners in Washington for the President's funeral.

Publications

By that fatal Friday in Dallas, Council had completed its usual mountain of Fraternity business. The new social log was finalized and pronounced ready for publication. And this was only one project of the expanding publications-public relations area. When it was decided to use Jackie Martin's services as public relations consultant, it was also considered the proper moment to add to the editor's duties that of Director of Public Relations. She would work with Jackie Martin and continue to head the publications department of Executive Offices. The obvious expansion entailed by this action made the addition of an editorial assistant necessary.

Manuals and handbooks to come

As work in this area progressed, others were

added to this staff for specific assignments, editing certain manuals and handbooks as they were scheduled. In fact, it was action at this Council meeting which set off a series of events which would result in a fine Fraternity reference library. The Executive Secretary proposed a consolidation of all necessary material for chapter officers into two manuals, one for collegiate chapters and one for alumnæ chapters, which would be the basis of all that might follow in the way of supplementary handbooks or instructions. Thus it was that Council approved a meeting in January, 1964, in the Executive Offices for the First and Second Vice-Presidents to work with the Executive Secretary on the initial steps of this lengthy project.

Council exercised the traditional "woman's privileges" and decided to change the site of Convention which had previously been scheduled for Washington, D.C. with Ruth Utz Russell, AP-Ohio Wesleyan as chairman. Instead, Convention would take place at the new Doral Beach Hotel, Miami Beach, Florida, June 25-July 1, 1964. Because of the distance from her home, Mrs. Russell resigned as Convention chairman, and Council appointed Floridian Mildred Moyer Baynard, K-Nebraska, a name familiar to Delta Gamma for the many areas in which she had served.

National Panhellenic Conference

Prior to this November, 1963, Council meeting, several of the officers had been in Hot Springs, Arkansas, at the Arlington Hotel, November 13-17, for the regular NPC biennium. Margaret Richardson Hay once more headed the Delta Gamma delegation with President Maisie Groves and First Vice-President Elizabeth Kloppenburg as her alternates. Treasurer Marjorie Van Ness also attended the meetings as a visitor and the Editor and Executive Secretary were present for their respective sessions.

For the first time at a National Panhellenic meeting an entire day was devoted to collegians and their problems, and all of the collegiate Panhellenic officers in a radius of 250 miles from Hot Springs, as well as their deans of women or advisers, were asked to attend. There were 34 schools in this area, and 23 accepted the NPC invitation. Seventeen NPC groups were represented by Panhellenic presidents, three of the latter being Delta Gammas; there were also two Delta Gamma deans and an assistant dean.

Much discussed at this NPC session was the decision of Panhellenic groups at Long Beach State College to operate off campus, severing their formal connection with the administration. Delta Gamma alone retained its campus status, continuing to operate in the usual manner.

Textured Flag

Making page one early in 1964 was the announcement by the Freedoms Foundation that one of its George Washington Medals would go to the Delta Gamma alumnæ of Oak Park-River Forest (Illinois) for their textured flag for the blind. Similar to reading braille in color, the blind person could distinguish the colors of the American flag by the changes of texture and so was "seeing" it for the first time. These flags were making ideal gifts for schools and classes for blind children or for blind centers. Since each flag was handmade, it was possible, too, for the group to furnish flags of other countries—which it was doing on special orders.

Council Meeting—Spring, 1964

Once more it was Council meeting time, and the officers met at the Pheasant Run Lodge, St. Charles, Illinois, April 15-19. For the last two days of the meeting the officers were joined by Jackie Martin and Fran Stevenson for finalizing Convention plans in the area of publications-public relations.

Manual progress report

The Executive Secretary presented the first progress report on the new series of manuals and handbooks. This was in what she called not finished, but thinking form. Contents were discussed and the proposed format and distribution arrangements were approved. Work to this point had been preliminary surveying and thinking, but Council agreed that the work on the manuals should be implemented immediately.

Publications expansion

Just prior to this Council meeting the Executive Secretary had learned that one large area of the second floor of the Executive Offices building would be vacated by its tenant early in the summer. Council immediately approved Delta Gamma absorbing this area for its own use, the area at the front to be used for archives development and on the side for the expanded publications facilities. This would enable the also rapidly growing auditing department to take over the publications area of the first floor north wing. It was further agreed that office space vacated by other tenants would be held for our own future use.

Field Secretaries—new concept

An entirely new concept of the Field Secretary program was proposed and agreed upon. Four Field Secretaries had been appointed for the coming year, and each chapter would be visited by one of them during the year. In previous years, Field Secretary visits had been, first, to offer special assistance in the case of special problems or in preparing a chapter for installation or assisting a new chapter with its early growing pains. It was agreed, too, that Mrs. Kloppenburg, First Vice-President, who would be going out of office at Convention, should take over the direction of the Field Secretaries. A training session for the four who had been appointed would be held in late August at the Executive Offices with Mrs. Kloppenburg directing the operation.

Forty-first Convention
1964—Miami Beach, Florida

The Doral Beach Hotel was new and luxurious and seemingly perfectly planned for the Forty-first Delta Gamma Convention. Chairman Mildred Baynard and the Florida Delta Gammas had, in spite of their delayed start, gone all out in decorations, entertainment and hospitality to make this Miami Beach meeting, June 25-July 1, a great success. And so it was—with only one minor deterrent: elevators whose pace was planned for a vacationer's leisure, not for the mass movement of Conventioners to top floor meetings.

Convention exhibits

Convention exhibits, depicting all phases of Delta Gamma activity, had been assembled under the direction of PR Consultant Jackie Martin and made the rear of the Convention Hall as spectacular as the platform—which was a spectacular itself. St. Petersburg Delta Gammas had created a huge three-dimensional anchor of gold and white satin over a styrofoam form, framed, against a dark blue backdrop, by cream colored roses. This indeed made a beautiful setting for all Convention meetings.

Workshops

Though workshops had become one of the most important parts of Convention and are generally a part of each day's program, this time an entire day was devoted solely to workshops. A number of "private" sessions, for collegiate delegates only, covered various areas of Delta Gamma programming and their own special problems. This was a valuable exchange, and it resulted in a number of resolutions presented to the assembly on the last day by the Collegiate Representatives for Council.

Panhellenic

The Panhellenic luncheon featured guest representatives from all other Panhellenic groups, and the Delta Gamma guest speaker was Margaret Long Arnold, P-Syracuse, retiring president of the General Federation of Women's Clubs, world's largest women's organization.

Guests and NSPB citation

Another guest speaker who came with a special duty was Dr. John W. Ferree, executive director of the National Society for Prevention of Blindness, who presented the Fraternity with a large citation honoring Delta Gammas contributions to the field of blindness prevention. Dr. Ferree appeared during the program devoted to the Delta Gamma Foundation when guest speaker, Lena Koch, IE student who had been with Gamma Mu during the year, completely captivated the audience with her charm and wit.

At the final general meeting, still another guest appeared. This was Dean May Brunson of the University of Miami, whose address seemed to tie Convention together as if she had attended each session and sometimes three workshops simultaneously.

Founder's daughter a special guest

As always, the banquet was memorable and beautiful. The awards program was an appropriate climax to Convention as were the gifts to outgoing Council members—miniature citations framed in sterling. And Delta Gamma heritage was personified by Convention guest Lena Boyd Ellington, daughter of Founder Anna Boyd Ellington.

Talks by the two Collegiate Representatives to Council who had been elected for the coming year were outstanding. Jeanne Swahn, BII-Texas, represented chapters living in their houses, and E. J. Holt, University of Miami, was elected by chapters not living in houses. E.J.'s mother, Jane Jones Holt, AM-Beloit, had been one of the busy Florida Convention committee.

Elections, 1964

For the first time an entire Council was to be elected (or re-elected) under the two-year term plan which had been put into effect in 1962. Those re-elected to Council were President Maisie Groves, Secretary Margery Hammill, and Marcia Strickland who was moving into the office of National Panhellenic Conference Delegate from the Third Vice-Presidency. New officers were Kathryn Bell Gary, M-Missouri, of San Marino, California, First Vice-President; Virginia Riesterer Gates, Σ-Northwestern, of Wheaton, Illinois, Second Vice-President; Eleanor Smith Slaughter, AΨ-Mississippi, of Columbus, Mississippi, Third Vice-President, and Carolyn Coffman Moorman, AO-Miami, of Dayton, Ohio, Treasurer.

Constitution

Much of the Constitutional revision covered at this Convention was clarifying in nature. A committee appointed as the result of a resolution adopted at the 1962 Convention had made a study of areas of the Constitution having to do with membership and this report was presented at this time. The clarifying amendments developed by this committee were adopted at this time.

It would be impossible to clock the hours of thinking and subsequent hours at the typewriter which this committee put into its task. The chairman, Louise Brown Christianson, Λ-Minnesota, accomplished what few are able to do in the expert direction she offered this long distance (continent-wide) committee meeting. The mountains of correspondence which remain attest to the clear thinking which brought about the well considered conclusions which were presented and incorporated to clarify wording in the Delta Gamma Constitution and By-Laws. If one can consider the belief that the right person is provided for a particular task at a particular time, then here, in the person of Louise Christianson as Constitution Chairman, is a first rate example.

Stern action on scholarship

An interesting facet of the Constitutional revision meetings at any Convention is guessing ahead of time which matter will become the point for a major debate. A member who surveys the proposed revisions prior to a Convention may try to predict which item this will be—and usually the prediction is wrong. In the case of the 1964 Convention, the greatest discussion time concerned a scholastic requirement which the Constitution committee had tried to ease for the chapters. The proposed amendment read, "A member whose scholastic average falls below 'C' at the end of the semester or quarter may not hold office . . ." After considerable discussion, then an adjournment and later further discussion, a collegiate-proposed amendment to the amendment was added: ". . . and will be deprived of her vote in chapter meeting except on the selection of members until she has regained a scholastic average of 'C'."

Collegiate resolutions

Further evidence of the great amount of collegiate participation in Convention sessions was the group of resolutions sponsored by collegiate delegates at the closing session. The collegiate delegates had been divided into committees, each committte concerning itself with one phase of chapter programming—rush, standards, scholarship, rituals, and pledge education. Each of these committees formulated several resolutions which were presented to the assembly by the two Collegiate Representatives to Council, E. J. Holt and Jeanne Swahn, who had earlier been elected by the collegiate delegates. The resolutions were recommendations for matters the collegiate chapters wished investigated by Council at its fall meeting. The recommendations, approved by the Convention, were in due course studied by Council, fully reported to the chapters, and several did form the basis for a policy change for the Fraternity.

The Office expands

Conventioners from Executive Offices were no sooner back in Columbus than moving day was upon them again. The second floor area into which publications would expand was available and the move began. It would be a true Communications and Information Center. This was a large "L", down the side and across the front of the building, and the front area was to be reserved for the Delta Gamma Archives which had been a slowly merging dream now beginning to take shape.

The Archives

Ever since 1905 when Blanche Garten had made her initial contact with the Mother Chapter and its early members, treasures of Delta Gamma's early days had appeared from time to time and had been in the care of various Fraternity officers. In the late 'thirties, after Delta Gamma had been re-established in Oxford, Mississippi, Minnie Wohlleben Carter gave to President Marguerite Winant the strong box in which all Delta Gamma papers had been kept during the days of the chapter at Lewis School. She had kept it safely in her attic since 1889 when Psi's charter had been withdrawn. From time to time old badges had been presented to the Office where they had been displayed in the Executive Secretary's office. These and many letters, Convention pictures and programs, and other mementoes had begun to accumulate, and always the Executive Secretary and Editor, as well as the various Councils, had hoped that some day the proper spot for display of these treasures could be made available.

During the winter of 1964-65 Archives plans began to take tangible form. To finance much needed display cases, the Office became a sales organization, offering an attractive line of monogrammed blouses and sweaters, the profits from which would go toward building the archives. At the same time, letters went to all living members who had been initiated more than fifty years, expressing the hope that some of them might be willing to part with more of these mementoes of their own times in college. The response was gratifying, and things began to appear that had been so long forgotten that there was no record of their having existed in the first place.

In the course of collecting archives items, it was also noted that the Archives would also receive gladly any clothing which might be appropriate for Convention historical pageants. This request also brought forth a great response.

The Archives will continue to grow through these donations from members, but the immediate goal of that winter was the proposed dedication of the Delta Gamma Archives which was scheduled to take place during the Leadership School in June. This it did, and it was launched with proper fanfare, President Maisie Groves charging the Executive Secretary and Editor with carrying the responsibility for its further development. Guest speaker for this event was, appropriately, former President Dorothy Knight Wildasin, who had done so much to re-establish Delta Gamma in Mississippi nearly thirty years before.

Council meeting—Fall, 1964

With four new members already deep into the affairs of their individual areas, Council held its fall meeting November 7-13, 1964, in Salt Lake City, Utah. Between meeting attention to the visiting officers was considerable for this was the first time that the Salt Lake Alumnæ and Beta

Gamma chapter had had the opportunity to entertain Council. During the sessions President Maisie Groves and First Vice-President Kathryn Gary were guests on two mid-day color TV programs, and Mrs. Groves had the opportunity to meet with Margaret Robinson Regan, BΓ-Utah, who had been appointed chairman of the Foundation Fund.

Attention to collegians

It was at this meeting that Council approved the final form for the Collegiate Chapter Officers Manual. The year 1964-65 may well be remembered as the year of the manuals, and the Executive Offices as the hub of the Delta Gamma universe. The Executive Secretary had presented the "thinking stages" as we have recorded at the spring, 1964 Council meeting. Council, field secretaries, chairmen, alumnæ and collegiate officers, members—all were contributing ideas and thoughts. The publications department was geared to receive this material and, now with approval, would complete the first of the intended series, the Collegiate Chapter Officers Manual.

In the collegiate field Council also reviewed and acted upon the recommendations from the collegiate committees at the Convention as well as the resolutions presented by the Collegians at this Convention. Council also heard the report of the two Collegiate Representatives for Council, E. J. Holt and Jeanne Swahn. These two had been working in several fields, but their particular interest had been in implementing a program for transfers.

A special fund was also approved to be used by the Treasurer, at her discretion, to aid collegiate members.

Since Coordinating Committees in large city-suburban areas have been successful, this program, Council decided, should also be implemented.

A wide variety of collegiate problems had been discussed—many the result of the recommendations and resolutions, and it was also decided that summer grades would be recognized by Council as fulfilling initiation requirements.

Memphis State University

On March 6, 1965, a new chapter joined the roll. This was Delta Zeta chapter at Memphis State University, Memphis, Tennessee. The colony had been formed nearly a year before by the colonization process, had been nurtured by an active group of local alumnæ, aided and trained by visiting field secretaries, and the charter was granted during installation festivities which began Friday, March 5, and concluded on Sunday.

Council meeting—Spring, 1965

Council gathered in Chicago a week later, March 14, for its spring meeting in the midst of one of Chicago's more spectacular blizzards. The Windy City added intense cold to its weather-fare and someone commented that the Council meeting looked more like an Indain council fire with each officer shrouded in a blanket—against the drafts which modern curtain-wall construction did not keep out.

Manuals and handbooks were once more the chief topic for discussion, and Council first viewed the final proof of the Collegiate Chapter Officers Manual and then progressed to the materials then in hand for accompanying handbooks in the areas of standards, rush, skits, rituals, and scholarship.

As always, full reports were given on all areas of Delta Gamma activity. Plans for the Foundation Fund drive were reviewed, and Council had the opportunity to view the new slides that are being circulated by the Sight Conservation and Aid to the Blind Committee.

The Manuals

Soon after Council meeting was over, the Collegiate Chapter Officers Manual was ready for distribution, with an Alumnæ Officers Manual soon to follow. This project was reviewed in the Summer, 1965, Anchora:

"Fifteen years ago, when a publications department became a part of the office to edit the Anchora, and as the Constitution provides, to 'be responsible for such other editorial duties as may be assigned by Council,' its duties were confined to editing in the strictest sense and to production. During the past year as an expanded Communications and Information Center, the publications staff has assumed much of the critical and creative in the production of manuals, handbooks, letters, certificates, speeches and a variety of other products. This is indeed an area where communications became education.

"The number one production during the 1964-65 year has been the Collegiate Chapter Officers Manual, which, from its beautiful cover (with absolutely correct colors for the crest) to its final page of obligations becomes the cornerstone of collegiate organization. This manual was to become the prototype product of the system: materials, which had been written by various officers gathered together, reshaped and molded to a predetermined editorial pattern, reviewed, evaluated, criticized for intent as well as content, test-used in a particular situation by an officer, a chapter, an adviser or field secretary, and then a repeat of the process of review, evaluation and criticism. Like other manuals and subsidiary handbooks this manual was the product of not one officer nor one term of office nor even one Council, but something which had been built upon, tested and which had evolved as the result of the thinking and knowledge and creativity of many individuals.

"Kathryn Bell Gary, our First Vice-President under whose administration this manual is issued, writes:

" 'It is with understandable pride and satisfaction that we announce the presentation of the

Collegiate Chapter Officers Manual to our collegiate leaders and their advisory boards. This Manual is the result of the vision and knowledge of many talented minds, representing long and varied experience in Delta Gamma collegiate chapter operation. It is our answer to the evident need for Fraternity direction, for clarification of Fraternity policy and for an outline of Fraternity procedures and regulations. With this Manual, the collegiate president and her officers will sail a 'tight ship.' Each officer will find a section of the Manual devoted to the philosophy and responsibilities of her office as well as clearly stated Fraternity Policies, procedures and regulations which she is to follow. The mechanics of the chapters' governing boards are explained and Fraternity organization is presented.' "

Following this plan, the Alumnæ Officers Manual was distributed in the fall of 1965, and the series of supplementary hand books kept a steady pace in the rate they followed.

Leadership School, 1965

When Collegiate Presidents and all Fraternity and Foundation officers came to Columbus for the biennial Leadership School, June 19-25, the Council-faculty offered a thorough schooling in the use of the new Manuals and handbooks.

For this Leadership School the facilities of Ohio State University were used once more, delegates residing in Bradley Hall and this time holding meetings at the Ohio Union—where fine food and excellent service helped contribute to the success of the school. The half-day spent at the Executive Offices was once more an important phase of the sessions, and the climax was the evening reserved for the dedication of the Archives. Columbus alumnæ who created decorations for the banquet preceding the dedication itself contributed to the beauty of the evening.

Continuing Education

Province Alumnæ Chairmen were offered a challenging new program for presentation in their alumnæ chapters and associations. Carolyn Benton Cockefair, M-Missouri charter member, for whom the Carolyn Benton Cockefair Chair of Continuing Education at the University of Missouri in Kansas City had been named, was a special guest. She presented the Continuing Education program, which she had promoted through the University, and which was being used currently by the Kansas City Delta Gamma Alumnæ with considerable success. Her presentation at Leadership School was followed in the fall by the special section in *Anchora*, and furthered in the winter issue.

Speak Up for Fraternity

Officer-delegates to the school also had another area of their duties aided with the presentation of "Speak Up for Fraternity," a speech-making booklet which had been completed by the Communications and Information Center during the spring. Since officers at all levels are frequently on speaking circuits, this aid service was one of the important items being offered by this division of the Executive Offices.

Design for Giving

Careful planning and skillful use of color, turned the fall issue into something of a spectacular. The cover featured the flags of the United States and Canada, the latter being the newly designed flag just adopted for use. This was appropriate not only from the standpoint of timeliness, but also as a special salute to a Canadian president—who had authored a section on Delta Gamma's Canadian chapters for this issue.

The focal point of the issue was the two-color center pull-out section, Design For Giving, featuring all phases of Foundation activities.

NPC, 1965

Once more National Panhellenic Conference convened in Williamsburg, Virginia, with meetings opening October 27. Again, the week-end found collegiate members within a 250-mile radius arriving for Saturday sessions and the NPC banquet that evening.

Marcia Connell Strickland represented Delta Gamma with her alternates, Kathryn Gary and Maisie Groves. Two other Council members, Ginny Gates and Eleanor Slaughter, also attended the conference.

At their respective meetings in conjunction with NPC were the Editor and Executive Secretary. Fran Stevenson was in charge of a portion of the Editor's program, and the guest speaker was another Delta Gamma, Polly Arbaugh Ward, Z-Albion, from the production department at AAUW national headquarters in Washington.

Once more Panhellenic delegates and visitors engaged in thoughtful discussion of the fraternity position of today. During the past ten years there has been continuing agitation to require fraternities to remove discriminatory rules and practices with respect to membership selection. These pressures have come mainly in the form of college regulations, but there have also been some attempts by federal agencies to investigate fraternities in this respect. In response to this agitation, at an earlier meeting, in 1957, NPC had adopted its Declaration of Freedom and a Statement of Rights designed to express the intent of the members of NPC to defend their rights of free association as private organizations. The Fraternity so far has been able to comply with regulations of all colleges where we have chapters. There was discussion, too, at NPC of the protection offered fraternities from federal regulation and control by provisions of the Civil Rights Act of 1964 and the Higher Education Act of 1965.

Again NPC members viewed statistical increases which contradicted the oft-heard statement that fraternities are on the wane. Total membership as of June 1, 1965, was 1,158,126. Since the 1963 Biennium 66 new chapters had been installed, 335 new alumnæ groups organized. Emphasis in reports was placed on the multimillion dollar philanthropic programs of the combined NPC groups, and a further resolution was adopted urging groups to further expand in this area.

Council meeting: The Guest House

When the Council members who had attended Panhellenic returned to Columbus and the remaining two met them there for their semi-annual meeting, November 1-5, another important event took place. For the first time the guest house, next door to Executive Offices, was open for occupancy during their meetings and for subsequent visitors to the Offices.

This small house had been purchased earlier to expand the property belonging to the Executive Offices and to serve as a buffer between the Delta Gamma building and whatever might in the future be constructed beyond this point. Though guest accommodations had been incorporated into the original EO plan, these were of course not adequate for an entire Council meeting—or for more than two guests at a time.

Therefore it had been decided to combine living area with meeting space in a guest house where Council members, field secretaries and other groups could meet for a period of several days. And it was during this Fall, 1965, Council meeting that the house, dubbed "Anchor In," was opened. It has since been used by a number of other small Delta Gamma groups visiting in Columbus to work at the Office—including many pledge classes and overnight chapter retreats.

Fraternity business, as usual

A tremendous amount of Fraternity business was handled as usual—business that includes not only the details of operation but continuing interest in each chapter and association, its progress and accomplishments, and in all phases of fraternity programming for the betterment of each member. An intensified emphasis on collegiate programming in the past few years had been so successful that this Council session voted to appoint a standing chairman in charge of alumnæ programs, one who would work under the direction of the Second Vice-President.

The handbooks were continuing to flow through the Communications and Information department, and Executive Offices had distributed several for use of specific officers as well as those for chapter use. These included Convention Planning, Province Collegiate Chairmen, Province Alumnæ Chairmen, Recommendations, Council, and Executive Offices.

Another area which had begun to expand with the speech materials which were being offered through the Office was visual aids. The project committee had more than ten years ago issued a movie, and its slide program was in circulation in 1965. At the same time the Secretary as Director of Housing had issued for circulation among chapters a program of slides picturing Delta Gamma houses and rooms across the continent.

As the year progressed, Communications and Information Center entered this field and planned for circulation during 1966 a program on Convention, another (premiered in March, 1966) on Executive Officers and Archives, and several series in the areas of fraternity education.

Sacramento State College

Wheels began to turn at this Council meeting toward the addition of a chapter (which would be Delta Eta) at Sacramento State College, Sacramento, California. In the following weeks a petition was accepted from the well-established local, Sigma Alpha Sigma, and the group was pledged on February 13, 1965. An early fall, 1966, installation makes Delta Eta chapter number 91 on the chapter roll.

Council meeting—Spring, 1966

The space between November and February for Council meetings seems short (and is!)—especially since December and the holidays are a universally agreed moratorium on Fraternity business. However, with a June Convention in view and many personal conflicts in scheduling later in the spring, it was deemed wise for Council to assemble February 22-28, 1966, for its spring meeting. The spot was the Mountain Shadows in Scottsdale, Arizona, which enabled—as usual—a number of profitable stops for each member en route to the meeting.

In spite of three members succumbing to the currently prevalent flu during the meeting, a great amount of business was taken care of. It was natural that considerable emphasis was on the plans for the Convention scheduled for June 19-25 in Portland, Oregon. The President, en route to and from her home in Vancouver, had made stops in Portland to meet with Chairman Chiane Gerow Anderson, ΔΔ-Oregon.

Forty-second Convention
1966—Portland, Oregon

As Convention opened June 19 at the Portland Hilton, Portland, Oregon, it was with a feeling of some satisfaction that officers and members viewed this biennium. In spite of ever-present problems, campus undercurrents and even riots, the Delta Gamma house was in order and a feeling of progress and accomplishment was present in all areas.

Chairman Chiane Anderson and her area committees made use of every delight the Portland area had to offer in providing not only a beautiful Convention ("They scatter roses like popcorn," said one delegate) but one with new surprises in decoration and entertainment each day. Special outings were a luncheon in the rose gardens at

Washington Park and a trip up the Columbia River gorge climaxed by a salmon bake.

The Portland Hilton offered the numerous Convention conveniences common in a modern mid-city hotel.

Since only one Constitutional revision had been offered (concerning fifth year student status), there was a minimum of business on the floor of Convention. Lest this suggests a leisurely Convention, free of business, let this historian state here for the record that probably more time was spent in workshops than in any previous conclave. Advisers were once more present and had their program—which sometimes took place with collegiate delegates and visitors and Province Collegiate Chairmen; more often it was a program geared to the needs of advisers. Once more collegiate delegates held their own private sessions and committee meetings from whence stemmed the collegiate resolutions presented at the final general meeting of the Convention. Alumnæ, too, had a more intensified program under the enthusiastic leadership of the Second Vice-President and her newly appointed programming chairman. Once more (as at the Leadership School in 1965) Continuing Education was presented and urged as part of the alumnæ program.

Alumnæ and Collegiate Dinners

As further emphasis on alumnæ and collegiate programs, separate dinners were planned one evening with special awards and exchanges being part of the programs which ensued.

Silver Anchors and Past Officers

Two "exclusive" luncheons which were among the gay events of the Convention were one for the Silver Anchor Sisters (those who have attended five Conventions or more) and another for all former officers (Fraternity, province, and chairmen) attending Convention. Reminiscences were a big part of both programs—not surprising when one notes that at the Silver Anchor luncheon every Convention as far back as 1907 was represented by someone present! Margaret Richardson Hay, Υ-Stanford, former Council member present as chairman of the 1966 Nominating Committee, had charge of these luncheons and programs.

Awards

Once more the long tables laden with silver trophies were a spectacular sight, and again the presentation of these awards, under the direction of LuAnne Lyen Leonard, ΑΣ-UCLA, was an important event.

Canadians honor "Maisie"

Not only was the Convention presided over by a Canadian president, but the hostess area also included a number of Canadian chapters, and they were the hostesses at a dinner to honor the Fraternity President. The Foundation awards and fellowships were announced at this time, and to climax the program an additional 1966-67 Fraternity Fellowship was announced, sponsored by the Ca-

nadian chapters and to be known as the Maisie Clugston Groves Fellowship for $350.

Guest speakers

Two special guests appeared on the program, one the night of the awards dinner—Dr. Franklin R. Thompson, president of the College of Puget Sound (a campus rapidly approved the next day at the Expansion session for a Delta Gamma chapter in the near future). Dr. Thompson's theme of "heritage and horizons" was an inspiration to the entire Convention program.

The second special guest appeared at the Panhellenic Luncheon the last day of Convention. This was J. Dwight Peterson, immediate past president of the Interfraternity Research Advisory Council. The nine Delta Gammas in his family, including his wife and two daughters among others, made him a very special Delta Gamma guest and at the close of his address he was presented with an "Anchor Man" certificate. Since this Convention

To serve as President of Delta Gamma, Elizabeth C. Kloppenburg, Γ-California, was elected at the 1966 Convention. She is the first President since 1954 to come to Delta Gamma's highest office after previous service in the area of collegiate affairs, having been a Province Collegiate Chairman and First Vice-President. Her daughter, Carolyn Kloppenburg Riggs, was a member of Beta chapter and was elected Collegiate Representative for Council at the 1960 Convention, later serving as a Field Secretary.

was being held in an urban area, nearly all of the National Panhellenic Conference groups were represented with one or more representatives at the luncheon. Since this festive luncheon took place on the last day of Convention—with the banquet scheduled for that evening, many Delta Gammas in the Washington-Oregon area arrived for this closing day of Convention.

Collegiate resolutions

One of the important portions of the final meeting of the past two conventions had been the presentation of a group of collegiate resolutions, recommendations to Council for study and/or action in various areas. These had been the products of "delegates only" meetings in which these delegates had been divided into committees to study different areas of the collegiate program—standards, scholarship, housing, pledge education, rituals, and Foundation. This type of collegiate action was urged by Council before the 1964 Convention to increase collegiate participation in the business of Convention. The actual presentation on the floor of Convention of these resolutions was made by the newly elected Collegiate Representatives for Council. In general, these resolutions have been affirmed by Convention for formal presentation to Council.

Elections

The slate of officers installed at the final session of Convention to serve for the 1966-68 period was as follows: President, Elizabeth Coffinberry Kloppenburg, Γ-California, of San Rafael, California; First Vice-President, Kathryn Bell Gary, M-Missouri, San Marino, California; Second Vice-President, Virginia Riesterer Gates, Σ-Northwestern, Wheaton, Illinois; Third Vice-President, Eleanor Smith Slaughter, AΨ-Mississippi, Columbus, Mississippi; Secretary, Janet Lau Sullivan, K-Nebraska, Braintree, Mass.; Treasurer, Carolyn Coffman Moorman, AO-Miami University, Dayton, Ohio, and National Panhellenic Conference Delegate, Marcia Connell Strickland, Ξ-Michigan, Bloomfield Hills, Michigan. The Secretary was the only officer new to Council; the President had previously served as First Vice-President, 1960-64, and all others were re-elected to their offices. It might be noted that for the first time since 1954 Delta Gamma would have a president whose previous offices had been in the area of collegiate affairs.

Collegiate Representatives

Collegiate Representatives to Council elected in 1966 were Barbara Carvill, Θ-Indiana, representing chapters living in their houses, and Sally Nutton, BP-George Washington, from the chapters not living in chapter houses.

Nominating Committee

The nominating committee, elected at the 1966 Convention to serve for the 1968 elections, would be headed by Florence Whitcomb Ebersold, E-

Ohio State, of Wilmette, Ill. Other members were Eva Williams Sackett, Φ-Colorado, Albuquerque, N.M.; Mary Ann Lummis Bowyer, BZ-Denison, Province VI Alumnae Chairman; Lynn Caswell Eavey, Π-Montana, Miami; and Ruth Rose Richardson, AΔ-Oregon, former Scholarship chairman.

Cavalcade of Conventions

A fitting conclusion to the 1966 Convention was the banquet whose program combined a "spectacular" and a surprise. The huge banquet hall was heavy with the scent of the thousands of roses provided for decorations, and the focal point was a rose-festooned gazebo at the center of the hall. This was the "stage" for the Cavalcade of Conventions, the historical pageant provided by the Archives, directed and narrated by Frances Lewis Stevenson, Z-Albion. As the pageant ended, the retiring President and her Council rose to make a special presentation. This was to Roberta Abernethy, E-Ohio State, honoring her twenty-fifth year as Executive Secretary—as well as the twenty-fifth year of the office which was voted into being at the 1942 Convention. To mark this anniversary the 1964-66 Council presented Miss Abernethy with a check for $1,500 and instructions for a month-long European vacation to be taken some time "before the next Convention."

Publication and printing

A new *History* of Delta Gamma appeared as the fall issue of *Anchora*. Though updating of Delta Gamma history had, in the long range plan, been scheduled for every decade, it had been eleven years since the previous edition. For the first time color was used in a number of sections, and the symbolic eagle of the 1870's was revived as a decorative piece on the cover and throughout the book. Following publication as an issue of the *Anchora*, the history was hardbound and would be included in a slip case with the *Shield*, a membership manual to appear the following year.

Though it was more exciting as a milestone for the editor than for most readers, the *History* opened another new era for *Anchora*. The fall *Anchora* was printed offset rather than the letterpress of the first 82 years of publication. In the introduction to the *History* the editor commented, "As we hope will become evident in subsequent issues, this process will allow greater latitude in layout and color. We might add that new equipment made available at the George Banta Company (geared particularly to fraternity needs, for the Banta Company is already among the largest offset printing establishments in the country) in 1966 was the chief reason for lengthening the ten years between histories to nearly eleven." Since the Communications and Information Center had been working with offset for some time, the transition was a happy one for the editorial department.

Days of unrest

The wonderful aroma of the thousands of roses which filled the hall for the 1966 Convention banquet lingers on for those who were there, and it will undoubtedly continue to linger in their memories well into Delta Gamma's second century. In the days ahead Delta Gamma leaders who were working closely with the nation's campuses would need to remember the reassurance of roses.

For those associated in any way with education, these final years of the 'sixties are likely to be remembered in one word: Rebellion. Rules and regulations had been flung aside, at first slowly and meeting with some resistance, but as the decade progressed, so did the momentum, and long established university policies were cast off with abandon. Firm and fixed hours had at first shaken and eased, and by the end of the decade were almost totally shattered. At first the demand was for keys to residences for seniors—then for junior honor students or for those over 21, then keys for any upperclassman, no sign out, and so on. From here the movement extended to the freedom to leave campus housing for an apartment, and so it went.

The sorority houses were the last bastions of resistance to this movement, largely because the young women who had chosen this way of life said they were glad "someone cares about where you are." However, the Delta Gamma Council at the fall, 1966, meeting found itself forced to face the issue squarely, and at this particular time they resolved that "before key systems may be instituted or hours cancelled for any age group or class, consent must be given by the advisory board and written approval obtained from the Province Collegiate Chairman."

In tune with the times

Through the years Delta Gamma has been particularly blessed, it has seemed, with leaders whose special attributes fitted especially well the needs of the times. Never was this more true than through this trying period. Between 1964 and 1970—and cresting between 1966 and 1968—hardly a mail arrived at the home of the President without communication from universities where we already had chapters, or from schools where we were considering chapters, which required our membership selection philosophy and procedures to be defined or interpreted. Add to this phone calls at all hours of the day—and sometimes night—from frantic chapters which had just received the same demands from campus organizations or administrations. With this came the questioning of members themselves and a rising number of resignations occurred during this period. Delta Gamma met these difficulties of the day in a manner which was frequently lauded by the university in question and continued, in spite of all, to progress and expand in a diversified range of activity.

Show and tell

By the fall of 1966 the Communications and Information Center of Executive Offices had added a new duty, the production and scheduling of slide programs in various areas of fraternity programming. The Housing Director had for some time been amassing a collection of slides of both exteriors and interiors of chapter houses, lodges, suites and rooms. These were filed with statistical material on each chapter residence and were used or loaned by her for chapter programs. Foundation, too, had its collection of slides and filed all donated slides with a listing of identities to be used, like housing, in an ad lib sort of program. Naturally, with a variety of slides representing each house or chapter quarters and usually a greater number reflecting a chapter or association philanthropic project, both of these programs had become rather lengthy. Thus, both of these shows as well as a new one on the Executive Offices were assembled in 80-slot Carousel projector trays with an accompanying script. Easily shipped about the country in film carriers, these became popular program materials. During the 1966-67 school year, an additional one portraying the convention in Portland was used by the field secretaries and circulated among alumnae chapters.

New Anchora editor

Increased activity in Communications and Information brought about a shift of responsibilities in this area. Fran Stevenson would continue as historian and director of this department with

Mary Ann Dalton, N-Idaho, assuming the editorship of the *Anchora* with the winter, 1966, issue.

Fall, 1966, Council meeting

For the first time in many years Council traveled to Nebraska for its fall meeting, gathering at the Indian Hills Inn, Omaha, October 27-31, 1966. The meeting was planned to include a visit with Lincoln alumnae (as well as Omaha) and with Kappa chapter. For the President and Executive Secretary it also included a special few moments with aging *Anchora* editor and 1915 historian, Ethel Tukey Korsmeyer, K-Nebraska. During Council's stay in Omaha they were invited to attend the city's famed Ak-Sar-Ben over which reigned Delta Gamma Mary Helen Durham, K-Nebraska, 1966 queen.

As usual, a variety of business consumed meeting days. At this point in time, American campuses were festering with movements which would become explosive within a few more years. The fraternity system was being needled with all manner of questions and requests for proof of non-segregation clauses in constitution and by-laws, even for open copies of fraternity ritual.

Simultaneously inquiries regarding the possibility of establishing a chapter on "our campus" continued to flow into the mail of the Expansion Chairman. At this fall, 1966, meeting, two such invitations were accepted: the petition of a colony at Georgia State College in Atlanta and an invitation to colonize from the University of Georgia at Athens.

Standing committee chairmen

Basic requirements were established for the qualifications necessary for appointees as standing committee chairmen: Responsibility, communication, required training period in Executive Offices, Council meeting attendance when necessary, attendance at Leadership School when required.

Grants and Loans

An expanded program of grants had been announced at Convention and was in operation in the fall of 1966: The Honorary Fellowship as well as the Memorial Fellowship would amount to $1,000 and would be awarded to Delta Gammas for study at any graduate level in any field. Twelve senior scholarships of $250 each would be awarded; these were subsequently raised to $300.

Survey of house loans

As a result of a survey made by the Trust Department of the Huntington National Bank of Columbus, Ohio, Council voted to limit the extent of co-signing on Fraternity housing loans to a maximum of $300,000, interest rate at 6%. It was further decided that to secure adequate protection for the Fraternity that a Joint Deed or other protective measure be exercised.

Sacramento State College

On November 5, 1966, another California chapter was added when Sigma Alpha Sigma, local sorority, became Delta Eta of Delta Gamma. Organized in 1954, Sigma Alpha Sigma had petitioned nearly two years earlier and had been pledged in 1965.

Final 1966 landmark

"Because Executive Offices will be involved in the new data processing system beginning the first of the year (1967), no extra printing will be done." Automation was here to stay, and to handle address files, mailing lists, and finally chapter bookkeeping efficiently, Delta Gamma joined the world of data processing. Local (Columbus) firms handled the process which for Executive Offices, like the rest of the world, had its initial headaches and provided the usual amount of material for computer jokes. This 1967 venture for Delta Gamma must have progressed handily during the early months, however, for the spring Council meeting received a report that four handbooks were in process (so extra printing could continue apace), and the two Council members who would colonize at the University of Georgia were invited to make full use of printing facilities at Executive Offices in preparation for colonization.

Council meeting, spring, 1967

For their spring Council meeting, officers met at the Fairmont Hotel, San Francisco, April 12-16, 1967. A west coast meeting site allowed officers from other areas to plan a wide variety of chapter visits en route, and before business was convened in San Francisco it allowed at least three to enjoy a special treat in Southern California. Roberta Abernethy, Carly Moorman, and Eleanor Slaughter were in Los Angeles with Kathryn Gary where all four were special guests at the Academy Awards presentations. Their host was Robert Metzler, Academy treasurer and husband of Beverly Williams Metzler, AN-Southern California, former Province Collegiate Chairman.

Virginia Gates resigns

This spring, 1967, Council session began on a decidedly sad note, for the Second Vice-President had submitted her resignation because of illness. A cancer victim, Virginia Gates maintained an active interest in her beloved alumnae chapters and associations until her death in November, 1967. The spring Council meeting appointed to the Second Vice-Presidency, at Mrs. Gates' recommendation, Mary Ann Lummis Bowyer, BZ-Denison, of Dearborn, Michigan. Mrs. Bowyer, a Province Alumnae Chairman since 1963, had been directing alumnae programming for Mrs. Gates.

Expansion

It was natural that much of this Council session be devoted to plans for the Leadership School which would assemble in Columbus, Ohio, in June. Considerable attention was also given to the forthcoming colonization at the University of Georgia and current activity at the University of

South Florida, recently approved as another field for expansion.

Gift to University of British Columbia

One session of Council meeting must become a board of directors meeting for the Delta Gamma Foundation. At this time the officers voted a $2,500 donation for the support of the Blind Center at the University of British Columbia. It will be maintained and serviced by Alpha Phi chapter and the Vancouver alumnae chapter.

Georgia State College

In May, following Council meeting, attention focused on the state of Georgia where both installation and colonization would take place. Kappa Chi Delta had organized at Georgia State College, Atlanta, in 1965 and was ready to petition Delta Gamma in 1966. Approval early in 1967 lead toward installation May 6, 1967.

University of Georgia

If Georgia State received more than the average number of visits for a petitioning group, it was because approval to colonize had also been accorded the University of Georgia. In January, 1967, the Executive Secretary and Treasurer traveled to Athens, Georgia, to study the housing needs and possible locations of the chapter house which must be built on the University of Georgia campus. This was an instance where a large chapter house was a primary need in carrying out the installation of a chapter—and a prime reason why such campuses cannot be entered frequently and often excludes other potential fields for expansion.* With the strong support of Dean Louise McBee and Panhellenic Adviser Caryl Lenahan, Delta Gamma's colonization at Georgia was accomplished with considerable flare. Two fraternity officers—Mrs. Strickland, National Panhellenic Conference Delegate and Director of Rush, and Mrs. Slaughter, Third Vice-President and Director of Programming—and their team of aides went to Athens in May to conduct rush with local alumnae assistance and to form a colony. They produced a strong group which would be prepared for installation the following February as Delta Iota chapter.

Anchor of Delta Gamma

As an added display brochure for the colonization at the University of Georgia, the Communications and Information Center at Executive Offices had produced a pamphlet, "The Anchor of Delta Gamma," which would hereafter also be included in the mailing to parents of new pledges.

*In this instance it was an invitation from the University of North Carolina which was necessarily refused, coming as it did on the heels of the University of Georgia and also being a campus where a fraternity-built chapter house would be in the scheme of things.

Alpha Psi building

Once more the Alpha Psi chapter house at the University of Mississippi was being rebuilt and enlarged. Though the former Memorial House was no longer financed and maintained by the Fraternity, the Council had responsibility for approving plans, particularly those concerning the Founders Room. The 1967 renovation would not include a Founders Room though it would be added within a few years. Council voted, therefore, to store the panelling, fireplace, and door frame from the Lewis School for future use in a new Founders Room. Attention was also given to the Memorial Window in the Ole Miss Geology Building. Once more rumor was about that the building would be razed, and it was hoped that the window could be preserved in some manner—either on the campus, at the Delta Gamma Executive Offices or as part of the future Founders Room at the Ole Miss chapter house.

Leadership School, 1967

The third biennial Leadership School found collegiate chapter presidents and Fraternity officers assembled June 18, 1967, in Columbus, Ohio, with school rooms in the Ohio State University Student Union, residences being OSU dorms, and field trip being a tour of the Executive Offices four miles away. The school once more emphasized the reciprocal value of such a gathering—to the Fraternity leaders in maintaining awareness of needs and wishes of collegiate members, and to the collegiate chapters in gaining a better understanding of the scope and values of the Fraternity.

The 1967 Leadership School was the first at which expert counseling was brought in to expose delegates to the group dynamics approach to leadership. Joy Herod, ΓN-North Texas, who was in the process of earning her doctorate, was present in 1967, at Convention the following year. Certainly both officers and collegiate presidents returned home aware of the impact of their leadership training and aware, too, of the officers' knowledge and interest in campus problems. Especially they were aware of the willingness of these women to listen and of the resources available to the chapters through their national organization.

Beside discussion groups and instructional sessions, a number of special programs reflected the times. Guest speaker included Dean Ruth Weimer of Ohio State on "Attitude toward Academic Excellence and Honoraries" and the University of Kentucky's Dean Doris Seward with a lively discussion of what might appear to be a dull subject—"From the Dean's Point of View." One afternoon session was devoted to a distinguished panel of experts discussing narcotics, the users and the effects.

Roberta Off to Europe

As the Delta Gamma headquarters celebrated its twenty-fifth anniversary in the summer of 1967, the Executive Secretary, Roberta Abernethy, went to Europe. This was the special gift, presented at the 1966 Convention, which Fraternity officers had planned for Roberta in celebration of this silver anniversary. When her plans were made and trip routed, Treasurer Carly Moorman purchased her own duplicate ticket to accompany Roberta.

National Panhellenic Conference, 1967

National Panhellenic Conference met for its fortieth biennium November 1-5, 1967, at the Royal Orleans Hotel, New Orleans, La. A total of 298 women attended, including not only the delegates and alternates but college panhellenic advisers and presidents of local college panhellenics in the area. Delta Gamma's official delegation to NPC sessions included National Panhellenic Conference Delegate Marcia Strickland; two alternates, Elizabeth Kloppenburg and Kathryn Gary; other Council members, Janet Sullivan and Carly Moorman; Roberta Abernethy, delegate to the Central Office Executives meeting; and Fran Stevenson and Mary Ann Dalton Shepard who attended the Panhellenic Editors Conference. At this biennium Mrs. Stevenson was elected vice-chairman of the Editors' group, and Mrs. Strickland was appointed Chairman of the NPC City Panhellenics Committee. Both Mrs. Stevenson and Mrs. Strickland appeared on a panel featured in one of the evening programs. Between 1965 and 1967 Mrs. Strickland had edited the City Panhellenics Newsletter with Executive Offices printing and mailing the "new look" publication.

Dedication at LSU

The convergence of all of Council in New Orleans by the close of the NPC meetings brought the group together to attend the dedication of the new Gamma Zeta chapter house at Louisiana State University in Baton Rouge on Sunday, November 6; from here they would continue on to the fall Council meeting. Until the preceding year the LSU campus had not had sorority houses, NPC groups being served by a Panhellenic Building which had become hopelessly overcrowded. At the 1961 National Panhellenic meeting the groups having chapters on the LSU campus had met to discuss the possibility of houses, and a few years later the decision was made to go ahead with the project. A choice piece of campus facing the lake was set aside, and a drawing for lots was held. All groups built simultaneously, and so Delta Gamma was not the only group holding a dedication ceremony on the weekend NPC adjourned in New Orleans eighty miles away.

Council meeting, fall, 1967

From Baton Rouge Council members and the Executive Secretary traveled to the Grand Hotel at Point Clear, Alabama, for Council meeting, November 6-10. After a busy and no-doubt colorful week in New Orleans, the group of eight women settled down in this quiet, off-season resort atmosphere to the routine business of running the Fraternity. To re-read the minutes it would appear that the group touched briefly on nearly every possible facet of fraternity, from

planning two installations and a Convention, as well as accepting an invitation to colonize, to approving housing, accepting resignations, and, in the Foundation session, raising the senior scholarship gift to $300. Having received many requests from other fraternity groups to borrow and use our publications, the officers also agreed that it would be good public relations to share Delta Gamma handbooks on request. It was also agreed that the fifty-year members should be eliminated from the annual alumnae billing, and a pension plan for Executive Offices staff members was to be investigated.

Emory University

Of primary importance was a discussion of the situation at Emory University as it affected Gamma Psi chapter of Delta Gamma. Since the climate seemed to continue to deteriorate, it was decided to notify Gamma Psi chapter that withdrawal was being considered. The grounds for removal (which was finally completed March 1, 1968) was that stated in the Constitution—"if it appears that the interest of the Fraternity will be served by the removal of the chapter." In this case the number of women at Emory choosing to go through rush did not seem sufficient to adequately supply all the Greek-letter groups established there.

Housing

Through the 'sixties the growing needs in the area of housing continued to be a prime topic for Council discussion and to occupy considerable space in Anchora. The oldest had become the newest in 1967 as the Zeta chapter lodge, occupied on the Albion College campus since 1896, was removed from the property and a new lodge constructed and dedicated on October 14, 1967. At the same time, the Beta Eta (Texas) house was totally transformed—to such an extent that its address changed from one street around the corner to another. Willamette Delta Gammas had occupied a new house, Beta Omega at Washington State was totally face-lifted, and Gamma Beta, celebrating its twentieth anniversary at Tulsa, had transformed its lodge to a house.

The Times

The Anchora pages these days discussed such varied matters as hippies, SDS, curriculum changes, campus living — apartments, keys to locked chapter houses, awareness, drugs and their increased use on campus, morals and attitudes. These were indeed days of turmoil and uneasiness which were destined to worsen before the decade ended.

Hannah

A beloved member of Delta Gamma for many years had been "Hannah" and 1967 found a revived interest and a new view of this famous member. Dede O'Shea, AI-Oklahoma, who later transferred to the University of Tulsa, had created for a rush party in 1959-60 a comic strip character, a "new Hannah." She used a typical member of her own chapter as a basic style and added other characteristics of chapter members. This Hannah was first introduced in a rush booklet similar to the popular "Peanuts" joke books. Hannah's fame received attention beyond the two Oklahoma campuses, was adopted by Executive Offices for rush materials being distributed on a national scale, and so she became a new tradition. All manner of new Hannah emblems—from keyrings to stuffed dolls—were created by other chapters so that Dede O'Shea's creation became something of a hallmark for rushing during the 'sixties.

Statistics, 1967

When the headcount was completed at the end of the 1966-67 school year, it had been noted that the number pledged was 2,536, down 46 from the previous year. However, largely because of pledging taking place on many campuses after prospective pledges had already made required grade averages, 433 more were initiated than the year before. Through these troublesome times the number of resignations had increased, too, but the continued rise in initiations each year far outdistanced a percentage rise in resignations.

Field Secretaries

During the 'sixties the concept of the field secretary program was gradually changing. The plan, established in 1963, by which each chapter would be visited at least once each year had proved successful. At first, it seemed that the work of the field secretary and the province collegiate chairman to some extent overlapped. Finally a clear-cut division of duties was set up by which the field secretary would inspect (and clear) chapter files, hold conferences with each officer, and generally offer in her report the opinion of a peer on the state of the chapter. This enabled the province officer to move forward from this point when she made her visit, to provide cures for ailments, to offer assistance where needed, and especially to train the members of the advisory board—individually and as a group. The field secretary's report also gave the province officer a better understanding of the campus and chapter itself before she made her visit.

The addition of the guest house, Anchor In, to the Executive Offices facility also contributed to the field secretary program. The comfortable and roomy quarters provided living space for not only four field secretaries but also for whichever officers were scheduled to be part of their training program. This included the First Vice-President who directed collegiate chapter administration including assignment of field secretaries. Midway through the school year it was later deemed advantageous to have what would be called an "In-gathering"—when field secretaries and officers and, on occasion, one or two Collegiate Representatives to Council met to re-assess the year and to project new ideas and new programs. A by-product of this in-residence period was a growing closeness among the field secretaries themselves, and frequently plans for "next year" were discussed privately. In 1968 one such

plan brought two of the four to Columbus to join the Executive Offices staff; a year or so later two took off for an extended tour of Europe together following their year as field secretaries.

Two installations—
University of Georgia
University of South Florida

Plans progressed for the installation of two new chapters in the month of February, 1968. Delta Iota at the University of Georgia would take place on February 17, 1968, in Athens, and Delta Kappa at the University of South Florida in Tampa was to be held on February 24 with the entire Council attending—having held spring, 1968, Council meeting in between.

The group at the University of Georgia was a healthy colony, having progressed well since its organization the previous May. Also early in 1967 the Council had approved, with an affirmative vote of the area, the establishment of a chapter at the relatively new University of South Florida. The University itself was unique. Having been founded in 1956, it opened to a charter class of 2,000 in the fall of 1960. Its home was a 1,734 acre tract of land eight miles northeast of downtown Tampa. It claimed to be the first state university to be totally planned and initiated within this century. This campus had no sorority houses, but members lived and met in university dormitories, and so this would afford a chapter with little expense. Since Delta Gamma colonizations in Florida were traditionally simple, due to large alumnae support, the future seemed bright for a Delta Gamma move into Tampa. Thus, Delta Phi Alpha local sorority had become a pledge chapter on September 10, 1967, and was ready now for installation as Delta Kappa chapter.

Council meeting, spring, 1968

This spring, 1968, Council meeting would be something of a session on the run. All members of Council had assembled in Athens, Georgia, for the Delta Iota installation. While Council meeting was not officially called to order at that time, it is certain that discussions of many Fraternity matters must have taken place before the officers traveled on to the Belleview-Biltmore at Bellair, Florida, for a week of meetings before the Delta Kappa installation. For the record, the meeting is listed as February 19-26, 1968, opened at the Belleview-Biltmore and finally adjourned at the International Inn, Tampa, where the group had moved for the installation of Delta Kappa chapter.

It was natural that a great deal of attention would be given to the continued nagging of campus situations as well as to the plans ahead for the June Convention. Once more Delta Gamma's special charm of having the right person appear at the right time for a position of leadership was working. If little seems to be written about the problems on campus at this time, it is because of the outstanding leadership of President Elizabeth Kloppenburg and her Council, each especially well suited to meet the demands of the day in her own area. The situation was indeed well in hand, and campus administrators frequently lauded the forward thinking of this group of women, remarking that Delta Gamma often stood alone in its sensitivity to the needs of the campus at this time.

One of the first actions of this Council session was a sad one: the vote to remove the charter of Gamma Psi chapter at Emory University as of March 1, 1968. Mrs. Gary and Mrs. Kloppenburg would visit the chapter and the campus following Council meeting.

Action necessary to forming a house corporation which could be responsible (for the Fraternity) for building a house for the new Delta Iota chapter at Georgia was also completed. Construction of this house would move ahead so that Delta Iota would have permanent housing as soon as possible.

Forty-third Convention
1968—Dallas, Texas

When your name is in lights, you must succeed, and so it was with the Forty-third Convention at the Sheraton in Dallas, Texas, June 16-22, 1968. Texas means big, and this Convention was —709 seated at the banquet on the closing evening. More important, the Texas-big adjectives seem to apply to every facet to create a biennium that was complete and full in every way.

First, "Delta Gamma" was in lights atop a downtown Dallas office building. For this first Texas Convention visitors were aware of the con tinued attendance and participation of Texas Delta Gammas throughout their days at the Sheraton. Convention production was superbly planned by Beverly Edlund Mertz, BK-Kansas, and her assistant, June McDonald Swanstrom, Φ-Colorado.

Program planning featured contrasts which may have been the secret ingredient which produced a successful conclave—starting with the opening session the first evening, the serious and sentimental combined in the President's address, followed by a Delta Gamma "Laugh In."

At the opening session officers departed from their traditional reports to list facts and figures against a background of history in the premiere performance of a slide program, "Portrait of Delta Gamma," which would become popular program material for chapters and associations in the ensuing years. To underline facts and figures delegates had heard and seen at this first meeting, the large Convention exhibits first displayed in 1964 had been updated and were on display just outside Convention hall.

Show and tell were woven throughout the Convention program, and few will forget Gamma Tau's "Thoroughly Modern Middie" rush show (written and directed by Diane Turner) or Joy Herod's demonstrations of how to conduct alumnae meetings. (Joy Herod, ΓN-North Texas, was part of the workshop programming as an expert in group dynamics.)

Memorable because of its sensible and sensitive view of the times was President Elizabeth Kloppenburg's Convention address on Campus Trends. After opening with "Please understand that I do not consider myself an expert on this subject . . . ", she went on to demonstrate, through a process of defining periods and patterns of unrest on campus, that she was possibly the most expert of all on this touchy subject. Her speech, reprinted by request in the fall, 1968, Anchora, is possibly one of the clearest and most accurate records of this decade on campus.

Seminars and singing, a barbecue fiesta, shopping trips to Neiman-Marcus which was happily nearby, two worthwhile guest speakers (Dr. Willis Tate of SMU and Mrs. Priscilla Jackson of Oakland University)—all were part of the busy week whose most important aspect was the action of the Convention body itself.

Each collegiate delegate was also president of her chapter, and these delegates were not just the chapter representatives who sat in the chairs bearing the right Greek-letter labels; these were working delegates who met, thought, discussed, and articulated their desires and ideas in the resolutions they presented at the final Convention session. Mandatory alumnae recommendations and the unanimous vote issues had continued to be of prime interest to the collegiate chapters because of the pressures from colleges and universities. These delegates pondered this problem throughout the six days in Dallas and submitted to the assemblage a resolution requesting a special committee to be appointed to investigate the problem thoroughly and report to the 1970 Convention two years hence. This resolution was passed with full support from alumnae delegates present.

Other Convention action
- Collegiate members would pay Fraternity dues of ten dollars annually, five of which would be allocated to the general fund and five to the Convention fund.
- The fee to be paid to the Fraternity for each pledge was raised from five dollars to ten.

Through business sessions alumnae had been wrestling with the knotty problem of the chartering of alumnae groups. An amendment had been proposed to increase the number necessary for the chartering of an alumnae chapter from 10 to 20, and for the certification of an alumnae association from 4 to 10, but this change was defeated.

Elections

The officers installed for the 1968-1970 term of office at the final session were: Marcia Connell Strickland, Ξ-Michigan, Bloomfield Hills, Michigan, President; LuAnne Lyen Leonard, AΣ-UCLA, Los Angeles, California, First Vice-President; Mary Ann Lummis Bowyer, BZ-Denison, Dearborn Heights, Michigan, Second Vice-President; Virginia Van Dyke Spaller, Ξ-Michigan, Dallas, Texas, Third Vice-President; Janet Lau Sullivan, K-Nebraska, Braintree, Massachusetts, Secretary; Carolyn Coffman Moorman, AO-Miami University, Dayton, Ohio, Treasurer; and Louise Callahan Call, E-Ohio State, Columbus, Ohio, National Panhellenic Conference Delegate.

Elected to the Nominating Committee for 1970 Convention elections were: Natalie Conrad Case, H-Akron; Dorothy West Bristol, ΓZ-LSU; Marilyn Witt Laird, Λ-Minnesota; Mary Elizabeth Falter Avery, AI-Oklahoma, and Elizabeth Coffinberry Kloppenburg, Γ-California, who would serve as chairman.

Collegiate delegates elected Margaret Talburtt, Ξ-Michigan, and Elizabeth Nelson, BP-George Washington, as Collegiate Representatives to Council, the former representing chapters living in chapter houses, and the latter those not living in chapter houses.

Crystal Banquet

Candles, crystal and roses created the Crystal Banquet for the final night of Convention, and once more an historical pageant was the program. This was theater in the round with Ludi Mai Sensabaugh Goode, ΑΥ-SMU, as producer, and Frances Lewis Stevenson, Z-Albion, as author-narrator of "The Girls Who Wear the Anchor."

Administrative transition

The administration transition between Mrs. Kloppenburg and Mrs. Strickland in the summer of 1968 was a smooth one in spite of the difficult situations which continued to face the Council. Mrs. Strickland had begun her official service to Delta Gamma twenty-five years earlier, and had served in nearly every area, having at this time been on Council in two positions during the preceding six years. Having served as Delta Gamma's National Panhellenic Conference Delegate since 1964 possibly was the best preparation she might have had to attain full awareness of the problems which might face her as President of Delta Gamma.

Council meeting—fall, 1968

Delta Gamma Councils through the years have had, in scheduling meetings, a magic touch for meeting events or extreme weather conditions head-on. It would not seem that scheduling the fall Council meeting for November 13-18 at the Americana Hotel in New York would bode such ill, but the session opened with two members absent and the Executive Secretary wearing a new cast and sling on her right arm. The absent ones, Mrs. Strickland and Mrs. Spaller, had been snowed in on chapter visits en route (the former at St. Lawrence and the latter at Syracuse) and arrived many hours late while Miss Abernethy had fallen on the steps to the hotel the evening before the meetings began.

Officers were entertained both by Omicron chapter at Adelphi and by the New York City alumnae during their stay, and they attended to a wide variety of fraternity business as well. An invitation to colonize at Mississippi State University was accepted, the Field Secretary In-gathering was planned, Council realignment of duties were discussed, and thought was given to future Convention sites.

Membership Selection Study Committee

Considerable time and attention was given to a discussion of the framework for the Membership Selection Study Committee, formation of which had been voted into being by the acceptance of the collegiate resolution on this matter at the 1968 Convention. The resolution had requested a committee composed of one alumna and one collegian from each Area, plus the Collegiate Representatives to Council, and to be chaired by the First Vice-President. Therefore, Council at this fall meeting chose representatives from each Area with consideration of geographical location, type of campus, alumnae background, and with attention to the areas already represented by the elected Collegiate Representatives. Thus, the committee would be composed of the following: Area A, Alpha Omicron president and Province I Collegiate Chairman; Area B, Alpha Psi president and Province III Alumnae Chairman; Area C, Tau president and Province VII Alumnae Chairman; Area D, Beta Chi president and Province XI Alumnae Chairman; and Area E, Alpha Nu president and the Grants and Loans Chairman. This committee would receive its instructions from the First Vice-President, Mrs. Leonard, and would meet during the Leadership School in Columbus in June.

Codes of Conduct

As campuses had continued to discard longstanding regulations covering the physical and moral existence of their students, chapters repeatedly expressed the need for something that went beyond "house rules" in defining standards and even identity. Louise Callahan Call, who had been Fraternity Standards Chairman before being elected to Council in June, 1968, had been particularly sensitive to this feeling among collegians and had introduced the idea of each chapter creating its own Code of Conduct. When these were compiled, they were an interesting reflection not only of individual Delta Gamma chapters but of the college woman of the 'sixties. Compiled exerpts from a number of the Codes of Conduct appear in the spring, 1969, *Anchora* and reflect a myriad of thoughts on personal integrity—honesty, dependability, self-respect, thoughtfulness, and cooperation; personal standards—appearance, virtue, morale, profanity, self-discipline; personal attitude—enthusiasm, positive mental attitudes, fulfillment of potential; personal etiquette on campus as well as in the chapter lodge, house, or rooms.

Council meeting, spring, 1969

When Council meeting had adjourned in New York in November, 1968, Mrs. Strickland had outlined to the other officers the areas for discussion and action which would receive major emphasis on the spring, 1969, Council meeting agenda. So when the officers arrived at Tan-Tar-A at Lake of the Ozarks, Missouri, for the March 4-9 get-together, they were prepared to give thought to Leadership School, Centennial planning, the realignment of Council duties, and alumnae-collegiate relationships as prime topics of interest over and beyond the routine business at hand.

Anchora

Before approaching these creative areas, however, Council as always attended to a quantity of business. The resignation of Mary Ann Dalton Shepard as *Anchora* editor would become effective in the fall, and the position would be offered to Barbara Carvill, Θ-Indiana, who had been Collegiate Representative to Council, 1966-67; a Field Secretary, 1967-68; and a member of the Executive Offices staff since the end of the school year in the spring of 1968. Mrs. Stevenson would continue as director of Communications and Information with Miss Carvill assuming the editorship of the *Anchora* with the winter, 1969, issue.

Realignment of Provinces

Once more, for the tenth time since their first mapping in 1917, provinces were realigned, the total now being eighteen.

Alcohol on campus

An area of collegiate activity which occupied considerable time for discussion and special attention at this meeting of Council was the use of alcoholic beverages in the chapter house or at chapter functions. With many campuses — and states — beginning to relax long-standing rules and even laws in the regard to drinking ages, chapters were beginning to express desire for the use of alcoholic beverages at parties. At this point in time this usually meant a request for special permission to serve punch or wine before a dinner party or beer or wine at an informal function. At this Council meeting, it was agreed that, while such permission could and, indeed, had been given, chapter funds should not be spent for alcoholic beverages. One year later the question would come before the group again as more chapters sought to dismiss the rule entirely since drinking was allowed on their campus and/or in their state. Council was inclined to agree that the chapters should be treated as adults, that state and campus regulations should be met, that in areas where the drinking age was 18—and where it was admissible everywhere else—these young women would handle the situation properly. For the time, however, traditional rules held, exceptions being allowed at the discretion of the Province Collegiate Chairman.

Rush

The lifeline of the fraternity system is, as it always has been, the acquisition of new members, and so rush took its place on the agenda—rush itself, rush schools, rush consultants (an officer or other responsible person assigned to be with a particular chapter during rush). It was even suggested, put into a motion which passed unanimously, that a rush consultant position should be created on the staff of Executive Offices. Though this action did not come to pass as planned, one member of the staff did assist with rush schools and later, Area Rush Forums,

in addition to her other duties in connection with collegiate services.

Field Secretaries

During the 'sixties the number of field secretaries had fluctuated from none to four, and their duties and assignments had varied considerably, too. It was agreed, however, at this Council meeting that the present system was so successful that five should be hired for the 1969-70 school year.

Housemothers

Mrs. Strickland had for some time urged that we offer more assistance to housemothers, and it was agreed that a newsletter should be prepared at regular intervals to be circulated among the housemothers.

Expansion

Within the three months following the spring Council meeting Delta Gamma found itself in a flurry of expansion. Colonization at Mississippi State University having taken place in February, petitions from three schools arrived in quick succession after the March meeting: Florida Atlantic University, Northern Illinois University, and Ball State University. All three were well-established locals, and all three were accepted by Council and offered for area vote which was affirmative in all three instances.

Editors honor Bachmann

Among the publications handled by Harold Bachmann as a service director at the George Banta Company were the quarterly magazines and other publications of twelve NPC groups. For more than forty years "Bach" had worked with a procession of editors, receiving their copy and overseeing it through the various printing stages until it was finally a finished publication and put into the mail. The twelve editors currently working with Bach had consulted with the company in planning their part in his retirement. To represent this group of editors and make their presentations, Fran Stevenson and Mrs. J. Stannard Baker, Sigma Kappa editor, were flown to Menasha as guests of the George Banta Company.

The Now Generation:
Leadership School, 1969

"The Now Generation"—featuring all the current words: project interaction, rap sessions, participant dialogues, innovative leadership—was the theme of the fourth biennial Leadership School in Columbus, Ohio, June 20-24, 1969. The school for collegiate chapter presidents and fraternity officers was as vital as it sounded.

The President in her address "Campus '70" discussed at length the student power movement and student demands facing college administrators and reviewed the background of the major student revolutionary groups. Moving on to campus situations which affect fraternities and sororities, the challenge against required recommendation and unanimous vote to pledge was discussed. Social trends were also brought out—the increased popularity of off-campus housing, drug use and abuse, participation in protest demonstrations.

School participants toured the Executive Offices, heard a group of distinguished speakers, exchanged thoughts and ideas with each other, but all agreed that the greatest out-put of the school was the bridge over the generation gap as students and officers shared fraternity concerns.

Council/Cabinet meeting

For the first time an open meeting for Council and its Cabinet (defined as province officers, Fraternity and Foundation Chairmen, the Foundation Director, Executive Secretary, and Editor) to openly discuss individual and general fraternity problems and plans together was on the agenda. The Executive Secretary jarred the Scioto Country Club a bit when she requested that the tables be arranged in a large open square with twelve or thirteen chairs on each side. The arrangement may have looked impossible, but it was a great success and the beginning of an annual meeting of this sort, at Convention or at Leadership School.

Rituals

From time to time since 1873 Delta Gamma's rituals have been revised and rearranged though the initiation service has never departed from its original base. The 'sixties were decidedly a time when change was in the air, and this feeling extended to the Delta Gamma rituals, especially the initiation service. Once again, it was not the basic ingredients chapters wished to change, but the embellishments which had been added at later dates. Pledge education and rituals had been under the direction of the Third Vice-President with no special chairman appointed to handle rituals as had been true in the past. To work with collegiate chapters, to listen to their suggestions for rituals changes, and to conduct a study and compilation of these suggestions, Elizabeth Needham Graham, Ξ-Michigan, was appointed Fraternity Rituals Chairman. What this meant for Mrs. Graham was a seemingly endless correspondence with ninety or more chapters, phone conversations, study of rituals and suggested changes, even visits to chapters who were doing experimental versions of a revised initiation service. Though the first two of these were approved for trial at the Council meeting at Leadership School, it would be two years before Mrs. Graham and her group of interested collegians would show the results of their labors.

Collegiate Representatives

The two Collegiate Representatives to Council for 1969-70 would be Jane Gegenheimer, X-Cornell, from chapters living in their houses, and Janan Mikkelsen, ΔK-South Florida, from chapters not living in houses.

Collegiate Comments

The fall, 1969, Anchora would include a new section which would appear regularly for the next few years as a mirror of collegiate thinking in Delta Gamma chapters. This was "Collegiate Comments" for which the editor had issued to all chapters a group of provocative questions which could be answered in brief form and which might reflect the thinking of the student of the times. The first questions were, "Whom do you admire?—Is idealism still alive?—What helps to relieve tension from college pressures?—What are your hopes for the future?" Perhaps a dozen individual (signed) replies to each question appeared, of interest now and bound to be of interest to the historian of the future.

National Panhellenic Conference

Six Delta Gammas were among the delegates to National Panhellenic Conference when it assembled at The Fountainbleau, Miami Beach, Florida, October 22-25, 1969, for its forty-first session. They were Louise Callahan Call, Delta Gamma's NPC Delegate and her two alternates, President Marcia Strickland and First Vice-President LuAnne Leonard; Roberta Abernethy attending the meetings of the Central Office Executives, and at the National Panhellenic Editors' Conference, Barbara Carvill and Fran Stevenson. At the close of the editors' session, Mrs. Stevenson was installed as Chairman for the 1969-71 biennium.

College panhellenic presidents and advisers had been invited to attend the NPC meeting in a day and a half of programs designed to increase communication between the college groups and the national organization. Delta Gamma had a large group of collegiate presidents of campus panhellenics present and several advisers.

Mississippi State University

This same weekend that NPC was meeting with collegians in Miami Beach, other Delta Gamma officers were in Starkville, Mississippi, to install Delta Lambda chapter at Mississippi State University. This group had been colonized in February and groomed for installation by Eleanor Smith Slaughter, AΨ-Mississippi, a former Council member who lived nearby in Columbus, Mississippi. Mrs. Bowyer, Mrs. Moorman, and Mrs. Sullivan had attended the complete installation weekend, and Mrs. Strickland, en route from Miami Beach, and Mrs. Spaller arrived in time for the reception honoring the new chapter on Sunday afternoon. The charter for Delta Lambda had been presented to the group on October 25, the day before.

Council meeting, fall, 1969

The officers who traveled to Starkville for the installation were not there for that purpose alone, for others were arriving in Mississippi, too. The fall, 1969, Council meeting was scheduled at the Alumni House on the University of Mississippi campus in Oxford, October 27-31. This in itself was part of a plan, for the President and her officers were interested in deciding what part Delta Gamma's birthplace might play in Centennial plans.

Two of the officers, Mrs. Moorman and Mrs. Sullivan, had stopped to meet with a local at Morehead State University, Morehead, Kentucky, on their way to Council meeting. After a favorable report, the Alpha Sigma Rho (Morehead local) petition was accepted and passed along for an area vote.

Expansion in general was discussed at length and an outline prepared which defined standards to be met by a pledge colony before installation would be scheduled.

Junior groups

For more than twenty years some of the large alumnae chapters had also supported groups of junior alumnae (usually out of school ten years or less) who planned their projects and programs as subsidiaries of the existing chapter. A set of standards and policies governing formation of these groups was outlined by Council at this meeting.

Area Rush Forums

Area Rush Forums had been proposed and were discussed by the Council. It was agreed that at least three would be held in the spring of 1970, in California, Florida, and Ohio. They would be attended by the chapter presidents, rush chairmen, rush advisers, assistant rush advisers, and advisory board chairmen. Each chapter would be obligated to bear its own expenses.

St. Lawrence University

The question of the continuance of a chapter at St. Lawrence University had been discussed on other occasions, but at this time it was voted unanimously to withdraw the charter of Gamma Omega chapter from that campus.

Realignment of Council

In years past Councils have been expanded and realigned to meet the needs of the day. It had been agreed for some time that a new realignment should be considered, and after much discussion—in several Council meetings—the following arrangement was outlined to be presented among Constitutional changes to come before the 1970 Convention:

President—*Anchora*, Constitution, Convention, Executive Offices.

Vice-President: Collegians—Substitute for President, overall chapter evaluation and control of Fraternity Chairmen and Field Secretaries.

Vice-President: Collegians—Province Collegiate Chairmen, advisers, housemothers, Collegiate Representatives to Council.

Vice-President-Alumnae — Province Alumnae Chairmen, Foundation.

Vice-President-Membership—Rush and Recommendations, Rush Consultants, Patronesses, Rush Forums.

Secretary-Treasurer—Collegiate Finance, House Corporations (Director of Housing and Finance).

National Panhellenic Conference Delegate — Director of Expansion (Investigation, colonizing, preparations and installation).

The wearing of the badge

One matter which received Council attention was that of the badge. Some years before it had been agreed that alumnae might convert their pins to charm bracelet ornaments—either alone, on a disc or within a ring. As the Centennial approached, members nostalgically pointed to the oldest Delta Gamma badges worn on collars, ties, or anywhere a small pin might be worn. This Council decided to discard the traditional "badge must be worn straight, over the heart, about six inches below the collar bone" and to encourage members to wear it as they would a scatter pin or even as a lavalier, but above all, to wear it.

The last of the Lewis School

Since Delta Gamma's founding in 1873 at the Lewis School, anyone who was interested and happened to be passing down University Avenue in Oxford, Mississippi, could see this building. It was true that in recent years its state of deterioration was appalling to many, but it was there, and one could easily picture it in its more prosperous days as a well-respected girls' school.

Finally, its state of dilapidation could no longer be either ignored or halted, and the building was razed so that Council, visiting the site during their stay in Oxford, found only a bare lot on University Avenue. Several were able to find in the grass one of the hand-wrought square nails which had been used in its construction more than a century before. They had, of course, approved earlier the storing of paneling and doors which might later be used in the Archives. During their stay in Oxford they also viewed the Memorial Window in the Geology Building and other Delta Gamma landmarks.

Florida Atlantic University

December 6 two chapters were added to the Delta Gamma roll, one in Florida and one in Illinois. The Florida state university and college system is a widespread one with a multitude of junior colleges as well as a group of state universities. Florida Atlantic University at Boca Raton was organized in 1961 as a senior university with neither freshman nor sophomore classes. In the early months of 1969 a local, Chi Delta, petitioned Delta Gamma after receiving presentations from a number of Panhellenic groups. Chi Delta had organized in January, 1969, for the purpose of becoming part of a national. The petition was accepted by Delta Gamma's Council and an affirmative area vote followed. Delta Mu chapter of Delta Gamma was installed at FAU on December 6, 1969.

Northern Illinois University

On the same day, December 6, a local at Northern Illinois University in DeKalb was receiving its charter as Delta Nu chapter of Delta Gamma. In the spring of 1969 a local, Chi Sigma

Phi, had petitioned Delta Gamma—making a considerable impression because of their housing. With no alumnae or house corporation to back them, the local had taken upon itself the acquisition of the house formerly occupied by a fraternity which had left the campus. Council voted to accept the petition and proceed with the necessary area vote which, of course, was affirmative.

In-Gathering, January, 1970

The Field Secretaries convened at the Anchor In at Executive Offices in January with four Council members—Mrs. Strickland, Mrs. Leonard, Mrs. Spaller and Mrs. Bowyer—exchanging experiences and thoughts with each other and with the officers. On January 23, Mrs. Moorman having joined the group as well as Editor Barbara Carvill, a special Council meeting was called to order to last until January 25.

Membership Selection Study Committee

The work of the Membership Selection Study Committee was reviewed by Mrs. Leonard who had been acting as its chairman. Since it had become apparent that, with the recommendation of this Committee, Convention would vote to make recommendations voluntary, some of the situations which would arise from this action were outlined.

Collegiate Representatives

Jane Gegenheimer, X-Cornell, 1969-70 Collegiate Representative to Council, arrived on January 24 for the remainder of this meeting. All present agreed that the potential of the work to be accomplished by the Collegiate Reps would certainly increase if their number were doubled, from two to four. This, too, would be recommended to the Convention.

Realignment vote by mail

Council members present voted to submit the Constitutional amendment necessary to cover the realignment of Council by mail for a chapter vote. In this way, assuming that the proposal passed (as it did), the Nominating Committee would be assisted in preparing the slate of officers for 1970-72.

Campus problems

Having the Field Secretaries and one of the Collegiate Representatives present brought forth an exchange of thought on liquor in the house, housing itself regarding the requirement of living in the chapter house, demonstrations, and visitation. Chapter structure also received the attention of those present—the size of the executive board, the time of elections, senior programming, Fraternity examinations, scholarship, Field Secretary visits and Collegiate Representatives to Council.

Membership Selection

The report and recommendations of the Membership Selection Study Committee were received by Council before they had met again, and the proposed amendments which would be presented at Convention were approved.

Ball State University

Not long after it was announced that more national sororities would be invited to the Ball State University campus in Muncie, Indiana, Delta Gamma officers received an invitation from one of the well-established (organized January, 1966) local groups, Sigma Beta Chi, to meet. Shortly afterward, early in 1969, Delta Gamma received a formal petition from Sigma Beta Chi, which, after Council approval, received an affirmative area vote. This local was installed as Delta Xi chapter of Delta Gamma on April 11, 1970.

Council meeting, spring, 1970

More often than not Council chooses the site for its semi-annual meeting in order to inspect a possible Convention location or because of convenience to another meeting such as National Panhellenic. When nothing of this sort dictates the choice of meeting place, the officers usually go to an area which has not been visited by Council members for some years. So it was that the Davenport Hotel, Spokane, Washington, was the site of the spring Council meeting, April 15-20, 1970. Mrs. Leonard and Mrs. Call came directly from the annual meeting of the National Association of Women Deans and Counselors in Los Angeles, and among the seven who traveled to Spokane, thirteen chapters had been visited en route.

Charters

Through the years the initiation of members of locals becoming chapters—including the initiation of members who had been graduated before the installation—had created a problem in the printing of charters: that of having enough space for all the names of members of the local who wished to be initiated as charter members. In some cases, the charter was issued to a group of officers or, if the number was not too great, to those in school at the time the charter was dated. This Council agreed that a charter certificate would replace the regular membership certificate for those persons initiated at an installation and that all names would be eliminated from the charter itself.

Badges and replica jewelry

Council voted that each person initiated into the Fraternity must purchase a badge, the badge no longer being an automatic charge to the initiation fee. The officers also agreed that the badge replicas which were pins, lavaliers and rings might be added to the jewelry line.

Policy review

With the current work on alterations in membership selection, it was decided that some policies might be reviewed as well. It was voted that pledges eligible for initiation would be permitted to participate in membership selection discussion but would not be allowed to vote until they had been initiated.

Meeting with alumnae

During Council's visit to Spokane they were entertained by the alumnae chapter and put into practice a programming routine which was becoming a familiar one whenever a group of officers visited a chapter or association. At a luncheon or dinner meeting one Council member was seated at each table of alumnae. Following the meal there was a period when general discussion with this officer could take place. At the end of a given period of time (five or ten minutes), the officers rotated tables so that at the end of the post-meal discussion period each officer had talked with the small group of members at each table. This enabled a more personal contact between members and officers than might be afforded by formal speeches.

Resignations

This was possibly the bleakest period the fraternities had yet faced with regard to resignations —the process referred to by students as "deactivation." This was part of the current individualism vogue—"do your own thing." We are now able to enjoy the perspective of a backward look and know that the 100 processed between the April Council meeting and Convention in June were the peak.

Morehead State University

A second chapter installation took place in the spring of 1970 when Alpha Sigma Rho at Morehead State University, Morehead, Kentucky, became Delta Omicron, Delta Gamma's ninety-seventh on its 1970 chapter roll. Alpha Sigma Rho, also known as CAPA, had been organized in 1962, the oldest local on the campus. Installation occurred on May 9.

Kent State, May 4, 1970

The war in Vietnam had dragged on for nearly a decade, and students across the nation had registered their displeasure with it as well as with a multitude of other wrongs in the world with campus demonstrations, riots, sit-ins, lock-outs, and draft card burnings. It is now a matter of history the events culminating on May 4, 1970, at Kent State University—the sit-in, burning of the ROTC building, calling in of the National Guard, and the deaths of four students. All of this occurred within 100 yards of the Delta Gamma house. Reaction on more than 100 campuses in all parts of the country was immediate, and many schools (including Kent State) closed before the end of the school year. As it turned out, "Kent State" proved to be the crest of this period of rebellion. There were threats that even worse would happen the following year and especially on May 4, 1971, to commemorate that date in 1970, but the fiery spirit of rebellion had ebbed. Most disruption of campus routine after the spring of 1970 was minor and finally non-existent.

Marcia Connell Strickland, Ξ-Michigan, was elected to Delta Gamma's Presidency in 1968 and served to preside at the Centennial Convention in 1972. Her Delta Gamma career had begun less than five years after graduation when she became Province Secretary, serving for the next twenty-five years in nearly every area of Fraternity activity and as the first Director of the Delta Gamma Foundation.

Forty-fourth Convention
1970—Lake of the Ozarks, Missouri

The campuses of the United States had just closed on this year of turmoil when Delta Gamma convened for the forty-fourth time at the Lodge of the Four Seasons, Lake of the Ozarks, Missouri, June 24-30, 1970. Kent State was a fresh memory, and the unknown lay ahead. It was a time of issues and general uneasiness. To meet the needs of this day a resort retreat had been chosen for a Convention site for the first time in eight years, and a Convention of workshops had been planned—possibly creating the most complicated program ever offered to delegates. The membership selection study requested by the 1968 Convention had been in committee for two years and was ready to be voted upon, and so interest in actions on the floor of Convention was high.

To review this—or any other—Convention the historian must return to the minutes, the *Anchora*, and any other existing records of the time. Personal memory helps, too, but today if one asked anyone who attended Delta Gamma's forty-fourth Convention at the Four Seasons what her first memory would be, nine answers out of ten would undoubtedly be "the power failure." Three hours before the banquet on the final gala evening of Convention, the electricity went off for a two hour period. This included not only the obvious light, air conditioning, and heat for cooking in the kitchens, but also the power to pump water to satisfy would-be bathers at the end of a hot summer day in central Missouri. Obviously this was not the most important thing that happened at the 1970 Convention, but it is certainly the best remembered.

For her opening address to set the tone of Convention, President Marcia Strickland had chosen the "Age of Aquarius" as reflective of the mood of the times, and she drew analogies from the currently popular show tune of this name. Focusing her attention on what she saw as the "two paramount issues of the next decade—the nature of change and the nature of power," she discussed the various changing institutions and mores of society approaching the Age of Aquarius —the desires of youth, the role of the university, ecological pollution including the pollutant effect of drug use and abuse, individuality, and the role of women, especially in their time-honored role as setters of standards.

"In Convention Assembled"

This was 1970, the decade of Delta Gamma's Centennial, and the President led the Fraternity in considering this Convention the threshold to the centennial years. With this in view, another new slide program was premiered at the opening business session — "In Convention Assembled" — reviewing the story of Delta Gamma's biennial meetings through its first century.

$50,000 Foundation gift

The biennial meeting of the Delta Gamma Foundation was part of the first morning's program, too, with guest speaker Dr. Richard L. Dreher, associate director and coordinator of special programs for Children's Mercy Hospital, Kansas City. At this time a surprise announcement was made, the presentation of $50,000 to Children's Mercy for the establishment of a Delta Gamma Fellowship in Pediatric Ophthalmology. The grant was committed to Children's Mercy for the purpose of initiating a new program emphasizing the educational aspects of pediatric eye care and would be issued in five annual gifts of $10,000, the first to be issued when the hospital had secured a qualified fellow. Children's Mercy Hospital had been chosen for this grant—which would be a continued commemoration through Delta Gamma's centennial years—because of its central location and because it was one of a limited number of medical training centers which emphasized pediatric ophthalmology.

To be best of the 'seventies

A popular Convention guest was Dr. Frederick D. Kershner, professor of American Social and Intellectual History at Columbia University and consultant for Operation Greek. Addressing the entire Convention assembly "On Being the Best Sorority of the 'Seventies," Dr. Kershner was also available for question/answer as he rotated among the discussion groups set up for this purpose after his formal address.

Workshops

In fact, it might be said that discussion was the name of the game at Convention 1970. More often than not fifteen groups of delegates were in workshop sessions simultaneously, three circles of collegian in discussion while three other groups found individual officers "at home" for talks at this time. The nine groups of alumnae were divided according to size and type of community they represented, and all nine groups were simultaneously focusing on the same subject —ways and means, Foundation, etc.

Convention action

Convention did, however, meet as the governing body and recorded a number of accomplishments, most concerning membership selection as had been prescribed by the 1968 Convention. The Membership Selection Study Committee had been at work for two years, and Convention 1970 was ready to receive its recommendations. In this area the following became part of the Delta Gamma Constitution:

- A prospective member must be "sponsored by a Delta Gamma" not necessarily recommended by an alumna member as previously required.

- No longer would it be necessary for a chapter to vote unanimously to pledge a prospective member—though each chapter still would have the option of retaining the unanimous vote if it wished. Its own bylaws would indicate the percentage of membership necessary for a membership vote.

Several clarification amendments were passed including the following:

- that a candidate for initiation must be registered in the college or university where she is to be initiated.

- permitting a chapter, with the approval of the Province Collegiate Chairman, to designate a scholastic average higher than a cumulative "C" for both members and officers.

- allowing that the Fraternity Constitution may be amended by mail regardless of war or other national emergency.

Special Awards

Awards night at Convention had several surprises beyond the usual anticipation of collegiate chapters which would be accorded special recognition, the highest of which awards, Parnassus, went to Phi chapter at the University of Colorado. Present at dinner for awards presentations was Catherine Leavitt Jones, AI-Oklahoma, whom it was announced would be the honoree for the 1971-72 Fraternity Fellowship.

Order of the Rose

It is indeed a special occasion when the Order of the Rose is presented at a Convention, and another special Delta Gamma was to receive this recognition at the Four Seasons. This was Patricia Reilly Hitt, AN-USC, Assistant Secretary of Health, Education, and Welfare, the highest

To talk and to listen — this was the day of keeping all lines of communication open, to discuss, to examine, to think, to learn . . . between alumna and alumna, collegian and collegian, and especially, alumna and collegian.

ranked woman in the 1968-72 Nixon administration.

Banquet

Aboard the Delta Queen was the theme of the Convention banquet which featured accolades for retiring officers and a toast to the future. As it turned out, the banquet committee from St. Louis earned its own special accolade having decorated tables by flashlight and candlelight in the darkness of the power failure.

Speaker of the evening was Howard E. Young, president of Phi Delta Theta. Further entertainment was provided by the St. Louis alumnae with their melodrama of Hannah the Housewife, a parade of wigs and fall fashions. A spontaneous collegiate skit was also part of the program.

Council/Cabinet

During the course of Convention the Council/ Cabinet had met not only for its scheduled session on the day chapter delegates were arriving at the hotel but also in an extended evening meeting. Campus issues aired by officers (attention centering on alcoholic beverages in chapter houses and visitation privileges) reflected such intense feelings in all degrees of opinion that discussions continued far into the night. Throughout this period the Council/Cabinet maintained year-round contact through "Capsule Comment," a periodic newsletter edited by the President and the director of Communications and Information.

Elections

The new Council alignment had been approved by mail vote prior to Convention, and the first group of officers elected after this change to serve for the 1970-72 biennium included: Marcia Connell Strickland, Ξ-Michigan, Bloomfield Hills, Mich., President; LuAnne Lyen Leonard, AΣ-UCLA, Los Angeles, Vice-President—Collegians; Virginia Van Dyke Spaller, Ξ-Michigan, Dallas, Vice-President — Collegians; Mary Ann Lummis Bowyer, BZ-Denison, Dearborn, Mich., Vice-

President—Alumnae; Louise Callahan Call, E-Ohio State, North Palm Beach, Fla., Vice-President—Membership; Mary Elizabeth Falter Avery, AI-Oklahoma, Oklahoma City, Secretary-Treasurer; and Eleanor Smith Slaughter, AΨ-Mississippi, Columbus, Miss., National Panhellenic Conference Delegate.

Nominating Committee, 1972

The Nominating Committee for 1972 would be composed of Carolyn Coffman Moorman, AO-Miami; Rebecca Fowler Hudson, AΨ-Mississippi; Carmalieta Dellinger Brown, Θ-Indiana; Beverly Edlund Mertz, BK-Kansas, and Kay Blankenship Lemmer, M-Missouri, with Mrs. Mertz as chairman. Later, Elizabeth Coffinberry Kloppenburg, Γ-California replaced Mrs. Lemmer from Area E.

Collegiate Representatives

The four Collegiate Representatives to Council were as follows: Northeast—Martha Milbourne, AP-Ohio Wesleyan; South—Ginny Green, AΥ-SMU; Midwest—Jean Hurst, BI-Purdue, and West—Dina Marengo, Γ-California.

Centennial ahead

At the final business session of Convention 1970 President Marcia Strickland had, as her first official act in her new term of office, officially launched the Centennial celebration plans by announcing the names of three chairmen who would be working with her: Margaret Richardson Hay, Υ-Stanford, former Council member and 1952 Convention Chairman, had accepted the chairmanship of the 1972 Convention in Los Angeles which would be the official celebration of the centennial to launch the centennial year. Judy Smith Moore, AΥ-SMU, who had produced the fabulous publicity covering the 1968 Convention, would be the chairman of the Century Fund, and Frances Lewis Stevenson, Z-Albion, of the Communications and Information Center at Executive Offices would be the Special Adviser to all Centennial Committees.

29—One hundred years of hope

Centennial Years

With the first Centennial committee chairmen appointed and with Fraternity officers who would serve through the 1972 Convention installed, all systems began to move forward into the Centennial years. Many have asked why the 1972 Convention was chosen as the official celebration of Delta Gamma's first century, since the actual anniversary would not occur until 1973 and since 1924 (rather than 1923) had been chosen for the fiftieth anniversary celebration. It was felt that a mighty celebration in Delta Gamma's most populous area, Southern California, would be a fitting way to launch a year dedicated to marking Delta Gamma's first century. Thus, a Centennial calendar was devised in the fall of 1970 to outline events leading up to Christmas, 1973, and pointing toward a time for review at Convention, 1974.

But these were plans yet in the future, for only the initial planning was under way in the fall of 1970. The daily business of the Fraternity continued as usual.

Council meeting—Fall, 1970

Council meeting had been scheduled for October 21-25 in Montreal, and, as was customary, each officer had planned a stop or two en route to visit chapters and to accomplish other business. Mrs. Avery and Mrs. Slaughter, newly elected to their offices, had planned to spend a few days at Executive Offices. While they were there, news focused on Montreal and the unrest in that city because of the separatist uprising. It seemed to the two officers and the Executive Secretary that the wise course to take would be to intercept other Council members in their travels and re-call the meeting to Columbus and Anchor In instead of meeting as planned in Montreal. Locating the five travelers was a challenge but was accomplished, and the meeting was called to order on Wednesday, October 21.

Off campus status

Council has always prided itself on its alertness to the needs of the campus, and an early note in the minutes of this meeting further reflects this. It had been increasingly evident that college women did not simply enter school, attend classes for four years, meet requirements and graduate. Many were involved in terms off campus — in another area of the country for special work or internship in their field or out of the country altogether—and a large percentage of seniors in education were doing practice teaching in a city out of commuting range of their campus. With all of this in mind, Council voted that "special status" would be granted collegiate chapter members who are required to be away from their chapter for periods during the college year. These members would pay chapter dues but would not count on limitation.

Centennial planning

A considerable portion of the Council meeting was devoted to preliminary Centennial planning with Fran Stevenson and Barb Carvill present to discuss the long range view of *Anchora* through this period. These two had prepared an outline for what would be called "Panorama of a Century," a special color section which would appear in ten *Anchoras,* one decade in each issue, to be concluded with fall, 1973, and interrupted only for similar coverage of Convention 1972 in the center section of fall, 1972.

Centennial colors would be gold and white—this and a multitude of other preliminary details were discussed and points settled. Special guests at Convention would be all past presidents able to come, and particular effort would be made to plan special historical exhibits for the Centennial which would then become a permanent part of the Delta Gamma Archives at Executive Offices. Diane Turner, ΓΤ-TCU, would be invited to write a Centennial song or group of songs and would also be asked to appear on the Convention 1972 program. There was some discussion of the wood from the Lewis School still in storage and of the possibility of a favor produced from this wood. The Centennial theme would be "One Hundred Years of Hope." This seemed a uniquely appropriate theme, for the anchor for centuries has been recognized as the traditional symbol of hope.

Century Fund

At this time it was also decided that no special financial goal would be named for Centennial giving. Instead, Council wished to emphasize the broadest possible base of participation with special reference to service of self, volunteer activity in special projects being an equally important goal. Three areas of activity would receive financial support to commemorate Delta Gamma's 100th birthday: gifts to provide financial assistance for collegians, gifts to the Foundation, and gifts to strengthen college panhellenic programs. The structure of a Century Fund would include chairmen to promote gifts to all of these worthy causes.

Visitation

There had been a time when a women's dormitory was just that; no men were allowed above the first floor public areas except for portage or maintenance service or for special open house occasions. In recent years, however, visitation—meaning boys entertained in girls' rooms and *vice versa*—had become a general thing, restriction of hours governed in many cases, but even this had become quite relaxed. This matter was discussed at some length by this Council and the policy restated that "in Delta Gamma chapter houses men are allowed in other than public areas of the house for maintenance, repair, or portage only, with the exception of traditional occasions." It was also noted that "chapters may recommend changes in policy, but the business of changing, waiving or adding to the policies is that of Council." The procedure to secure a waiver in the case of visitation was outlined. This was reviewed several times in ensuing years. While some chapters indicated interest in experimenting with limited forms of visitation, none have wished to open their houses to the extent dormitories have been open to general coming and going.

Housing matters

Housing matters in general were part of the discussion at each Council meeting during this period of change. Often the pendulum seemed to be swinging in two directions at once. There were some students who wished, often as seniors, to live in apartments, and often a resignation of membership would be traced to the choice between the desire to live off campus and "having to live in the house." On the other hand, on many campuses chapter houses had waiting lists because underclasswomen were so anxious to get away from the "open" dormitories. The safety

factor had entered the picture in the 'sixties, too. At first keys had been a privileged convenience for after-hour entry, and then they became a necessity as it was deemed wise to keep the house locked even during daylight hours.

Chapter relations

It had been discussed and generally agreed at Convention—and further endorsed by collegiate resolution—that "Standards Board" was a misleading title for this area of the chapter structure, and Council officially changed this name to "Chapter Relations" as recommended by the Convention resolution.

Rituals

Other collegiate resolutions from Convention were reviewed and assigned officers for further study, but the resolutions coming from the rituals workshops were discussed at this time. The recommendation to replace the Greek letters "Pi Alpha" with "Delta Gamma" on the pledge pin was rejected because it was in conflict with the Fraternity Constitution. The recommended change in the "Omega Toast" was accepted as well as alternate uses of the badge which had been suggested (rings, lavaliers, etc.). The initiation revisions which had been offered were added to those already under consideration by the special rituals committee which would report at the 1972 Convention.

Field Secretaries

Cecily Hoffius, ΓZ-LSU, who had been directing field secretary operations from Executive Offices joined Council for a session on this program. The success of the In-gathering in January was discussed, and it was decided that they would also report back to Columbus in May for a wrap-up of their traveling year.

Volunteerism

When, at the June Convention, Patricia Hitt had accepted her Order of the Rose, she responded with a brief discussion of Delta Gamma's relation to the volunteerism which was sweeping the nation at the time. This same message appeared in the winter, 1970, *Anchora,* and with it appeared a group of resumes of the activities of outstanding Delta Gamma volunteers, women who were giving countless hours to their chosen philanthropy. From both alumnae and collegiate reports it was evident that not only was our Delta Gamma Foundation benefiting from this enthusiastic period of volunteerism on the part of alumnae, but that collegians were spending more hours than ever before in aiding others through the Delta Gamma Foundation.

Implementation of Centennial

A month after the Council meeting Mrs. Strickland returned to Columbus to meet at Anchor In with her Centennial aides, Judy Moore and Fran Stevenson. Roberta Abernethy and Barb Carvill also took part in these Centennial brainstorming sessions which covered all areas of

Centennial planning from stationery to special events. They also designed a Centennial brochure which would be sent to every member of the Fraternity, and they considered each facet of the Centennial celebration in planning a Centennial packet which would go to every chapter and association early in 1972. When this appeared it was beautifully packaged in white with a shower of gold Centennial seals.

Panorama

It was the spring, 1971, *Anchora* which opened Centennial to the membership, the first pages featuring President Marcia Strickland's personally chosen headlined quotes to describe a centennial celebration. This was the first of a series of opening pages of *Anchora* which would focus on various aspects of Delta Gamma's Centennial. This issue also carried the first of the special center sections, "Panorama of a Century."

Comment

Anchora had carried its collegiate comments section for some time, and now the editor remarks that both collegiate and alumnae reaction has been such that the alumnae want equal time. This is the issue in which they have their opportunity—which, as the editor says, demonstrates that where or when you went to school "doesn't affect greatly your basic ideas and values."

Council meeting—spring, 1971

Council chose Oklahoma City for its spring, 1971, meeting and convened March 15-19 at the Lincoln Plaza Hotel. March 15 being Founders Day, all of Council was able to take part in observances both with Alpha Iota chapter at Oklahoma University, a short distance away in Norman, and with the Oklahoma City alumnae.

Collegiate Finances

There was general discussion of collegiate finances — rising costs, deficit budgets, below quota/limitation operation, house corporations, the possibility of life membership dues as well as some specific housing questions. It was agreed that the house corporations would be brought into a tighter structure by placing them under the supervision of the Province Alumnae Chairmen who would be required to meet with the house corporation boards on their regular chapter visits. If house corporation boards were not within a reasonable visitation distance, then a specific contact should be made by mail within each biennium.

Balfour suit

For many years Delta Gamma had dealt exclusively with the L. G. Balfour Company for its badges and other official jewelry though many chapters purchased favors for parties and other novelty items from other suppliers. Included in the Executive Secretary's report at this spring, 1971, Council meeting was an explanation of the lawsuit, charging monopolistic practices, against Balfour and currently pending in federal court. When this was finally settled in 1972, the L. G. Balfour Company was forced to divest itself of some of its interests.

Convention planning

Following Council meeting Mrs. Strickland, Mrs. Avery and Miss Abernethy met in Oklahoma City with the 1972 Convention Chairman, Mrs. Hay, for preliminary discussions. Arrangements were made for Council to meet with the Convention committee in Los Angeles in connection with the fall Council meeting.

University of Southern Mississippi

Delta Pi chapter was added to the chapter roll on May 1, 1971, when the colony at the University of Southern Mississippi, Hattiesburg, was initiated. This group had been colonized early in 1970 and had spent the following year "establishing themselves, both in the eyes of Delta Gamma and in the eyes of a campus which already had eight sororities."

Foundation activity

The work of the Delta Gamma Foundation Director and her chairmen is apt to be overlooked in the review of the day to day operation of the Fraternity. This is possibly because theirs is a steady, year 'round service which more often becomes spectacular in its totals than in its individual acts. One individual act did receive attention in 1971, however. This was the *Library Aids and Services Available to the Visually Handicapped*, compiled by Florence Hinshaw Maxwell, Sight Conservation and Aid to the Blind Chairman. This helpful volume contained a directory of all the resources available to blind persons. As a gift in honor of our Centennial, a copy of the manual was sent to the president of every university where we have a chapter with the request that it be placed in the school's library. The letters of response were heartwarming and appeared in *Anchora*.

Foundation totals

A new "Design for Giving" slide program would be shown for the first time at Leadership School in June with totals in time which were summed up in an astounding manner by Foundation Director Elma Brock Hendrickson, AI-Oklahoma, "Or tell it like it is—200 hours each day, every day of the year, our gifts through the Delta Gamma Foundation." This was reflective of the high-geared volunteerism of this day. The script also noted that during the last year alone through the Delta Gamma Foundation members had raised and given away just short of $100,000.

Leadership School, 1971

Leadership School convened in Columbus, Ohio, on the Ohio State University campus, June 23-27, 1971.

The school opened with a day of intensified training for province, Fraternity and Foundation chairmen, and while collegians were arriving and checking into the dormitory, the Council/Cabinet met for their annual exchange of ideas and thoughts.

Leadership School, in total, formally opened that evening with Marcia Strickland's address, "From One President to Another." Mrs. Strickland shared the platform with four collegiate presidents who also discussed leadership experiences.

The newly revised *Collegiate Chapter Officers Manual* was formally presented to the chapter presidents with its major conceptual change: chapter Executive Board would now be solely responsible for chapter administration while the Chapter Relations Board would be responsible for chapter programming.

Once more the total picture of Leadership School and the people who made it was described as "enthusiastic . . . practical . . . perceptive." Indeed, Fraternity members had worked together to achieve the goal Marcia Strickland had placed before them when she was installed as President: "a creative approach to our mutual concerns."

The 1971-72 Collegiate Representatives would be Anne Laing, Ξ-Michigan; Suzanne Sloan, BΨ-Alabama; Jonette Beaver, K-Nebraska, and Jan Royer, ΔE-Pacific.

Campus calendars

The 'sixties and early 'seventies have abounded in additions to the vocabulary of academia, and possibly some of the most interesting have dealt not with ideology but with the formerly simple matter of the college calendar. Generations of students had started school in September, followed either a two-semester or three-quarter plan, and concluded the academic year in June. The option of summer school was chosen by some while others sought employment or enjoyed travel during the summer months. Beginning with the introduction of the trimester early in the 'sixties, progressing to the addition of the mini-mester late in the decade, and arriving at the total rescheduling of the semester system in the early 'seventies, students could be found matriculating or taking finals in nearly any month of the year. Even the "school day" and "school week" were being revised. Saturday classes seemed to be nearly extinct, and sometimes Friday appeared to be the first full day of the weekend by 1970. More classes were meeting in the evening, but many observers concluded that this generation was spending less time in the classroom and more in independent study than in the past.

Services for the Greeks

Generations of fraternity men and women had known the name of Stewart Howe, and chapters across the country had used his services. During the late 'sixties several new names appeared in the spectrum, individuals and agencies who felt that their services offered the answer to the ills facing the Greek world at that time.

Operation Greek was composed of a small group of professionals in the fraternity and counseling field, men and women who believed strongly in the fraternity system and who offered a number of professional services to campuses and to individual fraternities. Their biggest name was Dr. Frederick Kershner who had been offering guidance and counseling to the Greeks for several years and who had become established as a leader in this area (see Convention, 1970). Circulating among the women's groups to promote Operation Greek was Caryl Lenahan, formerly Panhellenic adviser at the University of Georgia, who made a presentation at NPC in 1969 and was present again in 1971.

Wilson Heller's Fraternity Counselors and its periodic publication, "Fraternity Insider," offered another sort of guidance for action to individual groups. Along with his services came his rating sheets which provided a picture of the status of each chapter on every campus. Many groups subscribed to the "Insider", colorful and gossipy, as well as to his rating sheets on the individual chapters.

Entering the scene a little later was Robin Bell, a retired businessman who looked upon the operation of a chapter and its fraternity house as strictly business. Meeting the challenge of the needs of his own chapter at Ohio State, he achieved results impressive enough to draw others to seek his advice. He found himself suddenly in business; his "how to" manual followed, and the demands on his time and knowledge spread.

Students on the move

The college curriculum was no longer confined to the college campus—as Council had already noted in its granting of "special status" to students necessarily off campus. The *Anchora*, fall, 1971, views a group of these young women who, by choice or to fulfill curriculum requirements, were exploring educational experiences outside the classroom: independent study in Mexico and Guatemala, lobbying for the environment, dance study tour in New York, fine arts trip to London, a summer archaeology dig, a pair who took a semester off to see America first (via a series of Delta Gamma house stops), and a review of the choices of Denison Delta Gammas during their January 1970 mini-mester.

Virginia Polytechnic Institute and State University

A local sorority at Virginia Tech (Virginia Polytechnic Institute and State University) at Blacksburg had chosen the letters Delta Rho when it organized as the first sorority on campus in 1966. When it petitioned Delta Gamma to become a chapter, it happily fell into the Delta Gamma roll as Delta Rho chapter. It was installed on October 16, 1971.

Celebration plans

Fall, 1971, found Delta Gamma officers and the special Convention committees in California increasing the momentum of activities which pointed toward the June Centennial celebration dates. Attending an October banking convention with her husband in Los Angeles allowed Fran Stevenson to spend a week working with Convention committees before traveling on to Scottsdale,

Arizona, for National Panhellenic Conference. This included a day with the historical pageant committee and time with Elizabeth Kloppenburg to plan the special exhibit areas at the Century Plaza where Convention would be held. Convention Chairman Peggy Hay, her assistant, Kathryn Gary, and Fran were able to devote this entire week to Convention detail, no doubt eliminating volumes of correspondence. Following the NPC meetings in Arizona, Council was scheduled to come to Los Angeles for the fall meeting and to concentrate on further Convention planning. And through all of this, the day to day business of Fraternity operation continued as usual.

National Panhellenic Conference

National Panhellenic Conference met for its forty-third session at Mountain Shadows, Scottsdale, Arizona, November 5-10, 1971, when delegates were challenged to develop new and decisive patterns of action to fit the realities of today's campus and to serve the changing needs of collegiate and alumnae members.

Delta Gamma's delegation was headed by its official delegate to NPC, Eleanor Slaughter. Her two alternates were the President, Marcia Strickland (who had helped found and was now chairman of the NPC "Presidents' Club"), and Vice-President—Collegians, LuAnne Leonard, who had arrived a day early to attend the special meeting of the College Panhellenics Committee. Roberta Abernethy was present to attend the meeting of the Central Office Executives, and Fran Stevenson and Barb Carvill were part of the National Panhellenic Editors Conference of which Mrs. Stevenson was chairman for this 1971 session.

During the NPC meetings one resolution should be noted in this history of Delta Gamma: "Resolved that the National Panhellenic Conference express deep appreciation to the following for (their) endeavors toward making this a most successful and effective session . . . Delta Gamma for the offer of service and seed money to strengthen college panhellenics." Both a slide program and a college panhellenics newsletter had been suggested, and the NPC College Panhellenics Committee determined the newsletter to be a fundamental means of communication among Greek-organized campuses. With funds provided by Delta Gamma as well as the services of the Executive Offices, the first issues of this mailing piece were edited by the 1969-71 and 1971-73 chairmen of the College Panhellenics Committee (Mrs. Charles Chastang of Kappa Kappa Gamma and Mrs. Carr Dix of Pi Beta Phi) both of whom live in Columbus, Ohio, a short distance from Delta Gamma's headquarters. Fran Stevenson continues to handle the production of the newsletter — "Ph Factor" — the first issue of which appeared in 1972.

This Panhellenic meeting in Arizona also decided that NPC in the future would include an interim meeting in the fall of the even-numbered years and that the official group delegation to meetings in the future would include the delegate and three alternates instead of two. This change was to insure better working involvement within NPC committee assignments.

Panhellenic totals, 1971

For the preceding two years National Panhellenic statistics showed the following headcount for memberships of all member groups: in 1969, 1,309,486 members, and in 1970, 1,930,000. For the decade, 1961-1971, 647 new National Panhellenic group chapters had been installed while 248 were lost—a net increase of 399.

Council meeting—fall, 1971

Mrs. Bowyer had joined the other officers in Scottsdale at the NPC meetings, and at its close they traveled on to Los Angeles for the fall

The immense task of the Los Angeles Convention committee was guided to a spectacular conclusion by this trio: Convention Chairman Peggy Hay, left, her assistant, Kathryn Gary, and the production chairman, Beverly Metzler.

Council meeting at the 1972 Convention site, the Century Plaza hotel. The first day of this session was devoted to a meeting with the full Convention planning force headed by Peggy Hay and Kathryn Gary. Here the details of decorations and entertainment were reviewed and approved by Council. It was decided that to complete many of the mechanical details the Executive Secretary should remain after Council meeting to work with Mrs. Hay.

Badges

Until the 1966-67 school year, the official badge, plain or engraved, was supplied to each initiate, its price included in the total initiation fee. Since many members indicated that they would have preferred the option of buying at the time of initiation a jeweled badge (rather than having to order it later, thus becoming owners of two Delta Gamma pins), it was decided by Council that each initiate should have this choice. Thus, for several years this option had been open to the initiate. This fall 1971 Council meeting further authorized L. G. Balfour to sell official badges and other identifications through its retail stores with verification of membership being a requirement of sales.

Mortgage burning in Columbus

January, 1972, marked an important event at the Delta Gamma Executive Offices when, with the final mortgage loan payment made, the mortgage was burned. In less than ten years the building had been paid for and in many ways paid for itself. During the first few years of existence of this building, the entire second floor had been rented, and this income had provided funds to meet mortgage payments. Gradually the second floor areas had been allotted to Delta Gamma use, and by the spring of 1972 only two tenants remained—an International Harvester regional office which occupied the entire rear wing of the second floor and a small office used by a manufacturer's agent. The Ohio Society for Prevention of Blindness, which had established its first small office in the Executive Offices basement and then expanded through several moves in larger offices on the second floor, found it necessary to move to another building which could provide more space than Delta Gamma had available.

During its first decade the value of Delta Gamma Executive Offices property has more than doubled.

In-Gathering, January, 1972

Once more four Council members—Mrs. Strickland, Mrs. Leonard, Mrs. Call and Mrs. Slaughter—met with the field secretaries to listen to their views on campus trends and the fraternity situation at that moment. During the 1971-1972 school year Delta Gamma had five field secretaries traveling, with one assigned to colonization projects and special assignments. As usual, the five contributed considerably to the knowledge and understanding with which the officers would meet the problems of the day.

Children's Mercy Hospital Fellow

It had been nearly two years since the Delta Gamma Foundation had granted $50,000 to Children's Mercy Hospital in Kansas City for the establishment of a fellowship in pediatric ophthalmology. The Hospital was now ready to announce the name of the physician who would make use of the grant in pediatric ophthalmology: Dr. Lawrence W. Hamtil.

Junior Alumnae Chapters

For many years, junior alumnae groups had been operating as appendages of some of the larger alumnae chapters, particularly those located in large metropolitan areas. Possibly because the age group involved—usually the first ten years after graduation—represented the most mobile segment of society, these junior groups seemed to flourish for a few years and then drop into a decline from which they seldom revived. During the late 'sixties, however, junior groups were giving evidence not only of marked stability but also of great achievements. It was a point in time when their place in the organization and their contributions could not be ignored. Late in 1971 the Columbus, Ohio, juniors began to instigate a movement toward official recognition for junior chapters.

The Delta Gamma Constitution neither prevented their chartering nor did it provide for it. Alumnae chapters were chartered on a geographic basis—a point which could, of course, be circumvented by adopting another geographic name within the same community. It was agreed, however, that this was not the answer and that recognition of junior chapters would be desirable. Policies describing limitations within which they might be chartered were set, and each junior group existing in the spring of 1972 was given the opportunity to petition for a charter and thus to be seated at Convention as an equal to its parent chapter. Three groups completed the necessary steps and appeared on the roll of delegates at Convention, 1972: Columbus, Indianapolis, and Pasadena.

Council meets in Milwaukee

Each officer made at least one Province VIII visit en route to the spring Council meeting at the Hotel Pfister, Milwaukee, Wisconsin, April 11-18, 1972. Final details of the Centennial Convention, now only sixty days away, occupied a great amount of discussion, but a variety of other items appeared on the agenda as well.

Badges from Executive Offices

It was agreed that all badge orders would be received and handled by Executive Offices. Badge prices had remained relatively stationary through the years, but as the price of gold rose, the charge was set at $10 for a plain pin and $25 for a pearl-set badge.

Florida Atlantic University

Council had received in the fall of 1971 from Delta Mu chapter a request that its charter be suspended due to lack of interest in the Greeks on the FAU campus. At the fall Council meeting the officers had agreed that Delta Mu should proceed with suspension but could initiate its present pledge class. Phi Mu was the only other group on campus, and this chapter had been informed that it must continue to operate. Mrs. Call, who lived nearby, visited the university a short time later, and Delta Mu evidently responded to her optimism to such an extent that the members wrote Council asking that their request for suspension of the charter be withdrawn.

Graduate counselors

There was some discussion of reviving a graduate counselor program, and guidelines were tentatively established for proceeding with this.

Auburn University

Sororities had first entered Auburn University in 1922, and several times in fifty years Delta Gamma had been invited to consider this campus. An invitation in 1971 was accepted, and a colony was formed in February, 1972. This group was installed as Delta Sigma chapter on May 19, 1972, just in time to be seated as number 100 on the chapter roll at the 100th anniversary convention.

Centennial Convention
1972—Los Angeles, California

For the officers and Los Angeles committees who had spent so many months planning a perfect Convention as the official celebration of Delta Gamma's Centennial, mid-June, 1972, was rather like the moment just before the curtain rises on a premiere performance.

The dates June 19-23, 1972, had been circled on Delta Gamma calendars for months. The Century Plaza, Los Angeles, would be the place,

and two days before Convention was scheduled to open, all was in readiness. Arriving at Los Angeles International Airport ahead of other officers, Roberta Abernethy and Fran Stevenson were greeted by Kathryn Gary who whisked them to the hotel with the word that they were to have luncheon immediately with hotel officials who were already in conference with Convention Chairman Peggy Hay. A problem had arisen. The Mexican President, Senor Luis Echeverria Alvarez, would be a guest at the hotel and was to be entertained as was befitting a visiting head of state. This included a state dinner in the Los Angeles Room (the largest Convention hall) at the Century Plaza where the official host, the President of the United States, might or might not be present. If not, Governor Ronald Reagan would officially host the guests.

Thus, the formal opening of Delta Gamma's Centennial, scheduled at the same time and in the same room, would have to be moved to another location. If this caused the four Delta Gamma officials to groan inwardly, it was only for a moment. We would occupy the just-completed American Broadcasting Company theater opposite the Century Plaza for our opening meeting.

This was a happy arrangement, but all of that was two days away. Another hurdle had yet to be crossed. A one-day work stoppage by airline pilots had been scheduled for June 19—the day delegates and visitors were to arrive. Across the United States and Canada fingers were crossed. The airline difficulty was settled, the planes did fly, and on June 19 delegates did arrive. It may be the only time on record that Convention opened with the Marine Band playing and Secret Service men in attendance—all for the President of Mexico, not for Delta Gamma's Centennial, however. At Convention's end Mrs. Strickland received a letter of apology and appreciation for

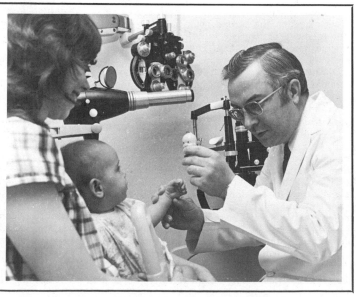

Named the Delta Gamma Fellow at Children's Mercy Hospital, Kansas City, was Dr. Lawrence W. Hamtil. Directing the Hospital's pediatric ophthalmology program, Dr. Hamtil gives particular effort to the education of medical students, interns, and residents to recognize and evaluate eye problems of infants and children.

Delta Gamma's gracious acceptance of this schedule change from California's Governor Reagan.

Panhellenic tea

Most Fraternity and Foundation officers arrived in time to hostess Delta Gamma's tea and open house at the new Alpha Nu chapter house at the University of Southern California on Sunday, June 18. Guests included representatives of all National Panhellenic groups, either officers living in the area or their personally chosen representatives, and University officials.

Tour of Los Angeles

For early arrivals the following day a tour of Los Angeles had been planned with stops at the USC and UCLA chapter houses and a party at the Blind Childrens Center. Aside from these tour buses on Monday, another shuttle bus was running throughout Convention. The UCLA house had been opened for collegians who preferred the economy of chapter house living for their stay in Los Angeles.

Convention programs of gold

This record of Delta Gamma's first hundred years and review of its first forty-five Conventions has done little in the way of comment on the physical nature of the program received by each conventioner to guide her through the days of meetings. Word of mouth undoubtedly sufficed at the first happy meetings of chapters in the 1880's. It is even probable that the elaborately handwritten (and often embroidered) banquet "programmes" of these days predated a program for the business sessions of Convention. In those days—and indeed for many years—everyone was a part of everything that happened at Convention; the division of collegians and alumnae for informal discussions came later, and workshops were the product of the period following World War I.

At any rate, even the rather complex program of the three-day meeting in Berkeley in 1915 occupied only a folded sheet about the size and weight of a first quality piece of notepaper. Paper quality and lavish printing reached one of its peaks in the 'twenties, and this is certainly reflected in Delta Gamma Convention programs. These became so elaborate that for several Conventions the program took the form of a large scrapbook to which a delegate could add her own snapshots and memories. "Cleverness" in themes took over (the symphony program of 1936) until World War II extinguished Conventions completely. Starting almost anew in 1946, the program became a formal presentation of officers and delegates pictures as well as a detailed schedule of the program of meetings. (It is interesting to note that conventioners did not have to be directed to breakfast until the 'fifties.) By 1958 delegates pictures were eliminated, and 1970 found Council appearing in a group picture. President Strickland declared this 1970 program both unique and beautiful and the most outstanding piece of printing to come from Delta Gamma Executive Offices' Anchor Press.

It was natural that great attention should be given to a beautiful keepsake program for this Centennial celebration. The Centennial seal had been embossed on the shimmering gold cover by the L. G. Balfour Company, and the binding of the contemporary square-shaped booklet was a gold spiral. A color reproduction of the portrait of the Founders appeared on the opening page, and a range of lavish printing devices were used to make each page a thing to notice. Facsimiles of the letters of greetings from President and Mrs. Nixon, Governor Reagan of California and Mayor Yorty of Los Angeles were included as well as a section of past Convention memorabilia. Since this Convention was possibly more pleasure than business, its official sessions were more limited than in past years, and each had its special highlight in speaker or announcement. This would not be a Convention of workshop or debate, but one of review and preview. Thus, the Convention 1972 program was a booklet to be treasured by the delegates and guests who received it in the gay plastic tote bags which were the Convention kits.

The Past Presidents

As a "prelude to Centennial," at Founders Day, 1971, in seven cities across the United States and Canada, seven past Presidents of Delta Gamma ceremoniously received a scroll inviting them to be special guests at the 1972 Convention. Six of them attended: Marguerite Dawson Winant, 1932-40; Edith Taylor Smith, 1947-50; Dorothy Knight Wildasin, 1952-54; Helen Million Preston, 1954-62; Maisie Clugston Groves, 1962-66, and Elizabeth Coffinberry Kloppenburg, 1966-68. Each had been asked to have a special part in the Convention program, each was honored for the contributions of her administration to the Fraternity, and each was enjoyed at this Convention for her presence alone.

Has-Beens

These past Presidents were more than special guests, however. In their Delta Gamma official lives they covered nearly fifty years of associations, not only as President but in the offices they had held prior to ascending to the highest post. And so it was that several other former officers spearheaded campaigns to gather together in Los Angeles as many as possible of the women who had served the Fraternity in official capacities during earlier years. From the West Coast, Convention Chairman Peggy Hay, herself fourteen years on Council, and her assistant, Kathryn Gary, a former First Vice-President, conducted their own campaign of letters to former co-workers. Simultaneously in the East, Jacque Buchenau Hawkins, Φ-Colorado, a recently retired province officer, was provided with a list of all former officers who were barraged with similar campaign literature. As a result of these two campaigns and the sparks of interest they ignited, more than 100 former officers were among the 1,123 officially counted on the 1972 Convention registration roll. Because of the special interest she had engendered in attendance, Mrs. Hawkins was appointed chairman of the Has-Beens/Silver Anchors luncheon, one of the festive affairs during the Convention.

The Opening Meeting

In the comfort and muted splendor of the ABC theater, delegates and visitors assembled at 8 p.m. on June 19, 1972, to hear the rap of the gavel and those time-honored words by the President, "We are now in Convention assembled." A huge replica of the Centennial seal was the only adornment at the center of the low stage. It was flanked by two round tables at which sat the current officers and the past Presidents with Mrs. Strickland at the podium. After the traditional preliminaries were completed—including the always impressive chapter roll call by the Secretary-Treasurer—it was Miss Winant, as the ranking President of the Fraternity, who delivered the President's address. It was she who had known the Founders, who had directed the construction of the Memorial House, and who had presided at the re-installation of a chapter in Oxford, Mississippi, and, in spite of her advanced years, the collegians found her as aware of today as themselves. The opening meeting provided the first of a series of memorable moments in Los Angeles. Following the formal session, an informal reception for the past Presidents was held back at the hotel. Instead of standing interminably in a tedious receiving line, the Presidents were spotted at separate locations through the area where they could individually greet old friends and meet new ones.

Happy Birthday Dinner

The business of Convention—province meetings and participatory dialogues of the collegians and alumnae—occupied the first full day of Convention, but the gala evening ahead was evident the moment conventioners entered the huge Los Angeles room for dinner. It was a giant birthday party, complete with Disneyland decorations (the real thing loaned by Disney Productions), balloons everywhere, a spectacular birthday cake, musical entertainment by Diane Turner and her group from Texas, a totally festive atmosphere. This was the moment that delegates had been instructed to bring their party-wrapped birthday gifts to the Fraternity to celebrate the one hundredth birthday. And so they did, each in turn bringing her colorfully wrapped gift to the long table at the front of the room—a sight to behold in itself. When the gifts were opened later by the Century Fund committee, they represented all manner of service and funds, the gifts of individual chapters to their communities in commemoration of Delta Gammas one hundredth birthday.

The Century Fund Committee

The birthday dinner was also the evening of recognition of the Century Fund committee: Judy Smith Moore, ΑΥ-SMU, chairman; Virginia Deal Williams, ΑΡ-Ohio Wesleyan, in charge of gifts from alumnae groups and provinces; Katie Scarborough, ΔΙ-Georgia, collegiate chapter gifts;

Gloria Fischer Dobbs, Μ-Missouri, individual gifts and gifts from special donors; and Marian Hill Keenan, Ω-Wisconsin, gifts from friends of the Fraternity, parents, and Mothers Clubs. All of these people were working in their particular areas promoting gifts to Delta Gamma's Century Fund, and all of these women were present at Convention at their own expense. Recording gifts at Executive Offices and mailing the recognition mementoes given for special donations was Priscilla Thompson Burgess, ΓΑ-Tennessee. The Century Fund recognitions were two-inch lucite cubes containing a Delta Gamma badge for gifts of more than $500 or containing a small gold anchor for gifts of $100 to $499.

After the birthday dinner the members of the committee amassed the birthday gifts in the First Century room to be opened and placed on display for the duration of the Convention.

First Century

One of the most memorable areas of the Convention was the room called First Century which housed the special Convention exhibits assembled there by Elizabeth Kloppenburg and Fran Stevenson. A Victorian breakfront was used to display a group of early, large badges, the original minute book, minutes of the first Convention, and a variety of other items of historical interest. The portrait of the Founders was displayed on an easel, and pictures of all Conventions were there for browsing. A complete and authentic outfit dating to the days of Delta Gamma's founding had been loaned by Dorothy Mardoff Jacobs, ΑΧ-Penn State, and was on display, too. A revolving display of Foundation history and good works had been designed and assembled by Carol Hoopingarner Hebert, ΑΙ-Oklahoma, of Houston. Of possibly most interest, however, were the twelve large exhibit screens, each 4 x 6 feet, containing period blow-ups of pictures of all areas of campus and chapter activity through the years. Particular care had been taken to include "famous Delta Gamma faces"—current officers during their school days and participating in the manner of those particular times. A full-page color portrait, a front page from the Chicago *Tribune* rotogravure section in 1939, of President Marcia Strickland as Big Ten beauty queen was a sample of the "finds" on display. One of the earliest candid shots was of a hayride at Indiana University in the early 1900's.

Convention action

The second general meeting on Wednesday, June 21, was the time chosen for the taking of the official Convention picture—the first recorded since Convention, 1962. This was the only session at which Fraternity business was featured, and action recorded at this time included:

- Alumnae per capita dues were raised from $3.75 to $5.00 for those alumnae paying through an organized chapter or association, and from $3.00 to $4.00 for those alumnae paying dues independently.

- Future expansion sites were discussed, and 34 campuses were approved for possible expansion during the coming biennium. (Council, of course, would not proceed with all 34, but Convention approval opened the way if an opportunity arose on any of these campuses.)

Silver Anchors—and Gold

It was at this general meeting that the Silver Anchors were recognized and the newly eligible were admitted to this elite group. A silver anchor is given to a person when she (or he) attends a fifth Convention. For the first time a gold anchor was given to those who had attended ten or more Conventions. All of the persons who have achieved these goals are recognized at some point in the Convention program. Two men have been admitted—Robert S. Baynard and James H. Clarke, both of whom, during their lifetimes, were regular conventioners with their wives, Mildred Moyer Baynard, K-Nebraska, and Ann Taylor Clarke, E-Ohio State.

Charrettes

A new word had been added to the group dynamics lingo—"charrettes." These were the discussions open to both alumnae and collegians on topics of interest for the day. In 1972 the choice was threefold: Rush and Panhellenic, DG Collegiate Chapters '72, and Service Involvement. Since many have already asked, it should be recorded here that "charrette" was a term gleaned by Mrs. Strickland from a news report of an architects' meeting where the term was defined as follows: "A charrette is a bringing together of a knowledgeable panel of resource persons for an in-depth discussion of a subject of interest with an audience which also wants to be involved in the subject and the discussion."

Story of the Ritual

A revision of the initiation service had been a four-year project under the direction of Elizabeth Needham Graham, Ξ-Michigan, who worked continuously with several college generations of collegians. The revised ceremony had been approved by Council and presented to collegians at the 1971 Leadership School. Since it allowed for individual chapter creativity as well, initiation through the 1972-73 school year had achieved a new and special meaning for each chapter. Mrs. Graham told the story of the ritual from the beginning in 1873, and with the aid of Carolyn Kloppenburg Riggs, B-Washington, and Kathryn Gary, presented the past, present and future as a single unit for all times.

Presidents' Dinner

Awards night is always a high point of Convention, and the Centennial celebration was possibly the highest of all. Century Plaza staging provided a dramatic setting, and, as always, the special awards were exciting. It was Gamma Rho chapter at Wittenberg University which received the Parnassus Award.

Each past President had a part in the evening's program, her toast to Centennial. As part of her toast, it was the happy task of Dorothy Wildasin to announce a surprise award—the presentation of the Order of the Rose to Delta Gamma's much loved Executive Secretary, Roberta Abernethy. The banquet room erupted with joyful applause as Mrs. Wildasin made the presentation and Fran Stevenson—the staff member who had worked most closely with Roberta for the longest period of time—stepped forward with the volume of testimonial letters and greetings from Roberta's many Panhellenic, university, business, and Delta Gamma friends. This award had indeed been a well-kept secret! Roses were presented by the two Columbus chapter presidents.

Foundation surprises

On Thursday morning delegates assembled for the biennial Delta Gamma Foundation meeting which opened with the showing of the Foundation slide program, "Design for Giving." This provided the background and many statistics for what was to come in current reports of Delta Gamma deeds. Dr. Lawrence Hamtil, Delta Gamma fellow at Children's Mercy Hospital, Kansas City, was presented, and he told of the promising future in the field of children's eye care and correction through advances in pediatric ophthalmology.

Another gentleman on the platform was there for another reason: Bradford Warner, President of the National Society for the Prevention of Blindness, who paid tribute to Delta Gamma by presenting the Mason Huntington Bigelow Award which honors a non-medical person or agency for a program or activity which has provided an outstanding volunteer community service in directly preventing blindness.

$50,000 for Home Kits

The surprise announcement of the meeting was a grant of $50,000 to the National Society for Prevention of Blindness to launch a program of Home Vision Screening. Made possible through the endowment of Margaret Price, Σ-Northwestern, Home Vision Screening Kits would be distributed nationwide by National Society for Prevention of Blindness affiliates and by Delta Gamma chapters to parents of pre-school children.

Woman Power

"Woman Power: What turns it on?" was the question discussed by a panel composed of keynoter Betty Furness, former TV-movie star turned consumer protection activist, and two Delta Gamma reactors, Gretchen Klaus Clarke, Σ-Northwestern, businesswoman-housewife-mother, and Jonette Beaver, K-Nebraska, former Collegiate Representative to Council and now first woman assigned to Ford Motor Company's marketing program.

Laurels Luncheon

Following this busy morning conventioners attended a Laurels Luncheon planned by Vice-President—Collegians LuAnne Leonard and honoring Rose, Shield and Cable award recipients, chapter charter members, fifty-year members, mothers and daughters, and chapters which had achieved in special areas. The oldest member present was honored—Irene Tomlinson Jackson, H-Akron, 1904 initiate. Luncheon entertainment was a fashion show provided by the Waltah Clarke shops of Hawaii and California.

The gavel falls on Century I

The last official meeting of Delta Gamma during the first century occurred on the afternoon of Thursday, June 22, 1972, when Convention business was completed, officers were installed and the next Convention announced for June 23-27, 1974, at the Doral Country Club, Miami, Florida.

Elections

Installed to serve through the Centennial biennium were: President, Kathryn Bell Gary, M-Missouri, San Marino, California; Vice-President—Collegians, Mary Ann Lummis Bowyer, BZ-Denison, Dearborn Heights, Michigan; Vice-President—Collegians, Marilyn Miner Hunt, AT-Butler, Noblesville, Indiana; Vice-President—Alumnae, Ruth Cope Mulvihill, Σ-Northwestern, Kent, Ohio; Vice-President—Membership, Louise Callahan Call, E-Ohio State, North Palm Beach, Florida; Secretary-Treasurer, Mary Elizabeth Falter Avery, AI-Oklahoma, Oklahoma City, Oklahoma; and National Panhellenic Conference Delegate, Eleanor Smith Slaughter, AΨ-Mississippi, Columbus, Mississippi.

Nominating Committee

The Nominating Committee for 1974 would be composed of: Helen Million Preston, Ξ-Michigan, chairman; Alice Beachler Gordon, BE-American; Helen Catherine Davis Stuart, K-Nebraska; Joyzelle Herod McCreary, ΓN-North Texas, and Dorothy Riley Milne, AΠ-Arizona.

Collegiate Representatives

Newly elected Collegiate Representatives to Council were Lynn Jaquay, X-Cornell; Beth Mitchell, AΨ-Mississippi; Susan Shirk, Φ-Colorado, and Susan Clouse, ΓΦ-Arizona State.

Banquet and Pageant

The traditional gala banquet closed the Centennial celebration Convention and featured, once more, the historical pageant, "The Girls Who Wear the Anchor" with models from the collegiate chapters in the Los Angeles area and Georgette Foster McGregor, AΣ-UCLA, narrator. Beverly Williams Metzler, AN-USC, and her husband, Bob, an Academy Award official, were able to provide Academy Award 1972 scenery for the background of this production. Costuming, furnished by the Delta Gamma Archives and by local contributors, was managed by Zada Pierce Folz, AN-USC. Following the banquet an informal reception was held in the foyer for retiring and newly elected Council members.

Once more a Convention had come to an end, an important Convention to end a Century and to launch a Centennial year of celebration.

Post-convention quiet

If the summer of 1972 was a fairly quiet one within the Delta Gamma world, it is understandable when one considers the frenzy of activity which preceded the Los Angeles Convention. Delegates had returned home with new inspiration for the year ahead, and officers were already looking forward to the Centennial events yet to come.

"Roberta is retiring . . ."

The name of Roberta Abernethy had become attached to Delta Gamma in much the same way "Betty Crocker" is identified with General Mills. It was not surprising then that her announcement of intended retirement at the close of 1972 was received with some shock by the post-Convention Council meeting. One of the first tasks of the newly elected officers would be to select a new Executive Secretary. This announcement was carried by the fall issue of Anchora, and a number of personal contacts were made, but it was not until the fall Council meeting that this action was completed.

NAME IN THE NEWS . . . In New York, Virginia Smith Boyce, ΓΩ-St. Lawrence, was appointed to the position of Executive Director of the National Society for the Prevention of Blindness. In May Mrs. Boyce had completed thirty-five years with the National Society, most recently as assistant executive director. In 1970 she was the recipient of Delta Gamma's Order of the Rose.

NPC interim meeting

National Panhellenic Conference met for its interim session October 12-14, 1972, on the University of Oklahoma campus with Mrs. Slaughter, Mrs. Call, Mrs. Gary, and Mrs. Avery representing Delta Gamma.

Council meeting—fall, 1972

Officers assembled for an October 16-22 fall meeting at the Warwick Hotel, Houston, Texas, a choice of location for the meeting which enabled the officers to hold an in-depth session with the Director of the Delta Gamma Foundation, Elma Brock Hendrickson, AI-Oklahoma. At some point during each Council meeting the officers are called to order as the board of trustees of the Delta Gamma Foundation. When this occurred at this meeting, Mrs. Hendrickson was asked to be present, and, after the minutes were read and approved, the meeting was turned over to her.

Cookbook

One of the first decisions made by this group was to update the Delta Gamma Cookbook in a reprinting and continue its sale. This would be under the direction of its 1966 editor, Margaret Robinson Regan, BΓ-Utah, of Salt Lake City.

International Education to be closed

The declining need for the International Education program had received attention for some time, and it was this meeting of the Delta Gamma Foundation board which finally agreed that it would be discontinued as of June 30, 1973.

For nearly 30 years the IE program had been a model of success. In recent years, however, there had been a decrease in the number of chapters able to hostess foreign students as universities became more and more reluctant to waive tuition fees, and the budgets of many chapters had become more stringent. It was agreed that chapters would be urged to develop individual programs which would enable them to maintain contact with the international students on campus. The board also voted that the Birthday Penny Fund, which had aided in supporting the International Education project, would also be discontinued in June, 1973.

Other new ideas

Two other changes in Foundation format were initiated at this time. The work-load of the chairman of Sight Conservation and Aid to the Blind had always been the heaviest of the three Foundation chairmen, largely because this was the area in which most Delta Gammas were able to participate. It was proposed—and the possibility would be investigated—to divide this committee so that in the future there would be an Aid to the Blind chairman and a Sight Conservation chairman. The division of duties was obvious, and this proposal was brought to actuality by the spring of 1973. Since both the International Education chairman and the Sight Conservation and Aid to the Blind chairman were completing terms and new appointments would be made in 1973, this was an ideal time to take this action.

New Foundation logo

There are fashions in printing just as there are in clothes, and it has been forever woman's way to change. Thus it was that the identification logo which had been designed for the Foundation in the 'fifties, it was felt, had served its allotted time. The steps toward a new logo were begun, and finally at Leadership School 1973 one was chosen, the design of Barbara Steiner Fuller, ΓP-Wittenberg.

Dr. Hamtil reports

Mrs. Hendrickson reported that both Dr. Hamtil and the Administrator of Children's Mercy Hospital had been asked to report quarterly to the Foundation. It was agreed that she should make a visit to Kansas City to talk personally with the Delta Gamma fellow and other members of the Hospital staff.

Money

It is interesting that during periods of extreme prosperity finances can become of as great concern as they are during periods of depression. At this point in time the Delta Gamma Treasurer reported that income is down and expenses are up; the key, it was agreed, to increased income is in payment of more alumnae dues. This would

Though President Kathryn Bell Gary was initiated at M-Missouri, she transferred to USC and affiliated with Alpha Nu chapter, married a native of Los Angeles, and has been a Southern Californian ever since. She is the third in a series of Presidents who began their Delta Gamma careers as PCCs. Her daughter Susan is a Delta Gamma, currently an adviser to her own Gamma chapter.

be an area of emphasis for Province Alumnae Chairmen during the coming year.

Field Secretaries

The changes in the school calendar already noted in this history once more came to the attention of Council when it was noted that so many schools were now taking final examinations before Christmas that it was almost impossible for the field secretaries to make effective visits in December. It was decided, therefore, that December 5-12 would be an ideal time for Ingathering during the 1972-73 school year instead of the January meeting held in previous years. Mrs. Bowyer, who directed field secretary activities, also proposed the possibility of a "Task Force" approach to chapter visits in a limited number of cases—two, or even four, field secretaries visiting a chapter at once. On some occasions in the past the plan had been used effectively for colonization, and it was decided to try the plan in the spring of 1973 for regular chapter visits.

After the Task Force plan was executed in March and April, 1973, it was agreed that while it was a delightful way for the field secretaries to travel, it created a number of problems for the chapters visited in this way. Housing one extra girl is not usually a problem, but housing four is. This seemed to apply to other aspects of the visit as well.

Hope groups of alumnae

For several years there had been small groups of alumnae in scattered areas across the continent, groups which met informally but were not listed as associations. For the first time in the summer, 1972, *Anchora* directory they were listed as Anchor Clubs, and readers were advised to write to the proper Province Alumnae Chairman for further information about the groups in these areas (seven were listed). This fall, 1972, Council meeting decided to christen these informally bound together circles of members as "Hope" groups. It was natural that the officers should voice the hope that the Hope groups would eventually become associations.

Life Management Counseling Program

Anyone scanning a college freshman handbook in these days would soon note that this publication had moved a long way from the days of "what to wear to the freshman mixer." Advice centered in many cases on lifestyle or what a woman's life held in store and what a college student should be doing about it. There was a discussion of these new attitudes at this Council meeting, and the two collegiate vice-presidents were to investigate a Life Management Counseling Program for the collegiate chapters with a professional in the field to set up the program.

Beta Alpha at McGill to be withdrawn

For some time the numbers interested in Greek participation at McGill University had been falling, and it had become obvious that it was no longer possible to operate a chapter on this campus. It was with deep regret that Council found it necessary to inform Beta Alpha chapter that it was considering withdrawal of the charter at the end of the sixty-day period required by the Delta Gamma Constitution. This action was completed in the spring of 1973.

Missouri Southern State College

Joplin Junior College was founded in 1937, and through the years passed through various stages of growth to become Missouri Southern State College in 1965. This was brought about through the combining of the junior college facilities with a two-year senior college as part of the Missouri educational system. A local sorority, Beta Sigma Phi, was established in 1969 by seven members. It grew quickly and in 1972, with a membership of 33, it petitioned Delta Gamma to become a chapter. The petition was approved and voted upon, the group became a Delta Gamma colony, and was installed on November 4, 1972, as Delta Tau chapter of Delta Gamma.

In Executive Offices . . .

A number of applications for the position of Executive Secretary had been reviewed by Council during the early fall, and several persons had been interviewed by the President and other members of Council prior to the fall Council meeting. Late in the Houston meeting it was learned that Carmalieta Dellinger Brown, Θ-Indiana, was immediately available. Mrs. Brown was a former Field Secretary and Executive Offices staff member and was currently on the staff at the office of the National Interfraternity Conference in Indianapolis—as well as serving as Delta Gamma's Chapter Relations Chairman. Council acted with both speed and enthusiasm, and in a matter of a few weeks Carmalieta Brown had moved to Columbus and was installed in the office where she would spend a month with Roberta Abernethy before the latter's retirement and departure for Florida.

Accolades for Roberta

Roberta's last days at Executive Offices was not entirely devoted to passing on her thirty years of knowledge to her successor, however. The In-Gathering early in December and the presence at that time of a representation of Council made this an ideal moment for the two Columbus alumnae chapters to hostess an open house in Roberta's honor. It could be said that "everyone" was there—most of her Ohio State pledge class, her associates at the University, all of the former Office staff members who were within traveling range, and many Delta Gamma friends, including immediate past President Marcia Strickland who came from Pinehurst, North Carolina, for this special weekend.

A more intimate group surprised Roberta with a party at the office on one of the last Friday afternoons of her career. The 150 Delta Gammas (representing 40 chapters) who had been staff members had been contacted by mail by the current staff. Many were able to come in person, and many others sent their greetings; nearly all of them had a part in the diamond watchband which was the parting gift of "The Staff"—all thirty years of it.

It's 1973!

For Delta Gammas who had worked with the date "1873" for many years, there was something magic about the turn of the calendar to 1973. With it came renewed activity and planning for the parts of the Centennial celebration yet to be observed. The Pilgrimage and the Leadership School were scheduled for June, 1973, in Oxford, Mississippi, and with the new year the momentum of motion in this direction once more increased.

Issue by issue of *Anchora* the "Panorama of a Century" had been moving forward so that now the editors were at work on the recent decades, the present one scheduled to close the series in the fall, 1973, issue. These two in the Communications and Information Center at Executive Offices were already at work on the updating of the *Delta Gamma History* which would appear as the winter, 1973, *Anchora*, the volume which would be the final record of the Fraternity's first century.

Council meeting—spring, 1973

When Council members landed at Detroit Metro airport to spend April 9-16 at Dearborn Inn, Dearborn, Michigan, they thought it was "spring" Council meeting. The week turned into winter's last blast, however, and so it was not as difficult as it might have been to stay inside and spend long hours around the council table.

Pension program

Pension programs and group health plans for the Office staff had been reviewed at many times in the past by various Councils, but each one had been rejected for one reason or another. A great portion of the first days of this Council session were devoted to this subject, and a plan in both areas to cover Executive Offices staff members was adopted.

Lifetime Participation

Another area which received a considerable amount of attention at this Council meeting was lifetime participation of members. It was agreed to appoint an Ad Hoc committee to study this subject and to appoint Elizabeth Finley Allen, X-Cornell, chairman.

Delta Alpha suspended

Council voted to notify Delta Alpha chapter that its charter would be suspended at the end of the school year in accordance with the Fraternity Constitution and due to the size of the chapter remaining below Fraternity standards. This chapter had been notified in November that the withdrawal was being considered, but in January Council decided to postpone the final vote until after the chapter's spring rush to ascertain if the number of members in the chapter had been increased.

To recolonize at Michigan State

Another chapter which was having difficult times was Beta Xi at Michigan State. This chapter, which had received the Parnassus Award as recently as 1968, had steadily decreased in number. Uncounted hours of special attention had been given it—as is the case with all faltering chapters—but without great success. It was decided that the chapter house would be closed at the end of the school year and Beta Xi would be recolonized during the 1972-73 school year.

Alpha Epsilon suspended

Numbers had been a problem for all groups on the Washington University campus for a number of years, and it was finally decided that it was no longer reasonable to try to operate a chapter under these conditions. Alpha Epsilon chapter, nearly sixty years old, would be suspended.

Consider Gamma Eta suspension

The possibility of suspending the charter of Gamma Eta chapter at San Jose had been discussed on several occasions, and this Council meeting decided to notify the chapter that this consideration was now official. On this campus the problem was a climate not conducive to the healthy life of a chapter though Delta Gamma might be said to be all that a chapter could be under these circumstances. In this case, Gamma Eta was willing to fight for its own survival, and so the suspension move was dropped, and the Gamma Eta delegate was seated at Leadership School in June.

Senior Scholarships

In recent years alumnae groups had been providing funds for senior scholarships beyond those allotted by the Fraternity. These were often Name Grants honoring some special member.

Retiring after thirty years as Executive Secretary, Roberta Abernethy was feted at an open house given by the two Columbus alumnae chapters. Alumnae and collegians from the Columbus area turned out to bid farewell before Roberta retired to Florida.

During the Foundation session at this spring, 1973, Council meeting it was agreed that the Foundation might award as many Senior Scholarships as are received from alumnae groups exceeding the twelve which are budgeted for the current year.

Indiana University-Purdue University at Fort Wayne

State university expansion in the state of Indiana has been, in the past few years, through the establishment of branches of the combined resources of Indiana University and Purdue University. Such was the case at Fort Wayne where Delta Gamma also counted a strong alumnae chapter with members representing 25 different collegiate chapters. It was not surprising that when nationals were admitted to the campus one of the first petitions was to Delta Gamma from Alpha Psi Omega, a well established local group. Installation of this local as Delta Upsilon chapter took place on May 12, 1973.

A Pilgrimage to Oxford

In many communities in the South today a pilgrimage is an annual occurrence—a time when the area's loveliest examples of ante-bellum homes are open to visitors. When the Delta Gamma Fraternity planned a Centennial Pilgrimage to Oxford, Mississippi, it was to see some of Oxford's finest old residences (opened annually for the Oxford Pilgrimage) because they had been the homes of Delta Gamma's early members, and to view other early Delta Gamma landmarks as well.

Since early in the fall of 1972 the correspondence had been humming between Columbus (the Executive Offices), Los Angeles (the President), and Oxford (the hostesses). Much credit must go to the latter who proved to be the key to the ultimate success of both the Pilgrimage on June 24, 1973, and the entire 1973 Leadership School which fell between June 20 when the officers sessions opened and June 27 when the last of the cabinet officers and collegiate presidents departed. It was certainly Delta Gamma's good fortune at this time that the staff of the University of Mississippi should include Dr. Judy Trott, AΨ-Mississippi, who had agreed to be the local coordinator of the Leadership School activities, and Sara Simmons Davidson, AΨ-Mississippi, who would be the Oxford chairman of Delta Gamma Pilgrimage day. These two, when asked the seemingly impossible by either Council or Executive Offices, became known for their standard reply: "It's no problem." They entertained the Executive Secretary, Carmy Brown, and Fraternity Pilgrimage Chairman, Fran Stevenson, for three days in April, working out final details and walking through what would become the Pilgrimage tour. They continued to handle a multitude of details on the scene up to the very eve of the Pilgrimage itself.

Any Delta Gamma pledge immediately identifies Oxford, Mississippi, with three names and a date: Anna Boyd Ellington, Mary Comfort Leonard, Eva Webb Dodd, and 1873. For ninety-eight collegiate chapter presidents and nearly fifty Council-Cabinet officers, it was indeed a special occasion which brought them to Oxford in 1973.

Council/Cabinet first

The Council arrived in Oxford on June 19 to hold its pre-Leadership School meeting the following day while the Foundation Director, province officers, and Fraternity and Foundation committee chairmen were arriving. The opening orientation meeting for this group—who were staying at the Ole Miss Alumni House—was held that evening, and the following day all officers became part of an intensified training period which would last through Saturday, June 23, the eve of Pilgrimage day.

Of this the fall, 1973, *Anchora* reported, "Operating the Fraternity is no small task, and it is upon the shoulders of the volunteer officers that the major responsibility falls. Thus, Officers Training School, under the direction of Council, was three days of concentrated discussion about the Fraternity's government and structure, policies and procedures, for collegiate chapters and alumnae groups, new ideas in programming and problem-solving."

Council/Cabinet meeting

During the course of each Convention or Leadership School a full morning or afternoon session is devoted to Council/Cabinet meeting. In the past these meetings had been held in the luxury of first class hotels (in Convention years) or at the Scioto Country Club when Leadership School was in Columbus. Though each of these settings was above reproach, all present agreed that the 1973 meeting site was the best of all: the beautiful and commodious Alpha Psi chapter room at the house. The Council/Cabinet gathered here for an afternoon session which closed in time for a buffet supper, on Friday, mid-way through the officers training period.

The Founders Room

Any Delta Gamma who comes to Oxford must see and admire the Founders Room at the Alpha Psi chapter house, and just before dinner the Council/Cabinet paused in their program to hear the President formally dedicate it. The present room set aside for this purpose is decorated in blues and golds, soft shades that go well with the original paneling and fireplace from the Lewis School. Its decorator, Sara Davidson, has carefully chosen pieces from this period which represent not the formal Victorian one might expect, but rather the simple and lovely things which, in that often over-decorated day, had been relegated to the schoolroom. The result is charming. The room also includes the portraits of the Founders painted in the early days of the Memorial House by Helen Humphreys Lawrence, Λ-Minnesota.

Pilgrimage Day

June 24—Sunday—was the day set aside for the

Delta Gamma Pilgrimage. The fall, 1973, *Anchora* reports, "Sunday, June 24, dawned warm and humid. The magnolia trees were still in bloom. It was to be a typical summer day in Oxford, Mississippi, except for the fact that a large group of Delta Gammas had gathered in town to celebrate the 100th anniversary of their Fraternity."

At 11 a.m. more than 100 Delta Gammas were present for services at the First Presbyterian Church, the church attended 100 years ago by Eva Webb, Anna Boyd, and Mary Comfort while they were students at the Lewis School. To those familiar with early Delta Gamma history it almost seemed as if some of the first members were present in the sanctuary, for this lovely church is lined on either side with memorial windows, each the gift of a local family. The family names were familiar ones, names which appear often in the original Delta Gamma minute book.

The church bulletin for Sunday, June 24, publicly acknowledged the presence of the large representation of Delta Gammas who had overflowed the sanctuary. The Reverend E. Stanley Smathers also noted the presence of the Delta Gammas and commented on the significance the church holds in the Fraternity's history. Two large vases of magnolias on either side of the altar were memorials to the many Delta Gammas who had attended services in this church one hundred years ago.

Following the church services, the pilgrims went to the nearby Holiday Inn for a buffet luncheon. Here the President, Mrs. Gary, officially welcomed the group present to Pilgrimage Day and directed them to the tour busses which would be their conveyances for the afternoon.

The tour guides for the two busses had combined their knowledge of Delta Gamma and Oxford, Fran Stevenson representing the Fraternity and Mrs. Bryan Tate, chairman of the annual Oxford Pilgrimage, from the community, and were able to discuss points of interest all along the way. Though many Delta Gamma landmarks and former residences were recognized along the way, time limited visits to only three homes.

The first stop was Rowan Oak, the home of William Faulkner, the Nobel Prize winner who made Oxford best known to many as "Jefferson." Estelle Oldham Faulkner and her sister, Dorothy Oldham, were both members of Alpha Psi chapter.

Next on the tour was one of Oxford's most elegantly restored ante-bellum homes, Shadow Lawn, where guests were greeted by Sara Davidson and her daughter Debra, AΨ-Mississippi. This, too, had been a meeting place for early Oxford Delta Gammas.

The third home was the Wright-Purser Home, just across the street from the site of the Lewis School. Its long shaded lawn and its proximity to the school must have made it a popular gathering spot for those first members. Here pilgrims were charmed by the two elderly ladies who reside there, one of whom is Oxford's oldest Delta Gamma, Matilda Kraus Fiske, Z-Albion.

Carmalieta Dellinger Brown, Θ-Indiana, was president of her chapter when she applied to Delta Gamma to become a field secretary for 1964-65. Thus began her Delta Gamma career; she was on the Executive Offices staff, 1965-67, and after moving to Indianapolis was a volunteer officer until she returned to Columbus in 1972 to become Delta Gamma's Executive Secretary. Her background in fraternity affairs was increased in recent years as a member of the Delta Upsilon headquarters staff and in the National Interfraternity Conference Office.

Dedication

The Lewis School had been razed in the late 'sixties and has now been replaced by a group of apartments. The 1973 pilgrims gathered to hear the President dedicate a plaque in the sidewalk which would mark the site of Delta Gamma's founding.

At this point in the tour visitors once more boarded the busses for a short ride back to the Ole Miss campus and the Geology Building to see the memorial window to which Psi chapter's treasury had been given when the chapter was removed from Oxford in 1889. In honor of its sizeable donation, a low panel in the window shows a Delta Gamma badge and its Psi chapter guard (see page 66).

The final stop of the afternoon was at the Mary Buie Museum, just outside the University gates. Mary Skipwith Buie, Ψ-Mother Chapter, had entertained the first Convention in her home in 1881 and had served as one of the first Fraternity officers. An artist of some note, she gave this Museum to the city of Oxford. Here the Delta Gamma pilgrims, after a warm and full afternoon, enjoyed not only the exhibits from the

Delta Gamma Archives as well as local items but also the punch and cookies served by the Oxford alumnae. Special hostess was Mrs. G. L. Eatman, curator of the Museum.

Founders relatives

A very special part of the Pilgrimage Day was the presence of a large representation of relatives of Delta Gamma's Founders. They were guests of the Fraternity for luncheon, the tour, and for the Mississippi Dinner that evening at the University.

Mississippi Dinner

During the course of the Pilgrimage Day the collegiate presidents who were delegates to the Leadership School had been arriving at Brown Hall at Ole Miss. These collegians would have their own Pilgrimage tours of the same homes and other landmarks on Monday and Tuesday with members of the Ole Miss chapter as their guides.

All had arrived by dinner time when more than 200 Delta Gammas gathered at the Commons on the Ole Miss campus for the Mississippi Dinner. Special guests were Chancellor and Mrs. Porter Fortune. The Chancellor of the University was a former president of the Mississippi Historical Society and well versed on the days of Delta Gamma's founding of which he spoke to the group assembled.

Leadership School

Throughout Monday and Tuesday the collegians went to school, both to learn and to share their ideas with Fraternity officers. It was an information packed two days, but ample time was planned, too, just for talk and exchange. A sunset supper at the Alpha Psi chapter house included a song exchange. Province awards, recognizing accomplishments within each Province were presented at the Province meetings, and special awards from the Fraternity recognized achievement in the areas of rush, chapter relations, chapter organization and structure, community and campus relations, and Panhellenic participation.

Certainly one of the highlights of the collegiate program during Leadership School was the Rush Simulation led by Vice-President—Membership Louise Call.

Collegiate Representatives

These 1973 collegiate delegates to Leadership School elected their Collegiate Representatives to Council for 1973-74: Cathi Hillen, BP-George Washington; Nancy Moore, ΓZ-LSU; Rosemary Ledvora, ΔN-Northern Illinois, and Leigh von der Esch, BΓ-Utah.

Christmas in June

When the Delta Gammas assembled in the crowded foyer were finally admitted to the Commons for the banquet on the final evening of the school, there was a momentary hush of surprise. Their programs had noted this event "To Mary, Eva, and Anna—with Love," but they were not

prepared for Christmas on a warm June evening. The Commons was lighted only by the candles in their Victorian chimneys on the tables, and the scent of Christmas greens filled the air. On the stage under one spotlight was a simple arrangement of furniture from the Founders Room and a six-foot Christmas tree bedecked with candles and gold ornaments in the style of the late 1800's.

When guests took their places at the tables, they found among the greens the sparkle of Christmas—a Delta Gamma Centennial ornament for each person present. It was almost too much that the dinner should be roast turkey and all the Christmas trimmings.

The special guest for the evening was Nancy Love Comfort Heilbronner, AΨ-Mississippi, who told of childhood memories of her aunt, Mary Comfort Leonard. The evening was climaxed by President Kathryn Gary's address, her letter "To Mary, Eva and Anna, with Love."

Century Fund reports

Following the story of the Pilgrimage and the Leadership School, the fall, 1973, Anchora included a report on the Century Fund. It says that money raised, with the final six months of 1973 yet to be counted, amounts to $294,500.82. Hours dedicated to projects commemorating Delta Gamma's Centennial total 208,222, and so far, 5,688 Delta Gammas have made individual contributions to the Centennial. This page of graphs further reports that 137 chapters and associations have initiated new projects in support of the Century Fund.

Rush figures up

Through the 1972-73 school year persons knowledgeable in fraternity affairs watched with guarded optimism reports of rises in numbers of students going through rush. When the figures were complete at the end of the year, it seemed fair to say that this trend was established. As of October 1, 1973 — with only a limited number of campuses reporting—rush increases are noticeably higher. Though these figures for the 1973-74 school year are far from final, it must be noted that among the schools reporting are those which seem to be the "first" in whatever the trend may be. University of California at Berkeley, for instance, reported highest rush figures in a decade while Big Ten schools with fall rush are noting spectacular rises.

The End—and the beginning

Thus, we reach today, this moment, in the chronology of the Delta Gamma Fraternity. Though this particular volume completes our first hundred years, no final chapter can be written for a Delta Gamma History. It is an ever progressing, ever growing thing, a story in which each member and each chapter has a part in writing the record. Even as this volume goes to press in time to reach its readers in the Christmas mail, National Panhellenic Conference will hold its forty-fourth session (in Memphis), and Council will gather in Kansas City for its fall, 1973, meeting. And so the record is never quite complete.

A Centennial is

not just one moment or event to commemorate a one hundredth birthday. It is a look to the past, a prelude to the future, a time and a mood, a way and the means for each Delta Gamma to share in the celebration of One Hundred Years of Hope....

The Lewis School, Oxford, Mississippi, Christmastime, 1873

Anticipating
the
Centennial

A commemorative grant to continue through the centennial years was the $50,000 gift to Children's Mercy Hospital, Kansas City, Missouri, to establish a program in pediatric ophthalmology. The announcement of the gift by Foundation Director Norris brought Dr. Richard L. Dreher, left, and Dr. Raymond B. Anderson to speak to the 1970 Convention.

Issuing the invitation for the 1972 Centennial Celebration Convention were the Southern California Delta Gammas at the 1970 Convention.

An early Century Fund donation was presented to President Strickland during 1971 Leadership School by Province II Alumnae Chairman Barbara Washburn, representing all Province II alumnae.

Centennial Calendar

Prelude	Leadership School, June 1971
Homecoming	Founders Day, March 1972
Official Celebration	Convention, June 1972, Los Angeles, California
Rededication	Founders Day, March 1973
Pilgrimage	Leadership School, June 1973, Oxford, Mississippi
Epilogue	Convention, June 1974

The Century Plaza Hotel, Century City, Los Angeles, California.

During the fall, 1971, Council meeting in Los Angeles, an entire day was devoted to meeting with the Convention Committee.

Looking ahead to the Centennial Celebration during the fall of 1971 were Mrs. Gary, Mrs. Stevenson, and Mrs. Kloppenburg as they made plans for the Convention historical exhibits.

Convention planning also required many meetings for committee members and the hotel staff. Discussing hotel arrangements with Century Plaza Sales Manager Patrick O'Daniel are Peggy Gault Kelly, AN-USC, left, Peggy Hay, and Jacquelyn Ford Walter, AN-USC.

The Celebration

The Centennial Celebration commenced as Presi-
dent Strickland escorted ranking past President
Marguerite Winant to the opening meeting. Miss
Winant subsequently gave the President's Address
to the Convention.

Former President Edith Smith found many old friends amid the Convention body.

Honored members of the Convention body were the Fraternity's Presidents. Seated from left: Elizabeth Kloppenburg, 1966-68; Maisie Groves, 1962-66; Marguerite Winant, 1932-40; Edith Smith, 1947-50. Standing, from left: Marcia Strickland, 1968-72; Helen Preston, 1954-62; Dorothy Wildasin, 1952-54.

A myriad of balloons, Walt Disney characters, a giant birthday cake, and lively music combined for a festive Happy Birthday Party dinner.

An array of gaily wrapped gifts adorned the stage following the Happy Birthday Party dinner.

First Century's historical displays presented a pictorial history of the Fraternity—the people, the campus, the chapters, and the times.

Amid the historical displays of First Century, former officers found a quiet atmosphere for chatting and relaxing.

First Century exhibits included photographs from previous Conventions, the original Minute Book, antique pins and jewelry, and other articles from the Archives, a costume from the 1870's, and the Founders' portrait.

Convention personalities

After accepting the Mason Huntington Bigelow Award from NSPB President Bradford A. Warner, President Strickland announced a $50,000 grant to NSPB to fund home eye testing kits.

Impressive and inspirational to all were the many former Fraternity and Province officers who attended Convention to celebrate the Centennial. From left: Audrey K. Wilder, Z-Albion; Mildred Quail, AK-Washburn; Mildred Baynard, K-Nebraska.

Commissioned to write songs for the Centennial, Diane Turner, center, and a group of Gamma Tau collegians entertained during collegiate workshops and the Happy Birthday dinner.

Champion Convention-goer Ruth French Shriver, Ψ-Goucher, attending her nineteenth convention, was escorted to the front of a general meeting by Executive Secretary Roberta Abernethy.

A surprise presentation of the Rose Award was made to the Fraternity's own Executive Secretary Roberta Abernethy.

The Century Fund Committee was present to make an interim progress report to the 1972 Convention. Century Fund Chairman Judy Moore is seated to the left of President Strickland.

Century Fund

The goal of the Century Fund was not a financial one but rather it was based on a commemoration of the one hundredth anniversary of Delta Gamma's Founding through service and aid in areas where need existed. The three areas of emphasis were aid to collegians through the awarding of Century Certificates and gifts to housing, the support of college Panhellenics, and as always, gifts through the Delta Gamma Foundation. As Christmastime, 1973, brings Delta Gamma's Centennial celebration to a close, nearly $300,000 have been given to the Century Fund and more than 200,000 hours of volunteerism have been dedicated to the Century Fund.

The Century Fund launched, Priscilla Thompson Burgess, ΓΑ-Tennessee, recorded and acknowledged every contribution received by Executive Offices. Mrs. Burgess also organized the chapter log pages presented at the Convention Birthday Party.

Delta Gamma

Century Certificate

This is to certify that

J. Lynn Jaquay

as a member in good standing of

Chi Chapter

has applied to the Grants and Loans Committee and been chosen as a recipient of the Delta Gamma Centennial Century Certificate.

This $100 grant to an active collegiate Delta Gamma, to be used for any purpose she so chooses, has been made possible through the bequests, donations and contributions to the Century Fund by Delta Gammas throughout the world, as their birthday gift of love.

The goal of collegiate assistance spearheads the aims of the Centennial celebration's three-pronged aim. No area is more worthy of the financial support than are you, the active Delta Gamma.

Century Certificates are the Fraternity's gift of love to our actives.

Kathryn Bell Gary
PRESIDENT OF DELTA GAMMA FRATERNITY

Judy S. Moore
CENTURY FUND CHAIRMAN

Bernadetta S. Brown
EXECUTIVE SECRETARY

A popular means for giving to the Century Fund were Century Certificates, $100 grants to deserving collegians. During the Centennial celebration ninety-six Century Certificate presentations were made by the Foundation Grants and Loans Committee.

Mississippi
Executive Department
Jackson

A PROCLAMATION

BY THE

GOVERNOR

WHEREAS, the Delta Gamma Fraternity was founded in Oxford, Mississippi in the year of our Lord, eighteen hundred and seventy-three; by the Misses Anna Boyd, Mary Comfort, and Eva Webb of the City of Kosciusko; and

WHEREAS, the above named Fraternity has flourished and extended into all parts of the United States and Canada; and

WHEREAS, that on a designated day, members of the Delta Gamma Fraternity will return in pilgrimage to Oxford to pay homage to the place of its birth:

NOW, THEREFORE, I, William L. Waller, Governor of the State of Mississippi, do hereby proclaim Sunday, June 24, 1973, as

DELTA GAMMA DAY

in Mississippi, and I call upon all members of the Delta Gamma Fraternity to observe this day.

IN WITNESS WHEREOF, I have hereunto set my hand and caused the Great Seal of the State of Mississippi to be affixed.

DONE at the Capitol in the City of Jackson, this 29th day of May in the year of our Lord nineteen hundred and seventy-three and of the Independence of the United States of America the one hundred and ninety-seventh.

William L. Waller

G O V E R N O R

BY THE GOVERNOR:

J Heber Ladner

SECRETARY OF STATE

Pilgrimage to Oxford

Relatives of the Founders were a special addition to Pilgrimage Day activities. From left: Betty Boyd Leonard Nelson, AΨ-Mississippi, great-granddaughter of Mary Comfort Leonard; Helen Lane Comfort Sanders, ΔΠ-Southern Mississippi, and Nancy Love Comfort Heilbronner, AΨ-Mississippi, nieces of Mary Comfort Leonard; Margaret Ray Buchanan, niece of Eva Webb Dodd; Evelyn Dodd Staehle and Virginia Dodd Devall, granddaughters of Eva Webb Dodd; Mary Mack Leonard Smythe, AΨ-Mississippi, great-granddaughter of Mary Comfort Leonard; William C. Leonard, grandson of Mary Comfort Leonard; and Charla Leonard, Φ-Colorado, great-granddaughter of Mary Comfort Leonard.

Outstanding among the restored ante-bellum homes in Oxford was Shadow Lawn, built around 1856 and occupied during its history by several Delta Gamma families. The Shadow Lawn gardens provided a cool retreat during the Pilgrimage tour of Oxford.

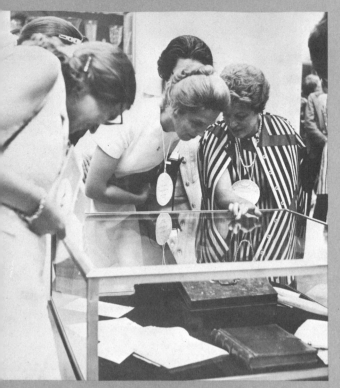

Touring Delta Gammas viewed items from the Delta Gamma Archives on display in the Mary Buie Museum, a gift to Oxford from Mary Skipwith Buie of the Mother Chapter.

Commemorating the Centennial, President Gary dedicated a plaque in the sidewalk on the lot where the Lewis School once stood.

Closing the Pilgrimage activities in Oxford was a Christmas dinner, at which time Nancy Love Comfort Heilbronner reminisced about her childhood and living next door to her aunt, Mary Comfort Leonard. Above, Mrs. Heilbronner shares some of her memories with President Gary and NPC Delegate Slaughter.

The Fraternity: Government and Officers

1873-74
Grand Chapter Officers
President—Anna Boyd Ellington
Secretary—Mary Comfort Leonard
Treasurer—Eva Webb Dodd

Convention Officers—1881
President—Mollie Laughead Jones, H-Akron
Secretary—Carrie Hawk Wolcott, H-Akron

1881-83
Grand Chapter, Psi, Oxford, Mississippi
Deputy Chapter, Eta-Akron

President—Lillie Wohlleben Hudson, Ψ-Mother
 Chapter
Vice-President—Minnie Wohlleben Carter,
 Ψ-Mother Chapter
Recording Secretary—Mollie Blakeley Chew,
 Ψ-Mother Chapter
Corresponding Secretary—Mary Skipwith Buie,
 Ψ-Mother Chapter
Treasurer—Julia Johnson Lipsey, Ψ-Mother
 Chapter
Historian—Delta Chapter, Tehuacana, Texas

Convention Officers—1883
President—Lillie Wohlleben Hudson,
 Ψ-Mother Chapter
Secretary—Mollie Schofield, H-Akron

1883-85
Grand Chapter, Omega-Wisconsin
Deputy Chapter, Eta-Akron

1883-84
Presidents
 Alice Lamb Updegraff, Ω-Wisconsin
 Fanchon Ellsworth, Ω-Wisconsin
 Florence Cornelius Flohill, Ω-Wisconsin
Vice-Presidents
 Belle Brown Flanner, Ω-Wisconsin
 Emma Goddard Marsh, Ω-Wisconsin
 Lizzie Hand Rowland, Ω-Wisconsin
Recording Secretaries
 Mary Dixon Edwards, Ω-Wisconsin
 Katherine Allen, Ω-Wisconsin
 Rose Fitch Briggs, Ω-Wisconsin
Corresponding Secretary—Marie Dahl Peterson,
 Ω-Wisconsin
Editor—Mary Thompson Stevens, H-Akron
 The officers were elected each term, in the
 fall, winter and spring, thus the frequent
 changes during the year.

1884-85
Presidents
 Edith Updegraff Simmons, Ω-Wisconsin
 Emma Goddard Marsh, Ω-Wisconsin
 Belle Brown Flanner, Ω-Wisconsin
Vice-Presidents
 Ada May Brown, Ω-Wisconsin
 Regina Lindeman Trowbridge, Ω-Wisconsin
 Mary Dixon Edwards, Ω-Wisconsin
Recording Secretaries
 Imogene Hand Carpenter, Ω-Wisconsin
 Emma Drinker Stearns, Ω-Wisconsin
 Sophie Lewis Briggs, Ω-Wisconsin
Corresponding Secretaries
 Emma Goddard Marsh, Ω-Wisconsin
 Belle Brown Flanner, Ω-Wisconsin
 Ella Spaulding Bunn, Ω-Wisconsin
Editor—Abbie Soule Schumacher, H-Akron

Convention Officers—1885
President—Emma Goddard Marsh, Ω-Wisconsin
Secretary—Mary Sibley Markley, H-Akron
Recording Secretary—Alida White Sherman,
 Ω-Wisconsin
Treasurer—Zoe Shimp Millard, A-Mt. Union

1885-87
Grand Chapter, Omega-Wisconsin
Deputy Chapter, Theta-Adelbert
1885-86
President—Katherine McDonald Jones,
 Ω-Wisconsin
Vice-President—Imogene Hand Carpenter,
 Ω-Wisconsin
Recording Secretary—Bertha Stiles, Ω-Wisconsin
Corresponding Secretary—Katherine Allen,
 Ω-Wisconsin
Editor—Bessie Kingsbury, H-Akron
1886-87
President—Imogene Hand Carpenter, Ω-Wisconsin
Vice-President—Ada May Brown, Ω-Wisconsin
Recording Secretary—Emma Drinker Stearns,
 Ω-Wisconsin
Corresponding Secretary—Belle Flesh Johnson,
 Ω-Wisconsin
Historian—Anna Hays Henshaw, Λ-Minnesota
Editor—Bessie Kingsbury, H-Akron

Convention Officers—1887
President—Sara McKinney Haserot, Θ-Adelbert
Secretary—Carrie Armstrong, A-Mt. Union
Treasurer—Anna Widman Bronson, X-Cornell

1887-88
Grand Chapter, Sigma-Northwestern
Deputy Chapter, Xi-Michigan

President—Caroline Hunt, Σ-Northwestern
Vice-President—Mary Richey Leslie,
 Σ-Northwestern
Recording Secretary—Camilla Ferris,
 Σ-Northwestern
Corresponding Secretary—Aurora Fiske Zeublin,
 Σ-Northwestern
Historian—Annie Kingsbury, H-Akron
Editor—Ima Winchell Stacey, Λ-Minnesota

Convention Officers—1888
President—Caroline Hunt, Σ-Northwestern
Secretary—Jennie Houghtaling Austin, Z-Albion
Treasurer—Louise Whitehead, Σ-Northwestern

1888-89
**Grand Chapter, Sigma-Northwestern
Deputy Chapter, Chi-Cornell**

From these a Council was to be chosen to govern between Conventions with the addition of a member from the Alumnae and one from the Editorial chapter; two to be chosen from the Grand Chapter and one from the Deputy, making five members.

President—Cornelia Wadhams Beardsley,
  Θ-Adelbert
Vice-President—Frances Flint Dean, X-Cornell
Secretary—Aurora Fiske Zeublin, Σ-Northwestern
Treasurer—Louise Whitehead, Σ-Northwestern
From Editing Chapter—Gratia Countryman,
  Λ-Minnesota
Historian—Emma Warren Ware, Z-Albion
Editor—Mary Mills West, Λ-Minnesota

1889-91
**Grand Chapter, Sigma-Northwestern
Deputy Chapter, Chi-Cornell**

President—Sara Foster Briggs, Σ-Northwestern
Recording Secretary—Carlotta Pope Creech,
  Ξ-Michigan
Vice-President—Almira Prentiss, Ξ-Michigan
Corresponding Secretary—Mary Power,
  Ξ-Michigan
Treasurer—Helen Babcock Latham,
  Σ-Northwestern
Historian—Phi Chapter
Editors—Lambda Chapter
  1890—Mary Mills West, Λ-Minnesota
  1891—Ina Firkins, Λ-Minnesota

Convention Officers—1891
President—Fannie Mulliken Thompson,
  H-Akron
Secretary—Minnie Buick Van Dusen, Ξ-Michigan
Assistant Secretary—Ida Hibbard Evenson,
  Ξ-Michigan

1891-93
**Grand Chapter, Xi-Michigan
Deputy Chapter, Eta-Akron**

President—Sara Foster Briggs, Σ-Northwestern
Vice-President—Lizzie Chaney Brandt, H-Akron
Secretary—Mary Power, Ξ-Michigan
Treasurer—Maude Parsons, Ξ-Michigan
Editor—Ina Firkins, Λ-Minnesota

Convention Officers—1893
President—Aurora Fiske Zeublin, Σ-Northwestern
Secretary—Josephine Cheney Brandt, H-Akron

1893-95
**Grand Chapter, Xi-Michigan
Deputy Chapter, Psi-Goucher**

President—Aurora Fiske Zeublin, Σ-Northwestern
Vice-President—Katherine Claggett Beck,
  Ψ-Goucher
Secretary—Lurene Seymour, Ξ-Michigan
Treasurer—Betsy Lee Hopkins, Ξ-Michigan

Editor—Ina Firkins, Λ-Minnesota
Historian—Josephine Tremain McCroskey,
  K-Nebraska

Convention Officers—1895
President—Ethel Baker Andrews, Σ-Northwestern
Assistant Secretary—Mary Mortensen,
  Λ-Minnesota

1895-97
From this time forward, a Grand Council replaced the Grand and Deputy Chapters.

President—Katherine Angell, Ξ-Michigan
  (resigned, 1896)
President—Mary Power, Ξ-Michigan
Vice-President—Betsy Lee Hopkins, Ξ-Michigan
Secretary—Helen Colgrove Nichols, X-Cornell
  (1897-98)
Secretary—Ruth Nelson Wetzel, X-Cornell
  (1898-99)
Treasurer—Mary Foster, Ω-Wisconsin
Fifth Member—Grace Tennant Adams,
  Λ-Minnesota
Historian—Mary Sloan Ayers, Φ-Colorado
Editor—Joe Anna Ross Pancoast, Ψ-Goucher

1899-1901
President—Nina Foster Howard, Σ-Northwestern
Vice-President—Ella Tyler Whiteley, Φ-Colorado
Secretary—Ina Godfrey Morris, Z-Albion
Treasurer—Mary Foster, Ω-Wisconsin
Editor—Jo Anna Ross Pancoast, Ψ-Goucher
Historian—Jessie Robinson Price, T-Iowa

1901-03
President—Edna Polk Wilson, K-Nebraska
  (resigned 1902)
President—Blanche Garten, K-Nebraska
Vice-President—Ella Tyler Whiteley, Φ-Colorado
Secretary—Ina Godfrey Morris, Z-Albion
  (resigned 1902)
Secretary—Belle Frost Richardson, Z-Albion
Treasurer—Genevieve Derby Woodrow,
  Ξ-Michigan
Editor—Joe Anna Ross Pancoast, Ψ-Goucher
Historian—Jessie Robinson Price, T-Iowa

1903-05
President—Blanche Garten, K-Nebraska
Vice-President—Grace Gibbs Yawger, X-Cornell
Secretary—Gratia Countryman, Λ-Minnesota
Treasurer—Genevieve Derby Woodrow,
  Ξ-Michigan
Editor—Joe Anna Ross Pancoast, Ψ-Goucher
Historian—Eva Lorenz Bailey, Δ-Mt. Union

1905-07
President—Rose Smith, Υ-Stanford
Vice-President—Grace Gibbs Yawger, X-Cornell
Secretary—Ruth Rosholt, Λ-Minnesota
Treasurer—Margarethe Sheppard Ferris,
  Σ-Northwestern
Editor—Grace Abbott, K-Nebraska
Historian—Eva Lorenz Bailey, Δ-Mt. Union

1907-09
President—Rose Smith, Υ-Stanford
Vice-President—Mary Rosemond, T-Iowa

Secretary—Ruth Rosholt, Λ-Minnesota
Editor—Grace Abbott, K-Nebraska
Treasurer—Margarethe Sheppard Ferris,
Σ-Northwestern
Historian—Mary Iredell Knight, H-Akron

1909-11
President—Imogene Hand Carpenter, Ω-Wisconsin
Vice-President—Mary Rosemond, T-Iowa
Secretary—Agnes Burton, Ξ-Michigan
Treasurer—Marguerite Lake Pendleton,
Ψ-Goucher
Editor—Edith Tukey Korsmeyer, K-Nebraska
Historian—Mary Iredell Knight, H-Akron

1911-13
President—Ada May Brown, Ω-Wisconsin
Vice-President—Lulu Parker Crawford, H-Akron
Secretary—Agnes Burton, Ξ-Michigan
Treasurer—Marguerite Lake Pendleton,
Ψ-Goucher
Editor—Ethel Tukey Korsmeyer, K-Nebraska
Historian—Alice Fieberger Meese, H-Akron

1913-15
President—Ada May Brown, Ω-Wisconsin
Vice-President—Lulu Parker Crawford, H-Akron
Secretary—Agnes Burton, Ξ-Michigan
Treasurer—Pauline Hagaman Faulkes, P-Syracuse
Editor—Ethel Tukey Korsmeyer, K-Nebraska
Historian—Edith M. Curtis, Θ-Indiana

1915-19
President—Jessie D. McGilvray Treat, T-Stanford
Vice-President—Frances Bragdon West,
Σ-Northwestern
Treasurer—Pauline Hagaman Faulkes, P-Syracuse
Secretary-Editor—Leulah Judson Hawley,
Λ-Minnesota
Historian—Jeanette Bartelle McNierney, Θ-Indiana
No Convention was held during World War I,
so the 1917 meeting was not held. The Vice-
President and Treasurer resigned and were
replaced as follows:
Vice-President—Hazel Whitaker Vandenberg,
Ξ-Michigan
Treasurer—Lenore Richards, K-Nebraska

1919-22
President—Gertrude Bradley Wilbur,
Σ-Northwestern
Vice-President—Hazel Whitaker Vandenberg,
Ξ-Michigan
Secretary-Editor—Leulah Judson Hawley,
Λ-Minnesota
Treasurer—Lenore Richards, K-Nebraska
Historian—Jessie Roberson Kingery, P-Syracuse
Lenore Richards resigned and Jean Burroughs
Reed, K-Nebraska, was appointed as Treas-
urer. The Historian's office was made part
of the Secretary-Editor's work at this time.

1922-24
President—Nancy Brown Woollett, Φ-Colorado
Vice-President—Alice Perry Gradle, Ξ-Michigan
Treasurer—Jean Burroughs Reed, K-Nebraska
Secretary-Editor—Leulah Judson Hawley,
Λ-Minnesota

Chairman Scholarship Advancement Committee—
Jessie Roberson Kingery, P-Syracuse
Installation Officer—Blanche Garten, K-Nebraska
Alumnae Representative—Irene Jenner Erlbacher,
Θ-Indiana
Changes were made in the installation and
ritual during this period; also special attention was given to alumnae organization;
scholarship advancement through a loan
fund was undertaken. Thus the addition to
the number of Council members.

1924-26
The above named officers served through the
four-year period, 1922-26

1926-28
President—Nancy Brown Woollett, Φ-Colorado
First Vice-President—Donna Amsden, T-Stanford
Second Vice-President—Irene Jenner Erlbacher,
Θ-Indiana
Secretary-Editor—Leulah Judson Hawley,
Λ-Minnesota
Treasurer—Alice Perry Gradle, Ξ-Michigan

1928-30
President—Mary MacHarg Halstead,
Σ-Northwestern
First Vice-President—Donna Amsden, T-Stanford
Second Vice-President—Marguerite Dawson
Winant, O-Adelphi
Secretary-Editor—Luelah Judson Hawley,
Λ-Minnesota
Treasurer—Alice Perry Gradle, Ξ-Michigan

1930-32
President—Mary MacHarg Halstead,
Σ-Northwestern
First Vice-President—Florence Cornell Bingham,
X-Cornell
Second Vice-President—Marguerite Dawson
Winant, O-Adelphi
Secretary-Editor—Luelah Judson Hawley,
Λ-Minnesota
Treasurer—Hazel H. Brown, AB-Swarthmore

1932-34
The Secretary-Editor's office was divided in
1932
President—Marguerite Dawson Winant, O-Adelphi
First Vice-President—Florence Cornell Bingham,
X-Cornell
Second Vice-President—A. E. Marie Parkes,
AΓ-Toronto
Treasurer—Hazel H. Brown, AB-Swarthmore
Secretary—Alice Perry Gradle, Ξ-Michigan

1934-36
President—Marguerite Dawson Winant, O-Adelphi
First Vice-President—Florence Cornell Bingham,
X-Cornell
Second Vice-President—A. E. Marie Parkes,
AΓ-Toronto
Treasurer—Hazel H. Brown, AB-Swarthmore
Secretary—Alice Perry Gradle, Ξ-Michigan

1936-38
President—Marguerite Dawson Winant, O-Adelphi

First Vice-President—Florence Cornell Bingham,
X-Cornell
Second Vice-President—Emma Sperry Robertson,
Φ-Colorado
Treasurer—Edith Taylor Smith, AB-Swarthmore
Secretary—Alice Perry Gradle, Ξ-Michigan

1938-40

President—Marguerite Dawson Winant, O-Adelphi
First Vice-President—Mary Myer Tobin,
E-Ohio State (resigned, 1939)
First Vice-President—Roberta Abernethy,
E-Ohio State
Second Vice-President—Emma Sperry Robertson,
Φ-Colorado
Secretary—Dorothy Brown Holland, K-Nebraska
(resigned, 1939)
Secretary—Alice Perry Gradle, Ξ-Michigan
Treasurer—Edith Taylor Smith, AB-Swarthmore

1940-42

President—Florence Cornell Bingham, X-Cornell
First Vice-President—Roberta Abernethy,
E-Ohio State
Second Vice-President—Jean Gooch Teall,
Γ-California
Secretary—Dorothy Knight Wildasin,
AO-Miami Univ.
Treasurer—Edith Taylor Smith, AB-Swarthmore

1942-46

No Convention was held in 1944 because of
World War II
President—Florence Cornell Bingham, X-Cornell
First Vice-President—Dorothy Glenn Holsinger,
I-Illinois
Second Vice-President—Jean Gooch Teall,
Γ-California
Secretary—Dorothy Knight Wildasin,
AO-Miami Univ.
Treasurer—Edith Taylor Smith, AB-Swarthmore

1946-48

President—Florence Cornell Bingham, X-Cornell
(resigned, 1947)
President—Edith Taylor Smith, AB-Swarthmore
First Vice-President—Dorothy Glenn Holsinger,
I-Illinois
Second Vice-President—Helen Russell Byars,
M-Missouri
Secretary—Dorothy Knight Wildasin,
AO-Miami Univ.
Treasurer—Edith Taylor Smith, AB-Swarthmore
(resigned, 1947, to become President)
Treasurer—Margaret Smallpage Banker,
Σ-Northwestern

1948-50

President—Edith Taylor Smith, AB-Swarthmore
First Vice-President—Dorothy Knight Wildasin,
AO-Miami Univ.
Second Vice-President—Helen Russell Byars,
M-Missouri
Secretary—Irene Howell Forman, AK-Washburn
Treasurer—Margaret Smallpage Banker,
Σ-Northwestern

1950-52

President—Helen Russell Byars, M-Missouri
(resigned, 1952)
First Vice-President—Dorothy Knight Wildasin,
AO-Miami Univ.
Second Vice-President—Helen Million Preston,
Ξ-Michigan
Secretary—Irene Howell Forman, AK-Washburn
Treasurer—Margaret Smallpage Banker,
Σ-Northwestern

1952-54

President—Dorothy Knight Wildasin,
AO-Miami Univ.
First Vice-President—Margaret Richardson Hay,
Υ-Stanford
Second Vice-President—Helen Million Preston,
Ξ-Michigan
Secretary—Irene Howell Forman, AK-Washburn
(resigned 1954)
Treasurer—Helen Bradford Anderson, M-Missouri

1954-56

President—Helen Million Preston, Ξ-Michigan
First Vice-President—Margaret Richardson Hay,
Υ-Stanford
Second Vice-President—Virginia Ungemach
Brown, Φ-Colorado (resigned, 1954)
Second Vice-President—Carolyn Boli Stanton,
AΥ-SMU
Secretary—Nancy Harris Cooper, AΣ-UCLA
Treasurer—Helen Bradford Anderson, M-Missouri

1956-58

President—Helen Million Preston, Ξ-Michigan
First Vice-President—Margaret Richardson Hay,
Υ-Stanford
Second Vice-President—Maisie Clugston Groves,
AΦ-British Columbia
Secretary—Laura Bertram Dillon, Z-Albion
Treasurer—Helen Bradford Anderson, M-Missouri

1958-60

President—Helen Million Preston, Ξ-Michigan
First Vice-President—Margaret Richardson Hay,
Υ-Stanford
Second Vice-President—Maisie Clugston Groves,
AΦ-British Columbia
Secretary—Laura Bertram Dillon, Z-Albion
Treasurer—Helen Bradford Anderson, M-Missouri
N.P.C. Delegate—Dorothy Glenn Holsinger,
I-Illinois (Died, October, 1958)
Ruth Canary Turpin, AN-USC (1958-59)
Margaret Richardson Hay, Υ-Stanford (1959)
(See History, 1958)

1960-62

President—Helen Million Preston, Ξ-Michigan
First Vice-President—Elizabeth Coffinberry
Kloppenburg, Γ-California
Second Vice-President—Kathryn Maple Roberts,
AH-Whitman
Secretary—Ruth Canary Turpin, AN-USC
Treasurer—Marjorie Reeves Van Ness, Θ-Indiana
N.P.C. Delegate—Margaret Richardson Hay,
Υ-Stanford

1962-64

President—Maisie Clugston Groves,
AΦ-British Columbia
First Vice-President—Elizabeth Coffinberry
Kloppenburg, Γ-California
Second Vice-President—Kathryn Maple Roberts,
AH-Whitman
Third Vice-President—Marcia Connell Strickland,
Ξ-Michigan
Secretary—Ruth Canary Turpin, AN-USC
(resigned Fall, 1962)
Secretary—Margery Sommers Hammill, AM-Beloit
Treasurer—Marjorie Reeves Van Ness, Θ-Indiana
N.P.C. Delegate—Margaret Richardson Hay,
Υ-Stanford

1964-66

President—Maisie Clugston Groves,
AΦ-British Columbia
First Vice-President—Kathryn Bell Gary,
M-Missouri
Second Vice-President—Virginia Riesterer Gates,
Σ-Northwestern
Third Vice-President—Eleanor Smith Slaughter,
AΨ-Mississippi
Secretary—Margery Sommers Hammill, AM-Beloit
Treasurer—Carolyn Coffman Moorman,
AO-Miami Univ.
N.P.C. Delegate—Marcia Connell Strickland,
Ξ-Michigan

1966-68

President—Elizabeth Coffinberry Kloppenburg,
Γ-California
First Vice-President—Kathryn Bell Gary,
M-Missouri
Second Vice-President—Virginia Riesterer Gates,
Σ-Northwestern (resigned, spring 1967)
Mary Ann Lummis Bowyer,
BZ-Dennison (1967-68)
Third Vice-President—Eleanor Smith Slaughter,
AΨ-Mississippi
Secretary—Janet Lau Sullivan, K-Nebraska
Treasurer—Carolyn Coffman Moorman,
AO-Miami Univ.
N.P.C. Delegate—Marcia Connell Strickland,
Ξ-Michigan

1968-70

President—Marcia Connell Strickland,
Ξ-Michigan
First Vice-President—LuAnne Lyen Leonard,
AΣ-UCLA
Second Vice-President—Mary Ann Lummis
Bowyer, BZ-Denison
Third Vice-President—Virginia Van Dyke Spaller,
Ξ-Michigan
Secretary—Janet Lau Sullivan, K-Nebraska
Treasurer—Carolyn Coffman Moorman,
AO-Miami Univ.
N.P.C. Delegate—Louise Callahan Call,
E-Ohio State

1970-72

President—Marcia Connell Strickland,
Ξ-Michigan

Vice-President, Collegians—LuAnne Lyen
Leonard, AΣ-UCLA
Vice-President, Collegians—Virginia Van Dyke
Spaller, Ξ-Michigan
Vice-President, Alumnae—Mary Ann Lummis
Bowyer, BZ-Denison
Vice-President, Membership—Louise Callahan
Call, E-Ohio State
Secretary-Treasurer—Mary Elizabeth Falter
Avery, AI-Oklahoma
N.P.C. Delegate—Eleanor Smith Slaughter,
AΨ-Mississippi

1972-74

President—Kathryn Bell Gary, M-Missouri
Vice-President, Collegians—Mary Ann Lummis
Bowyer, BZ-Denison
Vice-President, Collegians—Marilyn Miner Hunt,
AT-Butler
Vice-President, Alumnae—Ruth Cope Mulvihill,
Σ-Northwestern
Vice-President, Membership—Louise Callahan
Call, E-Ohio State
Secretary-Treasurer—Mary Elizabeth Falter
Avery, AI-Oklahoma
N.P.C. Delegate—Eleanor Smith Slaughter,
AΨ-Mississippi

Executive Offices

Though Leulah Judson Hawley, as Secretary-Editor from 1915-32, operated a "Centralized Office" from her home in Minneapolis, a Central Office, as a business center for the Fraternity, was not established until 1942. From 1942-55 the Central Office was located in a downtown office building at 50 West Broad Street, Columbus, Ohio. From 1955-61 the Central Office was located in a suburban office building at 1820 Northwest Blvd., also in Columbus, Ohio. On December 1, 1961, the Executive Offices, a building constructed by Delta Gamma Fraternity for this purpose, was opened at 3250 Riverside Drive, Columbus, Ohio 43221 (in the suburb of Upper Arlington).

Executive Secretary—
1942-72   Roberta Abernethy, E-Ohio State
1972-   Carmalieta Dellinger Brown,
Θ-Indiana

National Panhellenic Conference

Inasmuch as the women's fraternities were founded on similar ideals, they have developed along parallel lines, and have been closely associated through the years. Fraternity officers early realized that some joint consideration and action would make possible a solution of problems common to all. In 1891, Kappa Kappa Gamma invited women's Greek Letter fraternities to meet in Boston to discuss methods of inter-fraternity cooperation. Six fraternities — Alpha Phi, Gamma Phi Beta, Delta Gamma, Delta Delta Delta, Kappa Alpha Theta and Pi Beta Phi — accepted their invitation and attended the meeting in Boston on April 16 and 17, 1891. This first meeting of these seven groups was the forerunner of National Panhellenic Congress. Bertha Reed, X-Cornell, and Tirzah Sherwood, Ω-Wisconsin, represented Delta Gamma at this first meeting. No permanent organization was perfected at this time, but plans were made to hold another conference which did not materialize, however, in Chicago during the World's Fair in 1893. An exchange of fraternity magazines was recommended, and an Interfraternity Directory of national officers was advocated. Tirzah L. Sherwood was appointed a member of the "World's Fair" committee and Bertha Reed a member of the Greek Journalism committee.

In 1902, Alpha Phi called a conference to meet in Chicago to discuss the question of pledging and rushing. The same seven fraternities represented at the earlier meeting responded. Present were Alpha Phi, Gamma Phi Beta, Delta Gamma, Delta Delta Delta, Kappa Alpha Theta, Kappa Kappa Gamma, and Pi Beta Phi. Miss Nina Howard, Past President of the Fraternity, represented Delta Gamma at this conference. Again, the problem of rushing was discussed; action was advocated to require matriculation before pledging and to banish any part of the initiation ceremony in public. It was arranged that similar meetings be called by the several fraternities in rotation, annually. This meeting in 1902 is usually considered the first meeting of the organization that today is known as National Panhellenic Conference, as the earlier Boston meeting did not result in any definite permanent organization.

Gamma Phi Beta called the meeting in 1903. Miss Blanche Garten, President of the Fraternity, represented Delta Gamma at this meeting, where plans were made for the formation of college Panhellenic organizations wherever two or more fraternities were present on a campus. Alpha Chi Omega and Chi Omega were represented at this meeting in addition to the original seven.

Delta Gamma called the Third Inter-Sorority Conference, which met in Chicago, September 16 and 17, 1904. Grace Telling, Sigma chapter, presided as chairman of the Conference. Ten fraternities were represented, Alpha Xi Delta being added to the number that had met previously. Again, problems of rushing and pledging were discussed; the plan for rotation in office according to membership in the Conference was established; cooperation with the college authorities, especially the deans of women, was stressed; and a spirit of democracy with regard to general college activities was urged.

Meetings were held from 1902 to 1908 under the name of the Inter-Sorority Conference. In 1908, the name was changed to National Panhellenic Conference; in 1911 to National Panhellenic Congress; and in 1945 National Panhellenic Conference. In 1905, the standards for admission to National Panhellenic Conference were established. To be eligible for membership, a fraternity must have at least five chapters in institutions of collegiate rank. It must be general in character and not restricted in membership to any special interest or type.

The member groups assume office in rotation according to the sequence listed in the Constitution of the Conference. The ten groups attending the 1904 meeting of the Inter-Sorority Conference head the list, and other groups follow in order of the sequence of their admission to National Panhellenic Conference.

The object of the National Panhellenic Conference, as stated in the Constitution, is "to maintain on a high plane fraternity life and inter-fraternity relationship, to co-operate with college authorities in their effort to maintain high social and scholarship standards throughout the whole college, and to be forum for the discussion of the questions of interest to the college and fraternity world."

National Panhellenic Conference is a delegate body, each member organization being entitled to one vote, cast by its official representative. Its legislative power is limited to matters concerning its own organization. Recommendations from the Conference become law only after ratification by the member fraternities.

From 1902 to 1915, meetings were held annually, the first thirteen meetings being held in Chicago. Since 1915, the Conference has met biennially with an executive committee of three members functioning in the interim. The work of the Conference is furthered by standing committees, each fraternity having a representative on at least one of these committees.

In 1947 the membership of National Panhellenic Conference was expanded to include the educational, Catholic and Jewish sororities which have since had an active part in the organization.

Meeting as a part of each biennium are the Panhellenic Editors Association and the Association of Central Office Executives.

1902   Nina Howard, Σ-Northwestern
1903   Blanche Garten, K-Nebraska
1904   Grace Telling, Σ-Northwestern
          This Conference was called by the Delta Gamma delegate who then

presided at the meeting which established the principle of rotation in
office and determined the order of
sequence from the membership at
that time.

1905	Elizabeth Williams Chandler, Σ-Northwestern
1906-09	Margarethe Sheppard Ferris, Σ-Northwestern
1910-12	Marguerite Lake Pendleton, Ψ-Goucher Secretary of NPC, 1910 Chairman of NPC, 1911
1913-18	Pauline Hagaman Faulkes, P-Syracuse In 1914 Delta Gamma President Ada May Brown, Ω-Wisconsin, was President of the Congress
1918-19	Jessie McGilvray Treat, Υ-Stanford
1919-21	Gertrude Bradley Wilbur, Σ-Northwestern
1921-22	Hazel Whitaker Vanderberg, Ξ-Michigan
1922-28	Nancy Brown Woollett, Φ-Colorado
1928-32	Mary MacHarg Halstead, Σ-Northwestern
1932-40	Marguerite Winant, O-Adelphi
1940-47	Florence Cornell Bingham, X-Cornell
1947-50	Edith Taylor Smith, ΑB-Swarthmore
1950-51	Mavis Mann, ΑΞ-West Virginia
1951-56	Helen Russell Byars, M-Missouri Chairman of NPC, 1953-55
1956-58	Dorothy Glenn Holsinger, I-Illinois
1958-59	Ruth Canary Turpin, ΑN-USC
1959-64	Margaret Richardson Hay, Υ-Stanford
1964-68	Marcia Connell Strickland, Ξ-Michigan
1968-70	Louise Callahan Call, E-Ohio State
1970-	Eleanor Smith Slaughter, ΑΨ-Mississippi

The Anchora Editors

1884-1885	Mary Thompson Stevens, H-Akron Abby Soule Schumacher, H-Akron
1885-1887	Bessie Kingsbury, H-Akron
1887-1888	Ima Winchell Stacy, Λ-Minnesota
1888-1890	Mary Mills West, Λ-Minnesota
1890-1897	Ina Firkins, Λ-Minnesota
1897-1905	Joe Anna Ross Pancoast, Ψ-Goucher
1905-1909	Grace Abbott, K-Nebraska
1909-1915	Ethel Tukey Korsmeyer, K-Nebraska
1915-1934	Leulah Judson Hawley, Λ-Minnesota

Since the office of Secretary-Editor was separated in 1932, the editor has been appointed
by Council.

1932-1934	Leulah Judson Hawley, Λ-Minnesota
1934-1948	Alta Gwinn Saunders, I-Illinois

Guest Editors:
January, 1949—Roberta Abernethy,
E-Ohio State
March, 1949—Frances Holyoke McCoy,
K-Nebraska
May, 1949—Joan Murchison, M-Missouri

In 1949, the Editor became part of the Central
Office staff, as Editor of Publications, including all Delta Gamma publications in addition to *Anchora*.

1949-1956   Frances Lewis Stevenson, Z-Albion
Guest Editors:
Spring, 1955—Aubrey Hamilton Leonard,
Γ-California
Summer, 1955—Jean Hartman Culp,
Σ-Northwestern
Fall, 1955—Edith Murphy Sackett, ΑΛ-Drake
Fall, 1956—Aubrey Hamilton Leonard,
Γ-California
1956-1960   Nancy J. Gregory, Σ-Northwestern
Guest Editor:
Spring, 1961—Aubrey Hamilton Leonard,
Γ-California
1961-63   Frances Lewis Stevenson, Z-Albion

In 1963, Public Relations was combined with
Publications in the Executive Offices, as the
Communications and Information Center.
Since 1963 a Director and Editor have con-
ducted the operations of this Center.

Director:
1963-   Frances Lewis Stevenson, Z-Albion
Editor:
1963-66   Frances Lewis Stevenson, Z-Albion
1966-69   Mary Ann Dalton Shepard, N-Idaho
1969-   Barbara Carvill, Θ-Indiana

Field Secretaries

The field secretary program had its beginning
in 1941 when First Vice-President Roberta Abernethy sent Jean Pierce, E-Ohio State, then just
out of school, on a special assignment with Phi
chapter. When Miss Abernethy became Executive Secretary and opened the Central Office in
Columbus, Ohio, in 1942, Jean was her assistant.
For the next few years Jean was from time to
time sent out on rushing assignments or to visit
a chapter to handle some special problem. At the
end of the war, when Delta Gamma's enlarged
expansion program began, the need for such an
officer as a field secretary increased.

During this period field secretaries were
assigned to chapters as needed — to aid with
special problems or to assist with organization in
the case of new chapters. This system continued
for the next decade, with these energetic travelers
visiting many other chapters en route, all profit-
ing by the resulting exchange in information,
ideas, and thoughts.

In 1958, the first Collegiate Representatives to
Council recommended universal coverage of all
chapters during the course of the year by the
field secretaries, but this did not come about
until 1964 when the entire program was reviewed.

Field Secretaries

Since that time a coordinator of field secretaries has directed training, communicating, and scheduling of visits, each chapter having at least one field secretary visit during the course of the year. Her visits are planned so that she may become attuned to the chapter's needs and problems, if any. This enables the province collegiate chairman then to make greater contributions to the chapter during her subsequent visits.

Field secretaries are still assigned for longer periods of time to colonies, new chapters, or chapters with special problems

1945-46
Jean Pierce, E-Ohio State
Grace Barricklow, BZ-Denison
Mary Jeanne Barricklow Bohannan, E-Ohio State
Ruth Postle Lindecker, AP-Ohio Wesleyan

1946-47
Beverly Griffiths, AN-Southern California
Marianne MacDonald, AT-Butler

1947-48
Betty Ray, E-Ohio State
Lillian Newton, AΨ-Mississippi
Frances Lewis, Z-Albion

1948-49
Frances Lewis, Z-Albion
Patricia Hegman, Λ-Minnesota
Susan Langstaff, ΓA-Tennessee
Effie Ingalls, BΣ-Maryland

1949-50
Margaret Thomson, BΞ-Michigan State
Eleanor Higgons, BΣ-Maryland
Josephine Griffin, BΓ-Utah

1950-51
Eleanor Higgons, BΣ-Maryland
Jean Shade, E-Ohio State

1951-52
Joy Shreffler, AP-Ohio Wesleyan

1952-53
Barbara Brace, B-Washington
Polly Hager, AΨ-Mississippi

1953-54
Barbara Haney, AΛ-Drake
Jane Matthews, N-Idaho
Nancy Wedemeyer, BΞ-Michigan State

1954-55
Barbara Haney, AΛ-Drake
Patsy Robinson, I-Illinois
Ada Lee Oglesby, AΨ-Mississippi
Sharon Ruh, E-Ohio State

1955-56
Barbara Haney, AΛ-Drake
Marilyn Monahan, AΓ-Toronto
Mary Anne Lynn, P-Syracuse

1956-57
Beverly Bosh, AΘ-North Dakota

1957-58
Shirley Kubic, BK-Kansas

1958-59
Shirley Kubic, BK-Kansas
Leola Lorenzen, AΔ-Oregon
Julie Whitney, N-Idaho

1959-60
Julie Whitney, N-Idaho
Sue Stephens, E-Ohio State

1960-61
none

1961-62
Nancy Weigle, ΓΦ-Arizona State
Margaret Thompson, BΓ-Utah
Carolyn Kloppenburg, B-Washington

1962-63
Suellen Sutphen, E-Ohio State

1963-64
Mary Winegar, N-Idaho
Penny Patch, ΓH-San Jose
Gae Chatten, ΓX-Long Beach

1964-65
Carmalieta Dellinger, Θ-Indiana
Marjorie Hansen, ΓΛ-Fresno
Clyda Stokes, ΓM-Florida State
Tamara Sweeney, B-Washington

1965-66
Nancy Hinman, AΔ-Oregon
Penny Pagano, BE-American
Pamela Penner, Σ-Northwestern
Barbara Penson, BΨ-Alabama

1966-67
Joan Boyer, ΓΔ-Montana State
Judith Crist, E-Ohio State
Margaret Curl, ΓT-TCU
Pamela Slate, ΓΠ-Roanoke

1967-68
Barbara Carvill, Θ-Indiana
Jan Spring, E-Ohio State
Edwyna Williams, K-Nabraska
Mary Frances Wright, ΔB-Kentucky

1968-69
Sara Gentry, Φ-Colorado
Caroline Smith, AZ-Lawrence
Nancy Tuttle, AΠ-Arizona
Avice Whiton, BT-Miami

1969-70
Joan Duffy, B-Washington
Kathy Gahlon, Λ-Minnesota
Linda Johnson, ΓΔ-Montana State
Jody Lionberger, M-Missouri

1970-71
Carolyn Cheley, AN-USC
Marcia Hunsinger, M-Missouri
Katie Scarborough, ΔI-Georgia
Mary Swan, ΓT-TCU

1971-72
Sue Ann Austermiller, BM-Bowling Green
Carol Olney, AΠ-Arizona
Monne Ortner, BΩ-Washington State
Monica Postell, Σ-Northwestern
Winkie Wolfe, AΣ-UCLA

1972-73
Katherine Arzt, Λ-Minnesota
Martha Barnes, ΓO-Indiana State
Carol Fleenor, ΔI-Georgia
Anne Laing, Ξ-Michigan

1973-74
Deborah Andrews, BΠ-Willamette
Ann Bennett, BX-Denver
Carla Chenoweth, ΔI-Oklahoma

1960-61—Betty Lou Soehner Goodrich,
     ΑΤ-Butler
1961-65—Kay Blankenship Lemmer,
     M-Missouri
1965-67—LuAnne Lyen Leonard, ΑΣ-UCLA
1967-69—Natalie Conrad Case, H-Akron
1969-71—Beverly Edlund Mertz, BK-Kansas
1971-73—Gae Chatten Lach, ΓX-Long Beach
1973-   Dorothy Riley Milne, ΑΠ-Arizona

Fraternity Committees

Advisers

For twenty years chapter advisers worked under the direction of the Province Secretaries. In 1960 they were invited to come, at chapter expense, to Convention where special sessions had been planned for their benefit. The following year a Chairman of Advisers was appointed as one of the Fraternity Standing Committee chairmen. In 1964 her duties were absorbed by the First Vice-President as Director of Collegiate Chapters.

1961-63—Eleanor Smith Slaughter,
     ΑΨ-Mississippi
1963-64—Marion Hill Keenan, Ω-Wisconsin
1969-71—Marilyn Miner Hunt, ΑΤ-Butler

Awards

Selections for awards and the presentation thereof had, since Delta Gamma's founding, been made by the person or group sponsoring the award. In 1952 the Order of the Rose was established as a Fraternity award and a special chairman appointed to process nominations, information, and presentation of this award.

1953-57—Grace Jones Henley, X-Cornell
1957-61—Margaret Leamer Sadler, ΑΛ-Drake

Meanwhile, in 1957, all Convention Awards (except those for specific Provinces) were brought together under the direction of one committee. In 1961, the Fraternity Awards program was further expanded when the Shield and Cable Awards were established as individual recognitions, companion awards to the Order of the Rose. At that time the Rose Award committee was discontinued and all awards placed under the supervision of one Awards Chairman. Further information on the awards themselves may be found in the Awards section of this history.

1957-58—Fern Spolander Moseley, M-Missouri
1959-60—Kay Maple Roberts, ΑH-Whitman

Chapter Relations

Both the title and the concept of the Standards area of programming within collegiate chapters were re-evaluated in 1971, and Standards became Chapter Relations. The disciplinary aspects of chapter Standards Boards were returned to the Executive Board while creative aspects of chapter programming would be emphasized by the Chapter Relations Board.

1971-73—Carmalieta Dellinger Brown,
     Θ-Indiana
1973-   Katherine Whitacre Rossing,
     BZ-Denison

Collegiate Finances

Supervision of collegiate finances began in 1923 when Thomas M. Wallace's services were employed for the auditing of chapter books. His bookkeeping system was installed and used not only by Delta Gamma chapters, but it was also adopted by many other Greek-letter groups. Budgets are an important phase of proper financing, especially in the case of chapters operating houses. Therefore, in addition to Mr. Wallace's services, a Collegiate Finance committee, including House Budgets, was set up and operated until 1962 when Collegiate Auditing became a division of the Executive Offices directed by the Treasurer of the Fraternity.

1929-34—Maude Case, Λ-Minnesota
1934-42—Ruth Gates, Σ-Northwestern
1942-45—Kate Sexton Booth, B-Washington
1945-46—Gladys Hutchins Foster, E-Ohio State
1947-49—Elizabeth Doane West,
     Σ-Northwestern
1949-51—Lucile Roebuck Keeler,
     Σ-Northwestern
1951-53—Wilma Von Oven Walmsley,
     ΑM-Beloit
1953-55—Martha Giltner Rounds,
     ΑO-Miami Univ.
1955-59—Patricia Bailey Gilbert,
     ΑE-Washington Univ.
1959-61—Carolyn Sawyer Havens,
     E-Ohio State
1961-62—Judith Mills Edwards,
     Σ-Northwestern
1962-   —Responsibility of Treasurer

Constitutions and Bylaws Revisions

(Service to Conventions listed)

1888—Kate McGillicudy, H-Akron
1889—Sara Foster, Σ-Northwestern
1891—Ethel Baker, Σ-Northwestern
1893—Avis Winchell Grant, Λ-Minnesota
1895—Avis Winchell Grant, Λ-Minnesota
1897—Ruth Nelson, X-Cornell
1899—Bessie Lee Hopkins, Ξ-Michigan
1901—
1903—Elizabeth Harbert, Σ-Northwestern
1905—Frances Main, Ω-Wisconsin
1907—Ina Firkins, Λ-Minnesota
1909—Carrie Sewall, Φ-Colorado
1911—Lillian Ray Titcomb, Υ-Stanford
1913—Edith Jackson, B-Washington
1915—Susie Wegg Smith, Ω-Wisconsin
1919—Frances Bragdon, Σ-Northwestern
1922—Alice Perry Gradle, Ξ-Michigan
1924—Marguerite Winant, O-Adelphi
1926—Jessie McGilvray Treat, Υ-Stanford
1928—Nina Goodnow Belcher, Ξ-Michigan
1930—Hazel Brown, ΛB-Swarthmore
1932—Dorothy Ferrier, ΛΓ-Toronto
1934—Mary Power, Ξ-Michigan
1936—Beryl Barnett, ΛI-Oklahoma
1938—Mary Longbrake Harshman, Λ-Minnesota
1940—Hazel Brown, ΛB-Swarthmore
1942—Evelyn Niedecker Walbridge, Ω-Wisconsin
1946—Ruey Sieger Messenger, ΛB-Swarthmore
1948—Ada Applegate Hill, Γ-California
1950—Sarah Tilghman Hughes, Ψ-Goucher
1952—Mavis Mann, ΛΞ-West Virginia
1954-56—Margarita Espinosa, Υ-Stanford
1958-60—Margaret Clark Luikart,
ΛP-Ohio Wesleyan
1962-67—Louise Brown Christianson,
Λ-Minnesota
1967-69—Comora MacGregor Nash, BK-Kansas
1969-73—Madeline Graf Ettl, Θ-Indiana
1973- —Nancy Taylor Jones, BΓ-Utah

Conventions

1919—Lillian Smith Burwell, Λ-Minnesota
1922—Pauline Hagaman Faulks, P-Syracuse
1924-36—Mae Brown Tompkins, Υ-Stanford
1938—Beryl Barnett, ΛI-Oklahoma
1940—Alice Perry Gradle, Ξ-Michigan
1942—Council Members
1946—Margaret Tyndall Pyle, ΛΣ-UCLA
1948—Irene Howell Forman, ΛK-Washburn
1950—Helen Mahan Hill, ΛI-Oklahoma
1952—Margaret Richardson Hay, Υ-Stanford
1954—Marcia Connell Strickland, Ξ-Michigan
1956—Marian Hill Keenan, Ω-Wisconsin
1958—Virginia Leudemann Terry, O-Adelphi
1960—Jeanne Catlett Strong, Φ-Colorado
1962—Laura Bertram Dillon, Z-Albion
1964—Mildred Moyer Baynard, K-Nebraska
1966—Chiane Gerow Anderson, ΛΔ-Oregon
1968—Beverly Edlund Mertz, BK-Kansas
1970—Gloria Fischer Dobbs, M-Missouri
1972—Margaret Richardson Hay, Υ-Stanford
1974—Patricia Six Cook, BT-Miami

Expansion

During the few years prior to 1913, Delta Gamma had taken part in a flurry of expansion previously unknown to an ultra-conservative Fraternity. It was then that a need was felt for a committee which would be responsible for thorough investigation of potential fields. After 1921 this responsibility was assigned to a member of Council. This policy continued until 1973 when it was felt that a committee could assist Council in watching educational trends and in judging suitable fields for expansion as well as processing the large number of inquiries coming to the Fraternity from potential campuses. Thus a chairman was once more appointed.

1913-16—Omega Sigma (Milwaukee Alumnae)
1916-17—Edna Russell Seymour, Ω-Wisconsin
1917-19—Elinor Stephens Trump, Ω-Wisconsin
1919-   —Louise Craig Bell, Ω-Wisconsin
1919-20—Frances Bragdon, Σ-Northwestern
1920-21—Edith Cochran, Σ-Northwestern
1973-   —Carolyn Kloppenburg Riggs,
B-Washington

Fraternity Programs

At several times through the years an attempt has been made to coordinate fraternity programs particularly in the collegiate area, under a Fraternity chairman. In 1962 the Council was enlarged to include a Vice-President to direct fraternity programming. She has directed chairmen in the various programming area for collegiate chapters. At one point in the 'sixties a Province Alumnae Chairman was appointed to aid the Second Vice-President in enlarging alumnae programming.

Collegiate Programs
1953—Faith Ferbitz Frikart, ΛΠ-Arizona
Coordinator of Fraternity Programs
1961-62—Marcia Connell Strickland,
Ξ-Michigan
Alumnae Programs
1966-67—Mary Ann Lummis Bowyer,
BZ-Denison

Housing

Though the first Delta Gamma chapter house, a lodge, was constructed for this purpose before the turn of the century, this was not the practice until the 'twenties. By this time several other houses had been built, while other chapters continued to rent and operate homes, and a need was present for supervision of construction and operation programs. Another building boom occurred in the 'fifties (and continued through the mid-'sixties), and it became necessary to divide some of the responsibilities. When Margery Sommers Hammill, as Housing Chairman, was appointed to Council in 1962, she took her work with her and added Director of Housing to the Secretary's duties.

1928-30—Anna McCandlish Fankhauser,
Γ-California

1930-34—Edna Nowland, Θ-Indiana
1934-42—Ruth Darville, X-Cornell
1942-46—Irma Twining Madden, Θ-Indiana
1946-49—Fraternity Treasurer
1949-53—Margaret Owen Hildreth, ΑΜ-Beloit
1953-55—Margaret Rossiter Eilers,
　　　　ΑΕ-Washington Univ.
1955-57—Emily Steffan Siegerist,
　　　　ΑΕ-Washington Univ.
1958-66—Margery Sommers Hammill,
　　　　ΑΜ-Beloit

House Bonds (See History, 1960)
1960-62—Elizabeth Lewis Lang,
　　　　Σ-Northwestern

House Furnishings
1956-58—Jean Verborg Anderson,
　　　　ΑΕ-Washington Univ.
1958-60—Ardath White Lilystrand,
　　　　Ε-Ohio State

Housemothers

Interest in the training and direction of a housemothers program (as well as the handling of applications) grew during the 'thirties and was at that time among the duties of the First Vice-President. Though a chairman has been appointed from time to time to direct this area of activity, it has once more returned to the Vice-President—Collegians.

1948-49—Pearl McDonnell, B-Washington
1949-51—Grace Mark Dratz, Z-Albion
1957-60—Edith Hammond,
　　　　ΑΕ-Washington Univ.

Membership

The Membership Committee was formed in 1936 to both assist and coordinate the work of collegiate and alumnae chapters in rush. The chairman was aided by a committee whose natural division was "rush" and, when a recommendations system was initiated in 1937, "recommendations." In 1948 a separate Rushing committee was formed, and in 1949 rushing was reunited with recommendations to become Rushing and Membership.

1936-41—Maxine Daniels Baker, M-Missouri
1941-42—Ruth Ellenwood McGuyre, X-Cornell
1942-45—Mary Johnstone Morrison, Θ-Indiana
1945-49—Ardath White Lilystrand,
　　　　Ε-Ohio State

Mothers Clubs

Mothers Clubs have offered moral and physical support to their daughters' chapters. Directed by a chairman for many years, they are currently under the direction of the Vice-President—Collegians.

1936-38—Jessie Gibson Rathburn, K-Nebraska

1938-40—Harriette Tate Lewis, Υ-Stanford
1941-46—Josephine Cleaver Woodward,
　　　　Η-Akron
1946-57—Directed by the Second Vice-President
1957-59—Genevieve Piatt Allen, B-Washington
1959-60—Veneta Slack McFarland,
　　　　ΓΓ-Texas Western
1960-63—Louise Magee Oxman, K-Nebraska
1963-64—Ruth Baer Kirkpatrick, Φ-Colorado

Nominating

Until 1954 the Nominating Committee and its chairman were appointed by Council. At this time a system of area elections was begun. Check 1954-64 Convention business for details of these changes. Currently there are five areas, one representative from each area elected to serve on this committee whose chairman is appointed by Council.

(Service to Conventions listed.)

1888—Ima Winchell, Λ-Minnesota
1889—Louise Whitehead, Σ-Northwestern
1891—Clara Kellogg, Λ-Minnesota
1893—Nina Howard, Σ-Northwestern
1895—Caroline Pier, Σ-Northwestern
1897—Lois Tennant, Λ-Minnesota
1899—Jessie Tucker, Z-Albion
1901—Blanche Telling, Σ-Northwestern
1903—Nina Foster, Σ-Northwestern
1905—Marguerite Lake, Ψ-Goucher
1907—Flora Sauer, Σ-Northwestern
1909—Lois Tennant, Λ-Minnesota
1911—None indicated
1913—Blanche Garten, K-Nebraska
1915—Pearl McDonnell, B-Washington
1919—Edith Cochran, Σ-Northwestern
1922—Belle Krolik Scheyer, Ξ-Michigan
1924—Lydia Mullon, K-Nebraska
1926—Mary Longbrake Harshman, Λ-Minnesota
1928—Jessie McGilvray Treat, Υ-Stanford
1930—Vera Burridge Baits, Ξ-Michigan
1932—Evelyn Niedecker Walbridge, Ω-Wisconsin
1934—Audrey Wilder, Z-Albion
1936—Elizabeth Hough Doughty, ΑΣ-UCLA
1938—Hazel Brown, ΑΒ-Swarthmore
1940—Beryl Barnett, ΑΙ-Oklahoma
1942—Irma Twining Madden, Θ-Indiana
1946—Zora Laird MacPhail, B-Washington
1948—Audrey Wilder, Z-Albion
1950—Mae Pope Worden, Π-Montana
1952—Mary Frances Cornell Grubbs, Θ-Indiana
1954—Margaret Tindall Pyle, ΑΣ-UCLA
1956—Marian McGirr Cragin, B-Washington
1958—Patricia Bailey Gilbert,
　　　　ΑΕ-Washington Univ.
1960—Kathryn Maple Roberts, ΑΗ-Whitman
1962—Lucile Ingram Walton, ΑΗ-Whitman
1964—Janet Lau Sullivan, K-Nebraska
1966—Margaret Richardson Hay, Υ-Stanford
1968—Florence Whitcomb Ebersold, Ε-Ohio State
1970—Elizabeth Coffinberry Kloppenburg,
　　　　Γ-California
1972—Beverly Edlund Mertz, ΒΚ-Kansas
1974—Helen Million Preston, Ξ-Michigan

Overseas Alumnae Expansion

Following World War II when a great number of service men and their families were overseas, in addition to an increasing number of business representatives, an attempt was made to organize alumnae groups in the major cities or military installations. The transient nature of this population made this impractical—though Founders Day luncheons were reported from time to time in London or Tokyo or other spots where Delta Gammas were living.

1949-50—Helen Fuller Spencer, E-Ohio State
1950-55—Betty Ray Browne, E-Ohio State
1955-57—Gene Caldwell Moore, ΑΗ-Whitman
1957-   —Sylvia Sweetman Sunderlin,
        Π-Montana
1957-59—Elizabeth Alexander McQuiggan,
        ΑΡ-Ohio Wesleyan

Pledge Education

Pledge education programs were directed by the First Vice-President for many years until a Fraternity Chairman was appointed for this purpose. In 1961 this committee was combined with rituals and became the responsibility of the Council member who directed collegiate programming. In 1973 pledge education was once more assigned to a chairman.

1953-55—Betty Land Krueger, ΑΠ-Arizona
1955-60—Ruth Canary Turpin, ΑΝ-USC
1960-61—Julie Whitney, Ν-Idaho
        (1961 Pledge Education and Rituals)
1961-64—Jean Falconer Chase, Λ-Minnesota
1973-   —Virginia Gard Mastio, ΒΚ-Kansas

Public Relations

Public Relations—and accompanying publicity—has grown in scope probably more than any other area in the past thirty years. Starting with attention to the society page, this area now touches all areas of communication and is a division of the Executive Offices—the Communications and Information Center.

Publicity (1938-48)
1938-49—Ethel Castle, ΑΖ-Lawrence
1946-48—Elsa Haeger, ΑΜ-Beloit

Public Relations
1948-49—Jean Speiser, Κ-Nebraska
1949-51—Margaret Gabriel Corbett, ΑΤ-Butler
1951-55—Georgette Foster McGregor,
        ΑΣ-UCLA
1955-58—Frances Lewis Stevenson, Ζ-Albion
1958-61—Dorothy Wood Felton, ΑΩ-Arkansas
1961-63—Ercelle Caldwell Francis, ΑΠ-Arizona
1963-   —A division of the Executive Offices,
        Communications and Information
        Center, directed by Frances Lewis
        Stevenson, Ζ-Albion

Recommendations

Though this aspect of the rush system had been in existence almost from the beginning, it was not until 1953 that a chairman was appointed to direct the complex organization of State and City Recommendations Chairmen and their duties. In 1964, the Second Vice-President, as Director of Alumnae Chapters and Associations, became as well Director of Recommendations, with the Recommendations Chairman working under her supervision. With the Constitutional change in 1970 allowing any Delta Gamma to sponsor a prospective member, this aspect of rush came under the supervision of the Vice-President—Membership.

1953-55—Helen Smith Hodgdon, ΑΤ-SMU
1955-58—Martha Hunter Farrell, Ψ-Goucher
1958-61—Kay Blankenship Lemmer, Μ-Missouri
1961-64—Virginia Riesterer Gates,
        Σ-Northwestern
1967-70—Mary Elizabeth Falter Avery,
        ΑΙ-Oklahoma

Rituals

A chairman to direct rituals, even to include at some periods the issuing of equipment, has been an appointed office for fifty years. In 1961 her duties were combined with those of Pledge Education, and in 1964 both areas became the responsibility of the Council member who directed collegiate programming. In the late 'sixties, as collegians expressed the desire for major ritual changes, a chairman was once more appointed to coordinate and direct ritual changes.

1919-26—Blanche Garten, Κ-Nebraska
1926-30—Donna Amsden, Υ-Stanford
1930-38—Florence Cornell Bingham, Χ-Cornell
1938-42—Roberta Abernethy, E-Ohio State
1942-48—Dorothy Glenn Holsinger, Ι-Illinois
1948-51—Jane Cowell, ΑΧ-Penn State
1951-53—Edith Murphy Sackett, ΑΛ-Drake
1953-   —Katharine Fulkerson Jakosky,
        ΒΚ-Kansas
1957-59—Lucile Ingram Walton, ΑΗ-Whitman
1959-61—See Standards
1969-73—Elizabeth Needham Graham,
        Ξ-Michigan

Rush

Though rush was much discussed from the very beginning, and most analyzed for a number of years a little later, it was not until 1948 that a Fraternity Chairman was appointed to direct this aspect of fraternity life. At that time she was Chairman of Rush and Recommendations. In 1953, rush was separated from recommendations, and in 1963, Director of Rush was added to the title of the National Panhellenic Conference Delegate. In 1970, directing rush became one of the duties of the Vice-President—Membership.

1948-51—Dorothy Kremer Heideman,
        ΑΕ-Washington Univ.
1951-53—Carolyn Boli Stanton, ΑΤ-SMU

1953- —(Rushing separated, recommendations under separate chairman)
1953-54—Carolyn Boli Stanton, ΑΥ-SMU
1954-59—Isabell Worley McIlvaine, Φ-Colorado
1959- —Sally Addleman Shenk, ΑΔ-Oregon
1959-61—Eleanor Smith Slaughter, ΑΨ-Mississippi
1961-63—Gloria Schnaiter Blake, Θ-Indiana
1966-70—Carolyn Kloppenburg Riggs, Β-Washington

Scholarship

Scholarship—and the chapters' maintenance of academic excellence—has always been a concern of fraternity officers. For some years the First Vice-President assumed this concern among her other duties, and in 1930 it became the area of interest for a Fraternity Chairman.

1930-34—Harriet Cammack, Τ-Iowa
1934-36—Susan Lau Milligan, Κ-Nebraska
1936-38—Margaret Waltz Evenson, Β-Washington
1938-40—Florence Cornell Bingham, Χ-Cornell
1940-41—Sarah Trousdale Mallory, Ν-Idaho
1941-45—Vonna Lamme Brown, Φ-Colorado
1945-46—Josephine Rudy Beatty, Ε-Ohio State
1946-51—Audrey K. Wilder, Ζ-Albion
1951-55—Edith Hammond, ΑΕ-Washington Univ.
1955-57—Lucile Ingram Walton, ΑΗ-Whitman
1957-61—Margarita Espinosa, Υ-Stanford
1961-65—Ruth Rose Richardson, ΑΔ-Oregon
1965-69—Dorothy West Freeman Bristol, ΓΖ-LSU
1969-73—Joann Whitley Grimes, Ε-Ohio State
1973- —Gwynn Williams Wardwell, ΑΖ-Lawrence

Standards

A standards program was initiated in 1948 and a Standards Chairman was for the first time that year added to the slate of officers for each chapter. While the title sometimes implies that she is a disciplinary officer, her duties have expanded into one of the most creative of fraternity programs. (see Chapter Relations)

1948-51—Ada Applegate Hill, Γ-California
1951-55—Mildred Quail, ΑΚ-Washburn
1955-57—Fern Spolander Moseley, Μ-Missouri
1957-61—Berenice Livingston Paul, Γ-California (Rituals included 1950-61)
1961-62—Dorothy Johnson Davison, ΑΛ-Drake
1962-67—Elizabeth Needham Graham, Ξ-Michigan
1967-69—Alice Park Newman, Λ-Minnesota

Miscellaneous Committees

From time to time, chairmen have been appointed to supervise programs which were subsequently short-lived or later merged with the duties of a member of Council or another chairman.

Canadian Liaison
1960-63—Pamela Fraser Wetmore, ΑΦ-British Columbia

Field Secretaries
1964-65—Elizabeth Coffinberry Kloppenburg, Γ-California
1965-68—Suellen Sutphen Brown, Ε-Ohio State
After 1968, this duty was assigned to a member of the Executive Offices staff who worked under the direction of the Council Officer in charge of Field Secretaries.

Magazine Agency
1950-55—Prudence LaPlac Heeseler, Ο-Adelphi
Transfer Scholarships and Graduate Counselors
1961-65—Frances McCormack Tierney, ΑΗ-Whitman

Ways and Means
1968-71—Mary Anne Holt Mueller, Ζ-Albion

The Provinces

1917-1924
FIVE PROVINCES

(Province Secretaries only until 1947)

Province I
New York, Maryland, Pennsylvania, Eastern Canada, West Virginia
Esther Kelley Bill, Ω-Wisconsin, 1917-22
Janet Brown, ΑΒ-Swarthmore, 1922-30

Province II
Michigan, Indiana, Ohio
Helen Malcomson Gore, Ξ-Michigan, 1917-23
Marguerite Williams, Ε-Ohio State, 1923-28

Province III
Wisconsin, Illinois, Minnesota, North Dakota
Maude Case, Λ-Minnesota, 1917-26

Province IV
Iowa, Missouri, Nebraska, Colorado, Oklahoma, Kansas
Harriet Haw Wright, Σ-Northwestern, 1917-19
Mary Raymond Lambert, Σ-Northwestern, 1919-23
Corinne Dawson, Φ-Colorado, 1923-24

Province V
Montana, Idaho, Washington, Oregon, California
Pearl McDonnell, Β-Washington, 1917-28

1924-1940
SEVEN PROVINCES

Province I
New York, Maryland, Pennsylvania, Eastern Canada, District of Columbia
Janet Brown, ΑΒ-Swarthmore, 1923-28
Pauline Schmid, Χ-Cornell, 1930-33
Anne Wilson Bartels, Ψ-Goucher, 1933-34

Edith Taylor Smith, AB-Swarthmore, 1934-36
Elizabeth Welch Ingerle, I-Illinois, 1936-38
Margaret Dodds, BA-McGill, 1938-42

Province II
Indiana, Ohio, West Virginia, Mississippi
Marguerite Williams, E-Ohio State, 1924-28
Katherine Tinsley Hamer, Θ-Indiana, 1928-30
Elizabeth Weintz Wooding, Θ-Indiana, 1930-36
Dorothy Knight Wildasin, AO-Miami Univ.,
    1936-40

Province III
Wisconsin, Illinois, Michigan
Ethelwyn Anderson, Ω-Wisconsin, 1924-25
Adelaide Miller, Ω-Wisconsin, 1925-33
Elizabeth Ketchum Odegard, I-Illinois, 1933-34
Louise Cooley Sutherland, Ξ-Michigan, 1934-35
Elizabeth Welch Ingerle, I-Illinois, 1935-36
Jane Brooks Corl, Ξ-Michigan, 1936-38
Kathleen Carpenter Milliken, Ξ-Michigan,
    1938-39
Dorothy Glenn Holsinger, I-Illinois, 1939-42

Province IV
Iowa, Nebraska, Minnesota, North Dakota
Maude Case, Λ-Minnesota, 1924-26
Frances Herriott, AΛ-Drake, 1926-28
Pearl McDonnell, B-Washington, 1928-32
Julia Rider Rogers, K-Nebraska, 1931-35
Norma Grumman Rotton, K-Nebraska, 1935-36
Jean Rathburn Faulkner, K-Nebraska, 1936-37
Louise Brown Christianson, Λ-Minnesota, 1937-38
Dorothy Yetter Swisher, T-Iowa, 1938-40

Province V
(Divided into two sections in 1938)
*Missouri, Colorado, Kansas, Oklahoma, Texas,
Arkansas*
Jessie Fitzpatrick, Φ-Colorado, 1924-30
Beryl Barnett, AI-Oklahoma, 1930-34
Maxine Daniels Baker, M-Missouri, 1934-36
Marjorie Woodhead Kollmann, M-Missouri,
    1936-37
Maxine Bray Foulis, AE-Washington Univ.,
    1937-38
Ludi Mai Sensabaugh Goode, AT-SMU, 1938-40
    (southern section)
Martha Schultz Davidson, K-Nebraska, 1938-39
    (northern section)
Martha Cushing Quam, Φ-Colorado, 1939-40
    (northern section)

Province VI
*Montana, Idaho, Oregon, Washington,
Western Canada*
Pearl McDonnell, B-Washington, 1924-28
Nina Goodnow Gelcher, Ξ-Michigan, 1928-30
Genevieve Thorneley Draper, T-Stanford,
    1930-34
Helen Wheeler Livengood, N-Idaho, 1934-38
Kate Sexton Booth, B-Washington, 1938-40

Province VII
California, Arizona, Utah
Lillian Ray Titcomb, Υ-Stanford, 1924-28
Jane Hawk Schuessler, Γ-California, 1928-30
Dorothy Sanborn Harries, Γ-California, 1930-32
Elizabeth Hough Doughty, AΣ-UCLA, 1932-36
Betty Jones Christy, AN-USC, 1936-37
Margaret Tindall Pyle, AΣ-UCLA, 1937-40

1940-1944
NINE PROVINCES
Province I
New York, Eastern Canada
Margaret Dodds, BA-McGill, 1938-42
Grace Bedient Kraft, Z-Albion, 1942-48

Province II
*Maryland, Pennsylvania, West Virginia, North
Carolina, District of Columbia*
Ruth French Shriver, Ψ-Goucher, 1940-41
Phyllis Richardson Jacobs, Z-Albion, 1941-44

Province III
Michigan, Illinois, Wisconsin
Dorothy Glenn Holsinger, I-Illinois, 1939-42
Margaret Smallpage Banker, Σ-Northwestern,
    1942-47

Province IV
Ohio, Indiana
Helen Develling Miller, AT-Butler, 1940-42
Helen Reaver Culbertson, T-Iowa, 1942-44

Province V
Oklahoma, Texas, Arkansas, Mississippi
Vonna Lamme Brown, Φ-Colorado, 1940-41
Helen Russell Byars, M-Missouri, 1941-46

Province VI
Missouri, Iowa, Minnesota, North Dakota
Dorothy Yetter Swisher, T-Iowa, 1940-44

Province VII
Nebraska, Kansas, Colorado, Utah
Martha Cushing Quam, Φ-Colorado, 1940-41
Jane Robertson, K-Nebraska, 1941-44

Province VIII
*Montana, Idaho, Oregon, Washington,
Western Canada*
Zora Laird MacPhail, B-Washington, 1940-43
Lucia Fryer McKenzie, B-Washington, 1943-44

Province IX
California, Arizona
Helen Hopkins, AN-USC, 1940-43
Ada Applegate Hill, Γ-California, 1943-47

1944
TEN PROVINCES
Province I
New York, Eastern Canada
Grace Bedient Kraft, Z-Albion

Province II
*Maryland, Pennsylvania, West Virginia, North
Carolina, District of Columbia*
Jane Cowell, AX-Penn State

Province III
Illinois, Wisconsin
Margaret Smallpage Banker, Σ-Northwestern

Province IV
Ohio
Miriam Pratt Mathews, E-Ohio State

Province V
Oklahoma, Texas, Arkansas, Mississippi
Helen Russell Byars, M-Missouri

Province VI
Missouri, Iowa, Minnesota, North Dakota
Elizabeth Mackey Burns, AE-Washington Univ.

Province VII
Nebraska, Kansas, Colorado, Utah
Virginia Brand, Ψ-Goucher

Province VIII
Montana, Idaho, Oregon, Washington, Western Canada
Laura Crump, ΑΗ-Whitman

Province IX
California, Arizona
Ada Applegate Hill, Γ-California

Province X
Michigan, Indiana
Marcia Connell Strickland, Ξ-Michigan

1945-49
THIRTEEN PROVINCES

Province officers to handle alumnae affairs, to be known as Province Alumnae Chairmen, were added when Helen Russell Byars' alumnae expansion program was introduced in 1947.

Province I
Massachusetts, New York, Eastern Canada
Province Secretaries
Grace Bedient Kraft, Z-Albion, 1942-48
Theodosia Moran, P-Syracuse, 1948-51
Province Alumnae Chairman
Helen Million Preston, Ξ-Michigan, 1947-50

Province II
Maryland, Pennsylvania, Virginia, North Carolina, District of Columbia
Province Secretaries
Margaret Brinton Woodward, ΑΒ-Swarthmore, 1945-46
Florence Hobbs Fenn, Ν-Idaho, 1946-48
Northa Porter Mayo, ΑΛ-Drake, 1948-50
Province Alumnae Chairman
Ruey Sieger Messenger, ΑΒ-Swarthmore, 1947-50

Province III
Pennsylvania, West Virginia
Province Secretaries
Jane Cowell, ΑΧ-Penn State, 1945-48
Helen Hechler, ΑΧ-Penn State, 1948-49
Province Alumnae Chairman
Mavis Mann, ΑΞ-West Virginia, 1947-51

Province IV
Georgia, Tennessee, Alabama, Florida, Mississippi
Province Secretaries
Lillian Harward, ΒΘ-Duke, 1946-48
Marian Cupp Wallis, ΑΘ-North Dakota, 1948-49
Province Alumnae Chairman
Lucille Carroll Ballinger, ΑΡ-Ohio Wesleyan, 1947-50

Province V
Ohio
Province Secretaries
Betty Nilson Smith, ΑΡ-Ohio Wesleyan, 1945-47
Willametta Morris Sisson, ΑΟ-Miami Univ., 1947-49
Province Alumnae Chairman
Marian Ross Seibel, ΑΟ-Miami Univ., 1947-51

Province VI
Michigan, Indiana
Province Secretaries
Marcia Connell Strickland, Ξ-Michigan, 1945-48
Madeline Graf Ettl, Θ-Indiana, 1948-51
Province Alumnae Chairman
Margaret Schermack Rueger, Ξ-Michigan, 1947-51

Province VII
Wisconsin, Illinois
Province Secretaries
Lois Adams, Σ-Northwestern, 1945-48
Elizabeth Weinhagen John, ΑΚ-Washburn, 1948-50
Province Alumnae Chairman
Esther Rosenblatt Faville, ΑΜ-Beloit, 1947-51

Province VIII
Minnesota, Iowa, North Dakota
Province Secretaries
Vera Disbrow Wylie, ΑΘ-North Dakota, 1945-48
Betty Anderson, ΑΛ-Drake, 1948
Margaret Dolliver Anneberg, T-Iowa, 1948-51
Province Alumnae Chairman
Edith Murphy Sackett, ΑΛ-Drake, 1947-51

Province IX
Texas, Missouri, Oklahoma, Arkansas, Louisiana
Province Secretary
Florence Lund Black, ΑΖ-Lawrence, 1945-49
Province Alumnae Chairman
Carolyn Boli Stanton, ΑΥ-SMU, 1947-49

Province X
Colorado, Kansas, Nebraska, New Mexico
Province Secretaries
Virginia Brand, Ψ-Goucher, 1945-48
Gertrude Nance Marthens, Φ-Colorado, 1948-51
Province Alumnae Chairman
Nina Shaffer, ΒΔ-Colorado College, 1947-51

Province XI
Washington, Eastern Canada, Idaho
Province Secretaries
Laura Crump Peterson, ΑΗ-Whitman, 1945-47
Barbara Patton Shrock, Υ-Stanford, 1947-48
Carolyn Logan Smith, Ν-Idaho, 1948-51
Province Alumnae Chairman
Margaret Richardson Hay, Υ-Stanford, 1947-51

Province XII
Oregon, Montana
Province Secretaries
Ruth Radford Herman, Ω-Wisconsin, 1945-47
Mae Pope Worden, Π-Montana, 1947-51
Province Alumnae Chairman
Elvira Starz Smith, Π-Montana, 1947-51

Province XIII
California, Arizona, Utah, West Texas
Province Secretaries
Ada Applegate Hill, Γ-California, 1945-47
Georgette Foster MacGregor, ΑΣ-UCLA, 1947-49
Province Alumnae Chairman
Margaret Richardson Hay, Υ-Stanford, 1947-51

1949-51
A fourteenth province was added during 1950.

Province I
New York, Massachusetts, Eastern Canada,
Connecticut, New Jersey
Province Secretary
　　Theodosia Moran, P-Syracuse, 1948-51
Province Alumnae Chairmen
　　Helen Million Preston, Ξ-Michigan, 1947-50
　　Eleanor Meck Smith, AP-Ohio Wesleyan,
　　　1950-55

Province II
Maryland, Pennsylvania, Virginia,
District of Columbia
Province Secretary
　　Northa Porter Mayo, AΛ-Drake, 1948-50
Province Alumnae Chairmen
　　Ruey Sieger Messenger, AB-Swarthmore,
　　　1947-50
　　Margaret Leamer Sadler, AΛ-Drake, 1950-55

Province III
Pennsylvania, West Virginia
Province Secretary
　　Mary Reif, Ξ-Michigan, 1949-51
Province Alumnae Chairman
　　Mavis Mann, AΞ-West Virginia, 1947-51

Province IV
Georgia, Alabama, Tennessee, Florida, Mississippi
Province Secretaries
　　Marian Cupp Wallis, AΘ-North Dakota,
　　　1949-50
　　Nancy Harris Cooper, AΣ-UCLA, 1950-51
Province Alumnae Chairmen
　　Lucille Carroll Ballinger, AP-Ohio Wesleyan,
　　　1947-50
　　Mildred Moyer Baynard, K-Nebraska, 1950-53

Province V
Ohio, Kentucky
Province Secretary
　　Mary Jean Elder Downing, AΛ-Drake, 1949-51
Province Alumnae Chairman
　　Marian Ross Seibel, AO-Miami Univ., 1947-51

Province VI
Michigan, Indiana
Province Secretary
　　Madeline Graf Ettl, Θ-Indiana, 1948-51
Province Alumnae Chairman
　　Margaret Schermack Rueger, Ξ-Michigan,
　　　1947-51

Province VII
Wisconsin, Illinois
Province Secretaries
　　Elizabeth Weinhagen John, AK-Washburn,
　　　1948-50
　　Elizabeth Candee Lee, Ω-Wisconsin, 1950-55
Province Alumnae Chairman
　　Esther Rosenblatt Faville, AM-Beloit, 1947-51

Province VIII
Minnesota, Iowa, North Dakota
Province Secretary
　　Margaret Dolliver Anneberg, T-Iowa, 1949-51
Province Alumnae Chairman
　　Edith Murphy Sackett, AΛ-Drake, 1947-51

Province IX
Missouri, Oklahoma, Arkansas
Province Secretary
　　Lucile Perkins Carnegie, AZ-Lawrence,
　　　1949-51
Province Alumnae Chairman
　　Helen Bradford Anderson, M-Missouri, 1950-52

Province X
Colorado, Kansas, Nebraska, New Mexico
Province Secretary
　　Gertrude Nance Marthens, Φ-Colorado,
　　　1948-51
Province Alumnae Chairman
　　Nina Shaffer, BΔ-Colorado College, 1947-51

Province XI
Idaho, Washington, Eastern Canada
Province Secretary
　　Carolyn Logan Smith, N-Idaho, 1948-51
Province Alumnae Chairman
　　Lucile Ingram Walton, AH-Whitman, 1947-51

Province XII
Oregon, Montana
Province Secretary
　　Mae Pope Worden, Π-Montana, 1947-51
Province Alumnae Chairman
　　Elvira Starz Smith, Π-Montana, 1947-51

Province XIII
California, Arizona, Utah, Hawaii
Province Secretary
　　Faith Ferbitz Frikart, AΠ-Arizona, 1948-53
Province Alumnae Chairman
　　Margaret Richardson Hay, Υ-Stanford, 1947-51

Province XIV
Texas, Louisiana
Province Secretary
　　Dorothy Lee, AΥ-SMU, 1950-53
Province Alumnae Chairman
　　Carolyn Boli Stanton, AΥ-SMU, 1950-51

1951-57
FOURTEEN PROVINCES

Province I
Connecticut, Eastern Canada, Maine, Massachu-
setts, New Hampshire, New York, Rhode
Island, Vermont
Province Secretaries
　　Helen Rupert Pitcher, Λ-Minnesota, 1951-54
　　Kathryn Maple Roberts, AH-Whitman, 1954-57
Province Alumnae Chairmen
　　Eleanor Meck Smith, AP-Ohio Wesleyan,
　　　1951-55
　　Margaret Sorenson Rayner, AΓ-Toronto,
　　　1955-57

Province II
New Jersey, Pennsylvania, West Virginia
Province Secretaries
　　Mary Reif, Ξ-Michigan, 1951-52
　　Pauline Unger Parker, AX-Penn State, 1953-57
Province Alumnae Chairmen
　　Margaret Leamer Sadler, AΛ-Drake, 1950-55
　　Ruth Mason Pitkin, AX-Penn State, 1955-57

Province III
Delaware, District of Columbia, Maryland, North Carolina, Virginia
Province Secretaries
Alice Beachler Gordon, BE-American, 1951-52
Ethel Clapsaddle Stephens Aiken,
BΛ-Gettysburg, 1952-55
Edna Kate Hale, AΩ-Arkansas, 1955-57
Province Alumnae Chairmen
Ruth French Shriver, Ψ-Goucher, 1951-55
Mary Frances Grubbs, Θ-Indiana, 1955-59

Province IV
Alabama, Florida, Georgia, South Carolina, Tennessee (Mississippi added in 1955.)
Province Secretaries
Nancy Harris Cooper, AΣ-UCLA, 1950-54
Fern Spolander Moseley, M-Missouri, 1954-55
Frances Lee Sparzani, AΦ-British Columbia,
1955-56
Eleanor Smith Slaughter, AΨ-Mississippi,
1956-59
Province Alumnae Chairmen
Mildred Moyer Baynard, K-Nebraska, 1950-53
Virginia Leudemann Terry, O-Adelphi, 1953-57

Province V
Kentucky, Ohio
Province Secretaries
Sylvia Draper Carlson, BΓ-Utah, 1951-53
Pauline Sutton Cline, AP-Ohio Wesleyan,
1953-55
Catherine Carroll Taliaferro, H-Akron, 1955-57
Province Alumnae Chairmen
Jean Purdy McNeill, AP-Ohio Wesleyan,
1951-54
Frances Brackett Derr, Θ-Indiana, 1954-57

Province VI
Indiana, Michigan
Province Secretaries
Mary Jane Cornelison Buffum, AH-Whitman,
1951-55
Margaret Button Finkenauer, X-Cornell,
1955-59
Province Alumnae Chairmen
Marjorie May, Θ-Indiana, 1951-53
Laura Bertram Dillon, Z-Albion, 1953-56
Sarah Brecht Wert, AB-Swarthmore, 1956-59

Province VII
Illinois, Wisconsin
Province Secretaries
Elizabeth Candee Lee, Ω-Wisconsin, 1950-55
Eleanore Ramsay Conlin, Ω-Wisconsin, 1955-57
Province Alumnae Chairmen
Frances Holyoke McCoy, K-Nebraska, 1951-53
Min Smith, AZ-Lawrence, 1953-57

Province VIII
Iowa, Minnesota, North Dakota, South Dakota (Nebraska added in 1955.)
Province Secretaries
Bertha McKechney Johnston, AΘ-North
Dakota, 1951-55
Dorothy Johnson Davison, AΛ-Drake, 1955-57
Province Alumnae Chairmen
Gwendola Beasley Fox, Λ-Minnesota, 1951-52
Ma'ene Schaefer James, AI-Oklahoma, 1952-55
Virginia Marsh Horner, I-Illinois, 1955-57

Province IX
Kansas, Missouri, Oklahoma
Province Secretaries
Fern Spolander Moseley, M-Missouri, 1951-53
Betty McDonald Minkler, BΔ-Colorado
College, 1953-55
Martha Howell Berg, BΔ-Colorado College,
1955-57
Province Alumnae Chairmen
Helen Bradford Anderson, M-Missouri, 1950-52
Jody Slack McLernon, AI-Oklahoma, 1953-57

Province X
Arizona, Colorado, Nebraska (moved to Province VIII in 1955), New Mexico, Utah
Province Secretaries
Nina Shaffer, BΔ-Colorado College, 1951-53
June Mangel Vance, BΓ-Utah, 1953-57
Province Alumnae Chairmen
Ruth De Klotz Sowles, K-Nebraska, 1951-55
Veneta Slack McFarland, ΓΓ-Texas Western,
1955-57

Province XI
Idaho, Washington, Western Canada
Province Secretaries
Bernice Judson Campbell, B-Washington,
1951-55
Dorothy Scotton Cash, AΔ-Oregon, 1955-57
Province Alumnae Chairmen
Maisie Clugston Groves, AΦ-British Columbia,
1951-55
Genevieve Piatt Allen, B-Washington, 1955-57

Province XII
Montana, Oregon, Wyoming
Province Secretaries
Agnes Beach, Γ-California, 1951-52
Marcia Griffin Traynor, N-Idaho, 1952-55
Margaret Maddock Anderson, Π-Montana,
1955-57
Province Alumnae Chairmen
Nettie Porter Reynolds, Π-Montana, 1951-55
Agnes Beach, Γ-California, 1955-57

Province XIII
California, Nevada
Province Secretaries
Faith Ferbitz Frikart, AΠ-Arizona, 1949-53
Berenice Livingston Paul, Γ-California, 1953-57
Province Alumnae Chairmen
Marian McGirr Cragin, B-Washington, 1951-55
Sara Addleman Shenk, AΔ-Oregon, 1955-59

Province XIV
Arkansas, Louisiana, Mississippi (moved to Province IV in 1955), Texas
Province Secretaries
Dorothy Lee, AΥ-SMU, 1949-53
Polly Atkinson Jones, AI-Oklahoma, 1953-54
Grace Odem Doyle, BH-Texas, 1954-55
Betty Bransford Weaver, AΥ-SMU, 1955-57
Province Alumnae Chairmen
Polly Atkinson Jones, AI-Oklahoma, 1951-53
Dorothy Lee, AΥ-SMU, 1953-57

Provinces

1957-60
FIFTEEN PROVINCES

Province I
Connecticut, Eastern Canada, Maine, Massachusetts, New Hampshire, New York, Rhode Island, Vermont
Province Secretaries
Kathryn Maple Roberts, ΛΗ-Whitman, 1954-59
Marian Hill Keenan, Ω-Wisconsin, 1959-63
Province Alumnae Chairmen
Elizabeth Wright Babcock, P-Syracuse, 1957-59
Peggy Baker Blod, ΛΗ-Whitman, 1959-61

Province II
New Jersey, Pennsylvania, West Virginia
Province Secretary
Jean Falconer Chase, Λ-Minnesota, 1957-61
Province Alumnae Chairman
Beulah Saffel Talbott, ΑΞ-West Virginia, 1957-61

Province III
Delaware, District of Columbia, Maryland, North Carolina, South Carolina, Virginia
Province Secretaries
Betty Rockwell Eyler, ΒΣ-Maryland, 1957-59
Mary Frances Cornell Grubbs, Θ-Indiana, 1959-61
Province Alumnae Chairmen
Mary Frances Cornell Grubbs, Θ-Indiana, 1955-59
Helen Fuller Spencer, E-Ohio State, 1959-60

Province IV
Alabama, Florida, Georgia, Louisiana, Mississippi, Tennessee
Province Secretary
Eleanor Smith Slaughter, ΑΨ-Mississippi, 1956-59
Province Alumnae Chairman
Carolyn Stuhler Carter, T-Iowa, 1957-60

Province V
Kentucky, Central and Southern Ohio
Province Secretaries
Edna Ketterer Keyes, E-Ohio State, 1957-59
Lynn Caswell Eavey, Π-Montana, 1959-60
Province Alumnae Chairmen
Mary Jeanne Barricklow Bohannan, E-Ohio State, 1956-59
Jean Pierce Dredge, E-Ohio State, 1959-63

Province VI
Michigan, Northern Ohio
Province Secretaries
Margaret Button Finkenauer, Ξ-Michigan, 1955-59
Ruth Keller Stowell, ΑΟ-Miami Univ., 1959-60
Province Alumnae Chairmen
Sarah Brecht Wert, ΑΒ-Swarthmore, 1956-59
Josephine Montgomery Williams, ΑΟ-Miami Univ., 1959-60

Province VII
Indiana
Province Secretary
Gloria Schnaiter Blake, Θ-Indiana, 1957-61
Province Alumnae Chairman
Gloria Gundeck Wampler, ΑΠ-Arizona, 1956-61

Province VIII
Illinois, Wisconsin
Province Secretaries
Mildred Owens Newman, Σ-Northwestern, 1956-59
Margaret Kimback Erickson, Σ-Northwestern, 1959-60
Province Alumnae Chairman
Virginia Riesterer Gates, Σ-Northwestern, 1956-61

Province IX
Iowa, Minnesota, Nebraska, North Dakota, South Dakota
Province Secretaries
Dorothy Johnson Davison, ΑΛ-Drake, 1956-59
H. K. Davis Stuart, K-Nebraska, 1959-61
Province Alumnae Chairmen
Virginia March Horner, I-Illinois, 1956-59
Elizabeth Dorman Diehl, Σ-Northwestern, 1959-63

Province X
Arkansas, Kansas, Missouri, Oklahoma
Province Secretaries
Betty Hamman Hattan, ΒΚ-Kansas, 1957-59
Celia Regnier Pitney, ΑΚ-Washburn, 1959-63
Province Alumnae Chairmen
Hope Joslyn Rogers, M-Missouri, 1957-59
Adele Stocking Thompson, ΑΕ-Washington Univ., 1959-60

Province XI
Texas
Province Secretaries
Lady Perry McGinnis Camp, ΒΗ-Texas, 1957-59
Elloie Barkley Wilson, Λ-Minnesota, 1959-60
Province Alumnae Chairmen
Kay Blankenship Lemmer, M-Missouri, 1957-58
Nancy Davis Greenway, ΓΗ-San Jose, 1958-59
Jane Teagarden Brutsche, ΑΥ-SMU, 1959-63

Province XII
Arizona, Colorado, New Mexico, Utah, Wyoming
Province Secretaries
Elizabeth Schicht Bergstrom, I-Illinois, 1957-58
Isabel Worley McIlvaine, Φ-Colorado, 1958-61
Province Alumnae Chairmen
Veneta Slack McFarland, ΓΓ-Texas Western, 1957-59
Margaret Robinson Regan, ΒΓ-Utah, 1959-63

Province XIII
California, Nevada, Hawaii
Province Secretary
Marian McGirr Cragin, B-Washington, 1956-61
Province Alumnae Chairmen
Sara Addleman Shenk, ΑΔ-Oregon, 1955-59
Dorothy Harvey Mattern, ΑΛ-Drake, 1959-61

Province XIV
Idaho, Montana, Eastern Washington
Province Secretaries
Margaret Maddock Anderson, Π-Montana, 1957-58
Polly Thomas Price, N-Idaho, 1958-63
Province Alumnae Chairmen
Elinore Finch Brown, N-Idaho, 1957-59

274

Hildegarde Weisberg Turner, Π-Montana,
1959-61

Province XV
Western Canada, Oregon, Western Washington, Alaska (1959)
Province Secretary
Elizabeth Coffinberry Kloppenburg,
Γ-California, 1957-60
Province Alumnae Chairmen
Agnes Beach, Γ-California, 1957-59
Louise Kittell Schnatterly, ΑΚ-Washburn,
1959-63

1960-65
In the Fall of 1964 the title of Province Secretary was changed to Province Collegiate Chairman.

SIXTEEN PROVINCES

Province I
Connecticut, Eastern Canada, Maine, Massachusetts, New Hampshire, New York, Northern New Jersey, Rhode Island, Vermont
Province Secretaries
Marian Hill Keenan, Ω-Wisconsin, 1959-63
Maud Eichmann Johnston, Σ-Northwestern,
1963-65
Province Alumnae Chairmen
Peggy Baker Blod, ΑΗ-Whitman, 1959-61
Janet Lau Sullivan, Κ-Nebraska, 1961-65

Province II
Central and Southern New Jersey, Pennsylvania, West Virginia
Province Secretaries
Jean Falconer Chase, Λ-Minnesota, 1957-61
Peggy McCann Garland, Ψ-Goucher, 1961-64
Angela Pollis Lynch, ΒΝ-Carnegie Mellon,
1964-67
Province Alumnae Chairmen
Beulah Saffel Talbott, ΑΞ-West Virginia,
1957-61
Naomi Young White, Κ-Nebraska, 1961-65

Province III
Delaware, District of Columbia, Maryland, North Carolina, South Carolina, Virginia
Province Secretaries
Mary Cornell Grubbs, Θ-Indiana, 1959-61
Northa Porter Mayo, ΑΛ-Drake, 1961-63
Shirley Hintzelman Herron, ΒΖ-Denison,
1963-67
Province Alumnae Chairmen
Betty Rockwell Eyler, ΒΣ-Maryland, 1960-61
Elizabeth Boyton Holmes, ΑΔ-Oregon, 1961-65

Province IV
Alabama, Arkansas, Louisiana, Mississippi
Province Secretaries
Natalie Chadwick Wood, ΑΨ-Mississippi,
1960-62
Jo Anne Lockard Allen, ΑΨ-Mississippi,
1962-64
Elroy Scruggs Smith, Σ-Northwestern, 1964-65
Province Alumnae Chairmen
Frances Boldman Van Eps, Κ-Nebraska,
1960-63
Gloria Fischer Dobbs, Μ-Missouri, 1963-65

Province V
Kentucky, Central and Southern Ohio. (Provinces V and VI are under direction of Mary Ann Lummis Bowyer 1963-65 thus combining territories of Michigan and Ohio. Kentucky was moved to Province VII.) In 1965 territory was redivided, and Province V territory was Ohio.
Province Secretaries
Carolyn Coffman Moorman, ΑΟ-Miami Univ.,
1960-64
Louise Callahan Call, Ε-Ohio State, 1964-67
Province Alumnae Chairmen
Jean Pierce Dredge, Ε-Ohio State, 1959-63
Mary Ann Lummis Bowyer, ΒΖ-Denison,
1963-65

Province VI
Michigan, and Northern Ohio.
1963—Michigan and Ohio
1965—Michigan
Province Secretaries
Natalie Conrad Case, Η-Akron, 1960-63
Lois Gruhler Beattie, ΑΡ-Ohio Wesleyan,
1963-64
Phoebe Rowe Burt, Ε-Ohio State, 1964-66
Province Alumnae Chairmen
Josephine Montgomery Williams,
ΑΟ-Miami Univ., 1959-61
Nan Sumner Force, Η-Akron, 1961-63
Mary Ann Lummis Bowyer, ΒΖ-Denison,
1963-66

Province VII
Indiana, Kentucky was added in 1963.
Province Secretaries
Gloria Schnaiter Blake, Θ-Indiana, 1957-61
Ellen Marty Troup, ΑΖ-Lawrence, 1961
Jean Robinson Turner, Ι-Illinois, 1961-65
Province Alumnae Chairmen
Gloria Gundeck Wampler, ΑΠ-Arizona,
1957-61
Jean Robinson Turner, Ι-Illinois, 1961
Ellen Marty Troup, ΑΖ-Lawrence, 1961-62
Patricia Peterson Danielson, Θ-Indiana, 1962-65

Province VIII
Illinois, Wisconsin
Province Secretaries
Ruth Keller Stowell, ΑΟ-Miami Univ., 1960-61
Joan McCabe, ΒΤ-Miami, 1961
Wilhelmina Kettenbach Eberhart,
Β-Washington, 1961-63
Winogene Springer Yost, Σ-Northwestern,
1963-66
Province Alumnae Chairmen
Virginia Riesterer Gates, Σ-Northwestern,
1957-61
Maryella Cowles Peacock, ΑΜ-Beloit, 1961-63
Frances Garrett Crotty, ΒΕ-American, 1963-66

Province IX
Iowa, Minnesota, Nebraska, North Dakota, South Dakota
Province Secretaries
H. K. Davis Stuart, Κ-Nebraska, 1959-61
Harriet Minier Hallett, Κ-Nebraska, 1961-63
Dorothy Carleton Griffith, ΑΣ-UCLA, 1963-65

Provinces

Province Alumnae Chairmen
Elizabeth Dorman Diehl, Σ-Northwestern,
1959-63
Charlene Horne Hilton, T-Iowa, 1963-66

Province X
Kansas, Missouri, Oklahoma
Province Secretaries
Celia Regnier Pitney, AK-Washburn, 1959-63
Comora MacGregor Nash, BK-Kansas, 1963-67
Province Alumnae Chairmen
Betty Beach Norris, BK-Kansas, 1960-63
Marion Chesnut Steinmeyer, AI-Oklahoma,
1963-67

Province XI
Texas
Province Secretaries
Martha Boyd, BH-Texas, 1960-63
Rosanne Matofsky Milan, ΓB-Tulsa, 1963-65
Province Alumnae Chairmen
Jane Teagarden Brutsche, AΥ-SMU, 1959-63
Carolyn Ashcroft Newbold, AΥ-SMU, 1963-65

Province XII
Arizona, Colorado, New Mexico, Utah, Wyoming
Province Secretaries
Isabel Worley McIlvaine, Φ-Colorado, 1958-61
Georgene Kuhn Miller, AP-Ohio Wesleyan,
1961-65
Province Alumnae Chairmen
Margaret Robinson Regan, BΓ-Utah, 1959-63
Eva Williams Sackett, Φ-Colorado, 1963-67

Province XIII
*California, Nevada, Hawaii. Territory divided
North and South in 1963.*
Province Secretaries
Marian McGirr Cragin, B-Washington, 1957-61
Kathryn Bell Gary, M-Missouri, 1961-64
Dorothy Roushall Starr, ΓΛ-Fresno, 1964-67
Province Alumnae Chairmen
Dorothy Harvey Mattern, AΛ-Drake, 1959-61
North: Kathleen Jesse McCormack, AΔ-Oregon,
1961-65
South: LuAnne Lyen Leonard, AΣ-UCLA,
1963-65

Province XIV
*Idaho, Montana, Eastern Washington, Alberta
(added in 1963)*
Province Secretaries
Polly Thomas Price, N-Idaho, 1958-63
Gladys Pence Welker, N-Idaho, 1963-65
Province Alumnae Chairmen
Hildegarde Weisberg Turner, Π-Montana,
1959-61
Virginia Gaddis Van Vliet, AΔ-Oregon, 1961-63
Elaine Wheeler Blomquist, N-Idaho, 1963-67

Province XV
*Western Canada, Oregon, Western Washington,
Alaska (Alberta moved to Province XIV in
1963)*
Province Secretaries
Marcia Wright Holmer, AΔ-Oregon, 1960-63
June Day Anderson, B-Washington, 1963-67
Province Alumnae Chairmen
Louise Kittell Schnatterly, AK-Washburn,
1959-63
Chiane Gerow Anderson, AΔ-Oregon, 1963-65

Province XVI
Florida, Georgia, Tennessee
Province Secretaries
Joan McCabe, BT-Miami, 1960-61
Lynn Caswell Eavey, Π-Montana, 1961
Jean Shade Sheahan, E-Ohio State, 1961-63
Northa Porter Mayo, AΛ-Drake, 1963-65
Province Alumnae Chairmen
Carolyn Stuhler Carter, T-Iowa, 1960-61
Frances Monroe Bass, AΨ-Mississippi, 1961-64
Ellen Marty Troup, AZ-Lawrence, 1964-65

1965-69
SEVENTEEN PROVINCES

Province I
*Connecticut, Eastern Canada, Maine, Massachu-
setts, New Hampshire, Northern New Jersey,
New York, Rhode Island, Vermont*
Province Collegiate Chairmen
Patricia Eden Dayton, ΓΔ-Montana State,
1965-67
Joan DePass, BA-McGill, 1967-71
Province Alumnae Chairmen
Jacquelin Buchenau Hawkins, Φ-Colorado,
1965-69

Province II
*Central and Southern New Jersey, Pennsylvania,
West Virginia*
Province Collegiate Chairmen
Angela Pollis Lynch, BN-Carnegie-Mellon,
1964-67
Dorothy Van Fleet Hicks, X-Cornell, 1967-69
Province Alumnae Chairmen
Ardyth Schaffer Walker, BN-Carnegie-Mellon,
1965-67
Nancy Spencer Rudloff, AX-Penn State,
1967-71

Province III
*Delaware, District of Columbia, Maryland, North
Carolina, South Carolina, Virginia*
Province Collegiate Chairmen
Shirley Hintzelmann Herron, BZ-Denison,
1963-67
Elizabeth Riggs Wallace, AΞ-West Virginia,
1967-69
Province Alumnae Chairmen
Virginia Ford Benson, BP-George Washington,
1965-68
Elizabeth Finley Allen, X-Cornell, 1968-73

Province IV
Alabama, Arkansas, Louisiana, Mississippi
Province Collegiate Chairmen
Lynn Caswell Eavey, Π-Montana, 1965-66
Harriet Harrison McIntyre, AΨ-Mississippi,
1966-67
Mary Elizabeth Ford, AΨ-Mississippi, 1967-69
Province Alumnae Chairmen
Lucile James Rasmussen, AΩ-Arkansas, 1965-66
Nancy Brock Johnston, AΥ-SMU, 1966-69

Province V
*Ohio Alumnae; Central and Southern Ohio
Collegiate Chapters*
Province Collegiate Chairmen
Louise Callahan Call, E-Ohio State, 1964-67

Barbara Stellhorn Wuichet, BZ-Denison,
1967-71
Province Alumnae Chairman
Joann Whitley Grimes, E-Ohio State, 1965-69

Province VI
*Michigan Alumnae; Northern Ohio and Michigan
Collegiate Chapters*
Province Collegiate Chairmen
Phoebe Rowe Burt, E-Ohio State, 1964-66
Lois Gruhler Beattie, AP-Ohio Wesleyan,
1966-67
Virginia Block Buckley, ΓE-Kent State,
1967-69
Province Alumnae Chairmen
Mary Ann Lummis Bowyer, BZ-Denison,
1963-66
Ruth Mary Baldwin Atchison, Z-Albion,
1966-71

Province VII
Indiana, Kentucky
Province Collegiate Chairman
Olive Steinle Witt, AT-Butler, 1965-69
Province Alumnae Chairman
Patricia Ferguson Dunbar, AT-Butler, 1965-69

Province VIII
Illinois, Wisconsin
Province Collegiate Chairmen
Winogene Springer Yost, Σ-Northwestern,
1963-66
Polly Shank LeFaivre, E-Ohio State, 1966-70
Province Alumnae Chairmen
Frances Garrett Crotty, BE-American, 1963-66
Martha Stone Evans, AE-Washington Univ.,
1966-69

Province IX
*Iowa, Minnesota, Nebraska, North Dakota, South
Dakota*
Province Collegiate Chairmen
Dee Goreham Staples, AΔ-Drake, 1965-66
Alice Park Newman, Λ-Minnesota, 1966-69
Province Alumnae Chairmen
Charlene Horne Hilton, T-Iowa, 1963-66
Yvonne Cottingham Mattson, Σ-Northwestern,
1966-69

Province X
Kansas, Missouri, Oklahoma
Province Collegiate Chairmen
Comora MacGregor Nash, BK-Kansas, 1963-67
Virginia Gard Mastio, BK-Kansas, 1967-68
Mary Hait Swift, AI-Oklahoma, 1968-72
Province Alumnae Chairmen
Marion Chesnut Steinmeyer, AI-Oklahoma,
1963-67
Gloria Fischer Dobbs, M-Missouri, 1967-69

Province XI
Texas
Province Collegiate Chairmen
Betty Meek Patten, ΓT-Texas Christian,
1965-66
Virginia Van Dyke Spaller, Ξ-Michigan,
1966-68
Jeanne Littleton Golladay, M-Missouri, 1968-70

Province Alumnae Chairmen
Cynthia Veatch Glatte, AN-USC, 1965-69
June McDonald Swanstrom, Φ-Colorado,
1968-70

Province XII
Arizona, Colorado, New Mexico, Utah, Wyoming
Province Collegiate Chairmen
Anna Lou Meyer Chapman, BX-Denver,
1965-67
Betty Land Krueger, AΠ-Arizona, 1967-71
Province Alumnae Chairmen
Eva Williams Sackett, Φ-Colorado, 1963-67
Ellen Cunningham Freese, AI-Oklahoma,
1967-71

Province XIII
Northern California, Hawaii
Province Collegiate Chairmen
Dorothy Roushall Starr, ΓΛ-Fresno, 1964-67
Kathleen Jesse McCormack, AΔ-Oregon,
1967-69
Province Alumnae Chairmen
Dee Breaux Lindsay, Γ-California, 1965-67
Barbara Lucas Pease, AΔ-Oregon, 1967-69

Province XIV
Alberta, Idaho, Montana, Eastern Washington
Province Collegiate Chairman
Virginia Gaddis Van Vliet, AΔ-Oregon, 1965-69
Province Alumnae Chairman
Elaine Wheeler Blomquist, N-Idaho, 1963-67
Mary Elizabeth Brome Bielenberg,
Φ-Colorado, 1967
Barbara Borrevik Wiley, AΔ-Oregon, 1967-69

Province XV
*Alaska, British Columbia, Oregon, Western
Washington*
Province Collegiate Chairmen
June Day Anderson, B-Washington, 1963-67
Mary Sargent Neville, BΠ-Willamette, 1967-69
Province Alumnae Chairmen
Marguerite Clark Tinsley, Σ-Northwestern,
1965-67
Hildegarde Weisberg Turner, Π-Montana,
1967-69

Province XVI
Florida, Georgia, Tennessee
Province Collegiate Chairmen
Jane Jones Holt, AM-Beloit, 1965-67
Katherine Cannon Titzel, BZ-Denison, 1967-68
Jean Shade Sheahan, E-Ohio State, 1968-70
Province Alumnae Chairmen
Sally Collier Rector, AI-Oklahoma, 1965-67
Mary Jean Stewart Daneke, AK-Washburn,
1967-69

Province XVII
Southern California, Nevada
Province Collegiate Chairmen
Beverly Williams Metzler, AN-USC, 1965-67
LuAnne Lyen Leonard, AΣ-UCLA, 1967-68
Jacquelyn Ford Walter, AN-USC, 1968-71
Province Alumnae Chairmen
Frances Doan Turner, AΠ-Arizona, 1965-67
Susie Lynch Riegel, Υ-Stanford, 1967-71

1969
EIGHTEEN PROVINCES

Province I
Connecticut, Eastern Canada, Maine, Massachusetts, New Hampshire, Northern New Jersey, New York, Rhode Island, Vermont
Province Collegiate Chairmen
Joan DePass, BΛ-McGill, 1967-71
Judith Van Scoyk Waymire, ΓI-DePauw, 1971-73
Andrea Van Alstne Lutz, ΛO-Miami Univ., 1973-
Province Alumnae Chairmen
Frances Williams Damerell, BI-Purdue, 1969-73
Patricia Kindig Ross, BI-Purdue, 1973-

Province II
Central and Southern New Jersey, Pennsylvania, West Virginia
Province Collegiate Chairmen
Gwynn Williams Wardwell, ΛZ-Lawrence, 1969-73
Mary Pennell Simmons, ΛX-Penn State, 1973-
Province Alumnae Chairmen
Nancy Spencer Rudloff, ΛX-Penn State, 1967-71
Barbara Turner Washburn, Θ-Indiana, 1971-

Province III
Delaware, District of Columbia, Maryland, North Carolina, South Carolina, Virginia
Province Collegiate Chairmen
Jane McDonald Price, ΛΥ-SMU, 1969-71
Arlen Kelly St. John, BΣ-Maryland, 1971-
Province Alumnae Chairmen
Elizabeth Finley Allen, X-Cornell, 1968-73
Jane Richmond Bowers, BΣ-Maryland, 1973-

Province IV
Georgia, Florida
Province Collegiate Chairmen
Jean Shade Sheahan, E-Ohio State, 1969-70
Jane Jones Holt, ΛM-Beloit, 1970-71
Janet McFarlane MaCris, BΞ-Michigan State, 1971-73
Helen Fuller Spencer, E-Ohio State, 1973-
Province Alumnae Chairmen
Maryanna Chockley Contole, Ξ-Michigan, 1969-70
Sarah Moores Walker, ΛH-Whitman, 1970-73
Rosemary Young Littlefield, ΛK-Washburn, 1973-

Province V
Ohio Alumnae; Central and Southern Ohio Collegiate Chapters
Province Collegiate Chairmen
Barbara Stellhorn Wuichet, BZ-Denison, 1967-71
Sue Mueller Loomis, BI-Purdue, 1971-
Province Alumnae Chairmen
Ruth Cope Mulvihill, Σ-Northwestern, 1969-72
Constance Clark Lauderback, BΞ-Michigan State, 1972-

Province VI
Michigan Alumnae; Northern Ohio and Michigan Collegiate Chapters

Province Collegiate Chairmen
Marcia Endle Sutcliff, ΓP-Wittenberg, 1969-71
Carol Swisher Bigelow, BZ-Denison, 1971-73
Susan Goebel Boesch, BΞ-Michigan State, 1973-
Province Alumnae Chairmen
Ruth Mary Baldwin Atchison, Z-Albion, 1966-71
Mary Anne Holt Mueller, Z-Albion, 1971-

Province VII
Indiana
Province Collegiate Chairmen
Harriet Childs Nelson, Σ-Northwestern, 1969-71
Virginia Ruess, ΓO-Indiana State, 1971-73
Mary Ellen Guyer Davies, ΓI-DePauw, 1973-
Province Alumnae Chairmen
Barbara Dale Szumski, ΛT-Butler, 1969-73
Janice Sawyer Fellows, ΓO-Indiana State, 1973-

Province VIII
Illinois, Wisconsin
Province Collegiate Chairmen
Polly Shank LeFaivre, E-Ohio State, 1966-70
Katherine Whitacre Rossing, BZ-Denison, 1970-73
Judith Van Scoyk Waymire, ΓI-DePauw, 1973-
Province Alumnae Chairmen
Marjorie Pulliam Gustine, ΓZ-LSU, 1969-73
Helen Goodwill Slater, BI-Purdue, 1973-

Province IX
Mississippi, Alabama, Louisiana
Province Collegiate Chairmen
Lillian Newton Landrum, ΛΨ-Mississippi, 1969-70
Dorothy West Bristol, ΓZ-LSU, 1970-
Province Alumnae Chairmen
Donna Vicknair Moak, ΓZ-LSU, 1969-71
Sue Fournet Roshto, ΓZ-LSU, 1971-73
Virginia Farley McLeod, M-Missouri, 1973-

Province X
Oklahoma, Arkansas, Tennessee, Kentucky
Province Collegiate Chairmen
Rose Godwin Brown, ΛΨ-Mississippi, 1969-73
Jody Slack McLernon, ΛI-Oklahoma, 1973-
Province Alumnae Chairmen
Marilyn Walker Mooney, BΔ-Colorado College, 1969-70
Ann Davenport Dowling, ΛI-Oklahoma, 1970-72
Margaret Thomas Dunbar, BZ-Denison, 1972-73
Nyla Jaszkowiak Villiger, K-Nebraska, 1973-

Province XI
Texas
Province Collegiate Chairmen
Jeanne Littleton Golladay, M-Missouri, 1968-70
Gloria Fitzpatrick DeGroot, BH-Texas, 1970-73
Ruth Graham Smith, E-Ohio State, 1973-
Province Alumnae Chairmen
June McDonald Swanstrom, Φ-Colorado, 1969-70
Jane Ann Williams Currie, ΓT-TCU, 1970-71
Lane Smith Vaughan, BH-Texas, 1971-

Province XII
Kansas, Missouri
Province Collegiate Chairmen
Mary Hait Swift, AI-Oklahoma, 1968-72
Virginia Gard Mastio, BK-Kansas, 1972-73
Barbara Hamker Anderson, ΓΥ-Wichita, 1973-
Province Alumnae Chairmen
Beverly Jorgensen Frederick, M-Missouri,
   1969-70
Barbara Walters Schneider, BM-Bowling Green,
   1970-73
Mary Ann Morie Starbuck, AK-Washburn,
   1973-

Province XIII
*Iowa, Minnesota, Nebraska, North Dakota, South
Dakota*
Province Collegiate Chairmen
Janet McClung Westcott, K-Nebraska, 1969-71
Ruth Obrestad Core, AΔ-Drake, 1971-72
Barbara Griswold Laederach, Λ-Minnesota,
   1972-
Province Alumnae Chairmen
Sandra Lichtenberg Robinson, K-Nebraska,
   1969-70
Elizabeth Richter Ruedy, Λ-Minnesota, 1970-71
Joan Christiansen Green, AΔ-Drake, 1971-

Province XIV
Alberta, Idaho, Montana, Eastern Washington
Province Collegiate Chairmen
Janice Graves King, BΩ-Washington State,
   1969-71
Janice Graves Stewart, BΩ-Washington State,
   1971-73
Barbara Eagleson Hazzard, AΔ-Oregon, 1973-
Province Alumnae Chairmen
Phyllis Lytle Harris, Π-Montana, 1969-73
Marilyn Walton Chamberlin, AH-Whitman,
   1973-

Province XV
*Alaska, British Columbia, Oregon, Western
Washington*
Province Collegiate Chairmen
Lee Tinglestad Stortz, BΠ-Willamette, 1969-73
Cynthia Gift Hamp, Θ-Indiana, 1973-
Province Alumnae Chairmen
Dorothy Riley Milne, AΠ-Arizona, 1969-73
Claire Williscroft Hurley, BB-Alberta, 1973-

Province XVI
Colorado, New Mexico, Utah, Wyoming, Mexico
Province Collegiate Chairmen
Betty Land Krueger, AΠ-Arizona, 1969-71
Carol Geisler Stott, BZ-Denison, 1971-
Province Alumnae Chairmen
Ellen Cunningham Freese, AI-Oklahoma,
   1969-71
Pearl Kimball Millerberg, BΓ-Utah, 1971-72
True McKenry Anderson, BX-Denver, 1972-

Province XVII
Southern California, Arizona
Province Collegiate Chairmen
Jacquelyn Ford Walter, AN-USC, 1968-71
Marcia Balyeat Leonhardt, E-Ohio State, 1971-
Province Alumnae Chairmen
Susie Lynch Riegel, Υ-Stanford, 1967-71
Nancy Taylor Jones, BΓ-Utah, 1971-

Province XVIII
Northern California, Nevada, Hawaii
Province Collegiate Chairmen
Kay Blankenship Lemmer, M-Missouri, 1969-71
Phyllis Morgan Keller, AΔ-Oregon, 1971-
Province Alumnae Chairmen
Doris Easterly Porter, ΓH-San Jose, 1969-71
Mary Alice van Barneveld van Doorn,
   AΣ-UCLA, 1971-

Collegiate Representatives to Council

Anxious for collegiate chapters to voice opinions
and thoughts which might improve collegiate
programming and Fraternity progress, Collegiate
Representatives to Council were first elected at
the 1958 Convention. The first Collegiate Representatives represented chapters living in chapter
houses and chapters in lodges, suites, and rooms,
and were elected by the collegiate delegates at
Conventions. In 1970, the election was changed
to provide for four Collegiate Representatives,
each representing all chapters from a geographic
region, and the election was subsequently held
on an annual basis, at both Convention and
Leadership School.

1958-59
Chapters in houses — Barbara Wallenfang, BΨ-
Alabama
Chapters in lodges and rooms—Susan Daugherty,
AP-Ohio Wesleyan

1960-61
Chapters in houses — Carolyn Kloppenburg, B-
Washington
Chapters in lodges and rooms — Peggy Flowers,
ΓA-Tennessee

1962-63
Chapters in houses—Sally Myers, AΠ-Arizona
Chapters in lodges and rooms — Lois Haegley,
AX-Penn State

1964-65
Chapters in houses—Jean Swahn, BH-Texas
Chapters in lodges and rooms—Ellen Jane Holt,
ΓΘ-Florida*

1966-67
Chapters in houses—Barbara Carvill, Θ-Indiana
Chapters in lodges and rooms—Sally Nutton, BP-
George Washington

1968-69
Chapters in houses—Margaret Talburtt,
Ξ-Michigan
Chapters in lodges and rooms—Elizabeth Nelson,
BP-George Washington

*Though Ellen Jane Holt was initiated at ΓΘ-
Florida, she represented BT-Miami as that chapter's Convention delegate in 1964.*

1969-70
Chapters in houses—Jane Gegenheimer, X-Cornell
Chapters in lodges and rooms—Janan Mikkelsen,
  ΔK-South Florida

1970-71
East—Martha Milbourne, AP-Ohio Wesleyan
South—Ginny Green, ΑΥ-SMU
Midwest—Jean Hurst, ΒΙ-Purdue
West—Dina Marengo, Γ-California

1971-72
East—Anne Laing, Ξ-Michigan
South—Suzanne Sloan, ΒΨ-Alabama
Midwest—Jonette Beaver, K-Nebraska
West—Jan Royer, ΔΕ-Pacific

1972-73
East—Lynn Jaquay, X-Cornell
South—Beth Mitchell, ΑΨ-Mississippi
Midwest—Susan Shirk, Φ-Colorado
West—Susan Clouse, ΓΦ-Arizona State

1973-74
East—Catherine Hillen, ΒΡ-George Washington
South—Ann Elizabeth Moore, ΓΖ-LSU
Midwest—Rosemary Ledvora, ΔΝ-Northern
  Illinois
West—Leigh von der Esch, ΒΓ-Utah

Fraternity Awards

The Order of the Delta Gamma Rose

This award has been a part of Fraternity tradition since 1952. It was initiated at that time to recognize Delta Gammas who have distinguished themselves in their chosen fields. The following have been conferred:

BUSINESS
1955 *Ethel Barbara Dietrich*, Ω-Wisconsin, world trade and economics. Residing in Paris at time award was made.
1956 *Madelyn Coe Cummiskey*, Ξ-Michigan
1963 *Ruey Sieger Messenger*, ΑΒ-Swarthmore
1972 *Roberta Abernethy*, E-Ohio State

EDUCATION
1952 *Dr. Lillian Ray Titcomb*, Υ-Stanford, educator, formerly women's physician, UCLA, director of Los Angeles Nursery School for Visually Handicapped Children.
1952 *Ada Louise Comstock Notestein*, Λ-Minnesota, Dean of Women, University of Minnesota; Dean of Smith College; President Emeritus Radcliffe College; President AAUW.

1952 *Margaret Shove Morriss*, Ψ-Goucher, Dean of Pembroke College, Brown University; past president, American Association of University Women.
1952 *Adele Chomeau Starbird*, ΑΕ-Washington Univ., Dean of Women, Washington University.
1953 *Florence Cornell Bingham*, X-Cornell, lecturer, former President of PTA, former President of Delta Gamma.
1953 *Harriet Estabrook O'Shea*, Ω-Wisconsin
1954 *Marjorie Carpenter*, M-Missouri, teacher of humanities at Stephens College.
1956 *Cora Merriman Martin*, ΒΗ-Texas
1956 *Lois Kimball Rosenberry*, Υ-Stanford
1957 *Mary Effie Coleman Marsters*, Θ-Indiana
1957 *Oleda Schrottky*, ΑΖ-Lawrence
1962 *Alice Shepard Riggs*, P-Syracuse
1963 *Ruth Dixon Elder*, I-Illinois
1964 *Mary Adeline McKibbin*, M-Missouri, artist, educator
1965 *Dr. Marion Lane Conrow*, ΓΥ-Wichita, educator-missionary.
1968 *Katherine Bazore Gruelle*, E-Ohio State
1968 *Jean Hitchcock Baer*, N-Idaho
1972 *Elizabeth Ball Carr*, ΑΙ-Oklahoma

GOVERNMENT
1952 *Ruth Bryan Rohde*, K-Nebraska, diplomat, congresswoman, author, lecturer.
1970 *Patricia Reilly Hitt*, ΑΝ-USC

HUMANITARIANISM
1964 *Sylvia Hunt Nickoloff*, ΑΖ-Lawrence
1966 *Elizabeth Earhart Kennedy*, Ξ-Michigan

JOURNALISM
1953 *Inez Calloway Robb*, N-Idaho, reporter and columnist.
1953 *Margaret Aitken*, ΑΓ-Toronto, reporter and columnist, member of Canadian Parliament.
1962 *Gwen Dew Buchanan*, Z-Albion

LAW
1961 *Marguerite Raider Gariepy*, Σ-Northwestern

LITERATURE, SCIENCE AND ARTS
1953 *Elsie Singmaster Lewars*, X-Cornell, author
1953 *Audrey Wurdemann Auslander*, B-Washington, poet, Pulitzer prize in 1934.
1953 *Amanda Ellis*, ΒΔ-Colorado College, author, professor at Colorado College.
1957 *Mary Elizabeth Tennant*, Φ-Colorado
1960 *Clara Hardin*, Φ-Colorado
1962 *Miriam Clark Potter*, Λ-Minnesota
1962 *Cecilia (Jackie) B. Martin*, P-Syracuse
1963 *Helen Dyer*, Ψ-Goucher
1963 *Viola Graham*, X-Cornell
1964 *Mary Adeline McKibbin*, M-Missouri
1964 *Martha Ferguson McKeown Dana*, ΑΔ-Oregon
1967 *Nan Hayden Agle*, Ψ-Goucher
1967 *Ann Todd Dowden*, Φ-Colorado
1968 *Marica McCann Ely*, Γ-California

1971 *Virginia Rowe Holmes,* X-Cornell
1973 *Ruth Starkey Duncan,* ΑΙ-Oklahoma, artist
1973 *Elizabeth Davies Gould,* Ξ-Michigan, pianist
1973 *Alberta Pierson Hannum,* E-Ohio State, authoress

NATIONAL CLUBS PRESIDENTS
1953 *Judge Sarah Tilghman Hughes,* Ψ-Goucher, past president of Business and Professional Women's Clubs.
1953 *Lavina White,* ΒΔ-Colorado College, president of American Society of Medical Technicians.
1953 *Gratia Countryman,* Λ-Minnesota, president of American Library Association, Librarian of City of Minneapolis for 40 years.
1956 *Helen Russell Byars,* M-Missouri
1961 *Lucille Refshauge,* K-Nebraska
1963 *Margaret Long Arnold,* P-Syracuse
1964 *Annie Laurie Peeler,* ΒΘ-Duke, medical technologist
1973 *Dorothy Betts Marvin,* ΑΠ-Arizona

SOCIAL SERVICE
1952 *Edith Abbott,* K-Nebraska, social worker, professor and Dean Emeritus of School of Social Service Administration, University of Chicago.
1961 *Murdoch Sisters (Charlotte, Agnes, Margaret, and Mary,* all Ψ-Goucher), missionaries.
1970 *Virginia Smith Boyce,* ΓΩ-St. Lawrence

RADIO, TELEVISION, THEATRE
1952 *Virginia Sale Wren,* I-Illinois, American characterizations.
1959 *Cheryl A. Crawford,* H-Akron
1962 *Eva Marie Saint,* ΒΜ-Bowling Green, actress.
1966 *Martha Scott,* Ξ-Michigan, actress.

Delta Gamma Shield Award

This award was created in 1963 to honor those Delta Gammas who have achieved distinction in their fields and are held in high public esteem in their community and state.

Nina McGinnies Ancona, Φ-Colorado, 1966 — Musician
Margaret Wier Andrekson, ΒΒ-Alberta, 1970 — Civic and Community Leader
Jane Heiser Baker, P-Syracuse, 1972—Volunteer Service with Blind
Pearl Base, ΑΔ-Oregon, 1968—Banking
Mildred Moyer Baynard, K-Nebraska, 1973 — Civic and Community Leader
Florence Wilcoxson Berchtold, Σ-Northwestern, 1973—Civic and Community Leader
Dorothy Maywood Bird, Z-Albion, 1967—Education-Author

Marian Ellis Brenneman, P-Syracuse, 1963 — Education
Dr. Elizabeth Brown, ΑΧ-Penn State, 1965 — Medicine
Elizabeth Burgess, Ξ-Michigan, 1965 — Social Welfare
Carolyn Stuhler Carter, T-Iowa, 1965 — Clubwoman
Bettina Barrett Chapman, P-Syracuse, 1967 — Artist
Ruth Maurine Clow, ΑΘ-North Dakota, 1972 — Education
Carolyn Benton Cockefair, M-Missouri, 1963 — Education
Hope McMillan Corey, B-Washington, 1973 — Civic and Community Leader
Catherine Palmer Craig, ΑΞ-West Virginia, 1963 —Clubwoman
Molly Hunter Dobson, Ξ-Michigan, 1971—Civic and Community Leader
Carolyn Cray Donaldson, Θ-Indiana, 1971—Social Welfare
Margaret Steele English, Θ-Indiana, 1965—Clubwoman
Margarita Espinosa, Υ-Stanford, 1970—Education
Madeline Graf Ettl, Θ-Indiana, 1969—Law
Margaret Walz Evenson, B-Washington, 1969 — Civic and Community Leader
Ruth Garvey Fink, I-Illinois, 1970 — Civic and Community Leader
Luella Wheeler Finlinson, ΒΓ-Utah, 1971 — Church and Civic Affairs
Dr. Mona Fletcher, ΓΕ-Kent State, 1963—Education-Political Science
Hope Halladay Flynn, Ξ-Michigan, 1967 — Musician
Janet Edmiston Folsom, K-Nebraska, 1964 — Community Service
Roberta Foote, Z-Albion, 1964—Public Health
Patricia Bailey Gilbert, ΑΕ-Washington Univ., 1970—Civic Leader
Dr. Kathryn Heath, ΒΕ-American, 1960—Government-Education
Helen Welborn Hobart, ΓΠ-Roanoke, 1967—Education
Helen Doswell Hobbs, Θ-Indiana, 1969 — Civic Leader
Harriet Crawford Janney, Σ-Northwestern, 1970 —Social Welfare
Metta McDaniels Johnson, B-Washington, 1966—Scientist
Marjorie Macklem Jones, B-Washington, 1972 — Health and Social Welfare Volunteer Service
Dr. Miriam Eubank Jones, M-Missouri, 1971 — Medicine
Dr. Louise O. Kappes, Σ-Northwestern, 1970 — Medicine
Lois Peterson Keller, Θ-Indiana, 1970 — Theatre Arts
Maurine Fulmer Kennedy, H-Akron, 1973—Civic and Community Leader
Betty McClintock Kirby, Υ-Stanford, 1969—Civic and Community Leader
Adele Klumb, ΑΖ-Lawrence, 1963—Education
Elizabeth Stupp Kohl, ΑΕ-Washington Univ., 1969—Civic and Community Leader
Elizabeth Bollman Kummer, Λ-Minnesota, 1968 —Education

Susan Pain La Bahn, Φ-Colorado, 1966 — Social Welfare

Theo Cobb Landon, AK-Washburn, 1970—Civic Affairs

Betsy Greer Lane, AΦ-British Columbia, 1970—Civic and Government Affairs

Ruth Neal Leckie, Ψ-Goucher, 1972—Civic and Scouting Leader

Beverley Cunningham Lecky, AΦ-British Columbia, 1970—Civic and Government Affairs

Micaela Bidegaray Mathiesen, ΓΛ-Fresno, 1966 —Education-Social Welfare

June Harrison Mayer, AI-Oklahoma, 1967—Civic Leader

Marian Young Meditch, Σ-Northwestern, 1973— Civic Leader

Florence Terry Mercer, O-Adelphi, 1964—Education

Kathleen Carpenter Milliken, Ξ-Michigan, 1967— Social Welfare

Carolyn Coffman Moorman, AO-Miami Univ., 1971—Business and Civic Leader

Elizabeth Hoddick Morrison, P-Syracuse, 1970— Vocational Rehabilitation

Jackie White Nokes, AΣ-UCLA, 1973 — Radio/ Television

June Dunham Norris, Θ-Indiana, 1973 — Civic Leader

Ragnhild Christensen O'Donoghue, T-Iowa, 1964 —Civic Leader

Mildred Schwieder Pelzel, M-Missouri, 1973 — Artist

Julia Hoover Peterson, N-Idaho, 1967 — Social Welfare for the Visually Handicapped

Helen Peppard Quail, AK-Washburn, 1970—Education

Eleanor Richmond, AΨ-Mississippi, 1964—Education

Bessie Keernan Roberts (posthumous), Θ-Indiana, 1965—Journalism

Helen Shaffer Robertson, H-Akron, 1971—Civic Leader and Philanthropist

Elizabeth Jameson Rockey, AΛ-Drake, 1965 — Civic Leader

Martha Giltner Rounds, AO-Miami Univ., 1973— Education

Marguerite McGown Savage, M-Missouri, 1968— Journalism

Martha Steed Seaman, AO-Miami Univ., 1973— Civic Leader

Louise Kittell Schnatterly, AK-Washburn, 1972— Church and Civic Leader

Grace Montgomery Showalter, Θ-Indiana, 1967— Civic Leader

Ruth French Shriver, Ψ-Goucher, 1970 — Civic Leader

Ruth Alwyn Bragdon Slayden, B-Washington, 1971—Civic and Scouting Leader

Helen Bing Smith, AP-Ohio Wesleyan, 1964 — Civic Leader in Sight Conservation

Jane Knauss Stevens, X-Cornell, 1967 — Civic Leader

Ann E. Sumner, AΣ-UCLA, 1965—Journalism

Edith Wood Swanson, AZ-Lawrence, 1965—Vocational Guidance

Lulu Allt Stronge Tarbert, X-Cornell, 1966— Social Welfare for Visually Handicapped

Lois Keener Thome, AN-USC, 1970 — Social Welfare

Virginia Melick Turner, AB-Swarthmore, 1970— Civic and Community Leader

Winifred Wood Updike, AZ-Lawrence, 1970— Scientist

Bess Christine Dodson Walt, K-Nebraska, 1964— Author-Clubwoman

Aline F. Hollopeter Ward, P-Syracuse, 1966 — Government

Anita Smith Ward, E-Ohio State, 1973—Education

Barbara Whitley, BA-McGill, 1964—Civic Leader

Dorothy Knight Wildasin, AO-Miami Univ., 1966 —Clubwoman-Volunteer Service for Visually Handicapped

Irene L. Willson, H-Akron, 1966—Education

Kathryn Shea Wilson, Σ-Northwestern, 1969 — Business and Civic Leader

Delta Gamma Cable Award

The Cable Award was established in 1963 to give recognition to those Delta Gammas who had contributed in some immeasurable way to their Fraternity. Nominations are made by local chapters and approved by the Province Alumnae Chairman, and the presentation is made at Founders Day or another suitable time.

Josephine Breckinridge Adams, N-Idaho, 1968

Ethel Clapsaddle Aiken, BΛ-Gettysburg, 1967

Martha Arant Allgood, AΨ-Mississippi, 1969

Jean Swarr Andersen, K-Nebraska, 1973

Chiane Gerow Anderson, AΔ-Oregon, 1967

Helen Bradford Anderson, M-Missouri, 1964

Jean Verbarg Anderson, AE-Washington Univ., 1967

June Day Anderson, B-Washington, 1968

Valerie Himbert Ard (posthumous), ΓZ-LSU, 1972

Margaret Widner Andrews, BΥ-Oregon State, 1973

Carolyn Rea Ashcroft, AΥ-SMU, 1967

Ruth Mary Baldwin Atchison, Z-Albion, 1972

Marion Elizabeth Smith Aube, O-Adelphi, 1973

Bessie Wilde Bailly, Π-Montana, 1971

Lucille Carroll Ballinger, AP-Ohio Wesleyan, 1965

Martha Jane Estes Baker, M-Missouri, 1966

Virginia Dorsey Baker, Γ-California, 1972

Era Godfrey Banks, AΔ-Oregon, 1973

Betty Ramage Barker, AH-Whitman, 1972

Harriet Tuttle Barker, H-Akron, 1972

Ruth McRoberts Barnett, N-Idaho, 1973

Ruth Jones Barricklow, E-Ohio State, 1969

Phoebe Ann Thompson Bass, B-Washington, 1971

Mildred Moyer Baynard, K-Nebraska, 1964

Marella Quant Bell, Z-Albion, 1972

Grace Conner Beatty, AΠ-Arizona, 1972

Martha Gene Perkinson Beaty, AΥ-SMU, 1973

Carol Swisher Bigelow, BZ-Denison, 1971

Lilian Levermore Billman, O-Adelphi, 1964

Dorothy Kelsey Bise, B-Washington, 1968

Gloria Schnaiter Blake, Θ-Indiana, 1969

Florence Lund Black, AZ-Lawrence, 1969

Gertrude Leech Bliss, Z-Albion, 1973
Marion Dankworth Bobey, E-Ohio State, 1972
Elizabeth Seitz Bohren, AZ-Lawrence, 1966
Margaret Lee Carter Bolyard, AΞ-West Virginia, 1971
May Elliott Bostwick, B-Washington, 1967
Jane Richmond Bowers, BΣ-Maryland, 1971
Leah Kunsman Bradstock, ΓE-Kent, 1972
Marie Ryan Bremner, ΓK-Santa Barbara, 1967
Eunice Blaney Bracken, B-Washington, 1964
Virginia Eaton Brand, Ψ-Goucher, 1963
Marion Ellis Brenneman, P-Syracuse 1972
Dorothy Hunter Brentlinger, Λ-Minnesota, 1973
Jean Wilson Brown, Φ-Colorado, 1972
Jeane De Garmo Brown, BZ-Denison, 1973
Kathryn Ann Lynch Brown, Φ-Colorado, 1971
Louise Hubbell Brown, P-Syracuse, 1963
Elizabeth Ray Browne, E-Ohio State, 1966
Poiteaux Halstead Browne, M-Missouri, 1971
Icle Mussellman Brune, BK-Kansas, 1972
Virginia Block Buckley, ΓE-Kent, 1970
Mildred Elgin Bumphrey, ΓE-Kent, 1972
Lauraine Trotman Burleson, AΥ-SMU, 1970
Phoebe Rowe Burt, E-Ohio State, 1968
Bernice Judson Campbell, B-Washington, 1965
Dr. Marie Stanbery Carson, AΥ-SMU, 1963
Dorothy Scotton Cash, AΔ-Oregon, 1964
Kathryn Klaesson Cavanaugh, Ω-Wisconsin, 1965
Vera Morris Chapman, ΓE-Kent, 1972
Louise Brown Christianson, Λ-Minnesota, 1967
Eleanor Mueller Churchman, AT-Butler, 1973
Beulah Waltemate Clark, Π-Montana, 1965
Mary Clerin, AΔ-Oregon, 1964
Margaret Shreve Conn, AΠ-Arizona, 1972
Louise McComb Conrad, AI-Oklahoma, 1967
Kathryn Kidd Cornell, Λ-Minnesota, 1968
Marjorie Conrad Cotton, AΔ-Drake, 1968
Nellie Bly Cotton, BK-Kansas, 1972
Samantha Ford Cox, M-Missouri, 1965
Marian McGirr Cragin, B-Washington, 1973
Edith Kalny Crist, AΔ-Drake, 1972
Frances Garrett Crotty, BE-American, 1970
Mary Jean Stewart Daneke, AK-Washburn, 1973
Sara Simmons Davidson, AΨ-Mississippi, 1968
Betty Drummond Davis, AO-Miami Univ., 1973
Susan Marris Davison, AΔ-Drake, 1972
Dorothy Johnson Davison, AΔ-Drake, 1966
Roberta Gibson Denman, AK-Washburn, 1971
Gloria Gray Deuben, T-Iowa, 1971
Elizabeth Dorman Diehl, Σ-Northwestern, 1973
Geri Reswick Dines, B-Washington, 1972
Jennie Huggins Doran, AΔ-Oregon, 1967
Irene Bates Bonnett Dorris, Υ-Stanford, 1971
Mary Jean Elder Downing, AΔ-Drake, 1967
Gertrude Brown Drake, I-Illinois, 1963
Genevieve Thornley Draper, Υ-Sanford, 1966
Virginia Tibbals Drusendahl, AO-Miami Univ., 1969
Patricia Ferguson Dunbar, AT-Butler, 1973
Dorothy Luedke Dunn, Ω-Wisconsin, 1972
Elizabeth Wright Ebers, K-Nebraska, 1967
Florence Whitcomb Ebersold, E-Ohio State, 1970
Rosa Warner Egan, Ω-Wisconsin, 1972
Lena Boyd Ellington, AΨ-Mississippi, 1967
Marli Rossiter Eilers, AE-Washington Univ., 1972
Martha Stone Evans, AE-Washington Univ., 1967
Helen Dean Ewbank, Z-Albion, 1968
Martha Hunter Farrell, Ψ-Goucher, 1968

Elizabeth Keller Felton, AI-Oklahoma, 1966
Marjorie France Fessenden, H-Akron, 1972
Ruth Garvey Fink, I-Illinois, 1965
Margaret Button Finkenauer, X-Cornell, 1972
Carol Murphy Fleisher, Ξ-Michigan, 1973
Catherine Fleming, AΥ-SMU, 1969
Alice Elgin Fenn, ΓE-Kent, 1973
Marjorie Hahn Fletcher, T-Iowa, 1968
Vivian Whiggam Flickinger, H-Akron, 1969
Martha Forsythe, E-Ohio State, 1969
Violet Walgren Forsythe, BZ-Denison, 1972
Gladys Hutchins Foster, AI-Oklahoma, 1967
Mary Beall Sheridan Franklin, I-Illinois, 1971
Ellen Cunningham Freese, AI-Oklahoma, 1972
Mary Percival French, M-Missouri, 1964
Sharon Standish Frost, AK-Washburn, 1970
Elizabeth Gardner, AH-Whitman, 1971
Olive White Garvey, AK-Washburn, 1965
Betty James Gegenheimer, E-Ohio State, 1973
Sybil Pettus Gibbons, AΨ-Mississippi, 1963
Barbara Scholes Gibson, AX-Penn State, 1973
Patricia Bailey Gilbert, AE-Washington Univ., 1966
Ludi Mai Sensabaugh Goode, AΥ-SMU, 1967
Elizabeth Needham Graham, Ξ-Michigan, 1968
Marjorie Parmelee Green, ΓE-Kent, 1972
Pauline Stowell Greenwood, AK-Washburn, 1967
Mary Catherine Gregg, BΔ-Colorado College, 1967
Winifred Wright Geyer, BE-American, 1973
Rosemary M. Grieg, Γ-California, 1972
Mary Frances Cornell Grubbs, Θ-Indiana, 1967
Emma Wilhelm Gruenwald, AΩ-Arkansas, 1964
Betty DeMotte Guppy, ΓH-San Jose, 1967
Mary Onstad Hecker, Z-Albion, 1968
Marion Dwight Hall, Υ-Stanford, 1970
Elizabeth Cushman Hamlin, BΥ-Oregon State, 1971
Edith Hammond, AE-Washington Univ., 1964
Evelyn Deering Hair, BH-Texas, 1969
Frances Coryell Harris, K-Nebraska, 1972
Jean Fraser Hart, Ψ-Goucher, 1969
Margaret E. Hartley, Θ-Indiana, 1972
Margaret Bostian Havekorst, M-Missouri, 1972
Carolyn Sawyer Havens, E-Ohio State, 1973
Carol Williams Hawk, E-Ohio State, 1970
Jacquelin Buchenau Hawkins, Φ-Colorado, 1973
Margaret Richardson Hay, Υ-Stanford, 1965
Virginia Wigley Hazlett, H-Akron, 1969
Fanny Alexander Hecker, M-Missouri, 1963
Dorothy Kremer Heideman, AE-Washington Univ., 1972
Elma Brock Hendrickson, AI-Oklahoma, 1970
Shirley Hintzelmann Herron, BZ-Denison, 1971
Helen Tophoy Henry, AΠ-Arizona, 1966
Jeanne Andross Hexberg, Γ-California, 1972
Grace Griffin Hodnett, BΨ-Alabama, 1966
Mary Crocker Hoffman, M-Missouri, 1965
Marcia Wright Holmer, AΔ-Oregon, 1973
Elizabeth Boynton Holmes, AΔ-Oregon, 1970
Mary Welshaus Hood, AΞ-West Virginia, 1968
Grace Bull Hooten, AΠ-Arizona, 1973
Jane Gray Houston, AN-USC, 1969
Veramina Lewis Houston, M-Missouri, 1963
Virginia Munn Howard, Λ-Minnesota, 1969
Elizabeth Weaver Hull, BΛ-Gettysburg, 1969
Hilda Humphreys, AT-Butler, 1968
Elizabeth Cather Ickis, Φ-Colorado, 1968

Katherine Fulkerson Jakosky, BK-Kansas, 1965
Ida Pearl Oberg Jeffers, Φ-Colorado, 1970
Betty Lee Winfield Johnston, ΓE-Kent, 1972
Catherine Leavitt Jones, AI-Oklahoma, 1964
Fay Hamilton Jones, Υ-Stanford, 1969
Gertrude Kearns, Θ-Indiana, 1963
Maurine Fulmer Kennedy, H-Akron, 1971
Lillian Nelson Kent, Θ-Indiana, 1973
Helen Palmer Kettler, BE-American, 1971
Pauline Rector Kidd, AI-Oklahoma, 1966
Elizabeth Mears Kiely, X-Cornell, 1967
Louise Pierce Kierzek, BΥ-Oregon State, 1965
Phyllis Umfreys Kimmel, I-Illinois, 1970
Phyllis Lee Lambeth Kinast, Φ-Colorado, 1967
Irene Ebner Kirkley, Φ-Colorado, 1970
Martha Munz Klein, Λ-Minnesota, 1972
Susan Slocum Klingbiel, Ξ-Michigan, 1970
Elizabeth Coffinberry Kloppenburg,
    Γ-California, 1972
Geraldine Sales Knapp, AΠ-Arizona, 1973
Mary Iredell Knight, H-Akron, 1973
Marjorie Woodhead Kollman, M-Missouri, 1970
Ethel Tukey Korsmeyer, K-Nebraska, 1963
Jane Ellen Steen Kramer, AI-Oklahoma, 1973
Grace Mark Kuphal, Z-Albion, 1967
Lucile Stark Kurtz, Z-Albion, 1973
Betty Morrison Land, Θ-Indiana, 1972
Mary Lillian Newton Landrum, AΨ-Mississippi,
    1971
Harriet Damon Lanzit, AΣ-UCLA, 1964
Louise Bekman Larew, T-Iowa, 1968
Frieda Hildabrandt Latimer (posthumous), ΓΨ-
    Emory, 1973
Mary Sanford Lawry, AΠ-Arizona, 1967
Hazel Walliser Lee, P-Syracuse, 1965
Marianne Hollingsworth Lee, BΘ-Duke, 1973
Kay Blankenship Lemmer, M-Missouri, 1968
Nell Almyra Landham Leonian, AΞ-West
    Virginia, 1967
Edith Dawes Lewis, Π-Montana, 1972
Mildred Hoover Liles, AP-Ohio Wesleyan, 1972
Ardath White Lilystrand, E-Ohio State, 1972
Jane Debandt Lochmoeller, AE-Washington
    Univ., 1968
Mary Elizabeth Leonard Long, AΨ-Mississippi,
    1970
Sally Sheldon Louthan, BΔ-Colorado College,
    1969
Winifred Lovejoy, B-Washington, 1967
Margaret Clark Luikart, AP-Ohio Wesleyan,
    1972
Mabel Lyden, Π-Montana, 1964
Marguerite A. Lyden, Π-Montana, 1964
Phyllis Dunn MacKinnon, Ξ-Michigan, 1964
Ada Goldsmith Malone, AM-Beloit, 1965
Carol McNierney Malone, Θ-Indiana, 1972
Mary Lou Willoughby Mann, Ξ-Michigan, 1964
Gertrude Nance Marthens, Φ-Colorado, 1968
Virginia Gard Mastio, BK-Kansas, 1970
Florence Hinshaw Maxwell, AT-Butler, 1969
Jessie Stewart McConahay, BΥ-Utah, 1969
Kathleen Jesse McCormack, AΔ-Oregon, 1966
Esther Dangerfield McCullough, AK-Washburn,
    1969
Emma Jean Provost McDermott, AI-Oklahoma,
    1965
Galie McDougall, I-Illinois, 1973
Clayone Johnson McElhaney, Z-Albion, 1968

Veneta Slack McFarland, ΓΓ-Texas Western,
    1972
Helen Wheeler McKenzie, N-Idaho, 1972
Lucia Fryer McKenzie, B-Washington, 1968
Virginia Hunt McKinley, K-Nebraska, 1967
Jody Slack McLernon, AI-Oklahoma, 1966
Jeanette Bartell McNierney, Θ-Indiana, 1972
Carol Forester McSweeny, AE-Washington Univ.,
    1971
Janet McTavish, AΦ-British Columbia, 1965
Eloise Eicholz McWhirter, BΨ-Alabama, 1966
Rae Ferrell Meacham, AI-Oklahoma, 1967
Isabelle Wiese Middleton, AN-USC, 1967
Georgene Kuhn Miller, AP-Ohio Wesleyan, 1966
Dorothy Riley Milne, AΠ-Arizona, 1966
Elizabeth McDonald Minkler, BΔ-Colorado
    College, 1965
Elizabeth French Moore, AΩ-Arkansas, 1966
Jean Powlesland Moore, P-Syracuse, 1973
Katherine McAuliffe Moore, Z-Albion, 1968
Ruth Roberts Moreland, AΞ-West Virginia, 1965
Muriel Ball Morgan, AΘ-North Dakota, 1972
Margaret Purdy Moyer, Z-Albion, 1963
Mary Mahin Moyers, AK-Washburn, 1964
Katherine Sheldon Mudgett, Υ-Stanford, 1968
Barbara Ann Frey Mueller, Ξ-Michigan, 1969
Nancy McLynn Munson, AΔ-Oregon, 1968
Comora MacGregor Nash, BK-Kansas, 1970
Jean Coffman Neal, AK-Washburn, 1971
Helen Dutton Newcomb, AN-USC, 1973
Alice Park Newman, Λ-Minnesota, 1965
Jean Coffman Nisbet, B-Washington, 1971
Betty Beach Norris, BK-Kansas, 1972
Emily Carter Norton, AΞ-West Virginia, 1964
Mildred Caroline Kelly Olausen, AI-Oklahoma,
    1970
Jane Walker O'Neil, B-Washington, 1973
Phyllis Cossar Oulie, AN-USC, 1967
Marion Spratt Palmer, BΓ-Utah, 1969
Caroline J. Pardee, H-Akron, 1966
Isabella Price Parker, B-Washington, 1965
Berenice Livingston Paul, Γ-California, 1965
Marjorie Helen Snyder Peabody, BZ-Denison,
    1971
Ruth Grant Pearson, B-Washington, 1968
Dorothy Cattle Peery, K-Nebraska, 1968
Carlen Quarnberg Penfold, Φ-Colorado, 1969
Dorothy Stanley Pennington, I-Illinois, 1969
Phoebe Thelmer Chapman Perkins,
    Σ-Northwestern, 1967
Eleanor Short Peterson, H-Akron, 1970
Elizabeth Westin Pew, X-Cornell, 1966
Ruth Elizabeth Mason Pitkin, H-Akron, 1969
Jane McDonald Price, AΥ-SMU, 1973
Polly Thomas Price, N-Idaho, 1968
Helen Curtis Pohlman, AΞ-West Virginia, 1971
Margaret Tindall Pyle, AΣ-UCLA, 1972
Katherine Holbrook Ramsey, AX-Penn State, 1967
Sally Peterson Ravensburg, Θ-Indiana, 1973
Elizabeth Buckley Rea, Ω-Wisconsin, 1964
Margaret Robinson Regan, BΓ-Utah, 1969
Muriel Ansley Reynolds, AΣ-UCLA, 1965
Nettie Porter Reynolds, Π-Montana, 1971
Patricia Hegman Rhodes, Λ-Minnesota, 1972
Eleanor Gay Ribar, Φ-Colorado, 1966
Esther McRoberts Richter, N-Idaho, 1970
Marilyn McClintock Riddel, BM-Bowling Green,
    1968

Lauran Krudop Riley, BΨ-Alabama, 1966
Marion Prescott Ritner, Π-Montana, 1973
Kathryn Maple Roberts, AH-Whitman, 1971
Ruth McCoy Rockhold, AK-Washburn, 1970
Nancy Spencer Rudloff, AX-Penn State, 1972
Ruth Frances Utz Russell, AP-Ohio Wesleyan, 1966
Eva Williams Sackett, Φ-Colorado, 1963
Ruth Antick Sadler, Σ-Northwestern, 1973
Ruth Ross Sager, P-Syracuse, 1972
Frances McLaughlin Savory, ΓΛ-Fresno, 1972
Virginia Reed Scott, AE-Washington Univ., 1973
Vera Schmidt Schrader, X-Cornell, 1971
Martha Schultz, K-Nebraska, 1965
Sally Niehaus Shaefer, Φ-Colorado, 1968
Mary Kay McLain Shaw, AP-Ohio Wesleyan, 1972
Sarah Mae Addleman Shenk, AΔ-Oregon, 1966
Barbara Rivet Shoemaker, AM-Beloit, 1967
Ruth French Shriver, Ψ-Goucher, 1967
Jane Crawford Simons, AΣ-UCLA, 1972
Marilyn Young Sims, P-Syracuse, 1972
Nancy Jean Wedemeyer Sippel, BΞ-Michigan State, 1973
Eloise vanDiest Skilling, BΔ-Colorado College, 1970
Helen Roling Slaughter, BH-Texas, 1964
Eleanor Meck Smith, AP-Ohio Wesleyan, 1971
Elroy Scruggs Smith (posthumous), Σ-Northwestern, 1972
Florence Nippert Smith, Λ-Minnesota, 1970
Gloria Brittain Smith, AO-Miami Univ., 1966
Dr. Helen G. Smith, BΩ-Washington State, 1967
Ruth Graham Smith, E-Ohio State, 1967
Gertrude Smith Solms, Ξ-Michigan, 1970
Amy Lou Ware Spencer, AΔ-Oregon, 1973
Helen Fuller Spencer, E-Ohio State, 1971
Jean Slemmons Spencer, T-Iowa, 1968
Delores Goreham Staples, AΛ-Drake, 1972
Esther Bolles Starks, Φ-Colorado, 1973
Dorothy Roushall Starr, ΓΛ-Fresno, 1972
Ann Robinson Stausebach, P-Syracuse, 1972
Virginia Hardin Stearns, Φ-Colorado, 1970
Marion Chesnut Steinmeyer, AI-Oklahoma, 1972
Isabel Worley Stelzner, Φ-Colorado, 1970
Dorothy Kramer Stephan, E-Ohio State, 1969
Arlen Kelly St. John, BΣ-Maryland, 1971
Virginia Denning Stilson, BZ-Denison, 1972
Araminta McGinnis Straight, AP-Ohio Wesleyan, 1969
Jeanne Catlett Strong, Φ-Colorado, 1973
Helen Catherine Davis Stuart, K-Nebraska, 1969
Janet Lau Sullivan, K-Nebraska, 1971
Shirley Dancey Swancutt, Z-Albion, 1972
Mary Myer Tobin, E-Ohio State, 1969
Barbara Gleason Taggart, ΓM-Florida State, 1973
Ann Luedeking Taylor, BI-Purdue, 1973
Clem Cameron Taylor, AΔ-Oregon, 1967
Patty Buter Taylor, Z-Albion, 1965
Virginia Leudemann Terry, O-Adelphi, 1968
Frances McCormack Tierney, AH-Whitman, 1966
Marguerite Clark Tinsley, Σ-Northwestern, 1970
Pauline Perry Titus, BZ-Denison, 1973
Mae Brown Tompkins, T-Stanford, 1964
Nan Ritzhaupt Trimble, BM-Bowling Green, 1970
Helen Riley Trumbull, AΨ-Mississippi, 1971
Judith Harris Turbeville, ΓΠ-Roanoke, 1972
Frances Doan Turner, AΠ-Arizona, 1968

Frances Jean Robinson Turner, I-Illinois, 1973
Hildegarde Weisberg Turner, Π-Montana, 1973
Virginia Cory Tuten, AP-Ohio Wesleyan, 1973
Loretta June Mangel Vance, BΓ-Utah, 1969
Jean Witmer Vane, T-Iowa, 1968
Frances Boldman VanEps, K-Nebraska, 1965
Virginia Gaddis VanVliet, AΔ-Oregon, 1972
Marlene McCoy Vogelsang, AN-USC, 1969
Charleen Dabbs Wadleigh, AT-Butler, 1973
Katherine McCrosky Wait, B-Washington, 1971
Harriet Gordon Wakefield, AH-Whitman, 1971
Martha Ringel Walker, AΞ-West Virginia, 1971
Edna Abell Wallingford, AK-Washburn, 1968
Lucille Ingram Walton, AH-Whitman, 1967
Meredith McCaw Warner, AΛ-Drake, 1969
Lyda Olmsted Warnke, Φ-Colorado, 1964
Barbara Turner Washburn, Θ-Indiana, 1971
Marilyn Newell Wearda, AP-Ohio Wesleyan, 1967
Katherine Kennedy Webb, T-Stanford, 1970
Virginia Player Welch, I-Illinois, 1965
Marjorie Shewmaker Wernet, Θ-Indiana, 1967
Oma Juanita Johnson West, BΩ-Washington State, 1970
Alice Bowen Westcott, P-Syracuse, 1965
Lucille Hickman Westfall, AE-Washington Univ,. 1973
Pamela Fraser Wetmore, AΦ-British Columbia, 1972
Ingrid Ann White, AP-Ohio Wesleyan, 1973
Naomi Young White, K-Nebraska, 1970
Helen Swisher Whinery, T-Iowa, 1966
Harriet Lewis Williams, AΣ-UCLA, 1968
Olive Steinle Witt, AT-Butler, 1973
Deanna Floyd Woodham, BΨ-Alabama, 1965
Josephine Cleaver Woodward, H-Akron, 1973
Mae Pope Worden, Π-Montana, 1967

Collegiate Chapters

**Beta
University of Washington
Seattle, Washington**

Chartered—June 5, 1903
Local petitioning Delta Gamma—Delta Alpha Organized—October, 1900
NPC groups on the campus since 1903—Delta Gamma first to enter.
Housing—Rented, then bought house; present house built in 1936; addition in 1962; capacity 70.

Collegiate Chapters

Gamma
University of California
Berkeley, California

Chartered—April 12, 1907
Local petitioning Delta Gamma—Pie Del Monte, first woman's house club at California. *Organized*—May, 1900
NPC groups on the campus since 1880—Delta Gamma eighth to enter.
Housing—Present house built in 1914; additions in 1930, 1937, 1958; capacity 62.

Epsilon
Ohio State University
Columbus, Ohio

Chartered—March 17, 1911
  Local petitioning Delta Gamma, organized—1909
NPC groups on the campus since 1888—Delta Gamma fifth to enter.
Housing—Present house built in 1939; addition in 1956; capacity 32.

Zeta
Albion College
Albion, Michigan

Chartered—1883 (Original charter was stolen 10 years later and was replaced by the Grand Council without exact date)
NPC groups on the campus since 1883—Delta Gamma the first to enter.
Housing—Operated first Delta Gamma chapter house, 1889; lodge built in 1896; new lodge built in 1966.

Eta
University of Akron
Akron, Ohio

Chartered—March 15, 1879
Group of friends contacted Mother Chapter to establish a Northern Chapter.
NPC groups on the campus since 1877—Delta Gamma second to enter.
Housing—Rented lodge; bought lodge in 1942; new lodge built in 1971.

Theta
Indiana University
Bloomington, Indiana

Chartered—December 10, 1898
Local petitioning Delta Gamma—never named. *Organized*—1898
NPC groups on the campus since 1870 — Delta Gamma fourth to enter.
Housing—Rented and moved many times; present house built 1925-26; additions in 1949 and 1960; capacity 75.

Iota
University of Illinois
Urbana, Illinois

Chartered—May 12, 1906
Local petitioning Delta Gamma—Zeta Nu. *Organized*—April, 1905
NPC groups on campus since 1875—Delta Gamma eighth to enter.
Housing—First house rented; present house purchased in 1916; rebuilt in 1936; capacity 48.

Kappa
University of Nebraska
Lincoln, Nebraska

Chartered—October 19, 1888
Local petitioning Delta Gamma—never named.
NPC groups on the campus since 1884 — Delta Gamma third to enter.
Housing—Had various houses until present house was built in 1926; addition in 1960; capacity 53.

Lambda
University of Minnesota
Minneapolis, Minnesota

Chartered—December 18, 1883
NPC groups on the campus since 1880 — Delta Gamma second to enter.
Housing—Rented first sorority house on campus; built present house in 1917 on "Lot 1, Block 1, St. Anthony Falls, the first recorded lot in Minneapolis;" house remodeled in 1949; addition in 1962; remodeled in 1965; capacity 32.

Mu
University of Missouri
Columbia, Missouri

Chartered—April 15, 1909
Installed—May 9, 1909
Local petitioning Delta Gamma—never named, only goal was Delta Gamma. *Organized*—1908
NPC groups on the campus since 1875 — Delta Gamma fourth to enter.
Housing—Lived in various houses; house burned Christmas, 1934; present house built in 1935; capacity 52.

Nu
University of Idaho
Moscow, Idaho
Chartered—September 16, 1911

Local petitioning Delta Gamma—Beta Sigma *Organized*—1900
NPC groups on the campus since 1909 — Delta Gamma second to enter.
Housing—Present house built in 1920; additions in 1951 and 1958; capacity 52.

Xi
University of Michigan
Ann Arbor, Michigan

Chartered—1885
*Colonized by transfers from Akron, Fannie Mul-
liken and Mary Thompson, 1884-85. Clara
Grover was taken to the 1885 Convention and
initiated there.*
NPC groups on the campus since 1879 — Delta
Gamma second to enter.
Housing—Operated the first sorority house at
Michigan; rented many different houses; built
first house in 1911; present house built in 1958;
capacity 69.

Omicron
Adelphi University
Garden City, New York

Chartered—May 7, 1908
Local petitioning Delta Gamma—Phi Delta Phi
Organized—1903
NPC groups on the campus since 1908 — Delta
Gamma first to enter. (Kappa Kappa Gamma
had been on the campus previous to 1908 but
the chapter had been inactive since 1905.)
Housing—Chapter occupies room in a Panhellenic
building.

Pi
University of Montana
Missoula, Montana

Chartered—September 7, 1911
Local petitioning Delta Gamma — Sigma Tau
Gamma
Organized—1908 (sub rosa), recognized 1909.
NPC groups on the campus since 1909 — Delta
Gamma third to enter.
Housing—Rented for some time; present house
built in 1925; enlarged in 1934; remodeled in
1950; capacity 39.

Rho
Syracuse University
Syracuse, New York

Chartered—May 23, 1901
Local petitioning Delta Gamma—Delta Sigma Phi
Organized—November 28, 1899
NPC groups on the campus since 1872 — Delta
Gamma seventh to enter.
Housing—Rented various houses; bought first
house in 1913; bought present house in 1924;
remodeled in 1941; capacity 33.

Sigma
Northwestern University
Evanston, Illinois

Chartered—March, 1882
*Group of eight desired Delta Gamma chapter,
sent Catherine Stoneman and Lelia Crandon*

*to University of Wisconsin to be initiated by
Omega and returned to initiate others.*
NPC groups on the campus since 1881 — Delta
Gamma second to enter.
Housing—Had first sorority house at Northwest-
ern; owns section in the quadrangle completed
in 1928; enlarged in 1961; capacity 46.

Tau
State University of Iowa
Iowa City, Iowa

Chartered—November 9, 1886
*Local had been approached through correspon-
dence by several nationals, preferred Delta
Gamma.*
Organized—1886
NPC groups on the campus since 1882 — Delta
Gamma third to enter.
Housing—Built first chapter house in 1923; pres-
ent house built in 1966; capacity 46.

Phi
University of Colorado
Boulder, Colorado

Chartered—June 12, 1886
*Group organized itself to be Delta Gamma chap-
ter after correspondence with Omega, then
Grand Chapter.*
NPC groups on the campus since 1884 — Delta
Gamma second to enter.
Housing—Present house purchased in 1908; annex
purchased in 1951; capacity 80.

Chi
Cornell University
Ithaca, New York

Chartered—March 7, 1885
NPC groups on the campus since 1881 — Delta
Gamma third to enter.
Housing—Rented and then purchased house in
1920; present house built in 1940; addition in
1966; capacity 45.

Omega
University of Wisconsin
Madison, Wisconsin

Chartered—1881 (Original charter during pre-
ceding year turned in at end of school year)
*Group organized as Delta Gamma chapter through
Phi Delta Theta contacts.*
NPC groups on the campus since 1875 — Delta
Gamma second to enter.
Housing—Bought first house in 1904; built pres-
ent house in 1926; purchased annex in 1962;
capacity 42.

Collegiate Chapters

Alpha Gamma
University of Toronto
Toronto, Ontario

Chartered—June 26, 1913
Local petitioning Delta Gamma—Sigma Beta Pi
  Organized—1907
NPC groups on the campus since 1887 — Delta
  Gamma fifth to enter.
Housing—Chapter owns house; capacity 9.

Alpha Delta
University of Oregon
Eugene, Oregon

Chartered—October 17, 1913
Local petitioning Delta Gamma—Lambda Rho
  Organized—Fall, 1908, as ΥΧΔ Club, then
  Lambda Rho, December, 1909.
NPC groups on the campus since 1908 — Delta
  Gamma ninth to enter.
Housing—House built in 1928; addition in 1961;
  capacity 60.

Alpha Zeta
Lawrence University
Appleton, Wisconsin

Chartered—September 11, 1915
Local petitioning Delta Gamma—Theta Gamma
  Delta
  Organized—Spring, 1903
NPC groups on the campus since 1908 — Delta
  Gamma third to enter.
Housing—Chapter rents rooms from the University.

Alpha Eta
Whitman College
Walla Walla, Washington

Chartered—September 30, 1916
Local petitioning Delta Gamma—Gamma Kappa
  (earlier the Girls Ministerial Association)
  Organized—1903 (recognized in 1911)
NPC groups on the campus since 1916 — Delta
  Gamma first to enter. (Phi Mu had been on
  the campus previous to 1916 but the chapter
  had been inactive since 1913.)
Housing—Chapter has occupied section of Prentiss Hall since 1924.

Alpha Theta
University of North Dakota
Grand Forks, North Dakota

Chartered—December 16, 1916
Local petitioning Delta Gamma—Beta Gamma Psi
  Organized—1911
NPC groups on the campus since 1911 — Delta
  Gamma third to enter.
Housing—Had house as a local; built present
  house in 1926; addition in 1960; capacity 42.

Alpha Iota
University of Oklahoma
Norman, Oklahoma

Chartered—June 4, 1918
Local petitioning Delta Gamma—Phi Chi
  Organized—Winter, 1915-16
NPC groups on the campus since 1909 — Delta
  Gamma seventh to enter.
Housing—Rented; built present house in 1928;
  addition in 1949; extensive addition and remodeling in 1965; capacity 75.

Alpha Kappa
Washburn University of Topeka
Topeka, Kansas

Chartered—June 9, 1920
Local petitioning Delta Gamma — Kappa Kappa
  Chi
  Organized—November, 1910
NPC groups on the campus since 1914 — Delta
  Gamma third to enter.
Housing—Rented; bought house in 1921; built
  house in 1937—destroyed by tornado in 1966;
  rented house 1966-68; present house purchased
  in 1968; additions in 1969 and 1972; capacity
  23.

Alpha Lambda
Drake University
Des Moines, Iowa

Chartered—April 30, 1921
Local petitioning Delta Gamma—Iota Alpha
  Omega
  Organized—October, 1906
NPC groups on the campus since 1921 — Delta
  Gamma second to enter (simultaneously with
  Kappa Kappa Gamma and Kappa Alpha
  Theta).
Housing — Rented house from the University
  since 1944; now owns house; capacity 40.

Alpha Nu
University of Southern California
Los Angeles, California

Chartered—February 11, 1922
Local petitioning Delta Gamma—Beta Phi
  Organized—1902
NPC groups on the campus since 1922 — Delta
  Gamma first to enter.
Housing—Had house as a local; built house in
  1934; present house built in 1969; capacity 70.

Alpha Xi
West Virginia University
Morgantown, West Virginia

Chartered—February 18, 1922
Local petitioning Delta Gamma — Delta Sigma
  Delta

Organized—February 13, 1919
NPC groups on the campus since 1905 — Delta Gamma fifth to enter.
Housing—Present house built in 1940; addition in 1963; capacity 35.

Alpha Omicron
Miami University
Oxford, Ohio

Chartered—February 2, 1923
Local petitioning Delta Gamma—Beta Phi Sigma
Organized—February, 1920
NPC groups on the campus since 1902 — Delta Gamma fifth to enter.
Housing—Chapter has occupied suite in Hamilton Hall since 1940.

Alpha Pi
University of Arizona
Tucson, Arizona

Chartered—October 7, 1923
Local petitioning Delta Gamma—Alpha Gamma
Organized—March, 1920
NPC groups on the campus since 1917 — Delta Gamma sixth to enter.
Housing—Rented house; present house built in 1928; additions in 1941, 1951, and 1961; capacity 58.

Alpha Rho
Ohio Wesleyan University
Delaware, Ohio

Chartered—May 10, 1924
Local petitioning Delta Gamma—Phi Omega Phi
Organized—1903; off campus 1913-20; reorganized 1920.
NPC groups on the campus since 1880 — Delta Gamma sixth to enter.
Housing—Rented until present lodge was purchased in 1950.

Alpha Sigma
University of California at Los Angeles
Los Angeles, California

Chartered—March 21, 1925
Local petitioning Delta Gamma—Delta Phi
Organized—1919
NPC groups on the campus since 1921 — Delta Gamma twelfth to enter.
Housing—Present house purchased in 1929; addition in 1948 and 1960; capacity 60.

Alpha Tau
Butler University
Indianapolis, Indiana

Chartered—October 3, 1925
Local petitioning Delta Gamma—Sigma Delta
Organized—December, 1922

NPC groups on the campus since 1874 — Delta Gamma sixth to enter.
Housing—Rented; built present house 1935-36; additions in 1948 and 1963; capacity 50.

Alpha Upsilon
Southern Methodist University
Dallas, Texas

Chartered—October 16, 1926
Local petitioning Delta Gamma—Lambda Rho
Organized—1916 as Pickwick Club, then Rannau, 1921, Lambda Rho, 1922.
NPC groups on the campus since 1915 — Delta Gamma seventh to enter.
Housing—Rented; built present house in 1951; capacity 28.

Alpha Phi
University of British Columbia
Vancouver, British Columbia

Chartered—June 14, 1928
Local petitioning Delta Gamma—Theta Epsilon
Organized—November 10, 1919
NPC groups on the campus since 1928 — Delta Gamma second to enter.
Housing—Chapter occupies suite in the Panhellenic Building, built in 1958.

Alpha Chi
Pennsylvania State University
State College, Pennsylvania

Chartered—May 17, 1930
Local petitioning Delta Gamma—La Camaraderie
Organized—November 14, 1922
NPC groups on the campus since 1926 — Delta Gamma fifth to enter.
Housing—Chapter occupies floor and suite in Shulze Hall.

Alpha Psi
University of Mississippi
Oxford, Mississippi

Chartered—May 21, 1927
Alpha Psi's charter was held in abeyance from 1931 until it was reinstated in February, 1938.
NPC groups on the campus since 1899 — Delta Gamma fifth to enter. (An anti-fraternity bill passed in the state in 1912 forced the existing groups on the campus, Chi Omega and Delta Delta Delta, to become inactive until the bill was repealed in January, 1926.)
Housing—Memorial House built in 1937; additions in 1950, 1960, 1964 and 1968; capacity 35.

Alpha Omega
University of Arkansas
Fayetteville, Arkansas

Chartered—October 11, 1930

Collegiate Chapters

Local petitioning Delta Gamma—Delta Beta
  Organized—December, 1925
NPC groups on the campus since 1895 — Delta
  Gamma sixth to enter.
Housing—Present house built in 1941; addition
  in 1960; capacity 75.

Beta Beta
University of Alberta
Edmonton, Alberta

Chartered—May 9, 1931
Local petitioning Delta Gamma—Phi Gamma
  Organized—October, 1928
NPC groups on the campus since 1931 — Delta
  Gamma first to enter.
Housing—Chapter rents house; capacity 9.

Beta Gamma
University of Utah
Salt Lake City, Utah

Chartered—May 7, 1932
Local petitioning Delta Gamma—Gamma Sigma
  Organized—December 27, 1920
NPC groups on the campus since 1914 — Delta
  Gamma seventh to enter.
Housing—House built in 1937; additions in 1951
  and 1964; capacity 19.

Beta Delta
Colorado College
Colorado Springs, Colorado

Chartered—March 29, 1932
Local petitioning Delta Gamma—Minerva Club
  Organized—October 14, 1891
NPC groups on the campus since 1932 — Delta
  Gamma first to enter.
Housing—Present lodge built in 1963.

Beta Epsilon
The American University
Washington, D.C.

Chartered—March 21, 1936
Local petitioning Delta Gamma—Epsilon Kappa
  Organized—November 12, 1929
NPC groups on the campus since 1933 — Delta
  Gamma second to enter.
Housing—Chapter has room in a dormitory.

Beta Zeta
Denison University
Granville, Ohio

Chartered—May 13, 1938
Colonization—formal pledging February 5, 1938
NPC groups on the campus since 1928 — Delta
  Gamma seventh to enter.
Housing—Lodge on land leased from the University; built in 1939; addition in 1963.

Beta Eta
University of Texas
Austin, Texas

Chartered—April 21, 1939
Colonization—Pledged, May 7, 1938
NPC groups on the campus since 1902 — Delta
  Gamma fifteenth to enter.
Housing—Rented; present house built in 1941;
  addition in 1956; extensive remodeling—changing address from one street to around the
  corner—in 1966; capacity 65.

Beta Theta
Duke University
Durham, North Carolina

Chartered—June 1, 1939
Local petitioning Delta Gamma—Delta Chi
  Organized—March 20, 1938
NPC groups on the campus since 1911 — Delta
  Gamma twelfth to enter.
Housing—Rented suite from University; now use
  classrooms for meetings.

Beta Iota
Purdue University
West Lafayette, Indiana

Chartered—February 17, 1940
Local petitioning Delta Gamma—Pedallion
  Organized—1936, for purpose of petitioning
    Delta Gamma.
NPC groups on the campus since 1915 — Delta
  Gamma eighth to enter.
Housing—Present house built in 1958; capacity
  60.

Beta Kappa
University of Kansas
Lawrence, Kansas

Chartered—April 26, 1941
Colonization—October, 1940
NPC groups on the campus since 1873 — Delta
  Gamma tenth to enter.
Housing—House purchased the day of installation
  from a fraternity leaving the campus; capacity
  60.

Beta Lambda
Gettysburg College
Gettysburg, Pennsylvania

Chartered—October 7, 1939
Local petitioning Delta Gamma—Beta Lambda
  Organized—November, 1916
NPC groups on the campus since 1937 — Delta
  Gamma second to enter.
Housing—Chapter rents rooms from the College.

Beta Mu
Bowling Green State University
Bowling Green, Ohio

Chartered—November 6, 1943

Local petitioning Delta Gamma—Skol
   Organized—December 23, 1923
NPC groups on the campus since 1943 — Delta
   Gamma fourth to enter.
Housing—House is owned by the University and
   rented by the chapter; capacity 70.

Beta Nu
Carnegie-Mellon University
Pittsburgh, Pennsylvania

Chartered—January 29, 1944
Local petitioning Delta Gamma—Gamma Phi
   Sigma
   Organized—1934
NPC groups on the campus since 1943 — Delta
   Gamma second to enter.
Housing—Chapter occupies suite in a dormitory.

Beta Xi
Michigan State University
East Lansing, Michigan

Chartered—January 5, 1946
Colonized—June, 1945
NPC groups on the campus since 1921 — Delta
   Gamma fifteenth to enter.
Housing—House built in 1951; capacity 42.

Beta Pi
Willamette University
Salem, Oregon

Chartered—November 10, 1945
Local petitioning Delta Gamma—Delta Phi
   Organized—September, 1920
NPC groups on the campus since 1944 — Delta
   Gamma fourth to enter.
Housing—Owned house as a local; addition in
   1949; present house built in 1966; capacity 48.

Beta Rho
George Washington University
Washington, D.C.

Chartered—October 6, 1945
Local petitioning Delta Gamma—Themian
   Organized—1943
NPC groups on the campus since 1889 — Delta
   Gamma eleventh to enter.
Housing—Chapter rents an apartment.

Beta Sigma
University of Maryland
College Park, Maryland

Chartered—October 13, 1945
Colonized—May-June, 1945
NPC groups on the campus since 1924 — Delta
   Gamma twelfth to enter.
Housing—Rented; present house built in 1962;
   capacity 41.

Beta Tau
University of Miami
Coral Gables, Florida

Chartered—February 16, 1946
Colonized—Spring, 1945
NPC groups on the campus since 1936 — Delta
   Gamma eighth to enter.
Housing—Chapter occupies suite in the Panhel-
   lenic Building, constructed in 1957.

Beta Upsilon
Oregon State University
Corvallis, Oregon

Chartered—April 27, 1946
Colonized—Fall, 1945
NPC groups on the campus since 1915 — Delta
   Gamma fourteenth to enter.
Housing—Lived in former fraternity house; first
   house built in 1950; present house built in
   1969; capacity 60.

Beta Chi
University of Denver
Denver, Colorado

Chartered—September 28, 1946
Colonized—March, 1946
NPC groups on the campus since 1885 — Delta
   Gamma tenth to enter.
Housing—Lodge built in 1949; converted to a
   house with an addition in 1962; capacity 36.

Beta Psi
University of Alabama
Tuscaloosa, Alabama

Chartered—February 8, 1947
Colonized—May, 1946
NPC groups on the campus since 1904 — Delta
   Gamma fifteenth to enter.
Housing—House built in 1951; addition in 1966;
   capacity 44.

Beta Omega
Washington State University
Pullman, Washington

Chartered—November 2, 1946
Colonized—1945
NPC groups on the campus since 1912 — Delta
   Gamma thirteenth to enter.
Housing—House built in 1951; addition and ex-
   tensive remodeling in 1967; capacity 60.

Gamma Alpha
University of Tennessee
Knoxville, Tennessee

Chartered—May 10, 1947

Collegiate Chapters

Colonized—October, 1946
NPC groups on the campus since 1900 — Delta Gamma tenth to enter.
Housing—Chapter occupies a room in the Panhellenic Building, constructed in 1964.

Gamma Beta
University of Tulsa
Tulsa, Oklahoma

Chartered—March 22, 1947
Colonized—October-November, 1946
NPC groups on the campus since 1929 — Delta Gamma sixth to enter.
Housing—Lodge built in 1948; addition in 1965; converted to a house with an addition in 1968; capacity 32.

Gamma Delta
Montana State University
Bozeman, Montana

Chartered—January 31, 1948
Colonized—May, 1947
NPC groups on the campus since 1917 — Delta Gamma sixth to enter.
Housing—Chapter occupies two dormitory sections; capacity 46.

Gamma Epsilon
Kent State University
Kent, Ohio

Chartered—December 6, 1947
Local petitioning Delta Gamma — Sigma Delta Sigma (had previously been Sigma Sigma Sigma, national education sorority, before education groups became affiliated with NPC).
Organized—1924
NPC groups on the campus since 1947 — Delta Gamma fourth to enter.
Housing—Bought house in 1950; capacity 23.

Gamma Zeta
Louisiana State University
Baton Rouge, Louisiana

Chartered—March 20, 1948
Colonized—October, 1947
NPC groups on the campus since 1909 — Delta Gamma fifteenth to enter.
Housing—Occupied room in Panhellenic Building; house built in 1966; capacity 53.

Gamma Eta
California State University, San Jose
San Jose, California

Chartered—February 7, 1948
Local petitioning Delta Gamma—Kappa Society
Organized—1931
NPC groups on the campus since 1948 — Delta

Gamma entered simultaneously with eight other national groups.
Housing—House built in 1948; addition in 1959; capacity 60.

Gamma Theta
University of Florida
Gainesville, Florida

Chartered—April 9, 1949
Colonized—Fall, 1948
NPC groups on the campus since 1948 — Delta Gamma eleventh to enter.
Housing—Rented; built present house in 1952; capacity 38.

Gamma Iota
DePauw University
Greencastle, Indiana

Chartered—December 3, 1949
Colonized—Spring, 1949
NPC groups on the campus since 1870 — Delta Gamma tenth to enter.
Housing—First house purchased in 1949; present house built in 1957; capacity 60.

Gamma Kappa
University of California at Santa Barbara
Goleta, California

Chartered—January 28, 1950
Local petitioning Delta Gamma—Chi Delta Chi
Organized—May 1, 1941
NPC groups on campus since 1950—Delta Gamma seventh to enter.
Housing—Rented; present house built in 1958; capacity 60.

Gamma Lambda
California State University, Fresno
Fresno, California

Chartered—May 5, 1951
Local petitioning Delta Gamma — Omega Xi Omicron
Organized—1918 as Agenda
NPC groups on the campus since 1928 — Delta Gamma second to enter.
Housing—House built in 1962; capacity 42.

Gamma Mu
Florida State University
Tallahassee, Florida

Chartered—September 19, 1951
Colonized—Formal pledging March 5, 1951
NPC groups on the campus since 1904 — Delta Gamma sixteenth to enter.
Housing—Rented house; built present house in 1958; addition in 1966; capacity 48.

Gamma Nu
North Texas State University
Denton, Texas

Chartered—November 22, 1953
Local petitioning Delta Gamma — Phi Gamma Kappa
Organized—February 28, 1949
NPC groups on the campus since 1953 — Delta Gamma third to enter.
Housing—Previously occupied University-owned housing unit; since 1970, chapter occupies section of the College Inn.

Gamma Xi
Texas Tech University
Lubbock, Texas

Chartered—March 6, 1954
Colonized—October, 1953
NPC groups on the campus since 1953 — Delta Gamma sixth to enter.
Housing—Lodge built in 1973.

Gamma Omicron
Indiana State University
Terre Haute, Indiana

Chartered—May 15, 1954
Local petitioning Delta Gamma—Gamma Gamma
Organized—1902
NPC groups on the campus since 1949 — Delta Gamma seventh to enter.
Housing—Chapter has a room in Lincoln Quadrangle.

Gamma Pi
Roanoke College
Salem, Virginia

Chartered—November 5, 1955
Local petitioning Delta Gamma—name unknown
NPC groups on the campus since 1955 — Delta Gamma third to enter.
Housing—Chapter rents a room above the College Infirmary.

Gamma Rho
Wittenberg University
Springfield, Ohio

Chartered—March 10, 1956
Colonized—October 5, 1955
NPC groups on the campus since 1904 — Delta Gamma seventh to enter.
Housing—House built in 1962; capacity 40.

Gamma Sigma
University of Houston
Houston, Texas
Chartered—February 4, 1956
Local petitioning Delta Gamma—Pi Lambda Chi

Organized—1940
NPC groups on the campus since 1956 — Delta Gamma second to enter.
Housing—Chapter rents a lodge.

Gamma Tau
Texas Christian University
Fort Worth, Texas

Chartered—September 29, 1956
Colonized—February 22, 1956
NPC groups on the campus since 1954 — Delta Gamma ninth to enter.
Housing—Chapter occupies section in a University dormitory.

Gamma Upsilon
Wichita State University
Wichita, Kansas

Chartered—February 1, 1958
Local petitioning Delta Gamma — Alpha Tau Sigma
Organized—1909
NPC groups on the campus since 1958 — Delta Gamma first to enter.
Housing—Lodge built in 1941; addition in 1958.

Gamma Phi
Arizona State University
Tempe, Arizona

Chartered—May 10, 1958
Colonized—February, 1958
NPC groups on the campus since 1949 — Delta Gamma ninth to enter.
Housing—Chapter occupies rooms in Palo Verde Main.

Gamma Chi
California State University, Long Beach
Long Beach, California

Chartered—March 7, 1959
Colonized—September 27, 1958
NPC groups on the campus since 1954 — Delta Gamma sixth to enter.
Housing—Six unit apartment building purchased in 1969; capacity 15.

Delta Beta
University of Kentucky
Lexington, Kentucky

Chartered—March 3, 1962
Colonized—September, 1961
NPC groups on the campus since 1908 — Delta Gamma twelfth to enter.
Housing—House built in 1962; capacity 48.

Collegiate Chapters

Delta Epsilon
University of the Pacific
Stockton, California

Chartered—December 4, 1959
Local petitioning Delta Gamma—Epsilon Lambda
  Sigma
  Organized—1858 as Emendia
NPC groups on the campus since 1959 — Delta
  Gamma first to enter.
Housing—Owned house as a local, constructed in
  1924; addition in 1959; capacity 54.

Delta Zeta
Memphis State University
Memphis, Tennessee

Chartered—March 6, 1965
Colonized—April 5, 1964
NPC groups on the campus since 1947 — Delta
  Gamma fifth to enter.
Housing—Chapter occupies suite in the Pan-
  hellenic Building.

Delta Eta
California State University, Sacramento
Sacramento, California

Chartered—November 5, 1966
Local petitioning Delta Gamma — Sigma Alpha
  Sigma
Organized—1954
NPC groups on the campus since 1966 — Delta
  Gamma second to enter.
Housing—Chapter rents an apartment in the Pan-
  hellenic complex.

Delta Theta
Georgia State University
Atlanta, Georgia

Chartered—May 6, 1967
Local petitioning Delta Gamma—Kappa Chi Delta
  Organized—1965
NPC groups on the campus since 1955 — Delta
  Gamma seventh to enter.
Housing—Chapter occupies a room in the Student
  Center.

Delta Iota
University of Georgia
Athens, Georgia

Chartered—February 17, 1968
Colonized—May, 1967
NPC groups on the campus since 1921 — Delta
  Gamma eighteenth to enter.
Housing—House constructed in 1969; capacity 60.

Delta Kappa
University of South Florida
Tampa, Florida

Chartered—February 24, 1968

Local petitioning Delta Gamma—Delta Phi Alpha
  Organized—September 25, 1966
NPC groups on the campus since 1967—Delta
  Gamma fifth to enter.
Housing—Chapter meets in the Student Center.

Delta Lambda
Mississippi State University
Starkville, Mississippi

Chartered—October 25, 1969
Colonized—February, 1969
NPC groups on the campus since 1936 — Delta
  Gamma fifth to enter.
Housing—Chapter occupies suite in Rice Dormi-
  tory.

Delta Mu
Florida Atlantic University
Boca Raton, Florida

Chartered—December 6, 1969
Local petitioning Delta Gamma—Chi Delta
  Organized—January, 1969
NPC groups on the campus since 1969 — Delta
  Gamma entered first, simultaneously with Alpha
  Omicron Pi.
Housing—Chapter occupies a floor in Dorm 21.

Delta Nu
Northern Illinois University
DeKalb, Illinois

Chartered—December 6, 1969
Local petitioning Delta Gamma—Chi Sigma Phi
  Organized—December, 1966
NPC groups on the campus since 1944 — Delta
  Gamma eleventh to enter.
Housing—Rented house as a local; house pur-
  chased by House Corporation when chapter
  was chartered; capacity 58.

Delta Xi
Ball State University
Muncie, Indiana

Chartered—April 11, 1970
Local petitioning Delta Gamma—Sigma Beta Chi
  Organized—January 17, 1966
NPC groups on the campus since 1936 — Delta
  Gamma eleventh to enter.
Housing — Chapter occupies suite in Dehority
  Complex.

Delta Omicron
Morehead State University
Morehead, Kentucky

Chartered—May 9, 1970
Local petitioning Delta Gamma — Alpha Sigma
  Rho
  Organized—May, 1962
NPC groups on the campus since 1969—Delta
  Gamma sixth to enter.
Housing—Chapter occupies floor in Nunn Hall.

Delta Pi
University of Southern Mississippi
Hattiesburg, Mississippi

Chartered—May 1, 1971
Colonized—January, 1970
NPC groups on the campus since 1937 — Delta Gamma ninth to enter.
Housing—Chapter occupies a suite in the Panhellenic Dormitory.

Delta Rho
Virginia Polytechnic Institute and State
University
Blacksburg, Virginia

Chartered—October 16, 1971
Local petitioning Delta Gamma—Delta Rho
Organized—1966
NPC groups on the campus since 1971 — Delta Gamma second to enter.
Housing—Chapter meets in Squires Student Center.

Delta Sigma
Auburn University
Auburn, Alabama

Chartered—May 19, 1972
Colonized—February, 1972
NPC groups on the campus since 1922 — Delta Gamma fourteenth to enter.
Housing — Chapter occupies floor and suite in Elizabeth Harper Hall.

Delta Tau
Missouri Southern State College
Joplin, Missouri

Chartered—November 4, 1972
Local petitioning Delta Gamma—Beta Sigma Chi
Organized—September, 1969
NPC groups on the campus since 1972 — Delta Gamma first to enter.
Housing—Chapter meets in classrooms.

Delta Upsilon
Indiana University-Purdue University at
Fort Wayne
Fort Wayne, Indiana

Chartered—May 12, 1973
Local petitioning Delta Gamma—Alpha Psi Omega
Organized—1966
NPC groups on the campus since 1973 — Delta Gamma first to enter.
Housing—Chapter meets in a campus conference room.

Inactive Chapters

Alpha
Mount Union College
Alliance, Ohio
1882-1908

Delta (I)
Trinity College
Tehuacana, Texas
1880-1881

Delta (II)
Hanover College
Hanover, Indiana
1881-1887

Delta (III)
University of Southern California
Los Angeles, California
1887-1897

Theta (I)
Fairmont College
Monteagle, Tennessee
1877-1880

Theta (II)
Adelbert College
Cleveland, Ohio
1883-1888

Pi (I)
Fulton Synodical College
Fulton, Missouri
1882-1885

Upsilon (I)
Bolivar College
Bolivar, Tennessee
1878-1881

Upsilon (II)
St. Lawrence University
Canton, New York
1884-1887

Upsilon (III)
Stanford University
Palo Alto, California
1897-1944

Phi (I)
Franklin College
Franklin, Indiana
1878-1885

Alumnae Chapters

Chi (I)

Water Valley Seminary
Water Valley, Mississippi
1877-1880

Psi (I)

Lewis School
Oxford, Mississippi
1873-1889

Psi (II)

Goucher College
Baltimore, Maryland
1891-1950

Alpha Beta

Swarthmore College
Swarthmore, Pennsylvania
1912-1934

Alpha Epsilon

Washington University
St. Louis, Missouri
1914-1973
Charter being held in abeyance

Alpha Mu

Beloit College
Beloit, Wisconsin
1922-1963

Beta Alpha

McGill University
Montreal, Quebec
1931-1973

Beta Phi

University of Pennsylvania
Philadelphia, Pennsylvania
1946-1958

Gamma Gamma

Texas Western College
El Paso, Texas
1948-1959

Gamma Psi

Emory University
Atlanta, Georgia
1959-1968

Gamma Omega

St. Lawwrence University
Canton, New York
1960-1970

Delta Alpha

University of New Mexico
Albuquerque, New Mexico
1961-1973
Charter being held in abeyance

Alumnae Chapters

1908	Akron (1888)
1959	Albuquerque (1947)
1964	Ann Arbor (1948)
1947	Appleton (1915)
	Appleton-Fox Valley (since 1968)
1965	Arlington
1954	Atlanta (1947)
1951	Austin (1937)
1915	Baltimore
1962	Bartlesville (1953)
1954	Baton Rouge (1949)
1958	Bellevue-Mercer Island
1923	Berkeley (1914)
	Berkeley-East Bay (since 1962)
1946	Beverly-Westwood (1937)
	Beverly-Westwood-Santa Monica (since 1951)
1953	Birmingham (1950)
1955	Bloomington (1917)
1923	Boise (1919)
1927	Boston (1919)
1956	Boulder (1948)
1963	Bowling Green (1944)
1924	Buffalo
1958	Cedar Rapids (1946)
1970	Central Florida (1953)
1955	Champaign-Urbana (1947)
1951	Charleston, W. Va. (before 1946)
	Chicago Far West Suburban (see Wheaton-Glen Ellyn)
1941	Chicago North Side
	Chicago (since 1968)
1966	Chicago North Suburban (1962)
1964	Chicago Northwest Suburban (1950)
1904-65	Chicago South Side
1953	Chicago South Suburban
1929	Cincinnati (1923)
1972	Clearwater (1959)
1929	Cleveland East (1912)
1955	Cleveland West Shore
1932	Colorado Springs
1955	Columbia Regional (1948)
1922	Columbus (1914)
1972	Columbus Junior
1967	Corpus Christi (1951)
1947	Corvallis
1930	Dallas
1923	Dayton
1910	Denver (1904)
1949	Des Moines (before 1946)
1920	Detroit (1910)
	Dearborn (1953)
	Detroit-Dearborn (1963)
	Detroit West Suburban (since 1973)
1949	Edmonton (before 1946)
1950	El Paso (1947)
1948	Eugene (1946)
1921	Evanston North Shore
1922	Evansville (had been chapter 1912-17)

1952	Fairfield County
1960	Fayetteville (1947)
1953	Fort Lauderdale (1952)
1956	Fort Wayne (1927)
1954	Fort Worth (1937)
1951	Fresno (1948)
1950	Glendale (1939)
1955	Grand Rapids (1950)
	Greater Kansas City (see Kansas City)
	Greater Lansing (see Lansing)
1945-56	Gulf Coast
1949	Helena
1954	Hinsdale-La Grange-Western Springs (1952)
	Hinsdale-La Grange (since 1953)
1942	Houston (1934)
	Houston Central (since 1966)
1966	Houston Memorial
1912	Indianapolis
1972	Indianapolis Junior
1951	Iowa City (1886)
1965	Ithaca (1928)
1954	Jackson, Miss. (1952)
1954	Jacksonville (1951)
1971	Jefferson County
1953-58	Johnson County (1952; see Kansas City)
1972	Joplin Regional (1948)
1922	Kansas City
	Greater Kansas City (since 1958; merger with Johnson County)
1948	Kent
1948	Lafayette, Ind. (1940)
1962	Lake Charles (1950)
1946	Lansing (1918)
	Greater Lansing (since 1960)
1947	Lawrence (1941)
1969	Lexington (1961)
1958	Lincoln
1968	Little Rock (1929-50; chapter 1950-56; reorganized 1958)
1948	Long Beach (before 1946)
1937-64	Long Island (1932)
1949	Long Island North Shore
1909	Los Angeles
1952-65	Los Angeles-Wilshire
1965-69	Los Angeles Westside (1951)
1957	Louisville & Southern Indiana (1951)
	Louisville (since 1962)
1954	Lubbock
1919	Madison
1969	Marin County (1953)
1953	Maryland-Suburban (before 1946)
1961	Memphis (1949)
1926-37	Miami
1945	Miami (reorganized)
1910	Milwaukee
1904	Minneapolis-St. Paul
	Minneapolis (1947)
	Minneapolis-St. Paul (1969)
1937	Missoula
1936-43	Montreal (1932)
1953	Montreal (reorganized)
1948	Morgantown (before 1946)
1965	Moscow (1924)
1972	Nashville (1951; chapter 1953-55)
1951	New Orleans (1950)
1900	New York City
1951	Norman (1950)
1965	North Mississippi
1952	Northeast Mississippi
1953	Northern Virginia (1952)
1937-72	Oak Park-River Forest
1918	Oklahoma City
1947	Omaha (1902)
1951	Orange County (1939)
	Santa Ana-Newport Harbor (since 1957)
1970	Palm Beach County (1962)
1923	Palo Alto
1932	Pasadena
1972	Pasadena Junior
1949	Pasco-Kennewick-Richland
1914	Philadelphia
	Philadelphia Suburban (since 1963)
1948	Phoenix (1920)
1922	Pittsburgh (1908)
1959	Pittsburgh South Hills
1922	Portland
	Portland Suburban (since 1971; merger with Tualatin Valley)
1966	Pullman (1949)
1949	Richmond (1947)
	Riverside (see San Gorgonio)
1972	Roanoke Valley (1956; chapter 1959-61; 1961)
1938	Rochester, N.Y. (1924)
1947-61	Sacramento (Sacramento Valley 1934)
1965	Sacramento (1961)
1914	St. Louis City
1951	St. Louis County
1959	St. Petersburg (1948)
1947	Salem (1938)
1932	Salt Lake City
1950	San Antonio (1938)
1947	San Diego (1927)
1948	San Fernando Valley (1938)
1929	San Francisco
1939	San Francisco (reorganized)
1951	San Gorgonio (1941)
	Riverside (since 1956)
1948	San Jose
1950	San Mateo County (1936-46)
	Santa Ana-Newport Harbor (see Orange County)
1950	Santa Barbara (1950)
1907	Seattle
1955	South Bay (1950-51)
1959	South Bend (before 1946)
	South Bend-Mishawaka (since 1949)
1925	Spokane
1966	State College (1931)
1929	Syracuse
1931	Tacoma
1954	Terre Haute
1922	Toledo
1921	Topeka (1921)
1920	Toronto (1916)
1961	Trenton-Delaware Valley (1953)
1956-71	Tualatin Valley (see Portland)
1947	Tucson (before 1946)
1947	Tulsa (before 1946)
1963	Vancouver, B.C.
1965-67	Vicksburg Area
1937	Walla Walla (1916)
1918	Washington, D.C.

1948	Westchester County (before 1948)
1931	Wichita
1969	Wilmington (1954)
1948	Yakima
1970	Youngstown (1949)

Alumnae Associations

1955-64	Abilene
1950-72	Albany
1900	Albion
1956-59	Alliance
1951-56	Amarillo
1961	Amarillo (reorganized)
1948-73	Ames
1958	Anderson
1967	Athens
1973	Auburn Area
1949-50	Aurora
1951-73	Aurora-Fox Valley
1950	Bakersfield
1958	Battle Creek
1960-61	Beaumont Area
1949-55	Beckley
1923-67	Beloit
1958	Bergen County
1956-71	Billings (chapter 1953-56)
1951	Birmingham, Ala.
1946-50	Bismark
1973	Blacksburg
1950-54	Blytheville
1952-55	Bozeman
1957-58	Bozeman (reorganized)
1965-72	Bozeman (reorganized)
1911-67	Butte (chapter 1947-63)
1972	Calgary (chapter 1956-72)
1946	Canton-Massillon
1958	Carmel Area
1958	Carolina Piedmont
1968-71	Central Brevard
1942-44	Central New Jersey
1951-56	Chapel Hill-Durham-Raleigh
1958-59	Chapel Hill-Durham-Raleigh (reorganized)
1957-59	Charleston
1969	Charlottesville
1950-60	Chattanooga
1951	Chicago-Beverly Hills
1951-56	Clarksburg
1965-73	Columbus, Ind.
1959-64	Coos Bay Area
1966	Council Bluffs
1952	Decatur
1962-67	Delaware
1956-64	Denton
1967	Denton (reorganized)

1952	Duluth (chapter 1953-63)
1947-48	Durham (merged with Chapel Hill-Raleigh, 1951)
1965-59	Durango
1961-73	Elgin
1958	Elkhart County
1949-51	Enid
1952-55	Erie
1952-58	Erie County
1960-69	Erie County (reorganized)
1971-73	Escondido
1947	Everett
1959-73	Farmington-Livonia-Plymouth (merged with Detroit-Dearborn, 1973)
1966	Firelands
1946	Flint
1956-57	Fort Collins-Loveland
1966	Fort Smith (before 1946-48; chapter 1951-54)
1957	Fullerton-Anaheim North Orange County (since 1971)
1951	Gainesville
1968	Galesburg
1939-55	Gary
1939	Gettysburg
1962-66	Glenbrook Area (became Chicago North Suburban chapter)
1955	Grand Forks
1952	Grand Island
1959-65	Grand Junction
1956-72	Great Falls (1942-45; 1946-55)
1950	Greencastle-Putnam County (chapter 1952-73)
1970	Greenwood
1951	Grosse Pointe (chapter 1954-62)
1951-59	Hagerstown
1960	Hammond-Calumet Area
1951-55	Hannibal
1950	Harrisburg (chapter 1954-63)
1947-49	Hartford
1950	Hartford Area (reorganized) Northern Connecticut (1950) Hartford Area (since 1966)
1949-50	Hermosa Beach
1955-56	Hollywood
1926	Honolulu
1950-55	Hot Springs
1958	Hot Springs (reorganized)
1951-56	Huntington
1969	Huntington Beach
1963	Huntsville
1950-54	Hutchison
1951	Idaho Falls
1966	Indianapolis Suburban Southside
1965-70	Irving
1924-67	Jackson, Mich.
1970-71	Jefferson City
1958	Kalamazoo
1964-67	Kings-Tulare Counties
1951	Knoxville
1955-61	Kokomo
1957	La Canada-Flintridge
1966	Lafayette, La.
1953	Lancaster County
1953	Las Vegas
1950-64	Lehigh Valley (chapter 1953-59)
1961-67	Lima
1955-57	Longview-Kelso

1966-67	Manhattan
1971-73	Mansfield Area
1965	Melbourne
1968	Mexico City
1965	Middletown
1953	Mid-Hudson
1948	Midland
1966	Mississippi Gulf Coast
1959	Mobile
1964-69	Monroe
1959	Monterey Peninsula
1954-55	Montgomery
1964	Montgomery (reorganized)
1963-65	Morgan City Area
1958	Mt. Diablo
	Central Contra Costa County (1962)
	Mt. Diablo (since 1968)
1958	Muncie
1930	Muskogee
1963-73	Napa-Solano
1947	Newark-Granville
1958	New Castle
1949	New Haven
1956-58	Norfolk
1961-66	Norfolk (reorganized)
1958-61	North Sacramento Valley
1945-71	Northern New Jersey
1960-71	Northern Philadelphia
1957-59	Ogden
1954	Olympia
1957-58	Ontario Shore-North West
1960	Orinda
1953-70	Orlando-Winter Park
	Central Florida (1969)
1952-56	Oxford, Miss.
1953-62	Oxford, Ohio
1959-64	Panama City
1959-61	Parkersburg
1964	Parkersburg-Marietta
1971	Peachtree
1959-71	Pendleton
1955-67	Pensacola
1949	Peoria
1954-58	Pioneer Valley
1954-59	Pocatello
1954-68	Pomono Valley
1971	Ponca City
1961	Prosser-Grandview-Sunnyside
1955-65	Providence (chapter 1952-55)
1940-56	Pueblo
1957	Pueblo (reorganized)
1950-54	Queens
1967	Quint City
1969-71	Rapid City
1951-66	Reading
1935-53	Red Oak
1962-70	Red Oak (reorganized)
1957-61	Reno
1963	Richardson
1946	Richmond, Ind.
1958	Rochester, Minn.
1971	Rogue Valley (chapter 1958-71)
1961	Roswell
1964-71	St. Joseph Area
1956-69	St. Paul (merged with Minneapolis chapter, 1969)
1970	Saddleback
1956-73	Santa Rosa

1971	Salinas
1963	Sarasota
1949	Schnectady
1949	Scottsbluff
1950	Shreveport
1952-55	Sioux City
1956-66	Sioux City (reorganized)
1967	Southern Alameda County
1955	Southern New Jersey
1962	Springfield, Mo.
1968	Springfield, Ill.
1956	Stockton (chapter 1959-71)
1956	Summit-Westfield
1949-52	Swarthmore
1951	Tallahassee
1958	Tampa
1950	Twin Falls
1958-60	Tyler
1966	Tyler (reorganized)
1955-58	Valley Forge
1961	Vancouver, Wash.
1951	Victoria, B.C.
1947-49	Waterloo
1964-66	Waukegan Lake Shore (chapter 1962-64)
1949	Wheeling-Ohio Valley
1953	Whittier
1951-52	Wichita Falls
1961	Wichita Falls (reorganized)
1953	Williamsport
1953-65	Winter Haven
1952-64	Xenia
	Springfield-Xenia-Urbana (after 1955)

The *Foundation*

The Delta Gamma Foundation is the culmination of many years of fraternity service to campus and community, to university and nation. The Delta Gamma story of such service is not unique —it is a true reflection of the fraternity world at work, the story of men and women who have channeled their philanthropic efforts through their fraternities and realized works well done, in spite of stigmas and aspersions many times cast on fraternity membership.

In the case of Delta Gamma, as with the rest, the beginnings were humble, merely an earnest endeavor on the part of a small group of college women to do good, to give their best in any way that they were able. With the passing years and increasing membership, it was only natural that efforts and results together grew. Since the first tie of the fraternity is the college, it was natural, too, that service first become tangible in scholarships and loans to worthy undergraduates, the beginning of the Grants and Loans program.

Wartime emergencies, too, provided added fields of progress (hospital service in Holland, an orphanage in Belgium), and finally a Delta Gamma Project—Sight Conservation and Aid to the Blind, a goal which has provided the incentive for Delta Gammas to raise more than $6,000,000 for this project alone since its beginning. After World War II, the International Education project was added (discontinued in 1973), and in 1951 an incorporated Foundation became a necessary organization measure to handle the growing volume of philanthropic business.

The Council serves as Board of Trustees of the Foundation. Until 1951, the various Foundation committees had, of course, been Fraternity Standing Committees, and from 1951 until 1956 these chairmen worked directly under the Second Vice-President. In 1956 the first Foundation Director was appointed:

1956-62—Marcia Connell Strickland,
    Ξ-Michigan
1962-67—Fay Hamilton Jones, Υ-Stanford
1967-71—Betty Beach Norris, BK-Kansas
1971- —Elma Brock Hendrickson,
    AI-Oklahoma

Grants and Loans

Though the possibility of a student loan fund was first suggested in 1880, it did not take form until the 1909 Convention in Ann Arbor. Ruth Rosholt, Λ-Minnesota, was chairman of a committee to raise money for a Scholarship Loan Fund. In 1910, the first loan was made, and the program was under way. Fraternity loans have been available ever since.

In 1922 Delta Gamma undertook a gigantic fund raising program which would be climaxed at its Golden Jubilee celebration at the 1924 Convention. Its real goal was a Scholarship Endowment Fund, the financial aim being $50,000 for this purpose. This endowment fund was to be invested in chapter house mortgages, the interest to provide a rotating fund for student loans. Under Jessie Roberson Kingery's inspired direction, more than $57,000 was raised, and at this time the first Fraternity Fellowships were established.

This was the beginning of a series of Memorial and Honorary Fellowships, offered at the time on no regular schedule. When the great social worker, Grace Abbott, died in 1940, the Convention voted to establish an annual $1,000 fellowship in social service in her memory. This was to be given for second-year graduate study in this field and was to be available to any qualified woman in the United States or Canada.

The Grace Abbott Memorial Fellowship was awarded in this manner for ten years, and then the 1950 Convention voted to discontinue it in favor of an annual Memorial Fellowship, honoring an outstanding Delta Gamma by its name each year and awarded in much the same manner as the Grace Abbott Fellowship.

In 1956 a Fraternity Fellowship of $500 was added to Delta Gamma Grants, this for a Delta Gamma in her first year of graduate study. It would be named for a Delta Gamma who had made outstanding contributions to her Fraternity. Today, the fellowships are known as the Memorial Fellowship and Honorary Fellowship. Both are $1,000 grants and are awarded to Delta Gammas for any level of graduate study in any chosen field.

Following the 1956 Convention, the Board of Trustees of the Foundation (Council) decided to authorize the Grants and Loans Committee to offer two scholarships for undergraduates for the next year. The purpose of these scholarships was to give recognition and financial assistance to collegiate members who had made noticeable contributions to their college and chapter and to assist with the completion of their education. In 1958 the number was increased to six, and today twelve are awarded.

In addition, many alumnae and collegiate chapters maintain scholarship, loan, and emergency grant programs of their own. Through the years these have included the Minneapolis Alumnae Chapter Senior Citation; the Vera B. Baits Senior Award maintained by the Grosse Pointe Alumnae Association; and the Ruth Canary Turpin Memorial Senior Scholarship, provided by Southern California alumnae.

From 1909 until the establishment of the Delta Gamma Foundation in 1951, the Grants and Loans Committees (including Scholarship Fund Committee, Student Loan Committee, Grace Abbott Fellowship Committee, etc.) operated as a part of the Fraternity.

From 1910 when the first loan was granted through 1973, successive committees have administered funds in excess of $370,000. More important, Delta Gamma has been able to provide financial assistance to more than 950 students who would not have been able to complete their educations without this aid. As the need for student aid has increased, scholarship funds have continually been supplemented by Fraternity allocations and gifts from chapters and individuals. During this fiscal year, the Grants and Loans Committee will administer approximately $24,000 to an average of fifty students.

The Chairmen
  1909-11—Ruth Rosholt, Λ-Minnesota
  1911-19—Blanche Garten, K-Nebraska
  1915-19—Blanche Garten, K-Nebraska,
      Collections
      Lydia Mullon, K-Nebraska, Awards
  1919-24—Lydia Mullon, K-Nebraska
  1924-26—Jessie Roberson Kingery, P-Syracuse
  1926-28—Marguerite Winant, O-Adelphi
  1928-30—Florence Cornell Bingham, X-Cornell
  1930-36—Rose Witte Smith, Ω-Wisconsin
  1936-46—Edna Nowland, Θ-Indiana
  1946-49—Laura Bertram Dillon, Z-Albion
  1949-53—Marguerite Funk Cottingham,
      I-Illinois
  1953-55—Evelyn White Hacker,
      BΩ-Washington State

1955-59—Eleanor Greene Daugherty,
　　　　AP-Ohio Wesleyan
1959-63—Elinor Engel Andrews, Λ-Minnesota
1963-67—Betty Beach Norris, BK-Kansas
1967-71—Louise Kittell Schnatterly,
　　　　AK-Washburn
1971-　—Ruth Carter Thomas, BX-Denver

Loans

Student loans more than any one thing reflect the state of the economy. During one Depression beinnium, more than $14,000 was loaned in amounts averaging from $50 to $75. In good times the needs are small, and today, as the costs of education have risen, the demand for loans is great.

Delta Gamma Student Loans, up to $500, are available to upperclass and graduate students. Loans are extended to both members and non-members and are interest free if repaid within three years following graduation.

Following the 1932 Convention (when needs were great) the Delta Gamma Student Loan Fund received a $20,000 legacy, given to the Fraternity in memory of Vera and Corinne Dawson, two Delta Gamma sisters, members of Phi chapter, by Olive Dawson, another sister who was not a Delta Gamma but had always been interested in Delta Gamma's activities. Loans from this fund are available to sisters and children of Delta Gammas under the same terms as other loans.

Fellowships

Since 1924, Delta Gamma has established a number of fellowships, named in honor of women whose influence and service have meant much in the development of the Fraternity and presented to women who have received the bachelor's degree and give promise of leadership or distinction in chosen fields.

The Anna Boyd Ellington Fellowship

This was one of the three Founders Fellowships created by the 1924 Convention, in memory of the only one of the Founders who was at that time deceased. It amounted to $500 and was awarded in October, 1926, to Dorothy Burnette Townsend, X-Cornell, who spent time abroad in the study of history, received her Ph.D. from Cornell, and taught at Cornell until her marriage.

The Eva Webb Dodd Fellowship

The second of the Founders Fellowships established by the 1924 Convention also amounted to $500 and was awarded in 1927 to Hattie Gordon Wakefield, AH-Whitman, who received both a M.A. and Ph.D. in Latin from the University of California. She has been president of the Honolulu alumnae association and has helped to develop Delta Gamma project work there.

The Mary Comfort Leonard Fellowship

This was the third of the Founders Fellowships, and like the others established in 1924 amounted to $500. It was awarded in 1930 to Ida Auch Teanack, X-Cornell, who, after graduate work, entered the Wall Street world via an attorney's office.

The Lillie Wohlleben Hudson Fellowship

This fellowship was created at the 1930 Convention for graduate work for a Delta Gamma of marked ability. It was established in honor of the member of our Mother Chapter who served as President of the Second Convention, 1883, and contributed immeasurably to the Fraternity through the years. This $500 fellowship was awarded in 1931 to Gertrude Wilber, AI-Oklahoma, M.S. with highest honors in chemistry. She had completed part of her work toward her Ph.D., and in 1931 won the National Research Council Fellowship on condition that she fulfill the requirements for the M.D. degree before the fall of 1932. This the Lillie Wohlleben Hudson Fellowship enabled her to do.

The Jessie Roberson Kingery Fellowship

Through the untiring efforts of Jessie Roberson Kingery, Φ-Colorado, Delta Gamma raised during World War I the sum of $28,300.91 for the benefit of homeless children found in the Iron Ring in Belgium. At the time of the Fiftieth Anniversary of Delta Gamma, she directed the Endowment Campaign which made the Student Loan Fund what it is today. This $500 award, created by the 1928 Convention, was presented in 1938 to Jean Failing, AΔ-Oregon, who used it for work on her doctorate. She taught for some time at Cornell University.

The Leulah Judson Hawley Fellowship

For seventeen years Mrs. Hawley served as a Council member, from 1915-1932 as Secretary-Editor of the Fraternity, and when this office was divided in 1932, an additional two years as Editor—until her death in 1934. This $500 Fellowship was established by the 1934 Convention and was awarded in 1952 to Patricia Ann Browne, BZ-Denison.

The Corinne Miller Fellowship

To Corinne Miller's leadership in the Mother Chapter, Delta Gamma owes much. It was she who designed the Delta Gamma Anchor, directed the expansion work done by Psi chapter, and through her help that a Constitution was written in 1877 that could be used nationally. The Corinne Miller Fellowship was established by the 1938 Convention and was awarded in 1939 to Genevieve Walberg, BΔ-Colorado College, who accepted an assistantship in the office of the Dean of Women at Syracuse University and there completed Dean Hilton's course in counseling and guidance.

The Grace Abbott Memorial Fellowships in Public Welfare Administration

These fellowships, created by the 1940 Convention, honored Grace Abbott, K-Nebraska, a well known figure in the field of Public Welfare Administration, first through her work at Hull House, then the formation of the Immigrant's Protective League, and later as chief of the

Children's Bureau in the U.S. Department of Labor. Miss Abbott had also served her Fraternity as editor of the *Anchora*, 1903-07. These fellowships differed from the others previously established in that they were available to non-members of the Fraternity. They were for $1,000 each, this amount contributed in part by friends and admirers of Grace Abbott and in part by the Fraternity. They were awarded annually for the period 1941-51 and were administered by a special committee appointed for the purpose. The recipients were as follows:

1941-42—Anna Sundwall, Salt Lake City, Utah
1942-43—Verna Irene Esser, Prescott, Arizona
1943-44—Rebecca Nell Dickerson, Dallas, Texas
1944-45—Ruth Margaret Werner, Madison,
          Wisconsin
1945-46—Carolyn Bullard, Nashville, Georgia
1946-47—Annette Jackson, X-Cornell
1947-48—Grace E. Nichols, Sante Fe, New Mexico
1948-49—Virginia Posvar, Reno, Nevada, $500
          Dolores Fitzsimon, San Antonio, Texas,
          $500
1949-50—Louise Rainer, Montgomery, Alabama
1950-51—Kate Berry Shepherd, Jackson,
          Mississippi

These awards were made to "a woman graduate of an American college or university (including Canada) who has had experience in public social service and who submits an approved plan for a year of professional study with the object of returning to public welfare service."

The Alice Perry Gradle Fellowship

The election of "Dickie" Gradle, Ξ-Michigan, in 1922 to the office of First Vice-President was the beginning of sixteen years as a Council member. In 1926 she became Treasurer and served later as Secretary when the duties of Secretary and Editor were divided. She edited the *Anchora* during an emergency period and served as Secretary again 1939-40 and simultaneously as chairman of the 1940 Convention. This $500 fellowship was established as a memorial to Mrs. Gradle at the 1946 Convention, and was awarded to Shirley Wilson, ΑΗ-Whitman, in 1956.

The Alta Gwinn Saunders Memorial Scholarship

As Editor of the *Anchora*, Alta Gwinn Saunders, I-Illinois, served Delta Gamma from 1935 until she was killed in a plane crash en route to the 1948 Convention. This 1948 Convention voted to honor her by establishing a scholarship fund, preferably for journalism students. The awards, $100 each, were made in 1950 to the collegiate member in each province submitting the best chapter history in the province. These awards were as follows:

Province I	Helen Mary Malti, X-Cornell
Province II	Joan Moore, BΣ-Maryland
Province III	Barbara Ware Foulkrod, BΛ-Gettysburg
Province IV	No award
Province V	Mary Ann Lummis, BZ-Denison
Province VI	Carolyn Jane Robbins, BΞ-Michigan State
Province VII	Ardis Ann Miller, I-Illinois
Province VIII	Nancy Ratcliff, Λ-Minnesota
Province IX	No award
Province X	Margery Van Pelt, K-Nebraska
Province XI	Karen Hansen, B-Washington
Province XII	Martha Piper, ΑΔ-Oregon
Province XIII	Dorothy Harrell, ΑΠ-Arizona
Province XIV	Marion Buchanan, ΑΥ-SMU

Convention 1950 voted to establish a Memorial Fellowship to be awarded each year in memory of an outstanding Delta Gamma. The action was the result of the feeling of the delegates that this would be an appropriate and consistent way to recognize service to the Fraternity.

The Hazel Whitaker Vandenberg Memorial Fellowship for 1951-52

Wife of Senator Arthur Vandenberg of Michigan, Hazel Whitaker Vandenberg contributed untiringly to her country, her state, her university, her profession, her fraternity and her family. She served Delta Gamma for six years as First Vice-President, for nine years as a member and chairman of the Grace Abbott Fellowship Committee, and was active in the Washington, D.C. alumnae chapter. This $1,500 award, named at the 1950 Convention, was presented in 1951 to Mary Mildred Hurd.

The Blanche Garten Memorial Fellowship for 1952-53

This 1952-53 award was named for Delta Gamma's sixteenth President who held the gavel at the 1903 and 1905 Conventions. At the latter Convention, this official gavel was one which Blanche Garten herself presented to the Fraternity, one she had had made of wood from the house in Oxford, Mississippi, where Delta Gamma was founded. Later in 1922, when the number of Council members was increased from five to seven, she was included as Installation Officer. In 1915, she and Ethel Tukey Korsmeyer had collaborated to publish Delta Gamma's first complete and documented history. This $1,500 award was presented in 1952 to Elsa Tice McBride.

The Helen Humphreys Lawrence Memorial Fellowship for 1953-54

This Memorial Fellowship for $1,500 was named to honor a Delta Gamma artist, Helen Humphreys Lawrence, Λ-Minnesota. A noted portraitist, it was Mrs. Lawrence who painted the portraits of the three Founders which today hang in the Founders Room of the Alpha Psi chapter house. "Humpy," as she was known, was an active Delta Gamma and in 1948 received a special Convention award for having attended ten Delta Gamma Conventions, more than any other member at that time. Marjorie White Main received this award in 1953.

The Ruth Billow Memorial Fellowship for 1954-55

Blind since a childhood accident, Ruth Billow, H-Akron, was a graduate of the Ohio State School for the Blind and attended Akron University for two years. Active in many organizations in Akron, she held her membership in Delta Gamma as one of the dearest things in her life. She was a veteran Convention-goer and was among those who instigated the establishment of the Delta Gamma Project, Sight Conservation and Aid to the Blind, at the 1936 Convention. This $1,500 fellowship was awarded in 1954 to Jeannette Griffin.

The Ruth Bryan Rohde Memorial Fellowship
for 1955-56

Ruth Bryan Owen Rohde, K-Nebraska, the daughter of William Jennings Bryan, was well known in America and in Europe. Like her father, she was a fluent and persuasive speaker. She was the first woman sent to Congress from Florida and the first woman Democrat in Congress. She was the first woman to represent the United States abroad as Minister to Denmark. As a token of her success there she received the Distinguished Service Medal from King Frederick in 1954. The $1,500 was awarded to Dorothy Gross of Teaneck, New Jersey, for second year graduate study at Western Reserve University.

The Gratia Countryman Memorial Fellowship
for 1956-57

For more than forty years Gratia Countryman, Λ-Minnesota, was the honored and loved City Librarian of Minneapolis, a position in which her achievements earned mention in Who's Who. An outstanding Delta Gamma, she served her Fraternity as Editor in 1888, Secretary in 1903-05, organizing the files and documents entrusted to that officer with a hand firm enough to be felt throughout the chapters of the Fraternity. This $1,500 grant was awarded to Doris Fraser in 1956.

In 1956 the Honorary Fellowship was established to be awarded annually to a Delta Gamma for first-year graduate study in any field. This fellowship would be named to honor a living member who had demonstrated particular loyalty and service to the Fraternity.

The George Banta Memorial Fellowship
for 1957-58

By establishment of the George Banta Fellowship, Delta Gamma recognized the contribution of mind and spirit made by Mr. Banta during the early years of the Delta Gamma Fraternity. George Banta was Delta Gamma's only male member, accorded membership by the Mother Chapter in 1879 and given authority to establish several chapters in the North. Throughout a life in which he dedicated himself to the furtherance of the fraternity movement, Delta Gamma enjoyed the good fortune of his special interest in her welfare. The year of this fellowship, 1957-58, commemorated fifty years of business association of Delta Gamma with the George Banta Company as printer of the Anchora. This $1,500 fellowship was given to Margaret Radabaugh Vradenberg, ΑΡ-Ohio Wesleyan, for study at Western Reserve University.

The Roberta Abernethy Honorary Fellowship
for 1957-58

Executive Secretary of Delta Gamma since 1942, Roberta Abernethy, E-Ohio State, had served the Fraternity since college days in a variety of offices. She was First Vice-President at the time it was decided to establish a Central Office, and Columbus, Ohio, was the site selected partly because it was her home and because she was such a logical choice for this tremendous responsibility. This $500 fellowship was awarded to Evelyn Alessio, ΒΝ-Carnegie-Mellon.

The Carolyn Boli Stanton Memorial Fellowship
for 1958-59

Carolyn Boli Stanton, ΑΥ-SMU, was devoted to her Fraternity and dedicated herself to furthering its ideals. Her appointment to the office of Second Vice-President in 1954 was the climax of a long career of Fraternity service. This $1,500 fellowship was awarded to Grace Schumacher of Ft. Lauderdale, Florida, for study at the University of Denver.

The Audrey Kenyon Wilder Honorary
Fellowship for 1958-59

The record of distinguished and devoted service of Audrey Kenyon Wilder, Z-Albion, covers a wide area. Her special interests in the furtherance of the stature of women scholastically, socially and politically have applied to her special contributions to Delta Gamma. This $500 fellowship was awarded to Margaret Losey, ΑΙ-Oklahoma.

The Edith Abbott Memorial Fellowship
for 1959-60

Edith Abbott, K-Nebraska, shared with her sister, Grace Abbott, an intense interest in humanitarian reform, a field in which they both made distinguished contributions. A pioneer in social welfare administraton, she worked closely with Jane Addams in Chicago and taught on the University of Chicago School of Social Welfare staff. She became its dean in 1924, serving for nineteen years in this post, making the school a leader in its field. This $1,500 fellowship for 1959-60 was awarded to Anne Minahan, Ω-Wisconsin, for advanced study at Ohio State University.

The Pearl McDonnell Honorary Fellowship
for 1959-60

Pearl McDonnell, Β-Washington, demonstrated a true pioneering spirit through more than fifty years of devoted service to Delta Gamma. She was chairman of Delta Gamma's first group of province secretaries, doing much in this post to develop organizational strength in the collegiate area. She served in many other capacities. This $500 fellowship was awarded to Patricia Miller, Z-Albion.

The Dorothy Glenn Holsinger Memorial
Fellowship for 1960-61

Dorothy Glenn Holsinger, I-Illinois, demonstrated her capability for leadership within the Fraternity by her service as president of her collegiate chapter, president of the Oak Park alumnae, president of the Hinsdale-LaGrange alumnae, president of the Greater Chicago Alumnae Groups. She was a delegate to seven Delta Gamma Conventions, chairman of the Alta Gwinn Saunders Memorial Committee, Province Secretary, and Fraternity First Vice-President. She also represented Delta Gamma as NPC Delegate. This $1,500 fellowship was awarded to Ada E. Deer for advanced study at Columbia University.

The Bertha Rose Honorary Fellowship for 1960-61

Considered the matriarch of California Delta Gammas, Bertha Rose, Υ-Stanford, demonstrated through the years a special interest in each pledge and each member in her area which endeared her to everyone. She also served on the board of the Nursery School for Visually Handicapped Children from the beginning and held a variety of other Delta Gamma offices. This $500 fellowship was granted to Carol Pitts, BΨ-Alabama.

The Barbara Wallenfang Memorial Fellowship for 1961-62

A few young, fresh and wonderful years of Barbara Wallenfang's brief span of life were shared with Beta Psi chapter. She served as Standards Chairman and President. The Fraternity recognized her worth when she was elected in 1958 as one of Delta Gamma's first pair of Collegiate Representatives to Council. She died the following spring, before graduation —having earned Phi Beta Kappa, Mortar Board, and many other honors, and the University of Alabama conferred her degree posthumously. This $1,500 fellowship was awarded to Miriam H. Milgram for study at the University of Minnesota.

The Frances Lewis Stevenson Honorary Fellowship for 1961-62

Frances Lewis Stevenson, Z-Albion, might be called a career Delta Gamma, having served two years as field secretary before she became part of the Central Office staff to establish a publications department as Anchora Editor. Her Delta Gamma work in the community and on the Grants and Loans Committee continued after her resignation in 1956, and when this $500 fellowship was awarded to Ellen Thomas, ΑΙ-Oklahoma, she had just returned to active duty in the office.

The Nancy Brown Woollett Memorial Fellowship for 1962-63

Many and varied were the contributions of Nancy Brown Woollett Yawger, Φ-Colorado, to Delta Gamma. As President of the Fraternity from 1922-28, Mrs. Woollett foresaw the growth in size and scope of the fraternity system and laid strong foundations of finance and organization accordingly. Her personal guidance in later years helped in reestablishing the chapter and building the Memorial House at the University of Mississippi. The Birthday Fund, the first major fund from which all Delta Gamma Fellowships and Scholarships have followed, was established during her term of office. The $1,500 grant was awarded to Margaret Robison for advanced study at Smith College.

The Julia McCune Honorary Fellowship for 1962-63

Julia McCune, Z-Albion, had not only been a loyal and active Delta Gamma in her own com-munity and on the Albion College campus where she taught for many years, but she had since 1941 contributed her literary talents to the Anchora as Manuscripts Editor. Her own literary skill and knowledge of the field—and a phenom-enal memory for names—made this section not only popular but added to the Anchora's prestige. This $500 fellowship was awarded to Marcia Reiners, ΓΤ-TCU.

The Laura Bertram Dillon Honorary Fellowship for 1962-63

Sponsored by the Birmingham alumnae chap-ter, this was a surprise $500 fellowship an-nounced at the 1962 Convention banquet to honor Mrs. Dillon, Z-Albion, a member of the Birmingham (Michigan) chapter and chairman of the 1962 Convention. Mrs. Dillon has also served as Student Loan Chairman, Province Alumnae Chairman, and Fraternity Secretary. This fellowship was awarded to Elizabeth Kirk-patrick, Φ-Colorado.

The Jessie McGilvray Treat Memorial Fellowship for 1963-64

Jessie McGilvray Treat, Υ-Stanford, was Delta Gamma's World War I President, serving from 1915-19. Jessie met the exigencies of these years with a dynamic determination to guide Delta Gamma into the most effective channels of war service. Under her leadership, substantial sums were raised by the Fraternity for a number of humanitarian projects, notably the establishment of the Delta Gamma House at Ossendrecht, Holland, where many sick and destitute children were restored to health. This $2,000 fellowship was used by Marcia Rafinski at the University of Minnesota.

The Hazel H. Brown Honorary Fellowship for 1963-64

Hazel H. Brown, ΑΒ-Swarthmore, prepared for a career in astronomy, turned to social work and the law in search of a more fulfilling life, and served as Assistant District Attorney, County Court Judge, and President Judge in Pennsyl-vania. She was also Treasurer of the Fraternity 1930-36 and served in the Philadelphia area in many other ways. This $500 fellowship was awarded to Leola Lorenzen, ΑΔ-Oregon.

The Irene Howell Forman Memorial Fellowship for 1964-65

Possessing true ability, Irene Howell Forman, ΑΚ-Washburn, demonstrated a unique capacity for giving of herself. Following her term as Project Chairman 1946-48, she was Chairman of the 1948 Convention, at which time she was elected Fraternity Secretary, in which office she served until 1954. She also chaired the 1960 committee appointed by Council to study the nominating committee system. Devoted to the Project, she aided in the establishment of the Rochester Orthoptic Center and was elected to the Board of Directors of the National Society for the Prevention of Blindness, serving as vice-president until her death. This $2,000 fellowship was awarded to Elaine Pestorius for study at the University of Denver.

The Florence Sylvester Winchell Honorary
Fellowship for 1964-65

Florence Sylvester Winchell, Λ-Minnesota, records what she calls her "three lives,"—in which Delta Gamma is entwined in the second two. The first was as a child in Germany with her dentist father, the second her college and medical training and practice in the United States, and third her marriage and years of her family. Her service to Delta Gamma has continued since her initiation at Minnesota. This fellowship was awarded to Marilyn Taft, BN-Carnegie-Mellon.

The Florence Cornell Bingham Memorial
Fellowship for 1965-66

A brilliant woman with tremendous ability and drive, Florence Cornell Bingham, X-Cornell, served in many ways, wherever she lived and all her life. First Vice-President of Delta Gamma, 1932-40, and President, 1940-47, found her simultaneously serving as national President of PTA, consultant at the organizational meetings of the United Nations in 1945, writing, speaking, editing, traveling, all in many areas of educational interest during these years. This $2,000 fellowship was awarded to Melvena Green for advanced study at the University of Pennsylvania's School of Social Work.

The Marguerite Dawson Winant Honorary
Fellowships for 1965-66

Marguerite Winant, O-Adelphi, was a charter member of her chapter, and during a busy life contributing service to many organizations, she has given many years to Delta Gamma. She served as Second Vice-President, 1928-32, and President, 1932-40. She is especially known for her work in connection with the Beekman Tower, Panhellenic House, in New York City. These two $500 fellowships were awarded to Marjorie Hansen, ΓΛ-Fresno, and Andrea Goudie, Λ-Minnesota.

The Ruth Canary Turpin Memorial Fellowship
for 1966-67

Ruth Canary Turpin, ΔN-USC, served her Fraternity and her community in many ways all of her adult lifetime. Her Fraternity work was climaxed with her appointment as NPC Delegate and election as Secretary. It was from this office that she was forced to resign by the serious illness which led to her death. Not only has the Fraternity honored her memory with this fellowship, but Province XVII offers a Memorial Scholarship bearing her name and several local scholarships honor her in the Pasadena, California, area, recognizing her community service, particularly in education. This $2,000 fellowship was awarded to Carolyn Eck for study at Western Reserve University.

The Marguerite Williams Honorary Fellowship
for 1966-67

Marguerite Williams, E-Ohio State, is considered the matriarch of Epsilon chapter, for since her days in college as a charter member, she has lived and taught in Columbus, and her services to the chapter have been many. Beyond this, she was among the first province secretaries and attended many Conventions where she always found an active part. This $500 fellowship was awarded to Sharon Pope, M-Missouri.

The Maisie Clugston Groves Honorary
Fellowship for 1966-67

To honor the first Canadian President of Delta Gamma, the Canadian chapters sponsored this $350 fellowship for 1966-67, announcing it as a surprise at the Canadian dinner at the 1966 Convention. Mrs. Groves, AΦ-British Columbia, had previously served as Province Alumnae Chairman and Second Vice-President of the Fraternity. This fellowship was awarded to Sheila Begg, BB-Alberta, for work at the University of British Columbia.

The Jean Gooch Teall Memorial Fellowship
for 1967-68

Jean Gooch Teall, Γ-California, served as Second Vice-President of Delta Gamma during the difficult years of World War II and through the rapid expansion that followed. Not only did she demonstrate her abilities for individual leadership in her own area, alumnae organization, but especially as a contributing member of the Council. This $1,000 fellowship was awarded to Mary Anne Maginnis, AH-Whitman.

The Helen Rupert Pitcher Honorary Fellowship
for 1967-68

Helen Rupert Pitcher, Λ-Minnesota, had served as Province Secretary and had enthusiastically directed the International Education program for the Delta Gamma Foundation since 1964. She became seriously ill just prior to the 1966 Convention and was forced to retire from this office. This $1,000 fellowship was awarded to Laurin Reininga, M-Missouri, for work at Harvard University.

The Ethel Tukey Korsmeyer Memorial
Fellowship for 1968-69

Ethel Tukey was initiated into Kappa chapter at Nebraska when that chapter was the acknowledged leader among new innovations for Fraternity organization, and she became a member who lived this tradition. She followed Grace Abbott as editor of the Anchora, and in 1915 produced the first large and complete Delta Gamma history, one which was considered the bible of beginnings for many years. She always was active in the affairs of her own chapter as well as the Fraternity at large. This $1,000 fellowship was awarded to Susan Edmundson Trimble, ΓI-DePauw, for work at the University of Pennsylvania.

The Alice Reynick Morgan Honorary Fellowship
for 1968-69

Alice Reynick Morgan's sixty-six years active membership in Delta Gamma reflects all that is best in being a fraternity woman. She served as Xi's delegate to the 1905 Convention, as Detroit's first chapter delegate to Convention in 1922, and was Convention treasurer when Michigan was a hostess for the 1929 Convention at Mackinac. She was Convention banquet chairman in 1940, again at Mackinac. She has had a lifelong interest in education, served on Xi's chapter board for 20 years, first as treasurer and then president. She is both a Delta Gamma mother and grandmother. This $1,000 fellowship was given to Jane Cecilia Bryan, Γ-California, for work at the University of California.

The Virginia Riesterer Gates Memorial
Fellowship for 1969-70

The 1969-70 Memorial Fellowship was named for a Delta Gamma, who, though she had been forced to resign from her Council position, remained an active force almost until the day of her death. This was Virginia Riesterer Gates, Σ-Northwestern, who was elected Second Vice-President at the 1964 Convention, was re-elected in 1966, and then resigned in the spring of 1967 because of illness. Ginny had previously served four years as a Province Alumnae Chairman and then as Fraternity Recommendations Chairman for three years. This $1,000 fellowship was awarded to Rosemary Verdi, O-Adelphi, for work at Boston College.

The Caroline Pardee Honorary Fellowship
for 1969-70

Caroline Pardee is a name synonymous with Eta chapter of Delta Gamma. She was on the University of Akron staff for many years (secretary to the President) and at the same time a loyal and active Delta Gamma, serving her own chapter as well as the Fraternity at large and attending many Conventions. This $1,000 fellowship was awarded to Sharon Pope, M-Missouri, for work at the University of Missouri.

The Joe Anna Ross Pancoast Memorial
Fellowship for 1970-71

Jo Anna Ross Pancoast, Ψ-Goucher, made her mark among Anchora editors because during her term in the editor's chair (1897-1905) she not only produced a lively magazine but also introduced photographs to the publication. The petitioning group at Syracuse University received such support from Joe Anna Ross that it chose her initial "R" in choosing Rho as their chapter letter. This $1,000 fellowship was presented to Randi Loftsgaarden, X-Cornell, for study at the Columbia University School of Law.

The Joyzelle Herod McCreary Honorary
Fellowship for 1970-71

Joyzelle Herod McCreary, ΓΝ-North Texas, gave freely of her time and talents as a professional consultant in group dynamics at two Delta Gamma Conventions (1966, 1968) and has always made herself available for special service to Delta Gamma in this field. She has served in an advisory capacity to several collegiate chapters. This $1,000 fellowship was awarded to Judy Bell, ΑΥ-SMU, for work at the Johns Hopkins School for Advanced International Studies.

The Carolyn Benton Cockefair Memorial
Fellowship for 1971-72

Carolyn Benton Cockefair, M-Missouri, was a charter member at Missouri after the petitioning group had already become known on campus as "Carolyn Benton's Bunch." Her special teaching talents were recognized in the small Missouri town which was her home, and in the neighboring towns, until her university sought her out and placed her on their Extension staff. Her renown grew as a member of the faculty at the main campus in Columbia, and then on the University of Missouri-Kansas City campus where in 1960 her devoted students established the Carolyn Benton Cockefair Chair of Continuing Education. This $1,000 fellowship was awarded to Joan Ashley Nickerson, X-Cornell, for work at Cornell University.

The Catherine Leavitt Jones Honorary
Fellowship for 1971-72

Catherine Leavitt Jones, ΑΙ-Oklahoma, has supported unstintingly nearly every Delta Gamma program and project offered collegiate and alumnae members. A loved member of her chapter, she was present at the 1970 Convention where the announcement of this fellowship was made as a surprise to her. This $1,000 fellowship was given to Susan Lang, ΑΛ-Drake, for study at Indiana University.

The Alumnae Memorial Fellowship for 1972-73

In honor of Delta Gamma's Centennial year, the 1972-73 Memorial Fellowship was created in memory of all those Delta Gammas who have gone before to make the Fraternity what it is today. Thus, it was the $1,000 Alumnae Memorial Fellowship which was awarded to Suzanne Sloan, ΒΨ-Alabama, for work at the University of Alabama.

The Ruth French Shriver Honorary Fellowship
for 1972-73

Ruth French Shriver, Ψ-Goucher, through her lifetime has not only served her Fraternity in a wide variety of official and unofficial capacities, but she also holds the record of number of Conventions attended, covering a period from 1913 until 1972 with very few missed. This $1,000 fellowship was awarded to Karen Glover, ΑΗ-Whitman, for study at the Harvard University School of Law.

The Mary Thompson Stevens Memorial
Fellowship for 1973-74

Mary Thompson Stevens, though initiated by Eta chapter, is usually identified with Xi because she was one of its founders. She was the first editor of the Anchora, a post she gave up when she entered medical school. One of Detroit's first "lady doctors", she was one of the city's first physicians to specialize in pediatrics. This $1,000 fellowship was awarded to Deborah Rufner, ΒΞ-Michigan State, for her second year at the Ohio State University College of Medicine.

The Marcia Connell Strickland Honorary
Fellowship for 1973-74

Marcia Connell Strickland, Ξ-Michigan, over a 30 year period held nearly every Delta Gamma office open to a member except that of province alumnae chairman. She served as President of the Fraternity, 1968-72, officiating at the Centennial

Convention in 1972. This $1,000 fellowship was awarded to Teresa Gail Sosby, ΓM-Florida State, for study of law at Florida State University.

The Carolyn Coffman Moorman Memorial Fellowship for 1974-75

Carolyn Coffman Moorman, ΔO-Miami Univ., following a term as Province V Collegiate Chairman, became Fraternity Treasurer in 1964, serving in this office until 1970, at which time she became a member of the 1972 Nominating Committee. Just before this Centennial Convention she suffered a heart attack and died a few weeks later.

The Mildred Moyer Baynard Honorary Fellowship for 1974-75

Mildred Moyer Baynard, K-Nebraska, since her days in college, has been the sort of Delta Gamma who was available for the task at hand. She has served as Province Alumnae Chairman, Convention Chairman, as colonizer of Gamma Theta chapter, as President of the Florida Society for the Prevention of Blindness, and as a member of the National Society for the Prevention of Blindness Board of Directors.

Continuing Education Scholarships

In 1969, the Foundation Board of Trustees authorized the awarding of a Continuing Education Scholarship of $1,000. Recognizing the growing trend toward continuing education, this scholarship was to be available to women whose academic work had been interrupted and were returning to a campus for additional study, on either the undergraduate or graduate level. When the first Continuing Education Scholarships were awarded for the 1970-71 academic year, the Grants and Loans Committee made two $500 grants—as opposed to one $1,000 grant—and all subsequent Continuing Education Scholarships were awarded in this manner.

1970-71—Barbara Baxter Pillinger, I-Illinois, for work at Harvard University.
Patricia Hartlage Stanley, ΓP-Wittenberg, for work at the University of Southern Mississippi.

1971-72—Sue Baldwin Sherman, BK-Kansas, for work at McPherson College.
Dorothy Grant Schulz, M-Missouri, for work at the University of Missouri at Kansas City.

1972-73—Donna Vicknair Moak, ΓZ-LSU, for study at Loyola University.
Patricia Kelly, Π-Montana, for work at the University of Montana.

1973-74—Katherine Hendricks Gardner, Ω-Wisconsin, for the study of law at Boston University.
Jean Noonan, P-Syracuse, for work at Boston University.

Senior Scholarships

1957-58   Margaret Losey,AI-Oklahoma
Cheri Segar, ΛΛ-Drake

1958-59   Barbara Roome, BE-American
Betty Johnson, ΓP-Wittenberg

1959-60   Lucy Lee Berner, ΑΣ-UCLA
Linda Brainard, ΓI-DePauw
Dona Fundis, ΓE-Kent State
Gale Jackson, X-Cornell
Valeria Logan, ΑH-Whitman
Beverly Oneal, ΓN-North Texas

1960-61   Rita Cawley, Λ-Minnesota
Judith Clothier, ΑΠ-Arizona
Doris Kurzenknabe, ΒΔ-Gettysburg
Elizabeth Power, ΓE-Kent State
Gail Rahkola, ΑΔ-Oregon
Mary Jo Swing, ΓO-Indiana State

1961-62   Diane Dykes, AI-Oklahoma
Lilien Filipovitch, BP-George Washington
Patricia Anne Hall, BΩ-Washington State
Marianna Koch, BΠ-Willamette
Barbara Ellen Manson, Θ-Indiana
Jennifer Young, ΑΓ-Toronto
Gretchen Shellberg, K-Nebraska
Sharon Squibb, Λ-Minnesota
Cynthia Wilson, ΓΩ-St. Lawrence
Meredith Moore, BE-American
Citation of $50: Carolyn Bickerstaff, ΑΨ-Mississippi

1962-63   Jere Jane Allen, ΓΔ-Montana State
Heather Jean Begg, BB-Alberta
Mary Beth Bryan, Φ-Colorado
Diane Diamond, O-Adelphi
Diane Klinck, ΓM-Florida State
Susan Kroener, Θ-Indiana
Kathryn Madsen, K-Nebraska
Jo Ann Prouty, ΑΘ-North Dakota
Dorothea Striebel, ΓΔ-Montana State
Peggy Ann Sugars, BX-Denver
Judith Wilder, ΑΠ-Arizona
Citations: *Oak Park-River Forest alumnae* ($250) to Kathleen Bourke, ΑΓ-Toronto
Vera B. Baits Award by Grosse Pointe alumnae to Mary Ann Dean, ΑΔ-Oregon
Minneapolis alumnae ($250) to Esther Nielsen, BB-Alberta
Seattle alumnae ($100) to Celia Smith, ΓΔ-Montana State

1963-64   Sonja Flatness, ΓΔ-Montana State
Katherine Haynsworth, ΑZ-Lawrence
Lyn Hopkins, ΑΨ-Mississippi
Willie Linsenbardt, M-Missouri
Betty O'Berry, ΓM-Florida State
Clyda Stokes, ΓM-Florida State
Marilyn Taft, BN-Carnegie-Mellon
Constance Waddell, ΑΞ-West Virginia
Eleanor Wagner, H-Akron
Martha Washburn, E-Ohio State
Citations: *Portland alumnae* ($60) to Dona Blazier, BX-Denver

Portland alumnae ($60) to Heather Wilson, BΥ-Oregon State

Minneapolis alumnae ($250) to Jean Parker, AI-Oklahoma

1964-65 Georganne Banks, ΓP-Wittenberg
Reha Bristow, AI-Oklahoma
Judith Clark, AΔ-Oregon
Wendy Crawford, AH-Whitman
Marsha Cundiff, Φ-Colorado
Doris Farrington, BZ-Denison
Gail Hewitt, P-Syracuse
Nancy Gail Kaufmann, N-Idaho
Marjorie Moran, AX-Penn State
Nancy Rees, AΛ-Drake
Jeanne Swahn, BH-Texas
Bette Wagner, BI-Purdue

Citations: *Detroit-Dearborn alumnae* ($250) to Sue Bethel, ΓO-Indiana State

Minneapolis alumnae ($150) to Sandra Illing, BX-Denver

Delta Gamma Foundation ($150) to Wendy Soth, B-Washington

Vera B. Baits Awards by Grosse Pointe alumnae ($50) to Sue Mockridge, T-Iowa, and Sandy Atkinson, ΓΣ-Houston

1965-66 Karen Acord, AI-Oklahoma
Cynthia Blehn, AΘ-North Dakota
Joan Christianson, AΛ-Drake
Judy Coursey, AΨ-Mississippi
Sue Dieringer, H-Akron
Becky Fisher, ΓP-Wittenberg
Adele Orr, AX-Penn State
Sharon Pope, M-Missouri
Sharon Swenson, N-Idaho

Citations: *Minneapolis alumnae* ($200) to Becky Barnes, ΓO-Indiana State

Detroit-Dearborn alumnae ($250) to Sherry Hughes, Λ-Minnesota

Vera B. Baits Award by Grosse Pointe alumnae ($50) to Pamela Dean, BΠ-Willamette

Ruth Canary Turpin Memorial Scholarship by Province XIII ($250) to Patricia Doan, Γ-California

1966-67 Diane Deere, Φ-Colorado
Sponsored by Oak Park-River Forest Alumnae
Sandra Ledahl, AΘ-North Dakota
Ingrid Myklestad, ΓΦ-Arizona State
Vickey Noser, Λ-Minnesota
Sponsored by Minneapolis Alumnae
Laurin Reiniga, M-Missouri
Marguerite Fuzo, BΣ-Maryland
Evelyn Holliday Fraker Memorial Senior Scholarship, sponsored by Westchester County Alumnae
Hope McCulloch, ΓΩ-St. Lawrence
Mary Ann Munka, H-Akron
Jane Gill Eggers Memorial Senior Scholarship, sponsored by Cleveland West Alumnae
Margaret Pickett, BΨ-Alabama
Susan Sheppard, AI-Oklahoma

1967-68 Nancy Akels, Λ-Minnesota
Sponsored by Minneapolis Alumnae
Mildred Cooper, BΨ-Alabama
Joyce Coulam, BΓ-Utah
Joan Eismann, N-Idaho
Helen Gerber, H-Akron
Sponsored by Detroit-Dearborn Alumnae
Shyla Jones, ΓP-Wittenberg
Jane Gill Eggers Memorial Scholarship, sponsored by Cleveland West Alumnae
Katherine Loomis, ΓΩ-St. Lawrence
Mary Sheridan Franklin Honorary Scholarship, sponsored by Long Island-North Shore Alumnae
Judith McSpadden, ΓΔ-Montana State
Pamela Pinnell, AΣ-UCLA
Sponsored by San Mateo Alumnae
Peggy Shaffer, BΠ-Willamette
Maisie Clugston Groves Honorary Scholarship, sponsored by Canadian Delta Gammas
Elizabeth Webber, T-Iowa
Pamela Wood, K-Nebraska

1968-69 Patricia Sue Campbell, ΓO-Indiana State
Carolyn Murphy Van Dyke Memorial Scholarship, sponsored by Oak Park-River Forest Alumnae
Maridella Carter, M-Missouri
Catherine Conner, N-Idaho
Sponsored by San Mateo Alumnae
Nancy Grant, ΔΘ-Georgia State
Linda Idoine, ΓP-Wittenberg
Linda Rhein, Π-Montana
Sponsored by Minneapolis Alumnae
Carol Ringer, BM-Bowling Green
Beth Seifried, ΓE-Kent State
Jane Gill Eggers Memorial Scholarship, sponsored by Cleveland West Alumnae
Rosemary Verdi, O-Adelphi
Sammie Vinson, AI-Oklahoma
Barbara Lucas Pease Honorary Scholarship, sponsored by Palo Alto Alumnae
Carol Watson, ΔK-South Florida
Sharon Watson, BK-Kansas

1969-70 Janet Battisti, BN-Carnegie-Mellon
Barbara Rivet Shoemaker Honorary Scholarship, sponsored by Fairfield County Alumnae
Cynthia Clampitt, ΔZ-Memphis State
Carolyn Collie, ΓB-Tulsa
Virginia Longley, BK-Kansas
Jean Ann McCain, AT-Butler
Sue Ann Noll, BX-Denver
Sponsored by San Mateo Alumnae
Susan Packard, E-Ohio State
Ferne Taylor Hutson Honorary Scholarship, sponsored by Columbus Alumnae
Vicki Posegate, ΓΦ-Arizona State
Jane Crawford Simons Honorary

Scholarship, sponsored by Palo Alto Alumnae

Terry Price, AΨ-Mississippi

Kathleen Reidel, ΓΔ-Montana State
Frances McCormack Tierney Memorial Scholarship, sponsored by Seattle Alumnae

Jane Stampe, AΛ-Drake
Sponsored by Minneapolis Alumnae

Kathleen Wintering, BM-Bowling Green
Jane Gill Eggers Memorial Scholarship, sponsored by Cleveland West Alumnae

1970-71 Peggy Bullion, ΓZ-LSU
Partially sponsored by Long Island-North Shore Alumnae

Vicki Carlson, Λ-Minnesota
Sponsored by Birmingham Alumnae

Marg Crandall, K-Nebraska
Dorothy Halsey Honorary Scholarship, sponsored by Fairfield County Alumnae

Britta Gunderson, B-Washington
Sponsored by Seattle Alumnae

Cathy Kiser, AX-Penn State
Jane Gill Eggers Memorial Scholarship, sponsored by R. H. Eggers

Susan Lang, AΛ-Drake
Sponsored by Des Moines Alumnae

Stephanie Reed, AΥ-SMU
Martha Hunter Farrell Memorial Scholarship, sponsored by Dallas Alumnae

Nancy Rethmeier, AΣ-UCLA
Sponsored by San Mateo Alumnae

Cindy Savage, AΨ-Mississippi

Carolyn Schaperkotter, M-Missouri
Carolyn Coffman Moorman Honorary Scholarship, sponsored by Dayton Alumnae

Becky Schild, N-Idaho
Ruth Squire Beaver Honorary Scholarship, sponsored by Palo Alto Alumnae

Jean Symington, BB-Alberta
Sponsored by Minneapolis-St. Paul Alumnae

1971-72 Jonette Beaver, K-Nebraska

Gail Bei, ΓK-Santa Barbara
Virginia Dorsey Baker Honorary Scholarship, sponsored by Palo Alto Alumnae

Alexandra Cummings, BN-Carnegie-Mellon
Partially sponsored by Long Island-North Shore Alumnae

Sandra Gerolamy, BB-Alberta

Karen Glover, AH-Whitman
Sponsored by Seattle Alumnae

Kris Hadel, BK-Kansas

Kathryn Sanders, ΓO-Indiana State
Ruth Mary Baldwin Atchison Honorary Scholarship, sponsored by Province VI Alumnae

Linda Santschi, ΓE-Kent State
Jacque Buchenau Hawkins Honorary Scholarship, sponsored by Fairfield County Alumnae

Linda Sharp, AΩ-Arkansas

Suzanne Sloan, BΨ-Alabama

Jan Stephenson, ΓΞ-Texas Tech
Lauraine Trotman Burleson Honorary Scholarship, sponsored by Dallas Alumnae

Patty Williams, AΔ-Oregon
Sponsored by San Mateo Alumnae

1972-73 Lorraine Achtem, BB-Alberta
Margaret Richardson Hay Honorary Scholarship, sponsored by the Province XVII Coordinating Committee

Barbara Bick, AH-Whitman
Sponsored by San Mateo Alumnae

Stephanie Certain, BP-George Washington
Sponsored by Fairfield County Alumnae

Diane Dutton, ΔB-Kentucky
Carolyn Coffman Moorman Honorary Scholarship, sponsored by Dayton Alumnae

Adelia Griffin, ΔΛ-Mississippi State
Virginia Van Dyke Spaller Honorary Scholarship, sponsored by Dallas Alumnae

Sharon Holub, ΔN-Northern Illinois
Partially sponsored by Des Moines Alumnae

Nancy Long, BΣ-Maryland
Helen Million Preston Honorary Scholarship, sponsored by Long Island-North Shore Alumnae

Sara Suzan Stanley, BM-Bowling Green
Marian Dankworth Bobey Honorary Scholarship, sponsored by Cleveland West Alumnae

Donna Tatman, ΔO-Morehead
Kathryn Bell Gary Hororary Scholarship, sponsored by the Province XVII Coordinating Committee

Deborah Wilken, ΓΛ-Fresno
Frances Halstenrud Ragno Honorary Scholarship, sponsored by Palo Alto Alumnae

Sidni Wilkinson, Π-Montana
Irene Ebener Kirkley Memorial Scholarship, sponsored by Denver Alumnae

Cinthia Williams, Θ-Indiana
Sponsored by Detroit-Dearborn Alumnae

1973-74 Susan Aho, AΔ-Oregon
Florence Phipps Dingman Honorary Scholarship, sponsored by Palo Alto Alumnae

Paula Beard, ΔΘ-Georgia State

Susan Clouse, ΓΦ-Arizona State
Esther B. Starks Honorary Scholarship, sponsored by Denver Alumnae

Nancy Hodgson, BB-Alberta

Rosemary Ledvora, ΔN-Northern
Illinois
*Peg Conlon Herman Memorial Scholarship, sponsored by St. Louis City
and County Alumnae*
Elaine Madsen, Π-Montana
Vicki Marmonstein, AI-Oklahoma
Debbie McCown, BΩ-Washington State
Marsha Penham, ΔZ-Memphis State
Gail Sonneman, AZ-Lawrence
*Sponsored by Cleveland West
Alumnae*
Pamela Tarr, AΞ-West Virginia
Carol Zacher, BN-Carnegie-Mellon
Sponsored by Fairfield County Alumnae

Sight Conservation and Aid to the Blind

Though the desire for a Fraternity philanthropic project had been felt for many years—and discussion at Convention had been considerable—it was not until the 1936 Convention that conjecture became action.

Marguerite Winant, Fraternity President at this time, had urged such action during her term as Second Vice-President in the last 'twenties, and it was she who presided at the alumnae workshop when the subject once more arose. (Details of this workshop and its outcome are contained in the narrative portion of the history, 1936.)

Today it is impossible to consider a better choice for a Fraternity Project than Sight Conservation and Aid to the Blind has proved to be. It has allowed collegiate and alumnae groups to take part in a Delta Gamma project of international scope and at the same time watch their good deeds grow as they contributed within their own communities.

On the international level, Delta Gamma in the area of Sight Conservation has worked closely with the National Society for the Prevention of Blindness, many of its state and national officers having been Delta Gammas. In Aid to the Blind, both the Canadian National Institute for the Blind and, in the United States, the National Foundation for the Blind, have been supported actively.

To celebrate the Fraternity's centennial, the Foundation made two large grants in the field of Sight Conservation: $50,000 to the National Society for the Prevention of Blindness to fund the Home Eye Test for Preschoolers; and $50,000 to establish the Delta Gamma Program in Pediatric Ophthalmology at Children's Mercy Hospital, Kansas City, Missouri, dedicated to re-search, diagnosis, and treatment of vision problems of infants and children.

The committees directing and channeling work in the area of Sight Conservation and Aid to the Blind worked as a Fraternity Standing Committee until the Foundation was incorporated in 1951. The choice of chairman for a committee is based to a great extent upon the selection first of a location for the committee.

1937-40—Jane Hawk Scheussler, Γ-California
1940-44—Lois Robinson Richter, Λ-Minnesota
1944-48—Irene Howell Forman, ΔK-Washburn
1948-53—Marcia Connell Strickland, Ξ-Michigan
1953-57—Mary Lee Lyon Foor, AI-Oklahoma
1957-60—Maxine Ford Bray Foulis, AE-Washington Univ.
1960-62—Fay Hamilton Jones, Υ-Stanford
1962-65—Martha Stone Evans, AE-Washington Univ.
1965-69—Elma Brock Hendrickson, AI-Oklahoma
1969-73—Florence Hinshaw Maxwell, AT-Butler

In 1973, the direction of the Fraternity Project was divided between two administrative committees.

Aid to the Blind
1973- —Gretchen Worley Hamilton, E-Ohio State

Sight Conservation
1973- —Sarah Moores Walker, ΔH-Whitman

International Education

In 1945, President Florence Cornell Bingham decided that Delta Gamma should have an International Education program that would function under a national committee, and she asked Irma Twining Madden, Θ-Indiana, to be the Chairman. The plan was that if the universities would waive or give tuition scholarships to foreign students, those chapters which could afford to do so would offer room and board in their chapter houses for one college year to a student they would choose from files submitted by the Institute of International Education.

Originally the sponsoring chapters bore the entire expense of housing a student. The first gift to the I.E. Fund was a $500 check in 1947 from the Washington, D.C. alumnae chapter to be used as a loan fund to assist individual guests rather than to aid the sponsoring collegiate chapters. In 1956, the Trustees of the Delta Gamma Foundation voted to allocate annually $1,000 of the Foundation's funds to International Education. Four grants of $225 each were awarded to the chapters who had previously shown the most interest in the program. That same year, the Chairman, Cornelia Powell Draves, B-Washington, set up a Birthday Penny Fund program among alumnae groups to augment the appropriation from the Trustees to help more chapters have foreign student guests. In 1958, the Fairfield County alumnae chapter made the first full International Education special grant in honor of one of its members, a grant the group continued to make for the duration of the International Education program. In 1958, the Trustees increased the allocation from Foundation funds to $2,000, thereby providing a $250 grant to all sponsoring collegiate chapters.

The height of the International Education program came in the late 'fifties and early 'sixties as many foreign students were anxious to study in the United States, colleges and universities were cooperative in giving tuition scholarships, and collegiate chapters were willingly opening their doors to foreign student guests. In recent years, however, as fewer foreign students desired to study on American campuses and as the tightening of budgets forced colleges and universities to cut back on scholarships to foreign students, the International Education program declined. While retaining the commitment to world understanding to be gained through international education, the Foundation discontinued the International Education program with the end of the 1972-73 school year.

As the International Education program came to a close, 223 foreign students had been guests of Delta Gamma collegiate chapters while International Education residential grants totaled $56,100. Two chapters were consistent participants in the program, Phi and Pi hostessing twenty-three and twenty foreign student guests respectively.

The International Education Committee was appointed from one of the numerous alumnae groups in the New York City area (northern New Jersey, suburban Westchester, Long Island, and Connecticut) to enable the committee to have close touch with the foreign guests as they arrived in this country.

1945-51—Irma Twining Madden, Θ-Indiana
1951-55—Marjory Rice, Χ-Cornell
1955-59—Cornelia Powell Draves,
        B-Washington
1959-63—Ruth Utz Russell, AP-Ohio Wesleyan
1963 (Summer)—Virginia Beatson Case,
        AΓ-Toronto
1963-66—Helen Rupert Pitcher, Λ-Minnesota
1966-69—Aurel Sexton Brown, Σ-Northwestern
1969-73—Lorna Becker Harrington, Ξ-Michigan

The History of Delta Gamma, 1973

The gathering together of the final record of Delta Gamma's first hundred years has witnessed many scenes like this, Barbara Carvill, Θ-Indiana, and Frances Lewis Stevenson, Ζ-Albion, pouring over an aging treasure. The disintegrating scrapbook they share here was another former Editor's, belonging to Ethel Tukey Korsmeyer, Κ-Nebraska, who compiled the large 1915 History of the Fraternity. Barb is currently Anchora Editor, and Fran is Director of Communications and Information, and it might be noted that another former Editor has rejoined the staff and has been responsible for much proofreading and indexing of this volume—Mary Ann Dalton Shepard, N-Idaho.

Index of Subjects

Index of People